Contemporary U.S.–Latin American Relations

Cooperation or Conflict in the 21st Century?

Edited by

Jorge I. Domínguez and Rafael Fernández de Castro

Routledge
Taylor & Francis Group

NEW YORK AND LONDON

First published 2010
by Routledge
270 Madison Avenue, New York, NY 10016

Simultaneously published in the UK
by Routledge
2 Park Square, Milton Park, Abingdon, Oxon OX14 4RN

Routledge is an imprint of the Taylor & Francis Group, an informa business

© 2010 Taylor & Francis

Typeset in Minion by Swales & Willis Ltd, Exeter, Devon
Printed and bound in the United States of America on acid-free paper by
Edwards Brothers, Inc.

Library of Congress Cataloging in Publication Data
Contemporary U.S.-Latin American relations : cooperation or conflict
in the 21st century? /
    Jorge I. Domínguez and Rafael Fernández de Castro, [editors].
    p. cm. — (Contemporary Inter-American relations)
    Includes index.
    1. Latin America—Foreign relations—United States.
    2. United States—Foreign relations—Latin America.
    3. Latin America—Politics and government.
    4. United States—Politics and government.
    I. Domínguez, Jorge I. II Fernández de Castro, Rafael
    F1418.C8133 2010
    327.807309'05—dc22
    2009050147

ISBN 10: 0–415–87999–X (hbk)
ISBN 10: 0–415–88000–9 (pbk)
ISBN 10: 0–203–85047–5 (ebk)

ISBN 13: 978–0–415–87999–6 (hbk)
ISBN 13: 978–0–415–88000–8 (pbk)
ISBN 13: 978–0–203–85047–3 (ebk)

To Janet Kelly (1947–2003)
Distinguished scholar, public intellectual, and friend
At home in both Venezuela, where she lived for over
twenty years, and the United States
Colleague as an author in this project from its very start,
and forever

Contents

List of Tables

Preface

This project began in 1997 when two of its authors, Jorge Domínguez and Cristina Eguizábal, sat together during a long international flight and thought out loud about the state of scholarship on the international relations of the Americas. Each had connected to Rafael Fernández de Castro at the Instituto Tecnológico Autónomo de México (ITAM) who would become the linchpin of several subsequent related internationalist projects. Soon the notion evolved to produce eight books on U.S. relations with each of the main Latin American countries and two other books on U.S. relations, respectively, with Central American and Caribbean countries. Each book would be relatively short and seek to reach a broad audience. The focus would be on the world as it had become since the start of the 1990s, that is, after the collapse of the Soviet Union, the end of the Latin American economic depression of the 1980s, and the emergence of democratic governments everywhere in Latin America outside Cuba. Each book would have two authors, one from the United States and one from the partner Latin American country or a subregion.

Several related conferences (the first at the ITAM in Mexico City in June 1998) and other projects later, this fantasy had for the most part become a reality. Ten books have been published, each with two authors; two other books are nearing completion and two of the original books are being readied for a second edition. Two books have been published in Spanish and one in Portuguese. Many of the same individuals went on to found the journal *Foreign Affairs en español*, subsequently renamed *Foreign Affairs Latinoamérica*, and the Centro de Estudios y Programas Interamericanos (CEPI), housed at ITAM, as a means to sustain an international conversation on these topics.

This book brings together at least one and sometimes both of the authors from the original books, namely, Jorge Domínguez, Rafael Fernández de Castro, Mônica Hirst, Anthony Maingot, Cynthia McClintock, Marifeli Pérez-Stable, Carlos Romero, Francisco Rojas, Roberto Russell, and Fabián Vallas. They and the new authors gathered at the ITAM in January 2009 commented on each other's draft chapters in preparation for this book.

We are grateful to the Fundación Mayan, and its academic director Roberto Russell, for their support of the conference at ITAM and this project. We are also grateful to the Ford Foundation for its support of many of our projects over the years and to Cristina Eguizábal for her advice and assistance throughout this endeavor. The Academic Department of International Studies at ITAM hosted the project throughout its duration and its various international conferences, including the one in January 2009 under CEPI auspices. Harvard University's Weatherhead Center for International Affairs has supported aspects of this project, including several logistical aspects of the January 2009 conference. Diane Kuhn was a valued research assistant. We are particularly grateful to Kathleen Hoover at the Weatherhead Center for her work on this book and related projects. At Routledge (Taylor & Francis), Michael Kerns has thoughtfully and persistently encouraged us to remain productive and on schedule.

We honor the memory of one of the original authors in this project, Dr. Janet Kelly, who died in 2003 but whose many contributions to Venezuela and its people, and their relations with the United States, will live forever.

Contributors

Cynthia J. Arnson is director of the Latin American Program at the Woodrow Wilson International Center for Scholars. She has written frequently on Colombia's internal armed conflict and U.S.–Colombian relations. Dr. Arnson is editor of *Comparative Peace Processes in Latin America* (1999), co-editor (with I. William Zartman) of *Rethinking the Economics of War: The Intersection of Need, Creed, and Greed* (2005), and author of *Crossroads: Congress, the President, and Central America, 1976–1993* (2nd ed., 1993). She is a member of the editorial advisory board of *Foreign Affairs Latinoamérica* and a member of the advisory board of Human Rights Watch/Americas.

Javier Corrales is associate professor of Political Science at Amherst College in Amherst, Massachusetts. He obtained his Ph.D. in political science from Harvard University, specializing on the politics of economic and social policy reform in developing countries. He is the author of *Presidents Without Parties: The Politics of Economic Reform in Argentina and Venezuela in the 1990s* (2002). His research has been published in academic journals such as *Comparative Politics, World Development, Political Science Quarterly, International Studies Quarterly, World Policy Journal, Latin American Politics and Society, Journal of Democracy, Latin American Research Review, Studies in Comparative International Studies,* and *Foreign Policy*. He has written extensively on Venezuela, most recently, "Chávez, Still Facing Discontent," in the 2009 issue of *Current History*. In 2008 he testified before Congress on the political situation in Venezuela. He has also been a consultant for the World Bank, the United Nations, the Center for Global Development, Freedom House, and the American Academy of Arts and Sciences. He serves on the editorial board of *Latin American Politics and Society* and *The Americas Quarterly*.

Jorge I. Domínguez is Antonio Madero Professor of Mexican and Latin American Politics and Economics and vice provost for International Affairs at Harvard University. He is a former president of the Latin American Studies Association. He has served as general co-editor of the Routledge series of books on U.S. relations with various Latin American countries. His most recent books are (with Rafael Fernández de Castro) *The United States and Mexico: Between Partnership and Conflict* (2nd ed., 2009) and co-edited with Chappell Lawson and Alejandro

Moreno, *Consolidating Mexico's Democracy: The 2006 Presidential Campaign in Comparative Perspective* (2009).

Cristina Eguizábal is director of the Latin American and Caribbean Center at Florida International University. Before joining FIU she served as a program officer at the Ford Foundation working on Peace and Social Justice issues. She has held research and teaching positions at the University of Costa Rica, University of Bordeaux, University of Miami, and the Latin American Faculty of Social Sciences and has served as advisor at the Confederacy of Central American Universities, the Central American Institute for Public Administration, and the United Nations University. Dr. Eguizábal holds a Ph.D. in Latin American Studies from the University of Paris-Sorbonne-Nouvelle.

Rafael Fernández de Castro is foreign policy advisor to the president of Mexico. He is founder, and has been chair and full-time professor of the international Studies Department at the Instituto Tecnológico Autónomo de México (ITAM), since 1991. He is currently on leave from ITAM. Dr. Fernández de Castro was Robert F. Kennedy Visiting Professor at Harvard University and Fellow at Brookings Institution, Georgetown and Carleton Universities. He was editor and founder of *Foreign Affairs en Español* and has served, together with Jorge I. Domínguez, as general coordinator of the Routledge series of books on U.S. relations with various Latin American countries. He has written extensively on U.S.–Mexico relations and on Mexican foreign policy.

Claudia F. Fuentes Julio is a Ph.D. candidate in the Josef Korbel School of International Studies at Denver University and holds an M.A. in International Relations from the University of Kent, England. She worked for five years as a researcher at the Latin American Faculty of Social Sciences (FLACSO-Chile) on international politics, human rights, and security issues in Latin America. She has been professor of International Relations at Chilean and U.S. universities. Her publications include (with Francisco Rojas Aravena): *Promoting Human Security: Ethical, Normative and Educational Frameworks in Latin America and the Caribbean*, 2005.

Mônica Hirst is a Brazilian academic based in Buenos Aires as professor of International Affairs at the Torcuato Di Tella University. She has taught at the Argentine Foreign Service Institute of the Ministry of Foreign Affairs (1994–2008) and FLACSO-Argentina (1985–96). She also has been a Visiting Professor at Stanford (1992), the University of São Paulo (1994), and Harvard (2000). She is co-organizer of a Fellowship Program for Research on Intermediate Powers run by the Institute for Research of Rio de Janeiro. She has worked as a freelance consultant for the United Nations Development Program, Ford Foundation, Andean Development Corporation (CAF), and the Foreign Ministries of Argentina and Colombia. Professor Hirst currently coordinates the Political Cooperation Area of the Project "The Reconstruction of Haiti: Strengthening Argentina's Capacity for Effective Cooperation," run by FLACSO-Argentina and supported by IDRC. She has published extensively on

Brazilian foreign policy, Latin America-U.S. relations, regional security, and integration issues.

Anthony P. Maingot is professor emeritus of Sociology at Florida International University, Miami, Florida. From 1971 to 1974 he was an advisor to the prime minister of Trinidad and Tobago and a member of that country's Constitutional Reform Commission. He is a past president of the Caribbean Studies Association. His latest book (with Wilfredo Lozano) is *The United States and the Caribbean* (2005).

Cynthia McClintock is professor of Political Science and International Affairs at George Washington University and director of GWU's Latin American and Hemispheric Studies Program. During 2006–2007, Dr. McClintock was a fellow at the Woodrow Wilson International Center for Scholars. Also, she was the 1994–1995 president of the Latin American Studies Association. Dr. McClintock's most recent book (co-authored with Fabián Vallas) is *The United States and Peru: Cooperation—At a Cost* (2003 and Spanish edition, 2005). Her previous books include *Revolutionary Movements in Latin America: El Salvador's FMLN and Peru's Shining Path* (1998) and *Peasant Cooperatives and Political Change in Peru* (1981).

Marifeli Pérez-Stable is professor at Florida International University and vice president at the Inter-American Dialogue. She authored *The Cuban Revolution: Origins, Course, and Legacy* and edited *Looking Forward: Comparative Perspectives on Cuban Transition*. *Looking Forward* was a finalist in the ForeWord Magazine Book of the Year Award (2007). She chaired the task force on Memory, Truth and Justice, which issued the report, *Cuban National Reconciliation*. She is a member of the Council on Foreign Relations and an associate of COMEXI, the Mexican Council on Foreign Relations. Her *Miami Herald* column appears every other Thursday.

Francisco Rojas Aravena has been secretary general of the Latin American Faculty of Social Sciences (FLACSO) since 2004. He is the former director of FLACSO-Chile and has worked as a professor at the School of International Relations at the National University (UNA) in Costa Rica. His recent publications include: *Integration in Latin America: Actions and Omissions, Conflicts and Cooperation. IV Report of FLACSO's General Secretary.* (FLACSO-Secretaría General, Costa Rica, 2009); co-edited with Luis Guillermo Solís, *Crimen Organizado en América Latina y el Caribe.* (Catalonia / FLACSO-Secretaría General, Chile, 2008); and written with David Mares, *The United States and Chile: Coming in from the Cold* (2001).

Carlos A. Romero is professor at the Universidad Central de Venezuela. He has been visiting professor and research associate at several American, European, and Latin American universities, teaching and researching in the area of political science and international relations. He is a former adviser to the Ministry of Foreign Affairs of Venezuela. His most recent books are *Jugando con el Globo. La* *política exterior de Hugo Chávez* (2006), and *Venezuela. Una Integração Complexa* (2008).

Roberto Russell is president of Grupo Vidanta Foundation and professor and director of the M.A. Program on International Studies at Torcuato Di Tella University, Buenos Aires, Argentina. In 2006, he was distinguished with the Konex Prize in Political Science. He is former academic director of the Institute of the Foreign Service at the Ministry of Foreign Affairs of Argentina. He was visiting professor at the Universities of London, Georgetown, Beijing and Salamanca and at the Institutes Ortega y Gasset, Madrid, and Sciences Po, Paris. He has written extensively on Argentine Foreign Policy, United States–Latin American Relations, and Latin American International Relations.

Arlene B. Tickner is professor of International Relations in the Political Science Department at the Universidad de los Andes, Bogotá, Colombia. She is the co-editor (with Ole Wæver) of the Routledge book series, "Worlding beyond the West." Her most recent publications are (with Ole Wæver), *International Relations Scholarship around the World* (2009); "Latin American IR and the Primacy of 'lo práctico'," *International Studies Review*, 2008; "Colombia y Estados Unidos: una relación 'especial'," *Foreign Affairs Latinoamérica*, 2008; and "Aquí en el Ghetto: Hip-hop in Colombia, Cuba and Mexico," *Latin American Politics and Society*, 2008.

Fabián Vallas teaches International Communication and Political Communication at the Universidad de Lima in Peru. He is co-author (with Cynthia McClintock) of *The United States and Peru: Cooperation—At a Cost* (2003, and Spanish edition, 2005). He has written extensively op-ed articles on International Politics and Inter-American Issues for the Peruvian Official Newspaper *El Peruano*. He is coordinator of the journal *Dialogos de Comunicación* dedicated to Andean integration and communication (Latin American Federation of Faculties of Social Communication, FELAFACS, 2009)

Acronyms

AFL-CIO	American Federation of Labor and Congress of Industrial Organizations
ALBA	Bolivarian Alternative for the Americas, Alternativa Bolivariana para las Américas
ALC-UE	Latin America, the Caribbean, and the European Union
AMIA	Asociación Mutual Israelita Argentina
APEC	Asia-Pacific Economic Cooperation
APRA	American Popular Revolutionary Alliance, Alianza Popular Revolucionaria Americana
ARENA	Alianza Republicana Nacionalista
ARI	Alliance for a Republic of Equals
ATPA	Andean Trade Preference Act
ATPDEA	Andean Trade Preference and Drug Enforcement Act
AUC	Autodefensas Unidas de Colombia
BCC	border crossing card
CAFE	Central American Fingerprinting Exploitation Initiative
CAFTA	Central American Free Trade Agreement
CAFTA-DR	Central American-Dominican Republic Free Trade Agreement
CAN	Andean Community of Nations
CANF	Cuban American National Foundation
CARICOM	Caribbean Community
CARIFTA	Caribbean Free Trade Association States
CAVIM	Venezuelan Military Industry
CBERA	Caribbean Basin Economic Recovery Act
CBI	Caribbean Basin Initiative
CBTPA	Caribbean Basin Trade Partnership Act
CCAI	Coordination Center for Integrated Action
CLC	Cuban Liberty Council
CONGUATE	National Coalition of Guatemalan Immigrants in the United States
CPD	Concertación por la Democracia
CSME	CARICOM Single Market and Economy

DAS	Departamento Administrativo de Seguridad
DEA	Drug Enforcement Administration
DEVIDA	National Commission for Development and Life Without Drugs
DHS	Department of Homeland Security
DIA	Defense Intelligence Agency
DIRECON	Chilean Directorate for International Economic Relations
DOD	Department of Defense
DSP	democratic defense and security policy
ECLAC	Economic Commission for Latin America and the Caribbean
ELN	National Liberation Army
ENARSA	Energía Argentina Sociedad Anónima
EPR	Popular Revolutionary Army, Ejército Popular Revolucionario
EU	European Union
EZLN	Ejército Zapatista de Liberación Nacional
FARC	Revolutionary Armed Forces of Colombia
FAST	Free and Secure Trade
FBI	Federal Bureau of Investigation
FDI	Foreign Direct Investment
FIU	Financial Intelligence Unit
FMLN	Farabundo Martí National Liberation Front
FOL	Forward Operating Location
FTA	Free Trade Agreement
FTAA	Free Trade Area of the Americas
GDP	gross domestic product
GEIN	Special Intelligence Group, Grupo Especial de Inteligencia
GNP	gross national product
HTA	hometown association
IADB	Inter-American Development Bank
ICC	International Criminal Court
ICE	U.S. Immigration and Customs Enforcement
ICITAP	International Criminal Investigative Training Assistance Program
ILEA	International Law Enforcement Academy
ILO	International Labor Organization
IMF	International Monetary Fund
INS	Immigration and Naturalization Service
IRnet	International Remittance Network
JFT-Bravo	Joint Task Force Bravo
JLP	Jamaica Labor Party
LNG	liquid natural gas
LPG	liquefied propane gas
MERCOSUR (MERCOSUL)	Southern Common Market

MINREX	Ministry of External Relations
MINUSTAH	UN Mission for the Stabilization of Haiti
NACARA	Nicaraguan Adjustment and Central American Relief Act
NAFTA	North American Free Trade Agreement
NATO	North Atlantic Treaty Organization
NED	National Endowment for Democracy
NGO	non-governmental organization
NJM	New Jewel Movement
OAS	Organization of American States
OECD	Organization for Economic Co-operation and Development
OECS	Organization of Eastern Caribbean States
PAC	Citizen Action Party
PCC	Cuban Communist Party
PCCP	Plan Colombia Consolidation Phase
PDVSA	Petróleos de Venezuela
PEMEX	Petróleos Mexicanos
PFP	Federal Preventative Police, Policía Federal Preventiva
PNP	[Jamaica] People's National Party
PNP	[Peru] Peruvian National Party, Partido Nacionalista Peruano
PRI	Partido Revolucionario Institucional
PTPA	Peru-U.S. Trade Promotion Agreement
SEDRONAR	Secretariat of Planning for the Prevention of Drug Addiction and Drug Trafficking
SENTRI	Secure Electronic Network for Travelers Rapid Inspection
SICA	Central American Integration System
SOUTHCOM	U.S. Southern Command
TPS	Temporary Protected Status
TSRA	Trade Sanctions Reform and Export Enhancements Act
T.T.	Trinidad/Tobago
UNASUR	Union of South American Nations
USAID	U.S. Agency for International Development
USTR	U.S. Trade Representative
VRAE	Apurímac-Ene River Valley
WTO	World Trade Organization

1 The Changes in the International System during the 2000s

Jorge I. Domínguez

The magnitude of change in the international system during the first decade of the twenty-first century was less stark than what had occurred around 1990 but the new changes were significant nevertheless.[1] The impact of such systemic changes, at the worldwide and hemispheric levels, upon U.S. relations with key Latin American countries was clear: U.S. clout weakened, Latin American autonomy from the United States increased. In some cases, as in relations between the United States with Venezuela, the relationship turned adversarial. In most cases, and even in aspects of U.S.–Venezuelan relations, U.S.–Latin American relations still worked effectively to address shared concerns, as the chapters in this book make clear. But, on balance, the likelihood and practice of widespread U.S.–Latin American policy coordination, relying upon multilateral institutions and common objectives, declined markedly during the decade.

The shift from the 1980s to the 1990s had been dramatic. By the start of the 1990s, the Soviet Union had collapsed, thereby terminating the Cold War in Europe, which had prevailed since the end of World War II. Moreover, every Latin American country but Cuba had held open, competitive elections as part of a wide-spread process of democratization. In about a decade, Latin America stopped being the land ruled by military dictators. And the Latin American economic depression of the 1980s had also ended, accompanied in many instances by pro-market changes in the economic strategies that Latin American government pursued. In part related to these changes, in part responding to specific contexts and opportu-nities, relations had improved substantially between the U.S. government and most Latin American governments.

The international and internal wars that had bedeviled Central America for nearly a generation came to an end; for the most part, domestic political violence also ended in Peru. Latin American countries, led at first by Argentina, became active participants in United Nations peace keeping missions. Economies grew. The World Trade Organization (WTO) came into effect and, in the Americas, the North American Free Trade Agreement (NAFTA) and the Southern Common Market (MERCOSUR or MERCOSUL, the Spanish and Portuguese language acronyms, respectively) were created, while new dynamism was imparted to the long-established Central American Common Market, the Andean Community, and the Caribbean Community (CARICOM). International financial institutions played generally constructive roles and both the Inter-American Development Bank (IADB) and the Organization of American States (OAS) became more active and effective. A "liberal" ideational consensus prevailed, which favored democracy, markets, and international cooperation especially through international institutions.

Nothing so cumulatively momentous unfolded during the first eight years of the new century though, as this chapter shows, important changes occurred. China became an international economic powerhouse while the United States became politically much less influential, mainly because of Bush administration actions regarding various issue areas but also because of the response of other governments to U.S. policy and demeanor. The economies of Latin American countries grew rapidly, thanks mainly to a commodity export boom rather than to market efficiencies or productivity gains. Such economic strength bolstered international reserves, freed Latin American governments from International Monetary Fund (IMF) financial tutelage, and emboldened them to act with renewed independence. Several political systems became sharply polarized. No domestic or ideological consensus endured within several key countries, and certainly not in hemispheric international relations.

In 2008, a major financial crisis broke out in the United States; in the Fall 2009, it spread worldwide. The real economy was adversely affected as well, with economic growth rates plunging across the globe. Latin American economies had either been relatively well governed (Brazil, Chile, Colombia, Mexico, and Peru) or had been cushioned by surpluses acquired thanks to commodity booms (Argentina, Venezuela). None, however, could withstand the international financial earthquake. By the end of 2009, the macroeconomic crisis had abated, although unemployment and underemployment rates remained high. China, India, and the smaller East Asian countries led the world's economic reactivation; the United States and the industrial democracies followed in the economic recovery, albeit with a lag. In South America, Brazil's economic recovery led the continent. Among Latin America's larger economies, Mexico's may have been the hardest hit and the slowest to recover.

The impact of this crisis increased China's clout in the international financial system and, more generally, increased the power of East and South Asian governments with regard to worldwide macroeconomic policy coordination. For the most part, however, the relative distribution of political or economic power in the international system had not been much affected. No country was immune from the crisis; the relative distribution of capabilities between them remained approximately the same. The principal change was common across countries, namely, the increased role of states in their respective economies through regulation or nationalization of financial and other private enterprises, even in the United States.

The next sections of this chapter explore four broad changes. Two occurred in the international system worldwide, namely, the rise of China in world markets and the spread of "balancing" behavior to cope with U.S. pretensions to worldwide primacy. Two changes had lesser widespread geographic scope. The breakdown of the ideological consensus was noteworthy in Latin America but not elsewhere in the world, and the impact of U.S. securitization of many of its foreign policies had impact mainly on U.S. near neighbors or on Islamic countries.

The Rise of China in World Markets

China's transformation since the end of the 1970s greatly improved the wellbeing of many of its people but it also brought about a significant realignment in world markets. During the first decade of the twenty-first century, the increase in China's international trade affected all the Latin American countries that we examine in this book, albeit in varying ways. China's emergence in world markets (and its impact on Latin American trade) was the most enduring and most general of the international systemic changes at the start of the century. The 2008–2009 worldwide economic crisis made China's international role more salient.

Between 1990 and 2000, on the eve of its accession to the World Trade Organization in 2001, China's exports to the world increased from $62.7 billion to $249.2 billion; such exports reached $1,218 billion in 2007. China's imports from the world followed a similar trajectory, reaching $225.1 billion in 2000 and rising to $956 billion in 2007. In 2000, China exported $4.2 billion to, and imported $5.1 billion from, Latin America. In 2007, it exported $44.4 billion to, and imported $46.7 billion from, Latin America.[2] Those massive Chinese imports increased global demand and raised the worldwide price of many commodities that Latin American countries exported, creating a powerful benign exogenous shock to propel the growth of Latin American economies.

The data on the exports and imports between China and various Latin American countries between 2000 and 2008 appear in Tables 1.1 and 1.2.[3] The absolute value as well as China's share of the exports and imports of every one of these Latin American countries increased dramatically during these years. In 2008, the seven Latin American countries in Table 1.1 (not counting Cuba) exported $53.2 billion to, and imported $89.8 billion from, China. In 2008, China accounted for impressive shares of Argentine, Brazilian, Chilean, and Peruvian exports and imports. Chile and Peru consistently showed bilateral trade surpluses with China. (Argentina faced a bilateral trade deficit in 2008 and Brazil experienced such annual deficits between 2006 and 2008.) In 2008, Brazil by itself accounted for 46 percent of the exports to these seven Latin American countries to China.

In contrast, Colombia, Mexico, and (until 2008) Venezuela regularly had bilateral trade deficits with China. The bilateral trade deficit has been especially large in the case of Mexico. Each of the latter three countries exported 3 percent or less of their respective total exports to China (again, 2008 Venezuela excepted). In 2007 and 2008, Colombia and Mexico imported more than ten percent of their imports from China, in the same league as Argentina, Brazil, Chile, and Peru.

China thus became very important for Latin American trade. The reverse is not yet the case, however. In 2007, all of Latin America represented only 3.6 percent of China's worldwide exports and 4.9 percent of its worldwide imports. On the exports side, only Mexico reached as high as 1 percent of the market for Chinese exports. On the imports side, Brazil reached 1.9 percent and Chile 1.1 percent of

Table 1.1 Exports to China from Selected Latin American Countries

	Arg	Bra	Chi	Mex	Per	Ven	Col	Cuba
2000	797	1,085	906	204	446	23	29	n.a.
	(3.0)	(1.8)	(4.7)	(0.1)	(6.5)	(0.1)	(0.2)	
2001	1,124	1,902	1,015	282	426	42	20	n.a.
	(4.2)	(3.2)	(5.5)	(0.2)	(6.1)	(0.2)	(0.2)	
2002	1,092	2,520	1,233	654	599	91	30	n.a.
	(4.2)	(4.2)	(6.7)	(0.4)	(7.8)	(0.3)	(0.2)	
2003	2,478	4,533	1,847	974	680	165	83	77
	(8.4)	(6.2)	(8.6)	(0.6)	(7.7)	(0.6)	(0.6)	(4.6)
2004	2,628	5,440	3,212	986	1,240	277	138	0
	(7.6)	(5.6)	(9.9)	(0.5)	(9.9)	(0.7)	(0.8)	(3.4)
2005	3,193	6,834	4,390	1,136	1,886	293	237	105
	(7.9)	(5.8)	(11.1)	(0.5)	(10.9)	(0.5)	(1.1)	(4.9)
2006	3,473	8,400	4,933	1,688	2,277	145	452	244
	(7.5)	(6.1)	(8.6)	(0.7)	(9.6)	(0.2)	(1.9)	(8.3)
2007	5,170	10,749	9,980	1,895	3,352	2,731	785	928
	(9.3)	(6.7)	(14.8)	(0.7)	(12.1)	(3.1)	(2.6)	(25.2)
2008	6,390	24,611	9,839	2,045	4,251	5,573	443	677
	(9.0)	(12.4)	(14.8)	(0.7)	(13.5)	(6.0)	(1.2)	(18.4)

Source: International Monetary Fund, *Direction of Trade Statistics*, various years, for all countries except Cuba. For Cuba, Oficina Nacional de Estadística, *Anuario estadístico de Cuba, 2008*, Table 8.5, http://www.one.cu accessed 29 October 2009.

Note: For each year, the first row is the value and the second row the percent of each country's exports to China. The value in all cases but Cuba is in millions of U.S. dollars; the value for Cuba is in millions of Cuban pesos. n.a. means not available.

Table 1.2 Latin American Countries' Imports from China

	Arg	Bra	Chi	Mex	Per	Ven	Col	Cuba
2000	1,157	1,344	950	3,168	329	187	172	n.a.
	(4.6)	(2.2)	(5.1)	(1.6)	(4.1)	(1.2)	(1.5)	
2001	1,066	1,461	1,014	4,430	409	348	475	n.a.
	(5.2)	(2.4)	(5.7)	(2.3)	(5.2)	(1.9)	(3.7)	
2002	330	1,710	1,102	6,902	260	227	532	n.a.
	(3.7)	(3.3)	(6.5)	(3.6)	(3.2)	(1.8)	(4.2)	
2003	721	2,362	1,289	10,341	315	173	686	506
	(5.2)	(4.4)	(6.6)	(5.4)	(3.5)	(1.9)	(4.8)	(10.8)
2004	1,402	4,081	1,847	15,811	358	431	1,055	590
	(6.3)	(5.9)	(7.5)	(7.1)	(3.3)	(2.6)	(6.2)	(10.5)
2005	2,237	5,889	2,535	19,466	1,139	889	1,617	891
	(7.8)	(7.3)	(7.8)	(8.0)	(8.6)	(3.7)	(7.6)	(11.7)
2006	3,122	8,788	3,491	26,882	1,678	1,634	2,219	1571
	(9.1)	(8.7)	(9.7)	(9.5)	(10.3)	(4.9)	(8.5)	(16.5)
2007	5,093	13,880	4,886	32,718	2,233	3,081	3,327	1,518
	(11.4)	(11.0)	(11.2)	(11.0)	(10.6)	(6.7)	(10.0)	(15.1)
2008	7,103	26,603	6,667	38,159	3,048	3,686	4,549	1,483
	(12.4)	(14.6)	(10.8)	(11.7)	(10.2)	(7.4)	(11.6)	(10.4)

Source: International Monetary Fund, *Direction of Trade Statistics*, various years, for all countries except Cuba. For Cuba, Oficina Nacional de Estadistica, *Anuario estadistico de Cuba, 2008*, Table 8.6, http://www.one.cu accessed October 29, 2009.

Note: For each year, the first row is the value and the second row the percent of each country's imports from China. The value in all cases but Cuba is in millions of U.S. dollars; the value for Cuba is in millions of Cuban pesos. n.a. means not available.

Chinese imports but all other Latin American countries were minor suppliers of Chinese imports.

China's trade with Mexico, Venezuela, and Cuba raises additional issues. Mexico had been the last of the 141 members of the WTO to sign a bilateral agreement with China to clear its admission to the WTO. Chinese competition turned out to be real. By 2003, China had replaced Mexico as the second most important supplier of U.S. imports; by 2007 and 2008, China and Canada vied for the role of the world's most important seller of products that the United States imported. By 2003, 85 percent of shoe manufacturers in Mexico had already shifted their operations to China. Sony, NEC, VTech, and Kodak closed their Mexican operations and moved them to China, while twelve of Mexico's twenty most important economic sectors that export to the United States already faced some or substantial competition from Chinese exporters.[4] China does not buy petroleum or other natural resources from Mexico. Thus, Sino-Mexican trade most resembles trade between industrial countries. As a World Bank study puts it, "Mexico is the only country in Latin America and the Caribbean whose comparative advantage has been moving in the same direction as the comparative advantage" of India and China.[5] Yet, Mexico lacks the capacity to compete with India or China on the basis of low wages and would prefer not to lower its wage level in order to compete.

Notwithstanding President Hugo Chávez's enormous efforts to strengthen Venezuela's ties to China, in the Latin American context in 2008, Venezuelan exports to China ranked fourth and Venezuelan imports from China ranked sixth. The jump in the value of Sino-Venezuelan trade in 2007 and 2008 may have a lagged political explanation, that is, at long last Chávez's courtship of China may have had effect. Yet, even in 2007, Venezuela represented only a third of 1 percent of China's worldwide imports and mattered proportionately even less for China's exports.

Sino-Cuban trade, presented in Cuban pesos, shows a large Cuban bilateral trade deficit with China, which in 2008 took 18 percent of Cuba's exports and supplied a tenth of its imports. Cuba depends greatly on China though its trade significance for China is very small. Except in 2007, Cuba's deficit in its bilateral trade with China has consistently exceeded the value of Cuban exports to China. Cuba may be the only Latin American country regarding which politics is the best explanation for China's trade behavior. China enables Cuba to defer payments for Chinese exports for nonmarket reasons, thus helping the only remaining communist regime outside of East Asia.

Latin America's trade with China depended disproportionately on its exports of commodities. As the price boom for various commodities broke in 2008 and the world economy spiraled into a deep recession, Sino-Latin American trade held its own for the time being. China's new considerable importance for Latin America continues to grow and it was one of the factors in the region's economic reactivation.

Latin America's New International Independence

Latin America's good economic performance between 2000 and 2007 owes much to the rise of its trade with China. From the end of the recession in 2003 to the end of 2008—on the eve of the severe economic crisis at the close of the decade—Latin America's aggregate gross domestic product grew between 4.6 and 6.1 per cent every year. Among the countries studied in this book, Argentina, Peru, and Venezuela grew substantially above the Latin American median during those years; Colombia rose also above median; Brazil, Chile, and the aggregate of the Caribbean and Central America hugged the Latin American median; and Mexico lagged the median but still grew respectably. (Cuba probably grew above median but its gross domestic product data is more difficult to interpret.)[6]

Because this economic growth resulted to a large extent from an export boom, the international financial position of most countries in Latin America and the Caribbean also improved substantially. The international reserves increased for all the countries included in Table 1.3. Between 2001 and 2008, Brazil's international reserves increased by a factor of nearly six, exceeding $200 billion dollars in 2008. The international reserves of Peru quadrupled, those Argentina and Venezuela tripled, while those of Colombia and Mexico doubled. Only Jamaica was hit in 2008 so hard and early that its international reserves by end 2008 were below their level in 2001. The rate of increase was substantial throughout the decade, though Brazil's boom in international reserves is especially marked after 2005.

Thanks to the same international economic trends, Latin American governments became financially independent from support from the IMF and, as a consequence, did not need to follow the Fund's advice. As Table 1.4 shows, Chile, Costa Rica, Jamaica, Trinidad & Tobago and Venezuela had not been compelled to borrow at all from the IMF during the current decade. Argentina and Brazil did not require an IMF agreement since 2002 and 2003, respectively, and paid off their IMF debt earlier than the expiration year reported in Table 1.4. Indeed, prior to the outbreak of the financial crisis in 2008, only Peru among the large Latin American

Table 1.3 International Reserve Assets, 2001–2008 (billions of dollars)

	2001	2005	2008
Argentina	15.2	28.1	46.1
Brazil	35.9	53.8	207.3
Chile	14.4	17	22
Colombia	10.2	15	23.2
Costa Rica	1.3	2.3	3.7
Dominican Republic	1.1	1.8	2.5
El Salvador	1.7	1.8	2.4
Guatemala	2.3	3.8	4.7
Honduras	1.4	2.3	2.5
Jamaica	1.9	2.2	1.8
Mexico	44.8	74.1	89.7
Nicaragua	0.4	0.7	1.1
Peru	8.8	14.1	31.3
Trinidad & Tobago	1.9	4.8	8.7
Venezuela	12.3	29.6	37

Source: United Nations, Economic Commission for Latin America and the Caribbean, *Preliminary Overview of the Economies of Latin America and the Caribbean, 2008*, Table A-13.

Table 1.4 Years of Last Agreements between International Monetary Fund and Latin American and Caribbean Countries, 1989–2009

	Year of Last IMF Agreement	Expiration Year of Last IMF Agreement
Argentina	2003	2006
Brazil	2002	2005
Chile	1989	1990
Colombia	2005	2006
Costa Rica	1995	1997
Dominican Republic	2005	2008
El Salvador	1998	2000
El Salvador	2009	2010
Guatemala	2003	2004
Honduras	2004	2007
Honduras	2008	2009
Jamaica	1992	1996
Mexico	1999	2000
Mexico	2009	n.a.
Nicaragua	2007	2010
Peru	2007	2009
Trinidad & Tobago	1990	1991
Venezuela	1996	1997

Source: International Monetary Fund, Members' Financial Data by Country, as of February 28, 2009, http://www.imf.org/external/np/fin/tad/ accessed April 6, 2009.

Note: n.a. = not available.

countries, and Honduras and Nicaragua among the smaller countries, continued to depend on the IMF. In 2009, only the Dominican Republic was scheduled to repay the IMF for funds borrowed earlier in the decade. For the first time in a generation, therefore, Latin American governments could set their economic policies as they deemed fit, for good or ill—the IMF had been relegated to the sidelines and, as a result, the U.S. government could not influence Latin American economic policies through this indirect route either.

By greatly increasing the international revenues of most Latin American countries, China contributed, albeit indirectly, to strengthening Latin American economies and thus the international political capacity of Latin American states. Brazil came to play a new leading role in South America, especially in 2007 and 2008, thanks in part to its economic growth rate just below 6 percent and newly found international financial independence. Similarly, Argentina became independent from the International Monetary Fund and international lenders because, thanks to commodity exports to China, its economy grew above 8 percent each and every year between 2003 and 2007. During the course of the twenty-first century's first decade, the foreign policies of Latin American governments had become as independent as ever. China deserves their thanks.

Balancing against U.S. Influence

The second change in the international system was the change in the general response to the U.S. government's attempt to claim worldwide primacy. In the early 1990s, following the collapse of the Soviet Union and communist Europe, Kenneth Waltz argued that "the response of other countries to one among them seeking or gaining preponderant power is to try to balance against it."[7] Waltz's general systemic forecast did not apply for the most part in the 1990s but it has been prescient for the 2000s.

The sharpest alternative to Waltz's forecast dates from late 1990 when essayist Charles Krauthammer described the post-Cold War international system as "unipolar," that is, "The center of world power is an unchallenged superpower, the United States, attended by its Western allies." On the eve of the U.S. decision to go to war against Iraq, Krauthammer revised his earlier argument. In the winter of 2002–2003, he averred, "The unipolar moment has become the unipolar era." The "challenge to such unipolarity is not from the outside," contrary to Waltz's analysis, but "from the inside," by which he meant whether the United States would be governed by those willing to engage in the "aggressive and confident application of unipolar power." He closed his article by paraphrasing Benjamin Franklin: "History has given you an empire, if you will keep it."[8]

In March 2003, the United States went to war in Iraq. The Bush administration claimed that the government of Iraq's president Saddam Hussein harbored nuclear weapons and other weapons of mass destruction, conspired to support the terrorists who attacked New York and Washington on September 11, 2001, committed brutal crimes against its own people, threatened its smaller neighbors, and ruled Iraq in authoritarian fashion. The U.S. Senate supported the Bush administration's decision to go to war.

In due course, this U.S. decision would redeem Waltz's forecast about the international system. The United States did not obtain United Nations Security Council authorization for the war in Iraq, despite strong efforts to do so. Nevertheless, the United States went to war with the backing of influential countries such as the United Kingdom, Italy, Spain, and Japan, but over the opposition of other comparably influential countries including Germany, France, Russia, and Canada. By mid-2003, it had become clear that Iraq did not have weapons of mass destruction, nor had Iraq conspired to support the terrorists who attacked New York and Washington on September 11, 2001. Support for the Bush administration's war policy in Iraq weakened among its allies and within the United States. The "unipolar era" had ended.

Latin American countries divided in their response to the U.S. decision to go to war in Iraq. Mexico, Cuba, and most South American countries opposed the U.S. decision; the exception was Colombia, which supported the United States. Several smaller countries supported the United States decisively. In August 2003, Honduras and the Dominican Republic each deployed 368 and 302 troops, respectively, to Iraq. Nicaragua followed suit in September, with 230 troops. Nicaraguan forces served in Iraq until February 2004, and Honduran and Dominican forces did so until

May 2004. While in Iraq, Nicaraguan, Honduran, and Dominican officers were under the command of officers sent as part of Spain's deployment to the Iraq war.

El Salvador proved the most steadfast U.S. ally in Latin America—the only Latin American country to deploy to, and keep troops in Iraq, between 2003 and 2009. Between August 2003 and late 2008, it had rotated over 3,000 troops in Iraq. El Salvador's original deployment in Iraq was 380, reduced to 280 in 2007, and 200 in 2008; five Salvadorans died in Iraq. At first, the Salvadorans served as part of the Latin American Brigade alongside Nicaraguans, Hondurans, and Dominicans, under Spanish command. Upon Spain's withdrawal, El Salvador's "Cuscatlán" battalion came under Polish command.

In March 2003, two Latin American countries—Chile and Mexico—were members of the United Nations Security Council. Neither supported authorization for the U.S.-led coalition to go to war in Iraq (in the end, there was no formal Security Council vote because the United States and its allies withdrew the resolution). Their position symbolized the general view of the majority of Latin American governments. In time, the Iraq war would widen and deepen worldwide public opposition to the general policies of the Bush administration, which contributed to making the management of U.S. relations more difficult for the governments of other countries, including those in Latin America.

The willingness of other countries to oppose the United States grew. The Bush administration found it increasingly difficult to obtain support for its views regarding a new international trade agreement under the World Trade Organization, climate change, opposition to the International Criminal Court, international energy issues as prices rose dramatically throughout the decade until the last quarter of 2008, or endeavors to isolate the governments of Cuba, Venezuela, or Zimbabwe. The Bush administration also had to accommodate the preferences of others regarding policies toward North Korea.

The worldwide weakening of U.S. influence during the middle years of the century's first decade gave Latin American states good company as they defied the United States even on issues that were salient for the U.S. government. Thus Chile and Mexico did not stand alone in the UN Security Council in opposition to the U.S. war in Iraq but, rather, they joined forces with other countries, many of which were U.S. allies. Mexico also differed with the United States over migration issues, not just over war in distant lands. Brazil blazed new foreign policy initiatives just as France, South Africa, or India did in areas of respective interest to them. The U.S. government deferred to Brazilian government views with regard to the proper response to the expropriation of natural gas concessions in Bolivia in 2006 as well as the Brazilian assessment of the (minor) security threat posed by transnational criminal activity in the tri-border area where Brazil, Argentina, and Paraguay come together. Venezuela's President Hugo Chávez defied the United States the most. In general, most Latin American countries demonstrated independence such as their foreign policies had not since the 1970s, if then. They found it safe to engage in a "soft balancing" of the United States, thereby widening their margin of international autonomy.

One international actor deserves a special mention: Russia. Upon the collapse of the Soviet Union and well into the current decade, Russia's role in Latin America became negligible. In the 2000s, the rise of petroleum, natural gas, and other natural resource prices enriched the Russian government and helped it rebuild some of its international capacities. By the decade's second half, Russia developed an active relationship with President Hugo Chávez's Venezuela, which included weapons sales and Russian navy visits to Venezuela's ports. Russia also dusted off its relations with Cuba and welcomed President Raúl Castro to Moscow in his first visit in two decades.

The Breakdown of the Inter-American Ideological Consensus

As noted earlier, a "liberal" democratic, pro-market consensus, reliant on international institutions for the conduct of foreign policy, had developed in Latin America in the 1990s. That consensus broke down during the century's first decade. In most cases, there was no replacement of one ideological consensus by another but, rather, a deep internal polarization. The last presidential elections of the decade turned out to be extremely close in Mexico and Peru, for example. In Venezuela, two constitutional plebiscites were held on the prospects of the unlimited continuation of Hugo Chávez in the presidency; Chávez lost one by a whisker in December 2007 and won another one also by a whisker in February 2009.

The role of personalist political leaders regained strength. Chávez in Venezuela, Rafael Correa in Ecuador, and Álvaro Uribe in Colombia agreed on very little but each had a profound disdain for political parties, each acted to disorganize not only the parties of their opponents but even those electoral vehicles that first elected them to office, each sought to amend the constitution via plebiscite to suit their own preferences, each sought continuation in presidential office, and above all each insisted on a personal relationship between president and people. This is not liberal democratic constitutionalism, which emphasizes the consent of the governed through political parties and legislatures.

Greater heterogeneity appeared in economic policy preferences.[9] Several of the region's key governments—Brazil, Chile, Colombia, Mexico, Peru—retained pro-market policies, while most of these inserted new social policies to reduce poverty levels. Yet, there were also some notable shifts away from pro-market policies. Argentina's catastrophic economic crisis at the start of the decade turned the public sharply against the previous pro-market policies and against a U.S. government that seemed indifferent to their country's misfortune. Bolivia underwent a social revolution early in decade, galvanizing those who had felt marginalized by the political process and who then elected Evo Morales to the presidency. Bolivia soon polarized sharply, endowing its new political division with a territorial dimension that threatened the state's integrity. Venezuela had never liberalized its economy but had long been a bastion of democratic contestation; the political and social struggles there led in December 1998 to the election of Hugo Chávez, who would come to anchor a new political perspective in the region. Chávez did not formulate an elegant or new ideological vision but, rather, returned to the long-standing Venezuelan practice that the government should regulate the market economy and own and operate many enterprises (not just those in petroleum extraction). Chávez also became the voice of the resentment of those who had felt abandoned or looked down upon by former rulers and their U.S. allies.

Admittedly, some of the ways to describe the liberal consensus of the 1990s had not been credible. By some standards, President Carlos Menem in Argentina, President Carlos Salinas in Mexico, and the ARENA (Alianza Republicana Nacionalista) party in El Salvador were part of this liberal consensus just because of their embrace of pro-market policies. On the political side, each fell well short of liberal democratic standards—Menem dealt imperiously with Congress and the Supreme Court, Salinas depended on electoral manipulation from his own election and during his years in office, and ARENA was born in part out of a death squad.[10] Of these, ARENA proved the most impressive in its ability to win consecutive elections over two decades until March 2009, when it lost a presidential election for the first time since the end of the Salvadoran civil war in 1992.

The breakdown of the domestic ideological consensus also had international implications, most clearly in reducing the effectiveness of the Organization of American States in its work in defense of democracy, which requires consensus, and in fostering the creation or reactivation of other subregional associations of Latin American states, some just for South American states and others pan-Latin American. A similar weakening in the commitment to democracy was evident in the invitation to Venezuela to join MERCOSUR, which for a decade had had a clause demanding democratic fealty, Chávez's trajectory toward autocratic behavior notwithstanding.[11]

The Bush administration itself bears responsibility for the breakdown of the democratic consensus. It seems to have supported—or it was remarkably inept at signaling that it did not support—the efforts to topple constitutionally elected President Hugo Chávez in 2002 and it interfered in presidential elections in Bolivia, El Salvador, and Nicaragua in the early years of the decade. It tarnished the democratic credentials of the U.S. government and seriously impaired its inter-American credibility.

The Bush administration also turned out to be trade protectionist with regard to U.S. agriculture and, on a NAFTA-wide basis, the steel industry. The U.S. Congress raised subsidies for U.S. agricultural producers during the Bush administration and with its encouragement. The Bush administration in 2001 also adopted various measures to protect its steel industry in the face of competition from non-NAFTA members. The United States and the European Union, in particular, did not reach substantial agreement to create a stronger World Trade Organization. Within the U.S. Congress, support for free trade agreements was feeble at best. The United States turned away from worldwide or even hemispheric-wide free trade agreements to emphasize, instead, bilateral or minilateral (e.g. CAFTA) agreements, where the United States exerted maximum leverage on weaker trading partners, typically safeguarding U.S. agriculture from exposure to free trade.[12]

Consequently, at the Fall 2003 meeting in Miami of the international trade ministers of the Americas, the United States and Brazil presented a proposal that, in effect, killed the project for a Free Trade Area of the Americas (FTAA), which had first surfaced in the previous George H.W. Bush and Clinton administrations.

Brazil and the United States sketched an agreement from which member states would pick provisions *à la carte*, thereby ending the prospects of a continental free trade agreement and formalizing the breakdown of an inter-American consensus on trade. At the Mar del Plata inter-American summit in 2005, the heads of state deepened the breakdown of this consensus.

The breakdown of the inter-American ideological consensus does not represent a change in the international system as a whole but it was a decisive feature of a change in the system of international relations in the Western Hemisphere. It made international coordination more difficult. It removed the appeal to shared values as a basis for unity. It fostered the emergence of many bilateral disputes between South American states.[13] This breakdown was also one of the casualties of Bush administration policies, which contributed indirectly to the growing propensity in Latin America for governments to act in ways that would counter U.S. preferences.

Securitizing U.S.–Latin American Relations

On September 11, 2001, terrorists hijacked several aircraft, crashed two of them on the World Trade Center towers in New York, one on the U.S. Department of Defense Pentagon headquarters outside Washington, DC, while a fourth went down over fields in Pennsylvania, killing over three thousand people altogether. The United States received impressive worldwide condolences and support. In response to the terrorist attack, the United States went to war in Afghanistan to depose that country's Taliban government, which had hosted the terrorist organization that sponsored these attacks. The United States retained significant worldwide support for its decision to go to war in Afghanistan, including from its allies in the North Atlantic Treaty Organization (NATO).

Those terrorist attacks compelled the U.S. government to refocus its international priorities on the problem of international terrorism. Many U.S. policies toward countries near and far were subordinated to the "war on terror." President Bush had less time and interest to attend to other policies and, when the United States did focus on a bilateral relationship, a change in U.S. priorities, often called securitization, was a typical component of the content of U.S. policy.

For the duration of the Bush administration, no terrorist based in Latin America crossed into the United States. Yet, U.S.–Latin American relations would be affected by the new U.S. government prism on the world. If security concerns were not especially salient in the bilateral relationship, as between Argentina and the United States, the U.S. government gradually downgraded its relations. If security relations constituted one element, albeit minor, in the bilateral relationship, as in U.S. concern with the use of Paraguay for international smuggling and money laundering, that topic became the sole focus of U.S. policy. And, for the near neighbors in the Caribbean, Central America, Colombia, and Mexico, the U.S. security obsession became a salient element of relations with the United States.[14] Their bilateral relations were burdened with having to see many aspects of international policy through a security lens.[15]

The U.S. government made a significant material commitment to foster this dimension of its foreign policy. From its first year in office (2001) to 2007, U.S. military and police aid to Latin American governments doubled. Colombia received about half of the value of such U.S. assistance but Bolivia, Peru, and Mexico were also significant recipients. Much of the motivation for this assistance was, of course, to counter drug trafficking, though in Colombia it would also be used to counter insurgencies.[16] Indeed, the Bush administration often acted as if terrorists and drug traffickers were part of a combined enemy that its security policies had to combat.

U.S. foreign policy securitization had a major impact on U.S. relations with Colombia. Until this decade, the U.S. government had provided funding to support Colombian government operations against drug traffickers but not against Colombian guerrilla insurgencies. In this decade, with encouragement from the president, the U.S. Congress lifted the prohibition against U.S. support for counterinsurgency operations in Colombia. The United States formally labeled as "terrorist" the decades-old insurgencies in Colombia, thereby coupling Al Qaeda's Osama bin Laden and the FARC's "Tirofijo"[17]—two highly dissimilar political and military actors, one with a worldwide reach, and the other hobbled in the mountains and jungles of Colombia. The Bush administration thereby explicitly combined the efforts against terrorists, insurgencies, and traffickers.

Latin American countries were not the only ones to undergo this change in their relations with the United States. Of course, this phenomenon deeply affected U.S. visa policies worldwide, for example, but also general U.S. policies toward Muslim countries. Latin American countries were not uniformly affected by the securitization of U.S. foreign policies—generally least so the further south from North America—and thus this securitization of aspects of U.S. policy ranks lower in international systemic importance than the previous changes analyzed in this chapter.

Conclusion

The rise of China in world markets created opportunities for the growth of Latin American economies, making most of their governments more self-assured and independent in their international behavior. The United States and China had correct political relations while George Bush was president; thus improved Sino-Latin American relations did not come at the expense of relations with the United States. China's new international trade role also added to the view prevalent in some South American countries that the United States had become less important in the world economy and, for this and other reasons, was due less deference, generally and in bilateral relations.

The Bush administration's general international behavior especially during the president's first term, its conduct of the war in Iraq, and its disdain for international institutions and diplomatic consultation created an international milieu conducive to "balancing" U.S. power. Some governments balanced softly (France, Canada, Spain, and, for a time, Germany), while others balanced more forcefully (Russia, Iran, Venezuela). By the middle of the decade, the U.S. claim to primacy and deference was no longer credible in the Americas. This change brought to an end the era of U.S.–Latin American coordination that had flourished in the 1990s. The combination of enhanced capacities thanks to economic growth and the self-imposed and deepening isolation of the Bush administration generated Latin American foreign policies much more markedly independent of the United States than during the previous two decades.

Two other notable international changes made U.S.–Latin American relations more difficult during the century's first decade. One was the breakdown of the "liberal" consensus in favor of constitutional democracy, markets, and reliance on international institutions. This change did not occur generally in the international system—though reliance on international institutions for policy coordination did become markedly lower worldwide—but it was a clear characteristic of domestic and international politics in Latin America during the decade. The other change was the securitization of important aspects of U.S. foreign policy, which distorted and burdened U.S. relations principally with Mexico, Colombia, and the Central American and Caribbean countries.

In no case did the factors sketched in this chapter alone determine the course of relations during the decade between the United States and any one Latin American country. Other factors regarding specific context, policies, opportunities, and personalities, discussed in other chapters of this book, greatly matter to understand bilateral U.S. relations with any given Latin American country. Yet, these general systemic or quasi-systemic changes did help to shape the international relations of the Western Hemisphere during the century's first decade.

In addition, where its actions may be assessed—war, terrorism, international trade, the defense of constitutional democracy in other countries, reliance on international institutions—the behavior of the Bush administration typically added complexity and extra burdens to the existing difficulties in its bilateral relations in the Americas. At times during the decade, it felt as if the Bush administration were to have the deliberate intent of undermining its own inter-American objectives. That was a tragedy in hemispheric relations during the century's first decade and a challenge for the second decade.

Notes

1. I am grateful to the book's co-authors for excellent suggestions regarding this chapter. Mistakes are mine alone.
2. International Monetary Fund, *Direction of Trade Statistics*, various years. These numbers do not include Cuba because it is not a member of the International Monetary Fund.
3. I am grateful to Diane Kuhn for assistance in the preparation of these tables.
4. CEPAL, "Los efectos de la adhesión de China a la OMC en las relaciones económicas con América Latina y el Caribe," *Panorama de la inserción internacional de América Latina y el Caribe, 2002–03* (Santiago, 2004), 221.
5. Daniel Lederman, Marcelo Olarreaga, and Guillermo Perry, *Latin America and the Caribbean's Response to the Growth of China and India* (Washington, DC: World Bank, Latin America and Caribbean Region, 2006).
6. Naciones Unidas, Comisión Económica para América Latina y el Caribe, *Anuario*

estadístico de América Latina y el Caribe, 2008, Table 2.1.1.1, http://www.eclac.cl accessed March 24, 2009.

7. Kenneth Waltz, "The Emerging Structure of International Politics," in *The International System after the Collapse of the East-West Order*, ed. Armand Clesse, Richard Cooper, and Yoshikazu Sakamoto (Dordrecht: Martinus Nijhoff, 1994), 169.

8. Charles Krauthammer, "The Unipolar Moment Revisited," *The National Interest* 70 (Winter 2002–2003): 5–17.

9. For an analysis of changes in economic policy preferences, see Javier Corrales, "The Backlash against Market Reforms in Latin America," in *Constructing Democratic Governance in Latin America*, ed. Jorge I. Domínguez and Michael Shifter, 3rd ed. (Baltimore: The Johns Hopkins University Press, 2008).

10. I first heard this point made eloquently by Laurence Whitehead.

11. For an analysis of the weakening of the international commitment to defend democracy in the hemisphere, see Laurence Whitehead, "The Fading Regional Consensus on Democratic Convergence," in *Constructing Democratic Governance in Latin America*, ed. Jorge I. Domínguez and Michael Shifter, 3rd ed. (Baltimore: The Johns Hopkins University Press, 2008).

12. For analysis, see Nicola Phillips, "U.S. Power and the Politics of Economic Governance in the Americas," *Latin American Politics and Society* 47:4 (Winter 2005): 1–25.

13. See Carlos Pérez Llana, "Modelos políticos internos y alianzas externas," in *América Latina: ¿integración o fragmentación?*, ed. Ricardo Lagos (Buenos Aires: Edhasa, 2008).

14. For an analysis of security circumstances across the hemisphere, making clear the differential geographic impact of U.S. securitization policies, see Raúl Benítez Manaut and Arturo Sotomayor, "El dilema mesoamericano: entre la inseguridad externa y la vulnerabilidad interna," Mônica Hirst, "Seguridad en América del Sur. La dimensión regional de sus desafíos políticos," and Francisco Leal Buitrago, "Una mirada a la seguridad en la Región Andina," in *América Latina: ¿integración o fragmentación?*, ed. Ricardo Lagos (Buenos Aires: Edhasa, 2008).

15. For further discussion, see Francisco Rojas Aravena, ed., *La seguridad en América Latina pos 11 de Septiembre* (Caracas: Nueva Sociedad, 2003); and Wolf Grabendorff, *La seguridad regional en las Américas* (Bogotá: Fondo Editorial CREC, 2003).

16. Adam Isaacson, Joy Olson, and Lisa Haugaard, *Below the Radar: U.S. Military Programs with Latin America, 1997–2007* (Washington: Latin America Working Group Education Fund, Center for International Policy, and Washington Office for Latin America, 2007), especially 2–3.

17. Fuerzas Armadas Revolucionarias de Colombia. Tirofijo was the war name for the late Manuel Marulanda.

2 U.S.–Mexican Relations in the Twenty-First Century

Jorge I. Domínguez and Rafael Fernández de Castro

"You cannot imagine what a sensation it caused in Mexico when the president of the United States chose our family ranch in Guanajuato for his first foreign state visit." Mexican president Vicente Fox (2000–2006) chose those words to open the description of his presidency in his memoirs, *Revolution of Hope*. Only once every twelve years, Mexico and the United States inaugurate presidents within seven weeks of each other—Fox on December 1, 2000, and George W. Bush (2001–2009) on January 20, 2001. Fox and Bush had met and become quite friendly as governors of Guanajuato and Texas, respectively. Fox was touched by Bush's gesture— "the reason I will always be his friend, no matter how sharply we may disagree on Iraq."

At this meeting on February 16, 2001, Fox and Bush pledged to work together to address the questions of Mexican migration to the United States, a topic that would play a dominant role for the duration of their presidencies. More importantly, the presidents believed that the sun had just risen over a new, better relationship between the United States and Mexico and that they were the key actors at the dawn of a bright new future. Yet, coinciding with this bilateral summit, President Bush ordered an air strike on Iraq, and it was the bombing of Iraq that riveted the journalists who asked questions at the joint press conference. That foundational moment, which combined hugs and war, would shape and shake U.S.–Mexican relations for the balance of their presidencies.[1]

Four factors explain the pattern of U.S.–Mexican relations during the first decade of the twenty-first century. First, the changes in the structure of the international system—sketched in Chapter 1—deeply affected U.S.–Mexican relations. The U.S. government came to look at the world through the prism of the security concerns of terrorism, "securitizing" its policies with regard to the movement of goods and people and the management of border issues, thus narrowing its international agenda. The U.S. government also over-stretched its power and over-burdened the good will of others; Mexico briefly joined the endeavor to balance and contain U.S. power. A longer-term change in the structure of the international system was the rise of China's economic power and its implications for other countries. The effects from these international systemic changes upon U.S.–Mexican relations were the securitization of hitherto non-security bilateral issues, greater strains in relations between the two governments, and more anger over some adverse impacts of international trade, which were blamed on the North American Free Trade Agreement (NAFTA), not just on China.

Second, we argue that these changes in the international system's structure were differentially mediated through the bilateral institutions that were created in the 1990s. The bilateral economic institutions embodied in NAFTA performed well, rendering trade and investment disputes routine technical issues that rarely required presidential attention. The embryonic bilateral security institutions to foster cooperation to address international migration and counter criminal drug traffic atrophied, however. There was no bilateral institutional architecture to cope with the new U.S. security demons.

Third, we argue that transnational processes set the agenda for bilateral relations. Bilateral trade and investment boomed, enabling the Mexican economy, for the first time since the early 1960s, to make it through a U.S. economic recession without a financial panic. These good results under NAFTA contained the economic disputes that might have otherwise spun out of control. Illegal drug production and especially drug traffic continued to increase in response to persistently high U.S. demand for such substances and the relative absence of effective U.S. demand-reduction and prisoner rehabilitation programs. Undocumented migration continued; overcome by security fears, the United States reduced the number of authorized lawful Mexican immigrants, inducing even more to choose illegal migration. Absent effective bilateral institutions to address migration and criminal drug activities, both governments spent considerable time, diplomatic effort, and political capital focusing on these topics, with little good to show in the end. At the end of the Fox and Bush presidencies, these two problems were as intractable as they were on their respective inauguration days or worse than that.

Fourth, to our surprise, the domestic political context had only a modest impact on the conduct of bilateral relations. We do not discuss these topics in this chapter but have analyzed them elsewhere.[2] The following summarizes our main findings in another work: Public opinion turned somewhat adverse in both countries but in neither with sufficient force to prevent cooperation. Mexico's democratization led to a more independent Congress and Supreme Court and a more contentious Congress. But the Court remained supportive of presidential foreign policy and the Congress concurred with the presidency over the disposition of nearly every treaty. The main impact on bilateral relations stemmed not from Mexico's democratization but from changes in the United States. The U.S. Supreme Court made the management of U.S.–Mexican relations more complex and the newly created U.S. Department of Homeland Security made bilateral cooperation more difficult.

In this chapter, we examine these issues in U.S.–Mexican relations between 2000 and 2008. We pay special attention to the differences between the 1990s and the 2000s, in particular the greater impact of security issues in the bilateral relations and the higher priority that the Mexican government accorded to migration issues in its foreign policy design. The great successes of the 1990s—ending Mexico's international debt and financial crises, designing effective Mexican fiscal and monetary policies, and establishing a secure framework for the flow of trade and investment under the NAFTA—helped the two governments to focus more on the exigencies that security emergencies imposed on them and to address the unaddressed legacy of the previous century regarding the movement of peoples in North America.

International Security

International security issues remained a contentious arena in U.S.–Mexican relations whose management became more difficult because of the atrophy of the embryonic bilateral security institutions that had been created in the 1990s. The principal difference between the foreign policies of the Fox and Calderón administrations was their respective approaches to security policy implementation: the Fox administration was likely to react to U.S. security initiatives whereas the Calderón administration took security policy initiatives on its own. First, consider the problems.

The Fox administration's response to the terrorist attacks on September 11, 2009, was baffling. The initial expressions of horror at the terrorist attack were soon overcome by an unseemly public debate on whether Mexico would be drawn into the U.S. war on terrorism and whether Mexico would "submit" to the United States. Some Mexican politicians and mass media took the opportunity to criticize Foreign Relations Secretary Jorge Castañeda's instant and unequivocal expression of solidarity with New Yorkers, amidst whom he had lived and worked at various times. As it turned out, Castañeda had added to the bilateral U.S.-Mexican complexity because he had persuaded President Fox—during Fox's triumphant state visit to Washington on the very eve of the September 11, 2001, attack—to give formal notice that Mexico would pull out of the Inter-American Treaty for Reciprocal Assistance (Rio Treaty, signed in 1947).

Yet the oddest aspect of the official Mexican response was Fox's behavior. Here was a president who had worked for Coca Cola, spoke fluent English, and had made the improvement of U.S.–Mexican relations the main pillar of his foreign policy and a key element for the construction of a new Mexico. Fox had cultivated a personal friendship with his boot-wearing cowboy buddy, George W. Bush, as the symbol of, and the instrument for, new relations between Mexico and the United States. Fox, alas, allowed his cabinet members to squabble in public. It took Fox two weeks to order his cabinet Ministers to shut up to enable him to repair the damage to U.S.–Mexican relations.[3]

In contrast, British Prime Minister Tony Blair flew to New York. Brazil invoked the Inter-American Treaty for Reciprocal Assistance—the very Treaty from which Mexico had just announced it would withdraw—on the grounds that a country of the Americas had been subject to international attack: an attack on one was an attack on all. Blair and Brazilian leaders understood that the United States, above all, needed a hug.

Speaking in Tijuana on October 3, 2001, President Fox began to repair the damage to Mexico's relations with the United States:

> We consider that the fight against terrorism is part of Mexico's commitment with Canada and the United States to create a shared space of development,

well-being, and integral security within the framework of the North American Free Trade Agreement. The Mexican government assumes the fight against terrorists as an international mandate, which is incumbent on those countries that have signed the many juridical instruments of the United Nations, as Mexico had.[4]

It would not prove easy. The United States soon went to war in Afghanistan and prepared for the same in Iraq. President Fox personally opposed the U.S. war policy in Iraq. As the start of the war in Iraq neared, Fox spent much of his time in Mexico campaigning in opposition to the war; in so doing, he mobilized Mexican opinion in such a way that he left himself no political room to maneuver.[5] Three factors shaped his decision. One was a genuine opposition, based on his religious beliefs, to this war, which he perceived—correctly from the start—to be a "war of choice": there had been no prior Iraqi aggression. The second was the strong conviction—equally correct—that the United States had no persuasive evidence regarding Iraq's possession of weapons of mass destruction. The Mexican ambassador to the United Nations, Adolfo Aguilar, who represented Mexico on the UN Security Council, strengthened Fox's resolve. Mexico thus had good and sufficient reasons to oppose this Bush administration decision.

The third factor was Fox's belief, as he wrote in his memoirs, "the United States didn't really have much carrot, and no stick at all." The Bush administration would not pull out of NAFTA or cut back on U.S. Drug Enforcement Administration security support because interests were shared. Mexico had paid back all its loans to the U.S. Treasury and the International Monetary Fund from its 1994–1995 financial crisis and it did not depend on much U.S. assistance of any sort. In 2002 the Bush administration dropped its proposal to Congress for guest-worker reforms. Thus, Fox concluded, "Even if the Bush administration had wanted to punish us, there was little they could do."[6] In this last respect, Fox was not correct. He underestimated the opportunity costs to U.S.–Mexican relations. Mexico might have made headway in creating a development fund within the NAFTA framework; it did not. Mexico might have had a significant input when the Bush administration in 2004 presented its own immigration proposals to Congress; it did not. Mexico might have expedited the lawful crossing at the U.S.-Mexican border (see later discussion of SENTRI lines); it did not. There would be no progress in U.S.–Mexican relations for the remainder of his presidency—the cost to Mexico of opposing the United States. Even the right decisions have serious costs.

In March 2003, however, the Mexican government did understand that it could not oppose the U.S. decision to go to war in Iraq and simultaneously fail to address the risk that U.S. adversaries would use Mexico to attack the United States. Operationally, then, Mexico behaved like a U.S. ally. Immediately following the start of the war, Mexico launched Operation Sentinel to beef up security along its northern and southern borders and secure airports, ports, oil platforms, and other key installations. Ten thousand soldiers were deployed to the northern border, three thousand soldiers to the southern border, and roughly another five thousand to provide protection at specific sites. This was a very significant deployment, given the limited deployable logistical capacities of its armed forces (total number of active military personnel was about 240,000). Mexico intensified its cooperation with the U.S. Department of Homeland Security (DHS). As Government Secretary Santiago Creel put it: "Mexico is not going to be used as a transit point for any terrorist or anyone who wishes to harm the United States."[7]

Beyond terrorism and war, there were important security legacies in U.S.–Mexican relations. Drug traffic and its related violence still ranked high. In a long-term perspective, September 11 had a negligible impact on measurable counternarcotics operations in Mexico. That is the good news. The less good news is that the same evidence suggests that there is little relationship between policy efforts, on the one hand, and achievements, on the other. Table 2.1 indicates that, at best, opium or cannabis (marihuana) eradication efforts had no impact on the net cultivation of opium or cannabis or the potential for opium gum, heroin, or cannabis production. Indeed, opium, heroin, and cannabis cultivation and production likely increased during Fox's six years in office. During Calderón's first two years, opium, heroin, and cannabis cultivation and production increased again. The most clearly changed policy variable is that the number of Mexican nationals arrested for these crimes jumped markedly in 2004 and remained at the higher level, jumping early in the Calderón administration. Yet this change also failed to improve the outcomes that matter, namely, cultivation and production.

There were two political accomplishments. In September 2002, the U.S. Foreign Relations Authorization for Fiscal Year (FY) 2003, Section 706, formally suspended the previous U.S. drug certification and sanctions procedures that had bedeviled U.S. relations with other countries, including Mexico, in preceding years. Instead, the president was required to issue an annual report to spotlight countries that had "failed demonstrably to take appropriate counternarcotics measures." The Act lifted this dark cloud from U.S.–Mexican relations at last.[8] For its part, in 2004 Mexico's new National Security Law created a new National Security Council and provided means to organize anti-crime efforts and gather intelligence.

In 2005–2006, levels of drug crime-related violence escalated across Mexico, especially on the northern border with the United States, despite policy efforts.[9] Soon after his inauguration in December 2006, President Felipe Calderón launched a major assault on drug cartels and other violent organizations in Mexico. As Minister of Government Francisco Ramírez Acuña put it dramatically during a confrontational question-and-answer exchange in the Chamber of Deputies: "Organized crime was becoming the owner of the nation's territory . . . drug traffickers controlled the State of Michoacán, they controlled the State of Guerrero, they controlled the State of Tamaulipas . . ." and other states.[10]

President Calderón's objective was plain: the state must exercise its monopoly of force. He deployed 27,000 troops within eleven Mexican states to achieve this objective instead of continuing to rely on law enforcement agencies. Calderón ordered Mexican security forces to intensify their cooperation with their U.S. counterparts. Within the opening months of the new administration, as a result of systematic investigations, 284 Federal Preventative Police (Policía Federal Preventiva, PFP) and Federal Investigative Agents (Agencia Federal de Investigaciones) were

Table 2.1 Opium, Heroin, Cannabis, and Cocaine in Mexico, 1998–2008

	1998	1999	2000	2001	2002	2003	2004	2005	2006	2008
Opium net cultivation (HA)	5500	3600	1900	4400	2700	4800	3500	3300	5100	6900
Opium eradication (HA)	17449	15469	15300	19115	19157	20034	15925	21609	16889	12035
Potential opium gum (MT)	60	43	21	71	58	101	73	71	110	149
Potential heroin (MT)	6	4	2	7	5	12	9	8	13	18
Cannabis net cultivation (HA)	4600	3700	3900	4100	7900	7500	5800	5600	8600	8900
Cannabis eradication (HA)	23928	33583	33000	28699	30775	36585	30851	30842	31161	15756
Cannabis production net (MT)	8300	6700	7000	7400	7900	13500	10440	10100	15500	15800
Cocaine HCL seizures (MT)	22	33	18	30	12	21	27	30	21	19
Cannabis seizures (MT)	1062	1459	1619	1839	1633	2248	2208	1786	1849	1650
Opium seizures (KG)	150	800	270	516	210	198	464	275	75	168
Heroin seizures (KG)	120	258	268	269	282	306	302	459	351	192
Mexican nationals arrested	10034	10261	n.a.	9784	6930	8822	18763	19076	11493	26947

Source: U.S. Department of State, Bureau for International Narcotics and Law Enforcement Affairs, *International Narcotics Control Strategy Report, 2008*, vol. I, p. 182, http://www.state.gov accessed July 14, 2008; ibid., 2009, http://www.state.gov/p/inl/rls/nrcrpt/2009/vol1/116522.htm accessed October 1, 2009.

Note: MT = metric tons; HA = hectares; KG = kilograms; n.a. = not available.

dismissed, including all thirty-four regional PFP coordinators; thousands of other Mexican officials were also dismissed for drug traffic-related corruption.

The U.S. government responded eagerly. Cooperation with the Mexican Navy increased. U.S. agencies trained thousands of Mexican law enforcement agents in 2007, Calderón's first year in office. As the U.S. Department of State put it in its official report for 2007, "The Calderón Administration's courage, initiative and success have exceeded all expectations," in particular celebrating its "using the military to re-establish authority and counter the cartels' firepower."[11]

Bush and Calderón met in Mérida in March 2007. They expanded bilateral and regional counternarcotics and security cooperation. U.S. and Mexican officials met behind closed doors over several months to craft "Plan Mérida." On May 22, 2007, Mexico's full draft proposal called for the exchange of intelligence and focused on U.S. support for training Mexicans. Mexico insisted that no U.S. troops would enter Mexican territory, nor would U.S. civilian agents participate in operations in Mexico. On October 22, 2007, the two governments issued their first public joint statement, announcing the multiyear Plan Mérida to assist Mexico and Central American countries to combat drug trafficking and other criminal organizations.[12]

The Bush administration asked Congress for $500 million for Mexico and $50 million for Central American countries in the Fiscal Year (FY) 2008 supplemental and $450 million for Mexico and $100 million for Central America in FY09. The goal was to transfer $1400 million to Mexico over three years. In June 2008, the Congress approved $400 million for Mexico and other funds for Central America. The scale of the effort was much larger than in the past. U.S. aid to Mexico for these purposes had totaled just $65.4 million in FY07 and $50.6 million in FY08. Four-fifths of the new FY08 funds for Mexico were for equipment and technology infrastructure improvements for Mexican military and law enforcement agencies. The remaining fifth of the FY08 funds for Mexico was for institution building and law enforcement initiatives, including the office of the prosecutor, the courts, the prisons, and other law enforcement civilian institutions; less than 10 percent of the FY09 request was for this purpose.[13]

Critics of Plan Mérida argued that it principally provided more funds for the same strategy that had long been in place. Missing from Plan Mérida was funding to reduce the U.S. demand for drugs, improve access to high-quality treatment for drug addicts, programs to better address the incubation of drug criminals in prison (i.e. when common criminals such as thieves enter prison with no previous drug history and then emerge as traffickers), closer supervision of drug-involved offenders on probation or parole, or prevention of weapons smuggling from the United States to Mexico. Critics of Plan Mérida highlighted the very high profile for military efforts instead of civilian law enforcement and the insufficient attention to the substantial risk of human rights violations from security forces that were insufficiently trained to prevent such abuses. The repeatedly unsuccessful strategy, which was now to be better funded, had failed to prevent the drop in drug prices for consumers or dent the lucrative business.[14]

To make problem solving more difficult, the two governments had allowed the high-level bilateral institutions created in the late 1990s to fall into disuse, in particular, the High Level Contact Group to Control Drugs and the Binational Commission. The Fox and Bush administrations found it difficult to fashion a broad cooperative framework over security relations, in part because they disagreed over the Iraq war and the Mexican government feared that the United States would ask Mexico to deploy troops abroad. How far this bilateral institutional deterioration had unfolded became clear when U.S. Defense Secretary Robert Gates visited Mexico City in April 2008. No U.S. Defense Secretary had visited since 1996; Gates expressed his surprise at the lack of such contact. Asked at a press conference about military to military relations, the articulate Gates stumbled verbally, searching for words, referring to the bilateral military relationship as "not in its infancy, but is young." He acknowledged "the sensitivities here in Mexico" as his explanation for why "the relationship is limited."[15]

Such "sensitivities" also identified two security issues in Mexico that would not involve the United States. Fortunately for Mexico, the Zapatista insurgency (EZLN, Ejército Zapatista de Liberación Nacional) in Chiapas did not lead to violent incidents in the 2000s; Zapatismo's impact was confined to the State of Chiapas and to some neighboring southern states. The Mexican army's counterinsurgency work, facing the Zapatistas, began badly in 1994 but, in the end, was successful and impressive.[16]

Less fortunate for Mexico was the re-emergence of the EPR (Popular Revolutionary Army, Ejército Popular Revolucionario). The EPR had been a small insurgent organization in Guerrero and Oaxaca in 1996. It reemerged in 2007, carrying out violent attacks on the infrastructure and installations of the Mexican state oil enterprise, Petróleos Mexicanos (PEMEX), at three sites in two states in July and at six sites in two other states in September. Mexico would fight the EPR on its own. U.S. Defense Secretary Gates confirmed that the United States would "defer" to the Mexican government.[17]

The fear of international troop deployment paralyzed the Mexican government in other contexts as well. In early 2004, the United Nations Security Council authorized a peacekeeping force in Haiti to enable the United States to extricate its forces from Haiti, where they had been deployed as part of a maneuver to depose Haiti's constitutional president, Jean-Bertrand Aristide. The U.N. force, to be led by a Brazilian General, was constituted of forces from many countries but principally from Brazil, Argentina, and Chile. Consistent with its long-standing practices that well preceded these events, Mexico sent no peacekeepers to Haiti in 1994 or 2004.[18]

Mexico's strategy remained mindful of long-standing legacies in Mexican foreign policy. Security cooperation would never become an invitation to the United States to involve itself in Mexico's domestic security issues. And Mexico would for the most part not deploy its troops abroad.

Given the decay of bilateral institutions for security cooperation, the Fox and Bush administration relied, instead, on routine relations between the respective government agencies without attempting to make use, adapt, or replicate the overarching institutional architecture for security issues fashioned by the Zedillo and Clinton administrations. They formalized many of those low-level cooperative security relations in March 2005 when Presidents Bush and Fox and Canada's Prime Minister Paul Martin, meeting at Bush's ranch in Crawford, Texas, called them the Security and Prosperity Partnership.

The Plan Mérida agreement signaled a shift in Mexican international security policy, emphasizing even closer Mexico's security policy engagement with U.S. counternarcotics tactics. Mexico would also build up a substantial military capability to advance joint U.S.-Mexican goals in combating drug trafficking and tilted even more toward U.S. suppliers of weapons. The two governments recognized the need to establish bilateral institutional procedures to expand and deepen their cooperation, remedying the institutional decay of the preceding years. The Bush–Calderón agreement was wholly consistent with the institutionalist approach to foreign policy first developed under the Salinas and Zedillo presidencies.

The greatest utility of that strategy for Mexico under Zedillo had been to contain (though never terminating) U.S. unilateral actions with regard to Mexico. There was a new risk in the Calderón administration's approach to the bandwagoning strategy, however. Its scale was so much larger and the intimacy of cooperation with U.S. agencies so deep that this lone successful result of the old strategy might become unachievable. Would the new strategy succeed in curtailing drug-related violence, traffic, and consumption while also limiting U.S. unilateralism in Mexico? President Calderón knew that success was difficult but he believed that he had no choice but to counter the spike in criminal violence that his administration had inherited.

NAFTA: Its Impact, Disputes, and Dispute Resolution

In the 1980s, investment and especially trade disputes peopled the agenda of presidents and their advisers as Mexico and the United States faced each other. NAFTA was the remedy for that problem. In seeking its enactment, the presidents of Mexico and the United States sold NAFTA to their peoples as if it would cure all ills. In incautious moments, NAFTA advocates in the United States argued that the agreement would stem the flow of undocumented migrants from Mexico. In comparably incautious moments in Mexico, NAFTA advocates implied that Mexico would only benefit and incur no costs. The overselling of NAFTA created political ill will toward it in years to come. Yet, NAFTA addressed the problems for which it was designed. And, politically, NAFTA removed trade and investment issues from the contentious high-politics agenda by relying on routine institutionalized problem solving procedures.

NAFTA was, above all, a trade agreement. During the 1990s, NAFTA succeeded within its own terms. It fostered trade and investment impressively and made it much easier to resolve complex trade disputes through routine procedures. A decade later, the conclusion is the same. As Table 2.2 shows, U.S. exports to Mexico recovered from the economic recession at the start of the 2000s and reached a new very high level by 2007. Mexican exports to the United States were less affected by that recession and jumped dramatically by 2007. Gary Hufbauer and Jeffrey Schott, who have examined NAFTA in considerable detail, conclude: "It has worked."

Table 2.2 U.S. Top Trade Partners: Exports, Imports, and Trade Balance, 2000-2008 (billion U.S. dollars)

	U.S. Exports			U.S. Imports			U.S. Trade Balance		
	2000	2003	2008	2000	2003	2008	2000	2003	2008
Canada	176.4	169.5	261.1	229.2	224.2	339.5	−52.8	−54.7	−78.4
Mexico	111.7	97.5	151.2	135.9	138.1	215.9	−24.2	−40.6	−64.7
China	16.3	28.4	69.7	100.1	152.4	337.8	−83.8	−124.0	−268.1
Japan	65.3	52.1	65.1	146.6	118.0	139.3	−81.3	−60.9	−74.2

Source: U.S. Department of Commerce, Office of Trade and Industry. Information; http://tse.export.gov accessed July 14, 2008 and October 1, 2009.

North American firms have become "more efficient and productive, restructuring to take advantage of economies of scale in production and intraindustry specialization. U.S.–Mexico trade has grown twice as fast as U.S. trade outside of NAFTA, and foreign investment in Mexico has soared."[19]

More worrisome is that the growth rate of Mexico's gross domestic product (GDP) was modest in the 2000s. Mexico recovered quickly from its 1994–1995 financial crisis and grew during the balance of the 1990s. Its economy did not go bust at the start of the 2000s, as had happened repeatedly in the last quarter of the twentieth century when the U.S. economy suffered a recession. In the early 2000s, the Mexican economy joined the U.S. economy in the recession—but it was only a recession, not another panic. However, Mexico's economy should have surged in the 2000s, given NAFTA access to U.S. and Canadian markets, yet the growth of Mexican GDP in the 2000s just matched the growth rate of the U.S. economy.

NAFTA was not designed to have an impact directly on employment and wages, no matter what its advocates and detractors claimed. On balance, its impact on U.S. employment and wages was positive but modest. Mexican real wages have not risen since NAFTA went into effect in 1994; the low growth of Mexican productivity along with exchange rate effects rather than the effect of international trade are the main explanations.[20] The effect of technological change on the Mexican economy explain the wider wage gap between skilled and unskilled workers in Mexican manufacturing industries before and after trade liberalization; the latter helped to prevent the wage gap from becoming even wider.[21] Similarly, increased foreign direct investment flows into Mexico were associated with decreased income inequality within Mexico's thirty-two states.[22] The root causes of high inequality in Mexico precede NAFTA.

The impact of NAFTA on certain sectors of Mexican agriculture has been worrisome. The adjustment cost of NAFTA to Mexican agriculture was under-appreciated at the start; programs to alleviate this burden were under-funded. Corn, Mexico's largest crop, occupied two-thirds of the country's agricultural land. It is a major staple in the Mexican diet, especially important to the poor. It is also a significant cultural artifact, embedded within the nation's imagination. NAFTA greatly facilitated U.S. corn exports to Mexico. The more U.S. corn Mexicans imported, the less Mexican farmers planted; they could not compete on price or commodity quality control, even if they still could on taste. On the eve of NAFTA's implementation, U.S. corn imports supplied only 2 percent of Mexican consumption; ten years later, such imports accounted for one-fifth of Mexican consumption.[23] Agricultural liberalization under NAFTA enabled many Mexicans to purchase a much wider variety of food at lower prices but it generated hardship for many Mexican corn and some other agricultural producers.

NAFTA's direct impact on the environment in Mexico has been negligible. There is little evidence that NAFTA increased the likelihood that firms operating in Mexico have a superior environmental record or have improved their environmental performance. Similarly, NAFTA did not make Mexico a pollution haven; dirty industry in the United States did not flock to Mexico. Some environmental conditions did worsen in Mexico but that was because the governments did not implement effective environmental policies that might have led to better environmental outcomes. NAFTA was neither a blessing nor a curse.[24]

NAFTA was also a political accomplishment. Notwithstanding the enormous power disparity between Canada, Mexico, and the United States, all three countries complied. They eliminated tariffs and quotas and met market access commitments. There have been some notable instances of noncompliance with NAFTA. The United States resisted opening its borders to cross-border trucking despite its clear NAFTA obligation to do so. Seven years after it should have happened, on September 8, 2007, the first Mexican eighteen-wheeler cargo truck crossed into Texas at Laredo, headed for North Carolina as part of the implementation of a highly restrictive U.S. pilot program that permitted Mexican trucks to enter the United States. Yet, early in 2009, the U.S. Congress enacted a prohibition on such Mexican trucking and President Barack Obama signed the bill into law. For its part, Mexico delayed providing market access for U.S. express courier services, while Canada imposed restrictions on split-run periodicals. Given an agreement as vast as NAFTA, these violations are insignificant. Moreover, NAFTA was designed to increase the number of trade disputes because the larger the volume of trade, the more likely trade friction becomes. In general, dispute settlement has worked well. The judgments of NAFTA panels have been observed for the most part in compliance with the terms rendered.[25]

NAFTA channeled all but a few trade disputes into institutionalized channels for routine problem solving of disputes. At most a handful of trade disputes require the attention of the presidents or senior officials in the two governments. NAFTA has unburdened the bilateral agenda from a great many hitherto highly politicized trade disputes. Thus its final success is somewhat bittersweet: It freed the presidential agenda to permit presidents and their governments to focus on security and migration disputes between the United States and Mexico, in the knowledge that NAFTA would handle well nearly all trade disputes.

Evolution of Trade and Investment Patterns

Consistent with expected NAFTA effects, Mexico became and remained one of the principal U.S. trade partners. During the 2000s, as Table 2.2 shows, Mexico has been consistently second only to Canada in its importance as an export market for the United States. Since 2003, it has been third, behind China and Canada, as a source of U.S. imports. It has been a more important trade partner for the United States than Japan, Germany, or the United Kingdom.

As Tables 2.3 and 2.4 demonstrate, the United States became the destination of approximately four-fifths of the value of Mexican exports, though Mexico diversified its exports slightly during the 2000s. On the imports side, between 1995 and 2008 the value of Mexican imports from the United States increased fourfold, rising each and every year during the 2000s. Yet, Mexico succeeded in diversifying its sources of imports impressively during this decade. China and Canada (included in "Other") and, to a lesser extent, the European Union (EU) made significant strides. Between 1995 and 2008, Mexico's imports increased five-fold from the EU and fifty-seven-fold from China. China's share of Mexican imports was on track to exceed the European Union's share by the end of the century's first decade. (On Mexico and China, see also the previous chapter.)

Table 2.3 Main Sources of Mexican Imports (percentage)

Year	Total	US	EU[a]	LAC[b]	Japan	China	Other
1970	100	63.6	25.7	5.8	4.3	n.a	0.6
1980	100	66.9	13.7	5.7	5.4	n.a	8.3
1990	100	64.6	15.5	5.1	4.7	n.a	10.1
1995	100	74.4	9.4	2.1	5.5	0.7	7.9
2000	100	73.1	8.8	2.6	3.7	1.7	10.2
2006	100	50.9	11.3	5.4	6.0	9.5	16.8
2007	100	49.5	12.0	5.0	5.8	10.5	17.2
2008	100	49.0	12.7	4.5	5.3	11.2	17.2

Source: México, Secretaría de Economía, with data from Banco de México.

a Spain and Portugal entered in 1986; last expansion was in 2007 with Rumania and Bulgaria.
b Latin American and Caribbean countries; Panama included.

Table 2.4 Mexican Exports by Main Destination (percentage)

Year	Total	US	EU[a]	LAC[b]	Japan	China	Other
1970	100	68.2	7.8	13.3	6.1	n.a.	5.3
1980	100	65.4	—	7.1	4.5	n.a.	22.0
1990	100	70.7	12.2	7.3	5.3	n.a.	4.5
1995	100	83.3	4.2	4.8	1.2	0.0	6.4
2000	100	88.7	3.5	2.6	0.6	0.1	4.5
2006	100	84.7	4.4	4.6	0.6	0.7	5.0
2007	100	82.1	5.4	5.6	0.7	0.7	5.6
2008	100	80.2	5.9	6.4	0.7	0.7	6.1

Source: México, Secretaría de Economía, with data from Banco de México.

Note: Some rows may not add up to exactly 100 because of rounding errors.
a Spain and Portugal entered in 1986; last expansion was in 2007 with Rumania and Bulgaria.
b Latin American and Caribbean countries; Panama included.

Table 2.5 Mexico's Annual Foreign Direct Investment (FDI)

Year	Total FDI (millions of dollars)	United States FDI (millions of dollars)	U.S. FDI (percentage of FDI)
1994	$10,646.9	$4,966.5	46.6%
1995	$8,374.6	$5,514.8	65.9%
1996	$7,847.9	$5,281.1	67.3%
1997	$12,145.6	$7,420.3	61.1%
1998	$8,373.5	$5,467.0	65.3%
1999	$13,858.6	$7,499.8	54.1%
2000	$18,019.6	$12,939.1	71.8%
2001	$29,817.7	$21,415.2	71.8%
2002	$23,728.8	$13,019.7	54.9%
2003	$16,521.8	$9,208.2	55.7%
2004	$23,681.1	$8,638.5	36.5%
2005	$21,976.8	$11,650.3	53.0%
2006	$19,428.0	$12,443.1	64.0%
2007	$27,528.2	$11,666.0	42.4%
2008	$22,481.2	$9,096.8	40.5%

Source: Mexico, Secretaría de Economía.

The story of foreign direct investment in Mexico resembles the story of Mexican imports. Annual total inflows of foreign investment into Mexico doubled between the 1990s and the 2000s. Foreign direct investment flows from the United States followed the same pattern. The big story, however, was foreign investment from other countries, in particular from European Union countries. As a result, as Table 2.5 shows, the U.S. share of foreign direct investment in Mexico fell on average from about two-thirds in 1996 to about two-fifths in 2008.

In sum, trade and investment relations within North America were buoyant during the first decade of the twentieth century. NAFTA's liberal framework welcomed increased international economic transactions between the United States and Mexico, on the one hand, and, on the other, with other countries including China and the European Union. The experience of trade and investment in North America was one of generalized gains. This macro story affirms the within-NAFTA micro story. The governments of Mexico and the United States had been freed to focus on other challenges. We turn to analyze the most important of those challenges.

Failed Immigration Efforts: Bilateral (2001) and Unilateral (2004–2007) Initiatives

At the end of January 2001, while in Davos, Switzerland, Jorge Castañeda, just recently appointed Foreign Relations Secretary, received a phone call from Juan José Bremer, who had just been appointed Mexican Ambassador to Washington. Bremer told Castañeda that President Bush had accepted President Fox's invitation to travel to Mexico to visit Fox's ranch in San Cristóbal, Guanajuato. Bush's visit sent a clear message: relations with Mexico would be a priority for Bush's newly elected administration. Thus Castañeda advised Fox to take advantage of Bush's willingness to tackle the issue that had long been neglected by both countries—the increasing flow of undocumented Mexican immigrants to the United States—through a comprehensive immigration agreement.

Immigration issues had not been given such joint presidential priority since the 1960s.[26] Fox and Castañeda hoped to go down in history as the masterminds of a new immigration agreement whose significance would be comparable to that of NAFTA. The immigration agreement would affect the still-unfolding largest migratory flow from Mexico to the United States in the history of the two countries.[27] It would legalize millions of undocumented Mexicans who represented more than half of the largest undocumented immigration pool ever to have lived in the United States.[28]

The 2001 plan for a bilateral agreement over the movement of Mexicans to the United States would fail, however. President Bush's unilateral initiative, announced in 2004, for the United States to enact some reforms would fail as well. By the end of the Fox and Bush presidencies, Mexican immigrants to the United States still faced tough times.

The Bush immigration reform initiative, in particular, generated a heated U.S. national debate that lasted from January 2004 to May 2007, when the Senate majority leader dropped the attempt to bring the bill to a vote.[29] During this time, U.S. anti-immigrant groups seized the national spotlight. Moreover, upon the defeat of immigration reform in Congress, federal, state, and local governments took the opportunity to enact various anti-immigration initiatives. State and local governments wanted to limit health care and education services hitherto available to immigrants. Federal government policies sought further control over the U.S.-Mexican border and to enforce immigration laws at the workplace.

After years of exertion on behalf of immigration reform, Mexico and Mexican immigrants still faced the "stick" but had not gotten the "carrots" they most wanted—the regularization of undocumented workers and the enactment of guest worker programs.

The Fox and Castañeda Immigration Gambit

Four goals helped to shape Fox's and Castañeda's attempt to negotiate a comprehensive immigration agreement:

1   Solve the key pending issue in U.S.–Mexican relations—the migration of Mexicans.
2   Apply the same diplomatic approach first used in the early 1990s by President Salinas: institutionalize the management of bilateral issues through agreements and targeted mechanisms.
3   Take advantage of the positive momentum—the "honeymoon phase"—at the outset of the Fox and Bush administrations.
4   Move towards a greater integration of the countries in North America, the so-called "NAFTA plus" in Fox's diplomacy.

As the former governor of Guanajuato—a traditional region of emigration—Fox was sensitive about immigration issues and had first-hand knowledge of the troubles that Mexican immigrants faced in the United States. He thought that the prevalent status quo on immigration was unacceptable: in 2000 alone, 460 Mexicans had died trying to cross the border.[30] Two countries that had established sophisticated trade relations through NAFTA had to find better means to manage immigration flows. Therefore, when Bush came to Guanajuato three weeks after taking office, Fox took the opportunity to denounce the status quo on immigration and propose a comprehensive agreement to solve the immigration problem.

In the 1990s, however, changes in U.S. policy toward illegal immigrants had made the crossing more dangerous yet had failed to provide a satisfactory outcome for the United States. The Clinton administration tightened control over the U.S.-Mexican border in an effort to slow down the flow of illegal immigrants coming from Mexico and Central America. By 2000, however, it was clear that the physical barriers between Tijuana and San Diego and the sharp increase in border patrol staffing[31] had not stopped the flow of illegal immigrants. These U.S. measures had had three unexpected consequences. First, the routes that illegal immigrants followed shifted toward the less inhabitable parts of the border, especially the desert between Sonora and Arizona, resulting in more casualties as people tried to cross. Second, because it was harder to cross, people found a greater need to hire professional smugglers or "*polleros*," which increased the number of smugglers and strengthened this criminal activity. Finally, the migration flow of Mexicans to the United States lost its "circularity." Mexican migration to the United States from the mid-1990s onwards became the same as most other migration flows in the world: immigrants stayed in the host country. The attempt to shut down the border had little impact on the long-term movement of Mexican migrants to the United States and it decreased the likelihood that Mexicans would ever return home.[32]

Prior to becoming Foreign Relations Secretary, Castañeda had highlighted the necessity to improve the status quo of Mexican migrants to the United States through a new agreement. In 1996 he published an article that praised the Bracero programs (agreements between the governments of the United States and Mexico for Mexican contract labor, which lasted from 1942 to 1964) and argued that "Mexico should aim for the legal departure of a significant number of immigrants each year via negotiations with the United States."[33] He thus proposed to return to the approach initially employed by Carlos Salinas, which involved negotiating agreements to address salient issues in U.S.–Mexican relations. The Salinas administration had addressed trade and investment. The time had come to tackle the problem of immigration through a comprehensive agreement. Fox's victory over the Partido Revolucionario Institucional (PRI) helped to consolidate democracy in Mexico. Castañeda characterized Fox's popularity at the beginning of his term and the optimism that it generated as a "democratic dividend." He claimed that Mexico deserved "special treatment" for having achieved it, enabling both countries to conduct business as equals.[34]

The Fox-Castañeda proposal had five main components: (1) establishment of a guest worker program; (2) earned regularization of legal status for undocumented immigrants who complied with specified criteria; (3) socioeconomic development projects in Mexico's traditional immigrant-sending regions; (4) bilateral cooperation over border administration and security; and (5) facilitating family reunification. (In 2005, the size of the entire unauthorized population in the United States was estimated at 11.1 million people; some five million of these were Mexican.)[35]

Washington took seriously the ambitious immigration proposal that Fox and Castañeda put forth in February 2001. It was an opportunity for the Bush administration to show its interest in international issues and in Mexico.[36] Bush was personally receptive. As Governor of Texas, he came to respect Mexican-origin people and welcomed their contribution to economy and society in Texas. The United States had experienced an economic boom during the second half of the 1990s, which augured well for a bilateral migration agreement. By decade's end, the U.S. economy had only a 4.5 percent unemployment rate. This promising economic outlook explains the favorable views toward immigration expressed by key actors in U.S. politics. Allan Greenspan, Chairman of the Federal Reserve Board, highlighted the significant contributions of immigrants to the U.S. economy. The peak U.S. labor confederation, American Federation of Labor and Congress of Industrial Organizations (AFL-CIO), changed its anti-immigration stance to one that accepted allowing immigrants provided they were to take jobs that U.S. citizens did not want.

Fox's main foreign policy objective was to move toward a more integrated North American economic community. Castañeda described Fox's ideas as "a rosy picture of a hypothetical North American Economic Community, along European lines, associating Mexico with the United States and Canada."[37] As president-elect, visiting Bush in Dallas, Texas, in September 2000, Fox referred to his vision of Mexico and the United States having "open borders." An immigration agreement would be a key building block to construct an economic community in North America, incorporating a new social chapter into NAFTA.

The U.S. Response to the Mexican Proposal

The Bush administration, eager to reach an understanding with Mexico, soon became somewhat baffled by the Fox administration proposal upon closer examination. Consider the five key elements in that proposal, mentioned above. All but one required the United States to make all the concessions and Mexico to make none. As Bush administration officials saw it, the United States was responsible for actions; Mexico was responsible for applauding such U.S. actions. The United States would change its laws to:

1   Take in Mexican workers,
2   "Regularize" the status of undocumented migrants who had already broken U.S. law to enter the United States,
3   Facilitate family reunification, allowing the newly "regularized" Mexican migrants to bring their relatives into the United States, and
4   Invest vast sums to develop those Mexican regions, which are the sources of the largest numbers of potential violators of U.S. entry laws.

Admittedly, receiving guest workers is most likely in the U.S. interest, as it is in the U.S. interest to drain the pool of illegality that could breed further illegal behavior. Yet, the only hint that the Mexican government would actually contribute anything to address these U.S. problems was the suggestion that Mexican authorities would cooperate with the United States over border administration and security. In bilateral negotiations, U.S. diplomats underlined the importance of border cooperation as the one clear gain that the U.S. government expected from its cooperation with Mexico.[38] On balance, however, as U.S. Ambassador Jeffrey Davidow put it in his memoirs, the concept that there would be U.S.–Mexican negotiations over migration was little more than an "effort to convert American law into a grand bargain."[39]

Mexico might have but did not make formal proposals of interest to the United States. Mexico could have welcomed its U.S. and Canadian NAFTA partners to co-manage Mexico's southern border with Central America because it was the same southern border for all of North America. Mexico could have proposed the establishment of procedures at its northern boundary to deter the emigration of those Mexicans who lacked proper documentation to enter another country. Mexico could have offered to reform its labor laws to enable citizens of its NAFTA partners to work in Mexico, just as it was hoping that the partners would change their labor laws.

Equally baffling to the Bush administration was Secretary Castañeda's insistence that the migration negotiations depended on the rules of a "single undertaking" that characterized trade negotiations, namely, no part of the agreement would be approved until all parts were approved. Given the enormity of what the Fox administration was asking from the Bush administration, what Secretary Castañeda called colloquially the "whole enchilada" approach was unreasonable. Yet, the United States went along at first.[40]

On August 9, 2001, Secretary Castañeda and Government Secretary Santiago Creel met in Washington with their counterparts, Secretary of State Colin Powell and Attorney General John Ashworth. At a joint press conference, Secretary Powell tried to convey Washington's growing reservation about Mexico's full-court press for a rapid agreement on highly complex immigration issues. Powell said, "We are in no hurry."[41] The reason was plain. There had been very little progress on the key issues of regularization, temporary workers, and visa policy review. Given that Mexico had offered so little, the problem was entirely on the U.S. side. The Justice Department was reluctant to enact the changes that Mexico wanted. Republicans in Congress had informed the White House that legalization of undocumented aliens would alienate the president's political base. Very little had been accomplished since the Bush-Fox hugs in Guanajuato by the time when Fox visited Washington on a state visit in early September 2001. As Ambassador Davidow would put it, "It later became conventional wisdom in Washington and Mexico City to assert that the two governments might have reached an understanding on immigration if the terrorists had not struck. But this is not an accurate reflection of the likely possibilities at the time of the state visit." By that time, "the president's team decided not to risk support among his political base by developing a dramatic new plan in immigration."[42] The September 11 terrorists fired only the second shot that killed the bilateral immigration deal.[43]

From the Failed Bilateral Agreement to the Failed Unilateral Immigration Reform

The immigration problem did not disappear, however. President Bush called on Congress to enact an immigration reform bill, denouncing what he called an immigration system that does not work, which he eventually labeled a "broken immigration system."[44] In January 2004, Bush presented an immigration reform proposal, including the creation of a guest worker program and a tax-preferred savings account that the immigrants could access upon returning to their country of origin. The president did not shut the door to eventual citizenship but did not provide a blueprint for regularization. The proposal would also increase border enforcement and step up efforts to ensure that business firms would comply with U.S. law.[45]

In Congress, several attempts were made to change immigration policy. These bills fell into three categories. First, some aimed at a comprehensive pro-immigration reform; all of these eventually failed. The two most salient were sponsored by Senators Edward Kennedy (D-Mass.) and John McCain (R-Ariz.) in the 109th Congress, and by Senate Majority Leader, Harry Reid (D-Nev.) in the 110th Congress. The second group of bills included partial pro-immigration initiatives, all of which would also be defeated. Among these the most relevant were the Ag Jobs and the Dream Act. The first, introduced by Senator Kennedy and Senator Larry Craig (R-Idaho), aimed to regularize more than half a million agricultural workers. The Dream Act, introduced by Senator Richard Durbin (D-Ill.), sought to allow undocumented youths to attend U.S. state universities and colleges paying in-state tuition. Finally, various initiatives would toughen immigration enforcement. Two of these passed: the Real I.D. Act, also known also as the Sensenbrenner Bill (2005), and the Secure Fence Act (2006), which approved the construction of a 700-mile long fence along the U.S.-Mexican border.

The congressional activity caused a heated debate of truly national proportions. According to one poll, in mid-summer of 2007, 86 percent of the American public had followed the debate.[46] The anti-immigrant groups enjoyed two advantages: the focus on security created by the terrorist attacks of 9/11 and signals that the U.S. economy was slowing down in 2007. Anti-immigrant groups benefited greatly from popular radio and television pundits who used the immigration debate to increase the public's anxiety in the midst of concerns about international terrorism and the globalization of markets.[47]

The Mexican government did not help its own public relations case, however. It published a guide for Mexican migrants who were considering crossing the border. The guide warned that it was dangerous to cross the Rio Grande/Río Bravo alone and at night and also that heavy clothing picked up more water at the crossing, making swimming more difficult and sinking more likely. The guide advised, "If you cross the desert, be sure to walk during the time of day when the heat is not so intense." The guide also observed, "Salt with water helps to retain body liquids . . .

If you drink water with salt, the risk of dehydration is much less." The *Guía* insisted that it was not designed to promote the crossing of the boundary by Mexicans who lacked the U.S. entry documents. Rather, its aim was to inform about the risks implied in such crossings and to advise the migrants about their rights, regardless of their legal status.[48] The guide could be and was read, however, by anti-immigration radio and TV personalities as a how-to manual for illegal crossings.

Pro-immigration movements had moments of glory but not effectiveness. In the Spring 2006, millions of immigrants took part in street demonstrations in many U.S. cities to pressure Congress to abandon the severe measures (such as classifying illegal immigration as a felony) that the U.S. House of Representatives had approved in December 2005 (Sensenbrenner Bill). In Los Angeles and Chicago, more than 400,000 took to the streets. These protests inspired pro-immigration groups and lawmakers in Congress and helped to dilute the harshest provisions of the law. Immigrants lack lasting political power, however: they cannot vote in U.S. elections.

In March 2006, a national survey of 2,000 adults conducted by the Pew Research Center found that: "Americans [were] increasingly concerned about immigration. A growing number believe[d] that immigrants are a burden to the country, taking jobs, housing, and creating strains on the health care system. Many people also worried about the cultural impact of the growing number of newcomers in the US." When asked whether "Immigrants today are a burden because they take jobs, housing, and health care," in September 2000 only 38 percent agreed; in March of 2006, that percentage had risen to 52 percent. Similarly, in May 2007, a *New York Times*/CBS News nationwide poll of 1,125 adults asked, "How serious a problem do you think the issue of illegal immigration is for the country right now?" In response, 61 percent said "very serious" and 30 percent "somewhat serious." Nevertheless, the 2006 Pew survey also found that 80 percent of the public believed Latin American immigrants to be hard-working and possess strong family values; only 37 percent believed that immigrants often went on welfare while only 33 percent thought that they significantly increased crime.

The principal changes, however, were Bush administration actions, such as the increased frequency of immigration raids, tougher enforcement of the immigration laws at the U.S.-Mexico border and elsewhere, and implementation of the legislative mandate to build long stretches of fence along the border between Mexico and the United States in the Arizona-Sonora region.[49] These measures created a climate of fear among immigrants.

Bush administration decisions should be placed in perspective, however. Consider one indicator: border patrol funding and staffing. Between 1986 and 2002, border patrol funding rose 519 percent and border patrol staffing 221 percent. The upward trend was steady throughout that time.[50] Notwithstanding the president's hopes to change aspects of immigration policy, the Bush administration merely extended the long series of restrictive measures, none of which had stopped migration flows in the long run.

In sum, President Fox's initial efforts to change the immigration status quo failed. At the end of the second Bush administration, the immigration debate had led to a more adverse situation for Mexican immigrants in the United States, both for those already in the country as well as for those trying to enter. The new border barriers seem to have had a temporary deterring impact. According to the Pew Hispanic Center, in early 2007 there was downward trend in the flow of undocumented migration from Mexico as a result of the cumulative tightening of the border—the construction of fences, the increased presence of the border patrol, the posting of the National Guard, and the deployment of technology to secure the border.[51]

Yet, as we have noted, research on similar measures in place since the start of the 1990s indicates that the principal impact of such restrictive policies is to transform the long-standing seasonal, cyclical, or circular migration flow, whereby Mexicans entered the United States for a time and voluntarily returned to Mexico, into a permanent inflow. Once crossing into the United States becomes so difficult, if you succeed, don't go back—just stay. The wall strengthens the incentives for migrants to remain permanently in the United States once they have crossed successfully. If these past findings hold, then the net effect of these restrictive measures will be to increase the number of permanent Mexican immigrants in the United States.

The failed immigration reform did nurture a trend toward a consensus in the United States: in a world past September 11, the United States requires a legal and orderly migration flow. Many believe that there should be immigration reform in the United States to achieve greater order and legalization but there is no consensus on how to achieve this goal. This explains the impasse in Congress in 2007–2008.

Discussions of undocumented immigrants in the United States often obscure the fact that very large numbers of Mexicans enter the United States lawfully every day. Not fewer than four million Mexicans were admitted lawfully with U.S. nonimmigrant visas each and every year during this decade; in 2008, 7,273,511 Mexicans entered the United States with such visas. In 2008, 830 Mexicans per hour entered the United States as lawful nonimmigrants to visit, engage in business, shop, or study. Their engagement with the United States serves the interests of both peoples. In addition, over a million people per day cross the U.S.-Mexican border to do business in the region within twenty-five miles of the border.

There is a more problematic trend in the number of lawful permanent immigrants from Mexico to the United States. In the 1990s, their average annual number was 275,742. One additional impact of the U.S. security measures enacted in response to the terrorist attacks of September 2001 was to reduce that annual number to 173,632 between 2000 and 2008. In turn, fewer authorizations for legal permanent migration create incentives for migration without proper documents. The combination of reduced opportunities for lawful permanent migration and more restrictive border measures against undocumented migration makes it more likely that undocumented migrants who manage to enter the United States choose to remain in this country.

Yet another effect of the U.S. measures enacted in response to the September 11 terrorist attacks seems to have been the construction of even more obstacles for naturalization. The number of new naturalizations of Mexican-origin persons in the United States fell from 189,051 in 2000 to 55,946 in 2003, though it recovered to

122,258 in 2007 and 231,815 in 2008 as these Mexican-origin migrants chose permanency in the United States over returning to Mexico.[52]

The Border

The U.S.-Mexico border was the geographic site most affected by the U.S. response to the terrorist attacks of September 11, 2001. At the start of their respective terms, the Fox and Bush administrations had focused on the inefficiencies of border crossings, which were a bottleneck to NAFTA-facilitated trade expansion. There was a growing conviction that big investments in infrastructure were necessary at the border in order to grow the NAFTA trade (construct new and fix old bridges, build binational sewer systems, and so forth) in order to develop the border region as an integrated economic zone.

The terrorist attacks, however, compelled a sharp change in the perception of the border from Washington, from an economic region that badly needed investment to a vulnerable security zone. Ambassador Carlos Rico, President Calderón's Undersecretary for North American Affairs,[53] explains the transformation in Washington's perspective of the U.S.-Mexico border as follows: With the creation of the Homeland Security Department (DHS), other federal agencies—the Departments of Justice, Treasury, and State—almost vanished from the management of the border. DHS handles more than 90 percent of the total federal budget assigned to the border and classifies all border topics as matters of concern for domestic security; it sees all policy making through a prism of control and security. Thus DHS has stopped almost every attempt to improve the efficiency of border crossing.

Consider the Secure Electronic Network for Travelers Rapid Inspection lines, called SENTRI for short. The SENTRI system identifies travelers who pose no security risk and allows them to cross using dedicated commuter lanes. Program participants are issued machine-readable cards and transponders for their vehicles. SENTRI participants submit to extensive background checks, fingerprinting, photographing, and registration. SENTRI lines are excellent tools to speed up the border crossing process—usually taking only a few minutes—for businesses as well as persons with legitimate interests on both sides of the border. Yet, it took DHS almost five years to authorize the construction of three additional SENTRI lines (in 2008, there were altogether nine SENTRI lines operating along the entire U.S.-Mexican border).[54]

U.S. border crossing cards (BCCs) are another successful procedure to expedite lawful border crossings by Mexicans into the United States. BCCs are laser visas issued to frequent crossers to enter a defined "border zone" of 25 miles of U.S. territory north of the border for a period of 72 hours or less without a U.S. visa. In 2004, 6.8 million Mexican citizens held BCCs. Similarly, the Customs-Trade Partnership against Terrorism expedited customs procedures at ports of entry for businesses that voluntarily adopted security procedures under the direction of U.S. customs. Many of the largest businesses engaged in North American trade have registered; they are eligible to use FAST ("Free and Secure Trade") lanes at the border for expedited processing.[55]

Nevertheless, six years after September 11, 2001, a Mexican border think tank, El Colegio de la Frontera Norte, assessed the efficiency of five ports of entry at the U.S.-Mexico border, concluding that bottlenecks at U.S.-Mexico land ports increased since the September 11 attacks. These bottlenecks impeded bilateral commerce because time delays impose large operational costs on trans-border companies. Since 2001, there has been a shift to much harsher inspection policies at U.S. border points of entry, making it harder for binational commerce to develop. In Tijuana, Baja California, every year 64 million people, 5.5 million passenger vehicles, and 1.4 million commercial vehicles cross the border. At the Tijuana port of entry, the proportion of people who wait for 60 minutes or more to cross the border has gone up 12 percent; the proportion of vehicles that wait for 60 minutes or more has risen 32 percent. In another border state, Sonora, time delays occur because of the military presence. Across the border region, waiting time at the border is up by at least 6 percent at almost every crossing point.[56]

To be sure, the increased power of drug cartels and criminal organizations in areas along the Mexican side of the border has deepened the concern in both countries about border security and helps to explain the increased deployment of security personnel to the border region.[57] This is especially worrisome at three border towns, Nuevo Laredo, Matamoros, and Ciudad Juarez. Even though the crossing between Nuevo Laredo, Tamaulipas, and Laredo, Texas, accounts for the largest fraction of U.S.–Mexican trade, in 2007 exceeding $100 billion, drug traffickers and organized crime operate with impunity in this region.

As a result, in early 2005 U.S. officials claimed that Nuevo Laredo, Tamaulipas, was spinning out of control. This Mexican city alone accounted for twenty-seven kidnappings of U.S. citizens.[58] In response to this increased violence, in January 2005 U.S. Ambassador to Mexico, Tony Garza, sent an open letter to Mexican law enforcement officials expressing his concern about the increasing violence on the border. In February 2005, the State Department issued a travel advisory warning, informing U.S. citizens about the growing violence in some Mexican border cities.[59] In July 2005, after a very violent confrontation between drug traffickers, Ambassador Garza temporarily closed the U.S. Consulate in Nuevo Laredo, claiming that even its employees were at risk.[60]

In mid-2006, President Bush announced the deployment of 15,000 National Guards to help to patrol the southern border against both organized crime and undocumented migrants.[61] This was followed by the Secure Fence Act, signed into law by President Bush in October 2006, which mandated the construction of a 700-mile fence on the U.S.-Mexican border. This law required the DHS to install an intricate system of surveillance cameras along the Arizona-Mexico border.[62] And yet, consider the oldest fence at the U.S.-Mexican border, built in 1990 between Tijuana and San Diego. This concrete fence rises up to 15 feet. High-intensity lights bathe the area around the fence. The U.S. Border Patrol employs 24-hour surveillance cameras. Yet, border patrol agents report that individuals routinely manage to scramble over all of these fences in less than one minute.[63]

Upon his inauguration in December 2006, President Calderón agreed that lawlessness on the Mexican side of the border had become unacceptable for Mexico. As noted earlier, the president deployed tens of thousands of Mexican troops to combat organized drug cartels across Mexico. Many of these troops were deployed to Mexico's border cities in an attempt to restore public order.

A borderless North America was not in the making. "[T]he people who die in the desert" seeking to enter the United States without documents are not criminals, Vicente Fox wrote in his memoirs.

> They are sons and daughters, mothers and fathers. They are pioneers, like the brave people who built your country and mine, crossing deserts in search of a dream. Our sin was greater, mine and George Bush's, because in Mexico we have failed to provide them the jobs they needed to survive while, in the United States, businesses in the world's richest economy held out the promise of opportunity, then officers with guns arrest those who come in hope.[64]

Mexico's former president thus summarized well North America's daily tragedy and reiterated the urgent need for future governments to do better.

Conclusion

At the dawn of the second decade of the twenty-first century, Mexico and the United States had discovered yet again that changes beyond the control of their governments had decisive impacts on their relations. The terrorist attacks of September 11, 2001, and the transnational process involving drug traffic and unauthorized international migration changed the bilateral agenda of the two governments during the century's first decade. Their governments felt compelled to respond. The principal impact of the September 11 attacks on U.S.–Mexican relations was to fire the second shot that killed bilateral negotiations over migration. The principal impact of the disagreement over the war in Iraq, as noted, was to prevent improvements in bilateral relations.

The actions of governments mattered, to be sure. The choice of the Bush administration to go to war in Iraq transformed U.S. relations with most other governments, including Mexico's. Mexico chose to place the immigration issue on the agenda of its diplomatic negotiations with the United States, and the Bush administration subsequently launched a unilateral effort to change U.S. immigration policy. The endeavors of both governments in war and migration failed. The most impressive and effective governmental actions in bilateral relations had been inherited from the 1990s, however: NAFTA institutions worked well to address and solve bilateral trade disputes following their routine, technical procedures.

External shocks and governmental design changed the structure of the international system at the start of the century. Fortunately for U.S.–Mexican relations, NAFTA institutions held up, fostering a massive increase in bilateral trade and helping both countries to cope with the disputes that are a normal side effect of such trade growth. Unfortunately for bilateral relations, bilateral security institutions atrophied just as Mexico's internal security situation deteriorated. Mexico felt compelled to accommodate unilateral U.S. security preferences; the Calderón administration thus sought through Plan Mérida to recalibrate bilateral relations along an institutional design that resembled the one fashioned by the Clinton and Zedillo administrations.

As the United States inaugurated a new president on January 20, 2009, the two countries faced clear challenges. During the preceding decade, the effect of organized drug traffic crime had worsened and the pool of unauthorized Mexican migrants in the United States and the number of Mexicans who died upon attempting to cross the border had grown. This remained the bilateral agenda that was being carried forward. The bilateral security institutions built in the 1990s had atrophied and new ones had to be developed to cope with these increasingly serious issues. Fortunately, bilateral trade and investment had grown and NAFTA's problem-solving institutions had succeeded. Mexico's democratic institutions had also responded with effectiveness and responsibility as they faced the new foreign policy challenges. Mexico and the United States worked most effectively in the past when they jointly built bilateral institutions. They had no choice but to face up to their shared North American future together.

Notes

1. Vicente Fox and Rob Allyn, *Revolution of Hope: The Life, Faith, and Dreams of a Mexican President* (New York: Viking, 2007), 195–199, 205–210, quotations from 195, 196.
2. Jorge I. Domínguez and Rafael Fernández de Castro, *The United States and Mexico*, 2nd ed. (New York: Routledge, 2009), Epilogue.
3. For a description, see *The Economist*, October 6, 2001, 38; October 13, 2001, 39.
4. Vicente Fox Quesada, "Mexico's Participation in the Fight against Terrorism," in *Woodrow Wilson Center Update on the Americas: Mexico*, no. 2 (December 2001): 5.
5. See Luis Rubio's thoughtful "Mexico Alert: The Vote that Wasn't," *CSIS Hemisphere Focus* 11, no. 8 (March 28, 2003): 1–5.
6. Fox and Allyn, *Revolution of Hope*, 283–284.
7. Tim Weiner, "U.S. and Mexico Coordinate Military Efforts for Mutual Protection against Terror," *New York Times*, March 23, 2003, B13; Armand Peschard-Sverdrup, "Mexico Alert: The Impact of the War in Iraq on Mexico," *CSIS Hemisphere Focus* 11, no. 10 (April 8, 2003): 1–5; Jordi Díez and Ian Nicholls, *The Mexican Armed Forces in Transition* (Carlisle, PA: Strategic Studies Institute, U.S. Army War College, 2006), 36.
8. K. Larry Storrs, "Mexico-U.S. Relations: Issues for Congress," *Issue Brief for Congress* (Washington, C: Congressional Research Service, Library of Congress, January 30, 2003), 11.
9. Laurie Freeman, *State of Siege: Drug-Related Violence and Corruption in Mexico* (Washington, DC: Washington Office for Latin America, June 2006).
10. "Versión de la comparecencia del Secretario de Gobernación, Francisco Ramírez Acuña, ante el pleno de la Cámara de Diputados, con motivo del primer informe de gobierno del Presidente Felipe Calderón Hinojosa," Secretaría de Gobernación, http://www.gobernacion.gob.mx accessed July 20, 2008.
11. U.S. Department of State, Bureau of International Narcotics and Law Enforcement, *International Narcotics Control Strategy Report, 2008*, vol. I, 176–181, quotation from 180; http://www.stage.gov accessed July 14, 2008.
12. "Versión estenográfica de las palabras de la Embajadora Patricia Espinosa Cantellano, Secretaria de Relaciones Exteriores, en la reunión de trabajo de las comisiones unidas de

relaciones exteriores, y de relaciones exteriores, América del Norte, del Senado," Secretaría de Relaciones Exteriores, http://www.ser.gob.mex accessed July 20, 2008; Carlos Rico, "La Iniciativa Mérida y el combate nacional al crimen organizado," *Foreign Affairs en español* 8, no. 1 (2008): 3–13.

13. "Mérida Initiative. Background and Funding," *CRS Report for Congress* (Washington, DC.: Congressional Research Service, Library of Congress, March 18, 2008), 1–5.

14. Laurie Freeman, "La política antidrogas en la relación México-Estados Unidos," *Foreign Affairs en español* 8, no. 1 (2008): 15–23.

15. U.S. Department of Defense, Office of the Assistant Secretary of Defense (Public Affairs), News Transcript, April 2008, http://www.defenselink.mil/transcripts accessed July 20, 2008.

16. Raúl Benítez, "Seguridad y defensa en México," *Foreign Affairs en español* 3, no. 4 (2003): 162–163.

17. Secretaría de Gobernación, "No tiene ninguna razón válida el EPR para su campaña de hostigamiento contra el pueblo de México," *Boletín* no. 331–07 (December 7, 2007), http://www.gobernacion.gob.mx accessed July 20, 2008; "Versión de la comparecencia del Secretario de Gobernación, Francisco Ramírez Acuña . . ."; for Secretary Gates' comments, see U.S. Department of Defense, Office of the Assistant Secretary of Defense (Public Affairs), *News Transcript*, April 2008, http://www.defenselink.mil/transcripts accessed July 20, 2008.

18. For Mexico's complex policies on deploying its troops outside its borders, see Benítez, "Seguridad y defensa en México," 167–171.

19. Gary C. Hufbauer and Jeffrey J. Schott, *NAFTA Revisited: Achievements and Challenges* (Washington, DC: Institute for International Economics, 2005), quotation from 61.

20. Ibid., 38–54.

21. Gerardo Esquivel and José Antonio Rodríguez-López, "Technology, Trade, and Wage Inequality in Mexico before and after NAFTA," *Journal of Development Economics* 72 (2003): 543–565.

22. Nathan Jensen and Guillermo Rosas, "Foreign Direct Investment and Income Inequality in Mexico, 1990–2000," *International Organization* 61 (Summer 2007): 467–487.

23. James Austin, Michael Chu, and Cate Reavis, "FIRA: Confronting the Mexican Agricultural Crisis," Harvard Business School Case 9–304–032 (Rev. March 10, 2004), 1–20.

24. Kevin P. Gallagher, *Free Trade and the Environment: Mexico, NAFTA, and Beyond* (Palo Alto, CA: Stanford University Press, 2004).

25. Frederick Abbott, "NAFTA and the Legalization of World Politics: A Case Study," *International Organization* 54, no. 3 (Summer 2000): 519–547; Hufbauer and Schott, *NAFTA Revisited*, 54–55; "The Border: Free Trade and Fireballs," *The Economist*, September 15, 2007, 40.

26. For discussion of what came to be known as Mexico's policy of not having a migration policy, see Carlos Rico, "Migration and U.S.–Mexican Relations," in *Western Hemisphere Immigration and United States Foreign Policy*, ed. Christopher Mitchell (University Park, PA: Pennsylvania State University Press, 1992), 221–283.

27. Pew Hispanic Center, "Indicators of Recent Migration Flows from Mexico," *Fact Sheet*, May 30, 2007.

28. Jeffrey Passel, "Unauthorized Migrants: Numbers and Characteristics," Pew Hispanic Center, 2004, 5.

29. Tamar Jacoby, "Immigration Reform, a Bitter Tide Begins to Ebb," *Berkeley Review of Latin American Studies* (Spring 2008): 2.

30. Zreportage, Zuma Press, *Deadly Crossing*, April 24, 2006. www.zreportage.com/DEADLY_CROSSING/DEADLY_CROSSING_text.html.

31. Wayne Cornelius, Philip L. Martin, and James F. Hollifield, *Controlling Immigration, A Global Perspective* (Palo Alto, CA: Stanford University Press, 2004), 69–70.

32. Wayne A. Cornelius, "Controlling 'Unwanted' Immigration: Lessons from the United States, 1993–2004," *Journal of Ethnic and Migration Studies* 31, no. 4 (July 2005): 775–794; Wayne A. Cornelius and Idean Salehyan, "Does Border Enforcement Deter Unauthorized Immigration? The Case of Mexican Migration to the United States of America," *Regulation and Government* 1 (2007): 139–153.
33. Jorge G. Castañeda, *The Estados Unidos Affair. Cinco ensayos sobre un "amor" oblicuo* (Mexico: Aguilar, 1996), 63–84.
34. Jorge G. Castañeda, *ExMex, From Migrants to Immigrants* (New York: The New York Press, 2007), 70.
35. Jeffrey S. Passel, "The Size and Characteristics of the Unauthorized Migrant Population in the U.S.," Washington, DC: Pew Hispanic Center, March 2006.
36. Pamela Starr, "U.S.–Mexican Relations," *CSIS, Hemispheric Focus* 12, no. 2 (January 9, 2004), 3.
37. Castañeda, *ExMex,* 69.
38. U.S. Department of State, "U.S.–Mexico Migration Talks and Plan of Action for Cooperation on Border Safety," *Joint Communiqué,* June 22, 2001, http://www.state. gov/r/pa/prs/ps/2001/index.cfm?docid=3733 accessed August 25, 2001.
39. Jeffrey Davidow, *The US and Mexico: The Bear and the Porcupine* (Princeton, NJ: Markus Winner, 2004), 216.
40. U.S. Department of State, "Joint Statement of the U.S.-Mexico High level Working Group on Migration," *Press Statement,* April 4, 2001, http://www.state.gov/p/wha/ci/ mx/index.cfm?docid=2013 accessed August 25, 2001.
41. U.S. Department of State, Secretary Colin L. Powell, "Remarks with Attorney General John Ashcroft, Mexican Secretary Jorge Castañeda, and Mexican Interior Minister Santiago Creel," August 9, 2001, http://www.state.gov/secretary/rm/2001/indix.cfm? docid=4492 accessed August 25, 2001.
42. Davidow, *The US and Mexico,* 223–231, quotation from 230. See also Andrew D. Selee, "Political Failure, Policy Success? The U.S.-Mexico Migration Agreement," Paper presented at the International Congress of the Latin American Studies Association, October 3, 2004.
43. Fox's proposal to negotiate a bilateral immigration agreement generated an academic debate in Mexico over the wisdom of approaching the White House to the relative inattention of the U.S. Congress. See Jesús Velasco in "Immigration Agreement: The Weakness of Hope," and Andrés Rozental, "Fox's Foreign Policy Agenda: Global and Regional Priorities," both in *Mexico Under Fox,* ed. Luis Rubio and Susan Kaufman Purcell (Boulder, CO: Lynne Rienner, 2004).
44. The White House: "President Bush Attends National Hispanic Prayer Breakfast," June 8, 2006, and "Press Conference by the President at the Rose Garden," May 24, 2007.
45. The White House, "President Bush Proposes New Temporary Worker Program," January 7, 2004, http://www.whitehouse.gov/news/releases/2004/01/print/20040107-3.html accessed January 8, 2004.
46. As quoted by Jacoby, "Immigration Reform, a Bitter Tide Begins to Ebb," 13.
47. David Leonhardt, "Truth, Fiction, and Lou Dobbs," *New York Times,* May 30, 2007.
48. Secretaría de Relaciones Exteriores, *Guía del migrante mexicano* (Mexico, no date), 4, 6.
49. Julia Preston and Marjorie Connelly, "Immigration Bill Provisions Gain Wide Support in Poll," *New York Times,* May 25, 2007.
50. Independent Task Force on Immigration and America's Future, *Immigration and America's Future: A New Chapter* (Washington, DC: Migration Policy Institute, 2006), 55.
51. Pew Hispanic Center, "Indicators of Recent Migration Flows from Mexico," *Fact Sheet,* May 30, 2007.
52. U.S. Department of Homeland Security, Office of Immigration Statistics, *Yearbook of Immigration Statistics, 2008* (Washington, DC), Tables 3, 21, and 26; U.S.–Mexico Binational Council, *U.S. Mexico Border Security and the Evolving Security Relationship* (Washington, DC: Center for Strategic and International Studies, 2004), 3.

53. Personal interview with Ambassador Carlos Rico, July 15, 2008.
54. See Homeland Security, CBP Securing America's Borders, *SENTRI Program Description Secure Electronic Network for Travelers Rapid Inspection*, March 17, 2008 http://www.cbp.gov/xp/cgov/travel/trusted_traveler/sentri/sentri.xml. In 2007, three new sentry lines were approved and opened in Brownsville-Matamoros, Reynosa, and Mesa-Ottay.
55. U.S. Mexico Binational Council, *U.S.–Mexico Border Security and the Evolving Security Relationship*, 10, 12–13.
56. "Estudio de Puertos de Entrada," El Colegio de la Frontera Norte, December 19, 2007, 2–12.
57. For a thoughtful analysis, see José María Ramos García, "La política de seguridad fronteriza de Estados Unidos: Estrategias e impactos binacionales," *Foro internacional* 44, no. 4 (October–December 2004): 613–634.
58. "U.S.: Kidnappings High Along Mexico Border," *USA Today*, January 27, 2005.
59. U.S. Department of State, Office of the Spokesman, *Public Announcement*, February 2, 2005, http://travel.state.gov/travel/cis_pa_tw/pa/pa_2100.html.
60. "Garza debió usar otras palabras: Washington," *La Jornada*, August 19, 2005.
61. "Government Refuses Bush Request for Border Troops," *Los Angeles Times*, June 24, 2006.
62. For a discussion of actions by government and unauthorized civilian border patrol groups, see Roxanne Lynn Doty, "States of Exception on the Mexico–U.S. Border: Security, 'Decisions,' and Civilian Border Patrols," *International Political Sociology* 1 (2007): 113–137.
63. Peter Skerry, "How Not to Build a Fence," *Foreign Policy* (September–October 2006): 65.
64. Fox, *Revolution of Hope*, 343.

3 The United States and Cuba since 2000*

Marifeli Pérez-Stable

For the first time in more than fifty years, Fidel Castro is not presiding over Cuba. On February 24, 2008, the National Assembly of Popular Power named his younger brother, Raúl Castro, then seventy-six, president of the Council of State and the Council of Ministers. Since July 2006 Raúl had held interim power. Now he is formally in charge and, for the most part, substantively as well. As long as he is alive and mentally alert, however, the Comandante will remain a potent symbol and an influential voice.

Cuba is slowly starting down an uncharted path, not toward democracy but nonetheless toward something different from where the elder Castro was taking it before ill health felled him. Lacking his brother's charisma, Raúl must govern through institutions, especially the military and the Cuban Communist Party (PCC). This is nothing new. In the 1970s and early 1980s, the younger Castro led efforts to institutionalize the political system and somewhat loosen central control of the economy. In the early 1990s, Raúl and the generals were likewise instrumental in the modest economic reforms enacted after Germans tore down the Berlin Wall. On both occasions the Comandante stopped the reforms at his whim.

Since the nineteenth century, the United States has taken an inordinate interest in Cuban domestic matters. After 1959, the Eisenhower and Kennedy administrations sought to revert the revolution. In the aftermath of the Missile Crisis, however, Washington abandoned that goal, eventually pursuing a rapprochement with Havana during the Gerald R. Ford and James E. Carter administrations. After the cold war ended, regime change, in effect, returned to the heart of U.S. policy, conditioning a normalization of relations to a democratic transition on the island. The Barack H. Obama administration faces a fork in the road regarding Cuba. The first, hewing to the Helms-Burton Act of 1996—the Cuban Liberty and Democratic Solidarity (Libertad) Act—stands fast on maintaining the embargo until Havana moves to open politics and the economy. The second, which marked U.S. policy in the 1970s and, intermittently, in the 1990s under the William J. Clinton administration, takes a realpolitik approach. Washington need not be constantly shouting

* I am grateful to Landen Romei, Maïté Hostetter, and Emily Phan-Gruber for their research assistance.

its support of freedom and democracy in Cuba into an open microphone which, in any case, has not hastened either of them. The Cuban government not only survived the fall of the Soviet Union but is also managing the succession from Fidel to Raúl rather well. Under Raúl, Havana is set to be more predictable at home and abroad than it ever was under the larger-than-life Comandante.

A realpolitik approach means a realistic dialogue: neither Cuba's commitment to a democratic transition nor a unilateral lifting of the U.S. embargo need happen before Washington and Havana start stepping back from the long-standing dead end. That is precisely what the Obama administration did on April 13, 2009 by rescinding all restrictions on travel and remittances for family reasons—a campaign promise kept—and authorizing U.S. telecommunication companies to do business with Havana.[1] In Congress, bills to lift the embargo and the travel ban altogether are under consideration. While similar initiatives had been introduced in the past to no avail, Obama's inauguration has opened up vistas unthinkable under his predecessor.

The United States and Cuba: A Framework

The cold war, it is often said, has not ended for the United States and Cuba. Yet, the basic quandary of the U.S.–Cuba relationship—how a great power and its weaker neighbor relate to each other—well antedated the superpower conflict. During the nineteenth and early twentieth centuries, U.S. manifest destiny never contemplated the rightful interests of neighbors like Cuba.[2] For its part, Cuba viewed the United States with ambivalence: admiration for U.S. democracy and progress, mistrust of its presumptuousness. In short, the United States and Cuba have never had normal relations.

Before 1959, the two countries failed to establish a stable, mutually beneficial relationship as Mexico and the United States did after 1940. When the revolution aligned Cuba with the former Soviet Union, U.S.–Cuban relations grievously deteriorated. Two decades after the fall of European communism, Washington and Havana are still far from resolving their long-standing predicament: how the great power gains some consideration of Cuban sensibilities and the weaker neighbor turns geographic nearness into an asset. Because the cold war so estranged the two countries, normalizing relations after it has long been over—and it is for Cuba as well—has not been nor will it be easy. The two countries carry an exceptionally heavy historical baggage that cold-war legacies have gravely compounded.

Cuba and the United States at the Turn of the Century

In October 2000, Bill Clinton signed the Trade Sanctions Reform and Export Enhancements Act (TSRA) which authorized U.S. producers to sell agricultural commodities to Cuba while barring the Cuban government from U.S. public or private credits; TSRA also codified the travel ban. The House Republican leadership had given Cuban American representatives the last word on all Cuba-related legislation; credit prohibition and travel codification were their doing. Havana promptly rejected the change and declared that no purchases would be made; the embargo remained the central issue which TSRA did not address. On the day the U.S. Senate passed TSRA by an 86–8 vote, Fidel Castro led some 800,000 people in a protest march through Havana. After Hurricane Michelle battered Cuba in November 2001, however, the Comandante changed his mind. Declining the humanitarian aid offered by the George W. Bush administration, he announced: "We are ready, just for this once, to acquire certain quantities of food and medicine from the United States, paying them in cash."[3] In December, Havana put in an order for over $4.3 million. Between 2001 and 2008, U.S. exports to Cuba totaled just under $2.6 billion.[4]

Towards the end of his second term, Clinton reclaimed some executive prerogatives that the Helms-Burton Act had curtailed and, in the process, made Cuba policy more flexible. First, the president invoked the waiver of Title III. Had he not, U.S. citizens—including Cuban Americans who were citizens of Cuba at the time their properties were confiscated—could have brought suit in federal court against foreign companies which "trafficked" in confiscated U.S. properties.[5] Congress had, in short, extended the law's reach beyond U.S. national boundaries which U.S. allies found inadmissible. Second, Clinton largely disregarded Title IV which barred foreigners who "trafficked" in confiscated properties and their family members from entering the United States. Third, the administration made liberal use of Helms-Burton's limited licensing power to revise some sanctions. After Pope John Paul II's visit to Cuba in early 1998, licenses for charter flights, family remittances, and the sale of medicines were issued. A year later, the president allowed any U.S. resident to send remittances to individuals and independent organizations in Cuba, expanded two-way, people-to-people contacts, and authorized charter flights to Cuban cities other than Havana and from U.S. cities other than Miami.[6] Upon leaving office in 2001, Clinton bequeathed his successor a Cuba policy focused on a limited expansion of trade and broadened powers to increase contacts between the two countries. Without repudiating Helms-Burton, his administration mobilized trade and soft power to pry Cuba open. Without abandoning the goal of a democratic Cuba, the White House had started down a path of limited engagement.

In 1999–2000, two signal events marked U.S.–Cuban relations. In November 1999, Fidel Castro welcomed his fellow Iberoamerican heads of state to Havana. Since 1991, Spain, Portugal, and Latin American nations had held annual summits. The Comandante wryly noted that few had expected him to give the welcoming address when Cuba was selected as host seven years earlier. Iberoamerican heads of state sent Washington a twofold message: (1) With Castro at the helm, Cuba hosted their annual gathering; and (2) the Cuban government's survival after the cold war served the United States especially with an unanticipated fait accompli. The Cuban leadership had weathered the cold war's end without collapsing or making transformational changes. Even under adverse circumstances, Havana still managed to deal with the world largely on its terms.

The second happened shortly after the European and Latin American dignitaries had returned home from the Havana summit. Elián González, then five years old, was picked up in the Florida Straits and the Immigration and Naturalization Service

(INS) released him to his relatives in Miami. Elián's mother had perished in the passage, and his father lived in Cuba. For seven months, a custody battle raged between the boy's U.S. family and his remaining parent. Almost immediately, Havana mounted a campaign to have Elián returned to his father. Just as defiantly, Cuban Miami engaged in an effort to keep him in the United States. In the meantime, the Clinton administration and the Cuban government held talks throughout the ordeal. In early April, 2000, Elián's father, stepmother, and infant half brother traveled to the United States. A few days later, INS officials forcefully took the boy from his granduncle's Little Havana home and reunited him with his father in Washington. Upon learning of the father–son reunion, Castro remarked: "Today is a day of truce, perhaps the only one in the course of these 41 years of confrontation with the United States." Three months later Elián returned to Cuba with his family.

The saga over Elián brought unintended consequences that long endured. In Cuba, the custody battle afforded Castro an ideal opportunity to reignite the mobilization campaigns that best suited his leadership. For months, many Cubans genuinely responded to official demonstrations: Elián's father elicited widespread sympathy in his quest to get his son back. By July, however, the Comandante was embarking on the Battle of Ideas, an ideological struggle to reaffirm the revolution's spirit. From 2000 until his illness in 2006, institutions were partly relegated in favor of weekly gatherings in town after town, nightly roundtable discussions on television, loyalty pledges, and brigades of revolutionary vigilance. After 2000 Castro relished the almost nonstop performance of outward support from ordinary Cubans as evidence that the revolution lived on. In November 2005, he gave an address at the University of Havana—now almost certainly his legacy speech—in which he cautioned against the revolution's self-destruction. His antidotes lay in upholding correct ideas, championing social justice, keeping markets at bay, and never yielding to the United States on matters of principle. Ironically, the mobilization opportunities that Elián offered the elder Castro complicated the succession. The younger Castro's first order of business has been to restore *la institucionalidad* and sideline charisma's chaos.

In Miami, the struggle over Elián crystallized changes already in train. During the 1990s, the Cuban American National Foundation (CANF) had continued to hold sway in Washington. Chairman Jorge Mas Canosa, for example, often took part in White House meetings when Cuba was at issue. Still, time's passage was taking its toll. In 1997, Mas Canosa, 58, lost his battle against cancer. Younger CANF members rumbled in private over modifying the long-espoused hard-line. In 1998, many Cuban American Catholics traveled to Cuba at the time of the pope's historic visit. Already existing ties between island and Cuban American Catholics were strengthened and have continued to flourish. For Cuban Miami, Elián proved to be a fiasco in almost every sense. U.S. and international public opinion stood fast against denying a father rightful custody of his child for political reasons. Havana, in turn, won the public relations campaign by coining a new term for the *gusanos*: the worms metamorphosed into the Miami mafia. Yet, the fiasco also helped new currents to surface such as the creation of the Cuba Study Group—Cuban American businessmen supportive of a new U.S.-Cuba policy—and the split within

CANF which led hard-liners to form the Cuban Liberty Council (CLC). Between 1991 and 2000, moreover, Cuban American support for the embargo softened—from nearly 87 percent to 62 percent—while a majority (52 percent) favored a national dialogue among exiles, dissidents, and the Cuban government (up from nearly 40 percent). These trends have continued to develop.

All the same, the ill-fated fight to keep Elián in the United States soured Cuban Miami's mood towards the Democratic Party. Even though Democratic presidential candidate Al Gore supported the exiles' quest, more than 80 percent of Cuban American voters cast their ballots for George Bush. The sharp increase from the 65 percent Bob Dole had garnered in 1996 was a factor in the Republican winning Florida's then-twenty-five electoral votes. Without the butterfly ballot in Palm Beach County or the 96,000 Floridians who voted for Ralph Nader, Cuban Miami would not have mattered. But it did and not just on election day. Cuban Americans relentlessly supported the Bush campaign over the five weeks before the Supreme Court tendered its ruling. Thus, once in the White House, Bush owed Cuban-Americans a debt of gratitude, one that the community did not let him forget.

The Bush Administration, the Cuban Government, and Cuban Miami

Under Bush, Washington and Havana initially kept the late Clinton momentum going. The new administration maintained the somewhat relaxed embargo on agricultural commodities. In July 2001, the president waived Helms-Burton's Title III. Like Clinton after Helms-Burton's passage, Bush went on to waive Title III throughout his presidency which, in effect, rendered the controversial title dead letter. Obama is certain to uphold his predecessors' practice of postponing Title III. On trade, Bush largely continued the trends of the late 1990s, albeit instituting further strictures on Cuba's cash payment for U.S. food products. Under TSRA, shipments left U.S. ports before the financial transaction was completed. In February 2005, the Bush administration required Havana to complete the cash transaction before the vessels left for Cuba.[7]

In early 2002, Havana issued encouraging statements regarding relations with the United States. At a meeting in Havana of the U.S.-Cuba Sister Cities Association, Ricardo Alarcón—Cuba's veteran expert on relations with the United States—told the audience that Cuba wanted "a civilized relationship" and was ready to talk even with the embargo in place. He added: "Cuba is willing to discuss, negotiate and forge a joint cooperation in areas such as the struggle against terrorism, narcotrafficking, and human smuggling."[8] More than one hundred Americans from thirty-one cities and seventeen states participated in the association's sixth meeting. In January, more than 2,000 Americans—legislators and businesspeople among them—had traveled to Cuba, a number Alarcón termed unprecedented. Still, Cuba warned about the risks carried by the Bush administration's close ties with Cuban Miami and the high-level appointment of two hard-line Cuban Americans.[9]

Over the course of 2002, the Bush administration set Cuba policy on a track of its own, a hard line spurred by ideological conviction and political expediency. While many fellow Republicans had called for a change in Cuba policy since the late 1990s, Bush had stood firm on the embargo well before becoming president. Jeb Bush had also never wavered on Cuba. In 2002, moreover, he was seeking reelection to Florida's governorship and needed to keep Cuban Miami in his column. Whatever the continuities from Clinton to Bush on Cuba, there is no gainsaying the political and ideological sea change that Bush's election represented. During the 1990s, neo-conservative Republicans had issued a critique of George H.W. Bush's and, especially, Clinton's foreign policy that harked back to Reagan's appreciation of moral clarity and military might. Before September 11, 2001, administration realists and neoconservatives competed to win the president's ear. Afterwards, neoconservatives brought most of the realists to their side and held sway for the remaining of Bush's first term.[10] At the same time, between 2001 and 2007, Governor Bush and hard-line Cuban Miami had a direct line to the Oval Office on Cuban matters.

In May 2002, former President Jimmy Carter traveled to Cuba for five days. Though the private trip had been in the works since the mid-1990s, Carter never received the Clinton White House's blessing for it, which made Bush's consent all the more significant. A few days before Carter's arrival, Oswaldo Payá Sardiñas and other members of the Varela Project presented the National Assembly with a petition signed by 11,000 Cubans. Under the Constitution's Article 88, citizens can introduce a petition for the Assembly to consider if bearing at least 10,000 signatures. The Varela Project called for a referendum on political liberties, entrepreneurial rights, free elections, and release of political prisoners. Once in Cuba, the former president met with Payá and other opposition figures. In his address at the University of Havana broadcast live, Carter called on the U.S. Congress to lift the travel ban, open trade, and repeal the embargo, adding: "These restraints are not the source of Cuba's economic problems." Neither did he mince words on human rights, asking Cuba "to meet universally accepted standards in civil liberties, permit the International Red Cross to visit prisons, and to receive the U.N. Human Rights Commissioner." The former president praised the Cuban Constitution for Article 88 and the Varela Project for making use of it. "When Cubans exercise this freedom to change laws peacefully by a direct vote, the world will see that Cubans, and not foreigners, will decide the future of this country," Carter noted.[11]

The Bush administration, in the meantime, finished a review of Cuba policy. On May 20, 2002, the 100th anniversary of Cuban independence, the president announced an Initiative for a New Cuba: easing restrictions on humanitarian and entrepreneurial assistance to independent groups, offering U.S. scholarships to students and professionals committed to building autonomous institutions, modernizing Radio and TV Martí, and working with world leaders to empower Cuban civil society. Most noteworthy were his comments on Cuba's then-upcoming Popular Power elections:

> If Cuba's government takes all the necessary steps to ensure that the 2003 elections are certifiably free and fair and if Cuba also begins to adopt meaningful market-based reforms, then—and only then—I will work with the United States Congress to ease the ban on trade and travel between our two countries.

Bush asked Havana to invite "objective outside observers" to certify the election, while recognizing that "freedom sometimes grows step by step."[12] Though Bush's tone and most of his remarks hewed to Helms-Burton, his mention of the 2003 elections fleetingly accepted the Cuban Constitution as a starting point for change. His offer of "a meaningful American response" to "meaningful reform on Cuba's part," moreover, echoed Secretary of State Warren Christopher's "carefully calibrated steps" during the first Clinton administration. Neither the Cuban Constitution nor a step-by-step strategy abide by a strict reading of Helms-Burton, particularly with Fidel or Raúl Castro at the helm.

Bush's May 20th speech immediately became non grata within hard-core sectors in the administration and Cuban Miami. Administration hard-liners had already tried to derail Carter's visit. On May 6, John Bolton, undersecretary of state for arms control, stated: "The United States believes that Cuba has at least a limited offensive biological warfare research and development effort. Cuba has provided dual-use biotechnology to other rogue states."[13] Carter labeled the undersecretary's accusations—issued six days before his departure—"a suspicious coincidence." In his briefings by U.S. intelligence, the former president had been assured that Cuba was not involved in terrorist or biological warfare activities.[14] On May 13, Secretary of State Colin Powell distanced himself from Bolton: "We do believe Cuba has a biological offensive research capability. We didn't say it actually had some weapons."[15]

Back on the island, the Comandante could not let Carter's live-broadcast mention of the Varela Project nor, especially, Bush's Cuba initiative pass without a response. For three weeks in June 2002, the government mobilized ordinary Cubans, the party, the mass organizations, the National Assembly, and the media in a campaign to amend the Cuban Constitution. The reform's gist lay in making socialism "untouchable" and affirming that Cuba would never negotiate while under attack, threats, or pressures by a foreign power. Millions of Cubans lined up to sign the petition, the National Assembly admitted it, and the Constitution was duly modified in a special session. In November 2002, the National Assembly issued a report denying the Varela petition on procedural grounds.[16]

By the end of 2002, Bush's Initiative for a New Cuba had shed all inklings of moderation. The president's speech with the heterodox passages had long been buried. In early 2003, James Cason, chief of the U.S. Interests Section in Havana, visited opposition groups throughout the island, offered workshops at his home, and overall increased contacts with dissidents. Washington wanted to gauge the state of independent civil society so as to structure a more effective aid program. Havana labeled his actions "repeated provocations." As a matter of course, diplomats everywhere establish communication with a broad spectrum of the government, the opposition, and society. The Cuban government, however, does not accept universally accepted standards of civil liberties and, therefore, takes offense at overtures toward what it calls *grupúsculos* (miniscule groups), dismissing them as mercenaries beholden to the United States. In mid-March, Castro responded by arresting seventy-five peaceful opponents who were quickly convicted to long prison terms.

On April 2, the government arrested three men for hijacking a fifty-passenger ferry to cross the Florida Straits. Tried and convicted of terrorism, the men were executed on April 11, 2003. The political crackdown and the hijackers' swift execution brought Cuba a wave of international condemnation, including sanctions by the European Union.[17]

This time Cuban Miami and world public opinion agreed: Havana's actions were inexcusable. Yet, the Iraq War, which started on March 19, elicited mixed reactions from Cuban Americans. While strongly behind the president, the question—Why only Iraq?—was raised by many. Migration matters increased Cuban Miami's uneasiness with the Bush administration on Cuba. In July, two boats were hijacked: one incident ended violently with three fatalities; the other concluded when the U.S. Coast Guard picked up twelve hijackers. Washington agreed to their return on the condition that Havana punish them with prison, not execution. Before July was out, the Coast Guard intercepted another twelve Cubans driving a retrofitted 1951 Chevy truck in the Florida Straits; the men were sent back to Cuba and their ingenious contraption destroyed. In mid-August, thirteen state legislators from South Florida—10 Cuban Americans—wrote Bush a letter expressing "great disappointment and outrage" and noting the damage already inflicted on "the historic and intense support from Cuban American voters for Republican federal candidates, including yourself."[18]

The White House at last understood the frustration of Cuban Miami. On October 10, 2003, the president delivered a speech on Cuba, announcing a Commission for Assistance to a Free Cuba with Secretary of State Colin Powell and Secretary of Housing and Urban Development Mel Martínez as co-chairs. Over several months, the Commission mobilized one hundred federal employees in seventeen agencies. An administration official underscored its purpose: "There will be change in Cuba, and it will come under George Bush!"[19] In May 2004, the Commission issued *Report to the President*, a 423-page document that called for the "expeditious end of the Castro dictatorship"; the adjective "peaceful" is largely absent from the thick report. Some recommendations—disbanding Cuba's security institutions and prosecuting former regime officials, for example—would almost certainly prompt violence and social unrest. For the most part, the report reads like an occupation manual, even if written while the U.S. occupation of Iraq was already mired in violence. The Commission wrote as if someone other than the people of Cuba would determine their future. Its report gives minute guidance on a host of technical, economic, political, and social issues without recognizing the reservoir of human capital on the island. Subsequently, the Bush administration created the office of Cuban transition coordinator in the Department of State.

On July 31, 2006, Fidel Castro ceded power to Raúl Castro. Shortly, thereafter the younger Castro offered to open a dialogue with the United States, albeit couched in militant language. "At this stage of the game, they should understand that impositions and threats will achieve nothing with Cuba. We have always been willing to normalize relations on an equal plane. What we won't admit is an imperious and interventionist policy which the current administration frequently assumes."[20] A few days later, Assistant Secretary of State for Western Hemisphere Affairs Thomas Shannon recalled Bush's long-buried speech on Cuba:

> In May 2002 President Bush effectively made an offer to the Cuban regime. If Castro were prepared to free political prisoners, respect human rights, if he were prepared to permit the creation of independent organizations, and if he were prepared to create a mechanism and a pathway towards elections, then we would look in consultation with Congress for ways to lift the embargo and begin a deeper engagement with the Cuban state.[21]

Rhetoric aside, Shannon's mention of a Bush speech that had distressed hard-liners was also significant. Like the end of the cold war, Castro's illness stoked the anticipation that Cuba would finally change. Cuba policy, however, remained unchanged, immune to the reappraisal of U.S. foreign policy that the Bush administration carried out in the second term. The Cuban government sailed on.

Cuba in the International Arena

At the beginning, the U.S. embargo aimed to strangle the Cuban economy, isolate the island, and bring down the revolutionary government. It did not work. From the 1970s on, Fidel Castro and his closest associates engineered a foreign policy that undermined U.S. intentions and advanced Cuban interests.[22] Though dependent on the former Soviet Union, Cuba was never a Soviet satellite. After the cold war, Havana defied all expectations of a short lifespan. During the 1990s, a decade of thin cows, Castro once again showed his mastery of foreign policy. While the United States and most of its allies brought Cuba to task in the old U.N. Human Rights Commission, Havana mobilized almost unanimous condemnation of the embargo in the U.N. General Assembly. Deplorable as Cuba's record on human rights might be, time after time the world denounced the embargo more forcefully. As the Cuban Democracy and Helms-Burton Acts hardened the embargo, Canada, the European Union, and Latin America stayed the course of engagement, even if the Cuban government yielded precious little in return. In the 2000s, under either Castro, foreign policy has remained an all-important recourse for Havana. Unlike most areas of the Cuban state, the Ministry of External Relations (MINREX) works well and draws upon a capable cadre of diplomats. Like the Cuban Armed Forces, MINREX could also serve as a recourse for a democratic Cuba.

Cuba's standing in the international arena is, therefore, a factor for the Obama administration to consider as it reviews Cuba policy. The United States, Canada, the European Union (EU), and most of Latin America share the goal of a democratic Cuba. What has divided the United States from its allies is the means to get there: Washington has insisted on the embargo; the EU, Canada, and most of Latin America have opted for engagement. Neither policy has succeeded. U.S. allies have welcomed the Obama administration's recent moves. Spanish Prime Minister José Luis Rodríguez Zapatero, for example, praised Obama's "positive measures" and prompted Havana to respond by making economic reforms.[23] Thus, the incipient dialogue between Washington and Havana could foster a more favorable ambience for some U.S. allies to politely call on Cuba to engage in the inescapable give-and-take of diplomacy. A précis of some of Cuba's external relations follows.

- Brazil. In January 2008 President Luiz Inácio "Lula" da Silva visited Havana. The two countries agreed to increase their economic cooperation, especially in the sugar and oil industries. Brazil—the world's leading producer of cane-based ethanol—would not agree to cooperation in the sugar industry except in ethanol, notwithstanding the elder Castro's and Chávez's criticisms of biofuels. Brazil's oil company, Petrobras, has joined Cupet (Cuba Petroleum) in offshore exploration of oil fields estimated at no less than five billion barrels. In a May 2008 visit to Havana, Foreign Minister Celso Amorim expressed Brazil's desire to become Cuba's principal trading partner. In November, Lula returned to Cuba. Shortly thereafter, the Río Group announced that Cuba was joining its ranks. Brazilian–Cuban relations could lessen Havana's dependence on Caracas.
- Canada. Since the early 1990s, trade, investments, and tourists have marked relations between Canada and Cuba. Occasionally, human rights have caused tensions in the relationship. April–May, 2009 was one of those occasions. Before leaving for the Summit of the Americas, Conservative Prime Minister Stephen Harper said: "Cuba must embrace democracy." After the summit, Ottawa announced it would send the minister for the Americas on an official visit to Cuba. His trip, he said, aimed to "encourage productive, constructive responses to the U.S. gesture" and "to stress again our encouragement of the release of political prisoners and the opening of institutions to democratic practices." Havana cancelled the minister's trip. Not long after, Canada denied a visa to a Cuban cabinet minister who had planned to attend the annual shareholders meeting of Sherritt International, perhaps the largest foreign investor in Cuba.[24]
- China. In the past few years, China has emerged as Cuba's second largest trading partner. Chinese buses and locomotives have helped the government to improve its battered transportation infrastructure. Sinopec, China's state oil company, and Cupet are jointly exploring offshore in the island's western waters. The two countries are also pursuing joint ventures in biotechnology. Economic ties with China are based on economic interests, not political solidarity. China, moreover, does not impose political conditions. Visits by high-ranking officials to Beijing and Havana—including those of then-Defense Minister Raúl Castro in April 2005 and Chinese president Hu Jintao in November 2008—highlight the political ties between the two countries. Chinese–Cuban relations are rooted in institutions, not in the personal ties between their leaders.[25]
- European Union. Cuba's Black Spring in 2003 elicited the EU's condemnation. In June, the EU announced sanctions: no high-level official visits, scant participation in cultural events, and increased contacts with the opposition. Cuba's application to join the Cotonou Agreement—the EU economic cooperation

pact with African, Caribbean, and Pacific countries—was shelved. Havana immediately withdrew from consideration. On July 26, Castro rejected all EU humanitarian aid as a matter of "dignity"; during 1993–2002, EU aid had totaled 145 million euros. Subsequently most official contacts with EU embassies in Havana were frozen. With Zapatero's election in March 2004, Spain moved the EU towards easing strained relations with Cuba. By April 2005, Havana had reestablished official contacts with the Spanish and eight other EU embassies. Tensions did not dissipate as EU countries continued to cast their votes against Cuba in the old UN Human Rights Commission. In September 2006, Madrid came under fire when a high-ranking foreign ministry official met with dissidents in Havana. By 2007, however, Spain and then the EU started on a course to normalize relations. Havana's aversion to any conditions and EU expansion to include former Eastern European Communist countries rendered the negotiations difficult. The Czech Republic and Poland, in particular, held out for a tougher stance. In March 2009, EU–Cuban relations were normalized.[26]

- Iran. Since the 1979 revolution, Cuban–Iranian relations have been on a strong footing. In the 1990s, Havana and Tehran forged several cooperation agreements in biotechnology. These ties formed the basis for Undersecretary Bolton's claim that Cuba was providing "dual-use technology to rogue states"; no hard proof in that regard was ever put forward. Cuba has had strong political affinities with Iran, from supporting the Palestinian cause to espousing Tehran's right to develop nuclear power. In May 2001, Fidel Castro visited Iran and there said: "Iran and Cuba, in cooperation with each other, can bring America to its knees." After 9–11, some analysts saw a potential Cuba-Iran axis in the making. After his election in 2005, Mahmoud Ahmadinejad noted: "Iran's relations with Cuba are strategic and deep-seated." In September 2006, Havana hosted the Non-Aligned Movement's summit; Raúl Castro met privately with Ahmadinejad as he did with other heads of state in attendance. In January 2009, Tehran sent a special envoy to meet with the Cuban president; the agenda was not made public. In April 2009, Havana welcomed the Non-Aligned Movement's foreign ministers, and Castro met with Iran's. As with Russia, Iran sees Cuba as an important ally in the Americas. In general, the new Cuban president is not prone to take risks. While politically siding with Iran against the United States, this Castro is unlikely to engage in perilous behavior.[27]

- Russia. Since 2007, Russian–Cuban relations have noticeably improved from their post-Soviet trough. In November 2008, President Dimitry Medvedev visited Cuba, on the last leg of a Latin American trip that also included Brazil, Peru, and Venezuela. In early 2009, Raúl Castro spent a week in Russia and returned to Cuba with $354 million in new loans, mostly for purchasing agricultural, construction, and transportation equipment. Moscow had previously provided generous relief aid after the devastating 2008 hurricane season. Russia's national oil company and Cupet have signed agreements to explore offshore oil. Moscow sees Cuba as a "key ally" in the Americas, a region where it seeks to wield some influence. Raúl always had a soft spot for the former Soviet Union, which Vladimir Putin's Russia partly rehabilitated. Russia, in addition, can supply Cuba with spare parts for military and industrial equipment. After Russian military sources suggested Moscow might consider placing nuclear bombers on the island, Havana responded unequivocally. When asked about the "hypothetical possibility," then-Foreign Minister Felipe Pérez Roque answered: "The answer is 'No'." Still, Cuba supports Russian positions in Georgia and on U.S. anti-missile defenses in Central Europe. From Soviet days, Cuba owes Russia $20 billion, a matter that will not be resolved soon. Thus far, Cuba refuses to pay and Russia resists any talk of pardoning the sum.[28]

- Venezuela. Hugo Chávez's election tendered Havana a political and economic lifeline. After almost a decade of solitude, the Comandante found a soul mate in the Americas. Thus, Venezuelan–Cuban relations were initially established on the strong personal bond between Fidel and Hugo. Between 1999 and 2004, the bilateral relationship flourished as the two governments signed their first cooperation agreements: Venezuela's sale of oil at preferential prices and Cuba's dispatch of health-care personnel. Cuba also provides Caracas with military and security advisors. Since the advent of the Bolivarian Alternative for the Americas (ALBA) in 2004, Caracas and Havana have forged a regional network of allies and influence based on Venezuela's oil and Cuba's health-care services. Both countries likewise have military and intelligence ties with some allies—e.g., Bolivia and Nicaragua—though their extent is hard to determine. In 2007, trade in goods and services between Cuba and Venezuela reached $7.1 billion. Some 39,000 Cubans—31,000 in the health sector—are estimated to be in Venezuela. Cuban industries such as oil refineries, construction, and metallurgy are recipients of Venezuelan largesse. In December 2008, Raúl Castro paid an official visit to Venezuela before traveling to Brazil.[29] Raúl and Hugo are not soul mates but rather, at best, are in a marriage of convenience. As long as he lives, Fidel will issue reflections that keep the ALBA ideals of anti-imperialism and twenty-first century socialism alive. Raúl's foreign policy, nonetheless, is geared towards diversifying Cuba's partners in the international arena. Once the Comandante departs or, even before, if Havana succeeds in broadening commercial, aid, and investment ties with Brazil, Canada, Russia, and the EU, while easing tensions with Washington, Havana and Caracas might well develop normal relations. Given the intimacy of their current relationship, such a change would be remarkable.

A New U.S. Policy and Cuban Miami

U.S. policy toward Cuba cannot change without some support in the Cuban American community. Since 1991, Florida International University has polled Cuban Americans in South Florida. In the 2007 Cuba poll, 55.2 percent of respondents agreed with the statement, "The United States should allow unrestricted travel to Cuba." About 50 percent also agreed with ongoing U.S. sales of medicines and food to Cuba. Forty-two percent opposed the embargo outright, an increase of eight percentage points since the last survey in 2004. Cuban American public opinion is clearly shifting toward easing travel restrictions, with a hefty minority embracing the end of the embargo altogether. In 2008, the three Republican Cuban American members of Congress from South Florida beat back well-funded Democratic challengers. Their victory should be tempered by Obama's win in Florida: even though an estimated 65 percent of Cuban Americans in Miami-Dade County voted for John McCain, Obama won the county by a 58–42 margin, besting John Kerry's performance in 2004 by five points. An exit poll of voters in the 2008 general election showed movement in the Cuban American electorate.

- Only 31 percent of those born in Cuba voted for the Democrat, whereas 61 percent of those born in the United States did.
- Sixty-five percent in the 18-to-29 age group preferred Obama.
- Cubans who arrived in the 1990s were split 49 percent for Obama and 51 percent for McCain, whereas those who arrived in the 2000s broke 58 percent for Obama.
- Obama's 35 percent of the Cuban American vote is comparable to Bill Clinton's share in 1996, sixteen points better than Al Gore's in 2000, and ten points higher than Kerry's in 2004.

Simply put, Cuban Miami is not what it used to be. A 2008 Cuba/U.S. Transition Poll released in December 2008 further highlights the community's evolving views: 67 percent favored unrestricted travel to Cuba and 55 percent opposed the U.S. embargo. A poll conducted after the Obama administration lifted all restrictions on family-related travel and remittances underscored ongoing trends.

- Sixty-four percent favored the measures; nearly three-quarters of those between the ages of 18 and 49 did so while those arriving after 1980 overwhelmingly applauded the change. In all questions, responses by age and arrival decade were similarly lopsided toward openness.
- When asked whether they favored or opposed all U.S. citizens being able to travel to Cuba, 67 percent responded in favor of ending the travel ban.
- On the U.S. embargo, there was a virtual tie: 42 percent for continuing it, 43 percent for ending it with 15 percent answering don't know or nothing at all.
- Sixty-seven percent had a favorable or very favorable opinion of President Obama. Even the 50+ category gave Obama a 63 percent approval rating; the 18–49 category's was 71 percent.[30]

For the first time, Cuban Americans are expressing opinions that are trending—in some cases, strongly so—away from the familiar positions of traditional exiles. With generational turnover and newer arrivals from Cuba, change was bound to come. These trends, however, should not yet be considered permanent. Unforeseen events—in Cuba or in the United States—could stall or even partly revert them. In the U.S. Congress, Cuban American senators and representatives mostly oppose the Obama administration's overture toward Havana. Public opinion and the Cuban American political establishment are seemingly at odds, in part, because traditional exiles still constitute a majority of Cuban American voters. Given these exiles' staunch identification with the Republican Party, current trends should benefit the Democrats, particularly if those arriving in the 1990s and 2000s become citizens, register, and vote. Even if they do, these newer Cuban Americans may not vote solely on the issue of U.S. Cuba policy and enough may be swayed to back the incumbents for their record on domestic issues.

The Obama Administration, the Cuban Government, and the OAS

At the Summit of the Americas held in Trinidad-Tobago April 17–19, 2009, Barack Obama said: "The United States seeks a new beginning with Cuba. I know that there is a longer journey that must be traveled to overcome decades of mistrust, but there are critical steps we can take toward a new day."[31] The administration was prepared to engage the Cuban government on "a wide range of issues—from drugs, migration, and economic issues to human rights, free speech, and democratic reform." At a post-Summit press conference, the president acknowledged that "the policy we've had in place for 50 years hasn't worked," while stating that "the Cuban people are not free, and that's our lodestone, our North Star."[32] After he listened first-hand to several leaders at the Summit on the excellent work Cuban doctors do in their countries, Obama paid Havana a compliment of sorts. "It's a reminder for us in the United States," he said, "that if our only interaction with many of these countries is drug interdiction, if our only interaction is military, then we may not be developing the connections that can, over time, increase our influence and have a beneficial effect." A month later, the Department of State delivered a note to the Cuban Interests Section in Washington proposing that the two countries resume talks on migration.[33]

At an ALBA meeting in Cumaná, Venezuela, held before the Summit of the Americas, Raúl Castro took notice of Obama's April 13 policy overture : "We have conveyed to the U.S. government that we are open to discuss everything, human rights, press freedom, political prisoners, everything they want to discuss. But it should be on the condition of equality, without the slightest shadow over our sovereignty."[34] Raúl's statement and Obama's subsequent mention of Havana making a gesture such as freeing political prisoners prompted a barbed response from the elder Castro. "Without a doubt," Fidel wrote on April 21, "the president misinterpreted Raúl's declaration. It was a manifestation of courage and trust in the Revolution's principles. No one should be surprised that he mentioned pardoning those sanctioned in March 2003 and sending them all to the United States, if that country were willing to free the Five Heroes, Cuban antiterrorists."[35] A State Department official observed off the record: "Cuba's president hasn't told us we misinterpreted him." On April 29, President Castro addressed a meeting of Non-Aligned Movement foreign ministers in Havana:

> President Obama's recent measures, while positive, aren't far-reaching. The blockade remains intact. No political or moral pretext can justify continuing

with that policy. Cuba doesn't have to make gestures. As I said recently in Venezuela: we're ready to discuss everything, everything, everything, what pertains to us but also to them, on the condition of equality.[36]

On May 30, the Cuban Interests Section delivered a note to the Department of State accepting the Obama administration's proposal to resume migration talks. Havana also signaled a willingness to discuss direct mail service and cooperation on terrorism, drug trafficking, and hurricane disaster preparedness.[37]

On June 2–3 the OAS General Assembly met in San Pedro Sula, Honduras. Cuba was the sole item on the agenda. After much debate, the Assembly revoked the 1962 sanctions excluding the Cuban government from its ranks. The new resolution—which was unanimously passed—resolved:

1   That Resolution VI, adopted on January 31, 1962 at the Eighth Meeting of Ministers of Foreign Affairs, which excluded the Government of Cuba from its participation in the Inter-American System hereby ceases to have effect in the Organization of American States.
2   That the participation of the Republic of Cuba in the OAS will be the result of a process of dialogue initiated at the request of the Government of Cuba, and in accordance with the practices, purposes and principles of the OAS.[38]

Except for the United States, all countries in the region now have normal relations with Cuba. During 2009's first semester, ten Latin American presidents traveled to Cuba on official visits. Without Barack Obama's proclamation of "a new beginning, " however, rescinding Cuba's OAS exclusion would have been unthinkable.

In 1962, the resolution excluding the Cuban government was approved after Havana sided with the Soviet Union and lent support to guerrillas in Latin America. Under the Río Treaty (1947), such conduct imperiling hemispheric security merited expulsion from the inter-American system. At the time, the cold war was at its height. In 1964, the OAS called on member states to break diplomatic and commercial ties with Havana; all but Mexico complied. Eleven years later, however, the General Assembly resolved to end collective sanctions against Cuba and set member states free to restore relations with Havana. The Ford administration, which had opened a discreet dialogue with Havana, green-lighted the OAS move. Still, the 1975 resolution passed only with the requisite two-thirds majority. Chile, Paraguay, and Uruguay, then military dictatorships, voted No; military-led Brazil and Anastasio Somoza's Nicaragua abstained.

"What is the next step for us? Nothing," OAS Secretary General José Miguel Insulza said after the annulment of the 1962 expulsion. National Assembly president Ricardo Alarcón called the move "a major victory," but quickly added that Cuba had no plans for rejoining the OAS. Dan Restrepo, senior director for Western Hemisphere Affairs at the National Security Council, noted: "We did exactly what we stated we would do here, which was stand up for the core values of democracy and human rights." Senator Robert Menéndez (D-N.J.) warned: "If the OAS allowed Cuba back in the fold without the government in Havana demonstrating a commitment to democracy, then I seriously would have to question why the U.S. government would want to pay 60 percent of an organization that is not committed to democracy, human rights, and the rule of law." Ecuadorean Foreign Minister Fender Falconi lauded the resolution for being free of "conditions of any kind, which is a good sign, because an historic error has been corrected." Honduran president Manuel Zelaya declared: "We begin a new era of fraternity and tolerance."[39] The resolution's meaning is, indeed, in the eye of the beholder.

At first glance, the discussion in San Pedro Sula was about revoking Cuba's suspension. While conditions were not directly imposed, the resolution does establish a process which only Havana can trigger. If and when it does, the OAS would host a dialogue based on its "practices, purposes, and principles"—democracy, human rights, and the rule of law—to bring about the "participation of the Republic of Cuba." At another, however, the crux lies with the Inter-American Democratic Charter (2001); Article 3 reads:

> Essential elements of representative democracy include, *inter alia*, respect for human rights and fundamental freedoms, access to and the exercise of power in accordance with the rule of law, the holding of periodic, free, and fair elections based on secret balloting and universal suffrage as an expression of the sovereignty of the people, the pluralistic system of political parties and organizations, and the separation of powers and independence of the branches of government.

In the 2000s, some governments—Venezuela, Bolivia, Ecuador, Nicaragua, and perhaps Honduras—have, in practice, rejected representative democracy and put forward an alternative model of participatory democracy. Should Havana take the initiative to open a dialogue as per the resolution's second point, the OAS would be in a bind that might well bury it. Member states would no longer be able to avoid facing the challenges that the ideas and practices of participatory democracy have lobbed at the Democratic Charter. Inevitably, the issue would also be competing views of the United States: partner or empire?

In lifting the 1962 expulsion, the OAS states gave Cuba the power to provoke what almost certainly would be a major crisis. While Chávez, Correa, and the others may well be itching for that fight, Havana will unlikely knock anytime soon. True, the Cuban government spares no epithet against the OAS. For the time being, however, it almost certainly would not undermine the opportunity of improving relations with the United States. After all, Havana's most important relationship—whether in enmity or friendship—is Washington's. Thus, if the two countries make progress in easing their estrangement, Cuba may well curb the enthusiasm of Venezuela and its allies. On the other hand, should this Cuban government take the initiative offered by the new resolution, it would be in a context of troubles everywhere: the OAS, U.S.–Latin American relations and, especially, the fledgling U.S.–Cuba rapprochement.

Regarding the United States and Cuba, Latin America and the Caribbean should take a deep breath. Neither country is set on a fast-track to mend their long-standing tensions. With the revocation of the 1962 OAS resolution and the offer of a path for the Republic of Cuba's readmission, the region should take its cues from Havana and Washington. The principals, moreover, have never expressed an interest in mediation by third parties. Neither end of the U.S. embargo nor respect for human rights in Cuba will happen quickly. Obama's new beginning and the OAS vote, however, may create opportunities to raise political matters with or about Havana which Bush administration policies precluded. Canadian Prime Minister Harper's comment on democracy and Spanish Prime Minister Zapatero's call for a Cuban gesture are cases in point. Down the road, some Latin American governments—those which support the Inter-American Democratic Charter—might yet find ways of broaching such matters with Havana.

The United States and Cuba, no doubt, will walk over jagged terrain before reaching fully normal relations. How could it be otherwise after having been so long estranged? Finding the trust necessary to talk is the first step. Presidents Obama and Castro have agreed to talks on migration and other issues where cooperation might be relatively easy and, thus, agreements would establish some ground in common. Both governments, however, are trapped in a rhetorical vicious cycle. Washington frames a new beginning in terms of the Cuban people's freedom while Havana stands fast on the United States respecting Cuban sovereignty. If both sides are serious about mending tensions, neither should lose opportunities to advance mutual interests while not forsaking their respective ideals. Washington may do more for the Cuban people's human rights by lowering the volume than the Bush administration ever did by carrying a big stick and speaking harshly. Havana released political prisoners in the 1970s without diminishing Cuban sovereignty. In the end, a democratic Cuba will ultimately come from within or not at all. For now, the Obama administration should mind Henry Kissinger's advice at the start of the quiet talks of 1974–1975: "Behave chivalrously; do it like a big guy, not like a shyster."

Notes

1. Between 1998 and 2004, U.S. citizens and residents could travel once a year to see family and send them remittances of up to $300 a quarter per household. In 2004, the Bush administration restricted travel to once every three years but only to direct-lineage family members with remittances allowed strictly to these members, e.g., grandparents, parents, siblings, children, grandchildren, spouses.
2. Ramiro Guerra, *La expansión territorial de los Estados Unidos* (Havana: Editorial de Ciencias Sociales, 1975); Lars Schoultz, *That Infernal Little Cuban Republic: The United States and the Cuban Revolution* (Chapel Hill: The University of North Carolina Press, 2009); Louis A. Pérez, Jr., *Cuba and the United States: Ties of Singular Intimacy* (Athens: University of Georgia Press, 1990).
3. "Easing of Embargo Rejected by Havana," *Latin American Regional Report: Caribbean & Central America* (October 31, 2000), 6.
4. "Castro Welcomes One-Off US Trade," *BBC Americas*, November 17, 2001, http://news.bbc.co.uk/2/hi/americas/1662346.stm.
5. U.S.–Cuba Trade and Economic Council, "2008 U.S. Export Statistics for Cuba," http://www.cubatrade.org/CubaExportStats.pdf.
6. Robert L. Muse, "A Public International Law Critique of the Extraterritorial Jurisdiction of the Helms-Burton Act (Cuban Liberty and Democratic Solidarity Act (LIBERTAD)

Act of 1996)," *The George Washington Journal of International Law and Economics* 30, no. 2/3 (1996–1997): 207–270.

7. Patrick J. Haney and Walt Vanderbush, *The Cuban Embargo: The Domestic Politics of an American Foreign Policy* (Pittsburgh: University of Pittsburgh Press, 2005), 110–118.

8. "Castro in Quotes," *The Guardian,* February 19, 2008, http://www.guardian.co.uk.

9. Discurso pronunciado por Fidel Castro Ruz, Presidente de la República de Cuba, en el acto por el aniversario 60 de su ingreso a la universidad, efectuado en el Aula Magna de la Universidad de La Habana, el 17 de noviembre de 2005, www.cuba.cu/gobierno/dis-cursos/2005/esp/f171105e.html.

10. Institute for Public Opinion Research and Cuban Research Institute, Florida International University, *2000 FIU/Cuba Poll,* http://www.fiu.edu/~ipor/cuba2000/index.html.

11. United States International Trade Commission, *U.S. Agricultural Sales to Cuba: Certain Economic Effects of U.S. Restrictions* (July 2007): 3–5 and 3–6, http://www.usitc.gov/publications/pub3932.pdf.

12. "La Habana dispuesta a negociar pese al embargo," *El Nuevo Herald,* February 19, 2002.

13. In 2001–2005, Mel Martínez led the Department of Housing and Urban Development. Otto Reich first served as Assistant Secretary of State for the Western Hemisphere under a recess appointment and then as U.S. Special Envoy for the Western Hemisphere. Both left after Bush's first term, Reich for private life and Martínez for the Senate.

14. Robert Kagan and William Kristol, eds. *Present Dangers: Crisis and Opportunity in American Foreign and Defense Policy* (New York: Encounter Books, 2000); James Mann, *The Rise of the Vulcans: The History of Bush's War Cabinet* (New York: Vintage Adult, 2004).

15. Remarks by former U.S. president Jimmy Carter at the University of Havana, Cuba, May 14, 2002, http://www.cartercenter.org/news/documents/doc528.html.

16. Remarks by the president on Cuba Policy Review, Washington DC, May 20, 2002, http://www.cubanet.org/CNews/y02/may02/21e5.htm.

17. "Cuba: Bioweapons Threat or Political Punching Bag?," Terrorism Project, Center for Defense Information, Washington, DC, http://www.cdi.org/terrorism/cuba-pr.cfm#_ftnref1.

18. Rosa Townsend, "Powell se retracta de las acusaciones de bioterrorismo contra La Habana," *El País,* May 15, 2002.

19. David González, "Carter and Powell Cast Doubt on Bioarms in Cuba," *New York Times,* May 14, 2002.

20. Ley de Reforma Constitucional, http://www.granma.cubaweb.cu/terrorismo/artic-ulo0173.html; Respuesta confeccionada por la Comisión de Asuntos Constitucionales y Jurídicos de la Asamblea Nacional que le fue entregada a Oswaldo Payá acerca de su proyecto el 18 de noviembre del 2002 y enviada posteriormente por correo el 26 de noviembre del mismo año, http://cuba-l.unm.edu/?nid=19534&cat=cd.

21. David González, "Cuba Arrests a Score of Dissidents Linked to a U.S. Diplomat," *New York Times,* March 20, 2003; Tim Weiner, "Cuba Arrests 8 in Hijacking of Havana Ferry," Ibid., April 5, 2003; Anita Snow, "Cuba Executes Three Men for Ferry Hijacking, *The Independent,* April 12, 2003, http://www.independent.co.uk/news/world/americas/cuba-executes-three-men-for-ferry-hijacking-594227.html; Gabriela Cañas, "La Unión Europea adopta sanciones diplomáticas contra Cuba," *El País,* June 6, 2003.

22. Daniel P. Erikson, *The Cuba Wars: Fidel Castro, the United States, and the Next Revolution* (New York: Bloomsbury Press, 2008), 78–81.

23. Ibid., 82.

24. Lázaro Barredo Medina, "Ningún enemigo podrá derrotarnos," *Granma,* August 18, 2006, http://www.granma.cubaweb.com.

25. Briefing on U.S. Policy Toward Cuba by Thomas Shannon, Assistant Secretary of State for Western Hemisphere Affairs, August 23, 2006, http://uruguay.usembassy.gov/usaweb/paginas/2006/06-312EN.shtml.

26. Jorge I. Domínguez, *To Make a World Safe for Revolution: Cuba's Foreign Policy* (Cambridge: Harvard University Press, 1989).
27. Lesley Clark, "Obama Aims to Renew Migration Talks with Cuba," *Miami Herald*, May 23, 2009; "Zapatero: le toca a Cuba 'mover ficha' en diferendo con Estados Unidos," *El Nuevo Herald*, May 25, 2009.
28. Jeff Franks, "Cuba Oil Claims Raise Eyebrow in Energy World," *Reuters*, October 24, 2008. Cuba announced that the offshore fields could contain 20 billion barrels which oil experts considered "hard to believe but not out of the realm of possibility."
29. "Ingresa Cuba al Grupo Río," *Granma*, November 14, 2008.
30. Mike Blanchfield, "Cuba Must Embrace Democracy, Harper Says," *National Post*, April 17, 2009, http://www.nationalpost.com/news/story.html?id=1504007; Blanchfield, "Minister to Make Rare High-Level Visit to Cuba," *National Post*, April 26, 2009, http://www.nationalpost.com/news/canada/story.html?id=1536145; Bill Curry, "Visa Delay Escalates Feud with Cuba," *Globe and Mail*, May 22, 2009, http://www.theglobe-andmail.com/news/politics/visa-delay-escalates-feud-with-cuba/article1147692/%23article.
31. "Cuba-China Relations," *Cuba Facts* 21 (May 2006), http://ctp.iccas.miami.edu/FACTS_Web/Cuba%2520Facts%2520Issue%252021%2520May%25202006.htm; Marc Lacey, "In Stores, Hints of Change Under New Castro," *New York Times*, May 2, 2008.
32. Bosco Esteruelas, "La UE congela su relación con Cuba por la represión de disidentes," *El País*, May 1, 2003; "La UE revisa su política frente a Cuba tras los últimos episodios de represión en la isla," Ibid., June 5, 2003; Mauricio Vicent, "Castro renuncia a la ayuda humanitaria de la UE y al diálogo político con los Quince," Ibid., July 28, 2003, "La Habana estima 'correcto' el intento de Madrid de favorecer el diálogo con la UE," Ibid., October 20, 2004, and "La UE reanuda la cooperación con Cuba después de cinco años de congelamiento de las relaciones," Ibid., October 23, 2008; Patricia Grogg, "Cuba-UE: Nuevos peldaños en la colaboración," *IPS*, March 20, 2009, http://cubaalamano.net/sitio/client/report.php?id=980.
33. "Cuban Policy in the Middle East: A Cuba-Iran Axis?" *Focus* 55 (June 7, 2004), http://ctp.iccas.miami.edu/FOCUS_Web/Issue55.htm; "The Growing Iran-Cuba Strategic Alliance," *Focus* 76 (May 16, 2006), http://ctp.iccas.miami.edu/FOCUS_Web/Issue76.htm; "Recibe Raúl a Presidente de Irán," *Granma*, September 16, 2006; "Recibió Raúl a Enviado Especial del Presidente iraní," Ibid, January 8, 2009; "Sostiene Raúl encuentros bilaterales como parte de la Reunión Ministerial del MNOAL," Ibid., April 30, 2009.
34. Oleg Mityayev, "Russian Revitalizes Relations with Cuba," *Ria Novosti*, February 4, 2009, http://en.rian.ru/analysis/20090204/119973885.html; "Raul's Pragmatic Approach," *Latin American Regional Report: Caribbean & Central America* (November 2008): 11–12 and "Cuba: Russian Tractors Re-seed Cuba," Ibid. (February 2009): 10–11.
35. Carlos A. Romero, "Venezuela y Cuba: 'Una seguridad diferente'," *Nuevo Mundo Mundos Nuevos* (March 30, 2009), http://nuevomundo.revues.org/index55550.html.
36. Institute for Public Opinion Research and Cuban Research Institute, Florida International University, *2007 FIU Cuba Poll* (www.fiu.edu/~ipor/cuba8/).
37. Bendixen & Associates, "Exit Polling in Florida and Miami-Dade County," (Miami: November 2008), http://www.bendixenandassociates.com/studies/Exit%20Poll%20of%20Miami-Dade%20County%20for%20the%202008%20Election.pdf. See also: Darío Moreno and María Ilcheva, "Cuban Americans in the 2008 Elections," *Cuban Affairs* (December 2008), http://www.cubanaffairsjournal.org.ezproxy.fiu.edu/Vol3Iss4/Vol3Iss4/Article-Moreno-FINAL.pdf, and Benjamin G. Bishin, Feryal M. Cherif, Andy S. Gomez, and Casey Klofstad, "Miami-Dade's Cuban-American Voters in the 2008 Election," Ibid. (February 2009), http://www.cubanaffairsjournal.org.ezproxy.fiu.edu/Vol4Iss1/Article_Gomez_FINAL.pdf.
38. Institute for Public Opinion Research, Brookings Institution, and Cuba Study Group,

2008 Cuba/US Transition Poll (www.fiu.edu/~ipor/cuba-t/Cuba-T.pdf). A competing poll showed solid support (72 percent) for the embargo, in part, because it surveyed only registered voters while the FIU sample was drawn among all Cuban American adults in Dade-County. Alfonso Chardy and Luisa Yanez, "Embargo Popular, New Poll Indicates," *Miami Herald,* February 4, 2009, Cuba Democracy Public Advocacy, Corp., "New Poll Finds Cuban-American Democrats Support Sanctions Against the Cuban Regime," http://media.miamiherald.com/smedia/2009/02/04/10/poll.source. prod_affiliate.56.pdf.

39. Bendixen & Associates, "National Survey of Cuban Americans" (Miami: April 20, 2009) http://www.bendixenandassociates.com/studies/National_Survey_of_Cuban_Americans _on_Policy_towards_Cuba_FINAL.pdf.

40. President Obama's Remarks at the Summit of the Americas (April 17), http:// www.whitehouse.gov/the_press_office/Remarks-by-the-President-at-the-Summit-of-the-Americas-Opening-Ceremony/.

41. Press Conference by the President (April 19, 2009), http://www.whitehouse.gov/the_ press_office/Press-Conference-By-The-President-In-Trinidad-And-Tobago-4/19/2009/.

42. After the 1994 *balsero* crisis, the United States and Cuba held biannual talks on migration until the Bush administration suspended them in 2004.

43. "Raúl Castro dice que Cuba está lista para hablar con EEUU sobre derechos humanos y presos políticos," *IBLNEWS* (April 17, 2009), http://www.iblnews.com/story.php?id= 46986.

44. Fidel Castro, "Obama y el bloqueo" (April 21, 2009), http://www.cubadebate.cu/index. php?tpl=design/especiales.tpl.html%26newsid_obj_id=14849. The "Five Heroes" were arrested, tried, and convicted of spying on anti-Castro groups in South Florida. Havana claims that the men's charge was to stop violence against Cuba, thus, the label of "antiterrorists."

45. Raúl Castro, "No hay pretexto político ni moral que justifique la continuidad del bloqueo" (April 29, 2009), http://www.cubadebate.cu/index.php?tpl=design/especiales. tpl.html%26newsid_obj_id=14915.

46. Matthew Lee, "U.S.–Cuba Talks on Immigration to Resume," *Miami Herald*, May 31, 2009.

47. General Assembly Thirty-Ninth Regular Session, *Resolution Through Which Resolution VI of The Eighth Meeting of Ministers of Foreign Affairs of 1962 Ceases To Have Effect*, San Pedro Sula, Honduras, June 3, 2009, http://graphics8.nytimes.com/packages/pdf/ world/OAS-statement.pdf.

48. Anthony L. Hall, "OAS Lifts Its Almost 50-Year Ban on Cuba," *Caribbean Net News,* June 5, 2009, http://www.caribbeannetnews.com/news-16906—6-6—.html; Thelma Mejía, "OAS Opens Doors to Cuba Without Conditions," *IPS*, June 3, 2009, http://www.ipsnews.net/news.asp?idnews=47090; Lesley Clark, "Cuba Critics Want to Punish the OAS," *Miami Herald*, June 5, 2009.

4 The United States and Central America since 2000

Free Trade and Diaspora Diplomacy

Cristina Eguizábal*

Central America emerged at the end of the Cold War as a region in peace. By the beginning of the twenty-first century, for the first time in its history, democratically elected men and women rule the six countries. Internationally observed elections have become the rule. Judicial systems have been overhauled. Civilian police forces have been established where they did not exist and strengthened where they did. The Guatemalan and Salvadoran military have been restructured. Truth Commissions have uncovered past abuses and the perpetrators have been named if not punished.

The negotiations leading to the signing and ratification of the Central American-Dominican Republic Free Trade Agreement, generally referred to as CAFTA-DR, by the governments of Guatemala, El Salvador, Honduras, Nicaragua, Costa Rica, the Dominican Republic and the United States implied a second generation of economic reforms in the six Latin American countries that deepened the transformations of their economies initiated under the Washington Consensus framework. Problems remain: governance is fragile, violence is widespread, inequality has grown, economic growth has been modest, but overall the region is in better shape than thirty years ago.

To most observers the relationship between the United States and the Central American Republics constitutes the perfect example of a hegemonic relationship resulting from the profound power asymmetry between the two poles of the relationship.[1] This chapter does not disagree with such an assessment. However, it argues that to examine the relationship exclusively through the lens of power and to analyze only formal diplomatic and economic relations is not enough and probably even misleading.

The point of departure in this chapter is that the extreme asymmetry of the relationship and the low priority the Central American countries constitute in the traditional U.S. foreign policy agenda hide a very dense and dynamic relationship between Guatemala, El Salvador, Honduras and Nicaragua and an increasing number of cities and counties in the United States. Despite having a more traditional state-centric relationship with the United States, Costa Rica is impacted by U.S. foreign policy in the direction of the other four (CA4) through its membership in the Central American Integration System (SICA), its incorporation in the Central America-Dominican Republic framework (CAFTA-DR), and its participation in Central American economic and political dynamics more generally.

In the following pages, in a first section this chapter will briefly go back to the Reagan years. Second, it will go over the three pillars of the relationship: trade, migration, and security cooperation. It will end with a discussion on possible future scenarios for the Obama administration.

Cold War Legacies

The dissolution of the socialist bloc and the disintegration of the Soviet Union made the peace accords possible and contributed to the democratization of the CA4. This chapter refers to that period not out of misplaced nostalgia, but because the foundations of the relationship pattern that currently determines CA-U.S. dynamics were established during those years, namely, the dominant trade patterns, the demographic interdependence between the CA4 and specific U.S. locales, and the security challenges.

During most of the Cold War, no other Latin American countries symbolized better the U.S. backyard than the Central American ones. The triumph of the Sandinista guerrilla over the Somoza dictatorship would transform the "backyard" into the last Cold War theater. The Reagan administration became obsessed with Central America, as did the neo-conservative intellectual elites and the foreign policy establishment. Many among the main characters at the time have been until recently important Washington foreign policy decision makers albeit not regarding Central America: John Negroponte, Thomas Pickering, and Elliot Abrams, to name a few.

A three-pronged strategy was implemented in the region to complement the U.S. sponsored counter revolution in Nicaragua: counterinsurgency in El Salvador and Guatemala, elections in those two countries plus in Honduras, and economic reforms in the CA4. Reasonably free elections were held and for the first time in decades civilian politicians would lead Guatemala, Honduras, and El Salvador. The three countries plus Costa Rica went through profound economic transformations following the premises of the Washington consensus.

In order to ease the burden on Central American and Caribbean countries going through the twin processes of structural adjustment and economic liberalization, the Reagan administration established the Caribbean Basin Initiative (CBI) in 1983, which gave tariff preferences to the exports of 27 nations and territories in the Caribbean. Nicaragua would not be designated as a "beneficiary country" until 1990 after the election of Violeta Chamorro. In 2000, the U.S.-Caribbean Trade Partnership expanded the CBI. It expired in September 2008, three years after CAFTA-DR was ratified.[2]

The U.S. became the main trading partner of the Central American economies at the beginning of the twentieth century and has remained so since. However, the economic reforms of the 1980s and the preferential trade agreement established through the CBI accelerated that trend. By increasing the importance of exports as the engine of economic growth and diversifying the pattern of trade with the introduction of U.S.-bound goods assembly plants (*maquiladoras*) and the development of non-traditional agricultural exports, trade relations with the United States increased even more their relative importance for the small Central American economies. CAFTA-DR is expected to further deepen their integration to the U.S. market.

Until the 1980s Central Americans had not migrated to the United States in large numbers. Prior to the armed conflict in 1969 that opposed El Salvador to Honduras, Salvadorans had been an important minority in Honduras, Nicaraguans routinely went to Costa Rica as seasonal laborers, Guatemalans picked coffee crops in Southern Mexico, but only a handful ventured farther north.

The contra war and the counterinsurgency strategies implemented in the region during the 1980s changed that. The first to come north were the Nicaraguan business elites and professionals deserting Sandinista Nicaragua. The vast majority of Nicaraguans settled in Miami and Los Angeles. Salvadorans and Guatemalans fleeing violence in their countries came shortly after. It is estimated that between 1981 and 1990, almost one million Salvadorans and Guatemalans came to U.S. cities such as Washington, DC, Los Angeles, San Francisco, Boston, and Chicago.[3] Were they economic migrants as the Reagan administration argued or war refugees as the opponents to the war considered them? Probably both.

U.S. public opinion was deeply divided regarding the country's intervention in Central America. In December 1990, a landmark immigration case, *American Baptist Churches vs. Thornburgh*, ruled that Salvadorans and Guatemalans had been discriminated against in the asylum adjudication process based on nationality and on how the U.S. government judged the ideological beliefs of the applicants. The Immigration and Naturalization Service was required to reopen 150,000 cases and hear petitions from 350,000 more.[4] That same year, Congress passed legislation allowing the president to grant Temporary Protected Status (TPS) to groups in need of a temporary safe haven.

Salvadorans and Guatemalans who had arrived in the 1980s were able to stay in the country. In the late 1990s the protected status of Salvadorans and Guatemalans was finally settled in a legislative agreement passed with the support of the Cuban American Florida legislators. The passage of the 1997 Nicaraguan Adjustment and Central American Relief Act (NACARA), although favoring mostly Nicaraguans, allowed Salvadorans and Guatemalans to apply for permanent residency as well.

Cultural practices traveled with the refugees. They brought with them as an organizing tool the Christian Base Community model that they had used back home. Religious and human rights activists, liberal lawyers, community organizers, and the refugees themselves incorporated the model to their activism in the United States, supporting new arrivals and organizing support for grass root organizations and political parties in their countries of origin. Over twenty years later, a number of those immigrant-led projects still exist as full-service non-profit legal and community service centers. Immigration from Central America has continued albeit at a lower rate. It has peaked following natural disasters, such as Hurricane Mitch in 1998, two earthquakes in El Salvador in 2001, and Hurricane Stan in 2005. Hondurans who did not emigrate during the war began doing it in large numbers after Hurricane Mitch devastated their country.

The Free Trade Agreement CAFTA-DR

In 1990, the first President Bush launched the idea of creating a free trade zone from Anchorage to Tierra del Fuego that he called Enterprise of the Americas. NAFTA would be ratified four years later, but the idea of creating a Free Trade Area of the Americas as President Clinton's administration renamed the initiative did not prosper despite his active support and that of the second President Bush.

In early 2002, at the Organization of American States (OAS), George W. Bush offered the Central American countries the possibility of negotiating a sub-regional free trade agreement. A year later, in San José, Costa Rica, Robert Zoellick, the U.S. Trade Representative at the time, and his Central American counterparts launched the process of formal negotiations with the explicit goal of reaching an agreement by the end of 2003.

Facing increasing difficulties in promoting a hemispheric free trade area, the Bush administration opted to establish a trade pact with the historic five Central American countries. During his father's administration, George W. Bush had been involved in the decision making regarding the settlement of the Central American conflicts and considered peace in the region a personal diplomatic achievement.[5]

Additionally, contrary to what the small size of the region's economies would suggest, as a whole it constitutes a relatively important market for U.S. exports. Buying more than $25 billion in U.S. exports, the CAFTA-DR region was in 2008 the third largest Latin American export market for the United States, right after Mexico and Brazil. Combined, the small Central America countries plus the Dominican Republic (DR) are a larger export market for U.S. goods than Russia, India, or Turkey. The United States exports more to Costa Rica or the Dominican Republic than to Sweden, Greece, or Vietnam. Moreover, unlike vis-à-vis Mexico, the balance of trade with all the CAFTA-DR countries favors the United States.[6]

After nine grueling rounds of negotiations, by December 2003, the United States and the CA4 had concluded negotiations on the U.S.-Central American Free Trade Agreement. The United States and Costa Rica settled the terms of the Central American country's participation in CAFTA on January 25 after an additional negotiating round. The United States and the Dominican Republic concluded market access negotiations in March 2004.

CAFTA-DR will liberalize bilateral trade between the United States and the region. It is also expected to further integration among the countries of Central America, as it removes barriers to trade and investment in the region by U.S. companies. CAFTA-DR will also require the countries of Central America to undertake a series of reforms in areas such as customs administration; protection of intellectual property rights; services, including financial services; investment; market access and protection; government procurements; and sanitary, phytosanitary and other non-tariff barriers.

The U.S.-Chile Free Trade Agreement served as the base document and legal framework for CAFTA's negotiations. In order to upgrade Central American negotiators' capacity, the United States established a Trade Capacity Building Assistance Act. USTR commissioned a needs assessment to the Inter American Development

Bank. The report concluded that two key areas should be targeted in the short term for capacity building assistance. One of those areas was a recognized government weakness in government outreach to civil society. The second was a deficit in capacity to analyze sectoral impacts of trade liberalization. A significant proportion of the aid provided to the Central Americans was designed to target the first issue.[7] Unfortunately, transparency was undermined after the U.S. negotiators requested that their Central American counterparts sign a confidentiality agreement "to ensure that what gets put on the table does not leave the room, or else the process would be interrupted."[8]

The "side rooms" established by the Central American negotiators as an informational mechanism designed for civil society and private sector observers became nothing more than window dressing. In most cases, the information shared was superficial, if not perfunctory. The quality of the exchanges also varied from country to country depending on the nature of the relationship between civil society and private sector groups and the official negotiating team. According to a Costa Rican participant in the side room, the relationship was good in the Costa Rican and Nicaraguan cases, bad in the others, particularly regarding governmental and private sector relations with civil society.

In exchange for lax labor and environmental safeguards the governments of El Salvador, Honduras, and Guatemala agreed to most of U.S. demands concerning trade liberalization, government procurement, and were ready to accommodate the U.S. insistence on closing the negotiations by the given December 2003 deadline. On the other hand, Costa Rica, which proved to be the most difficult negotiating partner for the United States, since the beginning openly criticized its counterparts in the region for closing deals bilaterally on terms that, according to Costa Rican negotiators, were not entirely favorable to the region.

In the end Costa Rica did not sign in December 2003. Its delegates had an additional negotiating round the following January where Costa Rica finally agreed to open the state monopolies of insurance, telecommunications, and utilities to private competition, thus lifting the main stumbling block to its participation in CAFTA. The Costa Rican delegation during the final round included 68 negotiators, 80 private sector representatives, and 11 congressional representatives.

The free trade agreement was signed on May 28, 2004 at the OAS by the five Central American governments. A second ceremony was held on August 5 that same year for the incorporation of the Dominican Republic. The first country to ratify the trade pact was El Salvador in December 2004, Honduras ratified it second, in March 2005, followed by Guatemala the same week. In 2005, the U.S. Senate approved the agreement 54 to 45 and the U.S. House of Representatives 217 in favor and 215 against it. Once approved by the U.S. Congress, it became Public Law 109–053. CAFTA-DR was ratified by the Nicaraguan Congress on October 2005 and by the DR legislature in March 2007.

A supra-national body, the Central American Free Trade Commission, with extensive attributions will "supervise the implementation of the agreement." Composed by cabinet ministers from the six countries, it will have the right to change, interpret, and generally oversee the operation of the agreement. The

Table 4.1 U.S. Exports to Central America, 2000–2008 (million U.S. dollars)

	2000	2001	2002	2003	2004	2005	2006	2007	2008
Guatemala	1900.7	1869.7	2044.4	2263.4	2551.3	2835.4	3511.4	4065.1	4718.3
Belize	208.4	173.3	137.5	198.8	151.8	217.6	238.8	234.2	352.7
El Salvador	1780.2	1759.4	1664.1	1820.9	1867.7	1854.3	2152.1	2313.1	2462.0
Honduras	2584.0	2415.8	2571.1	2826.2	3078.4	3253.8	3687.1	4461.4	4846.2
Nicaragua	380.1	443.0	437.0	501.7	592.4	625.5	751.6	890.0	1094.2
Costa Rica	2460.3	2502.3	3116.5	3413.5	3305.9	3598.6	4132.4	4580.5	5679.8
Panama	1612.3	1330.5	1406.6	1848.7	1772.5	2162.0	2660.1	3669.2	4887.3

Source: U.S. Census Bureau, Foreign Trade Division.

commission will be the first instance for dispute settlements. There are rights of arbitration under CAFTA-DR, but the Free Trade Commission is empowered to change, interpret, and generally supervise the operation of the pact. Whatever the countervailing forces, in the end, the Free Trade Commission will act as the court and legislature that issues administrative rules by which disputes have to be decided.[9]

Why did the CA4 want CAFTA so badly? Despite the obvious costs for the small agricultural producers and domestic industry oriented toward local markets, it was considered the only way to consolidate the advantages offered by the Caribbean Basin Initiative, attract investment into the growing *maquiladora* sector, and very importantly, take advantage of the expanded trade in goods and services that the Central Americans in the United States yearn for from their countries of origin— referred to as the "nostalgic trade." Trade between Central America and the United States has indeed grown rapidly since CAFTA-DR was ratified (see Table 4.1).

Labor and the Environment

U.S. opponents of the agreement criticized its weak provisions regarding labor and the environment. In order to increase the likelihood of congressional approval, U.S. negotiators insisted that labor and environmental clauses be included in the agreement. Those demands irritated the Central Americans who considered them as aggressive meddling in their internal affairs.

The International Labor Organization (ILO) has defined three "core international labor standards": (1) the right to associate, form unions, to bargain collectively; (2) the prohibition of prison and child labor; and (3) freedom from employment discrimination. In CAFTA-DR, each country has additionally pledged: to effectively enforce its own labor laws, to ensure that both ILO core labor principles and internationally recognized worker rights are recognized and protected by domestic law, not to waive its own labor laws to encourage trade or investment, and to establish mechanisms for cooperative activities and labor-related trade capacity building with the other countries. However, enforcement mechanisms are weak. CAFTA-DR establishes that, of these shared commitments, only sustained failure to enforce one's own labor laws is subject to binding dispute settlement and ultimately to fines or sanctions. Furthermore the maximum fine in a particular dispute is set at $15 million per year per violation, a part of which may be directed towards remedying the labor violation.[10]

In a report commissioned by the Central American governments during the negotiations, the ILO evaluated the labor laws of the five countries and found them largely compliant with international core labor standards. CAFTA-DR critics contend that the problem is not necessarily with the law but with the application and enforcement. Unionization, discrimination in the workplace, and the codification of the right to strike are particularly problematic. Generalized violence, corruption, impunity, weak judicial systems, and poor enforcement structures only add to the common violations of workers' rights.

Concerning the environment, the Central American isthmus is one of the most biodiverse regions of the world; unfortunately, with the exception of Costa Rica, the Central American countries have not behaved as responsible stewards of the natural riches bestowed to their territories. Four of the five Central American countries have been identified by environmental experts as "critical regions." The isthmus has lost much of its forest cover due to agriculture, overgrazing, and increased logging and mining. The depletion of forest coverage has led to increased soil erosion, the deterioration of watersheds, and decreased biodiversity. Urban pollution, insufficient sewage and solid waste treatment facilities, and chemical and pesticide runoffs into water supplies are rampant, particularly as rural-urban migration increases. Central America's coastal environment is contaminated with agricultural and industrial runoff and untreated sewage. Over-fishing has led to the depletion of many valuable fish stocks. In Guatemala and Honduras, even the most basic environmental laws are still lacking in many instances. The other countries lack enforcement capacity.

CAFTA-DR is expected to open Central America to substantial changes in industrial and agricultural development, many of which would exacerbate the existing problems in the region if left unregulated. Despite extensive lobbying from environmental groups, the agreement does not clearly require any country to maintain and effectively enforce a set of basic environmental laws and regulations. CAFTA-DR also lacks an enforceable set of standards for corporate responsibility on environmental issues. The trade agreement does include a process that allows citizens to make submissions alleging government failures to effectively enforce environmental laws. However there is no dedicated source of funding for environmental cooperation, capacity building, and objective monitoring of environmental progress.

The Costa Rican Exception

In order to be able to renegotiate its external debt and to have access to U.S. economic aid, during the 1980s Costa Rica implemented the reforms prescribed by the Washington consensus, albeit in a milder version than other Central American countries. The country maintained a much larger public sector. With higher salaries and a better educated population, it opted for a high-end type of *maquiladora* (electronics) and does not have a sizeable migrant population in the United States. The structure of its relationship with the United States is

Table 4.2 U.S. Imports from Central America, 2000–2008 (million U.S. dollars)

	2000	2001	2002	2003	2004	2005	2006	2007	2008
Guatemala	2607.5	2588.6	2796.4	2946.8	3154.0	3137.4	3102.3	3026.1	3462.7
Belize	93.5	97.5	77.6	101.4	107.0	98.3	146.9	105.0	154.0
El Salvador	1933.0	1880.3	1982.3	2019.8	2052.2	1988.8	1856.8	2043.5	2228.0
Honduras	3090.1	3126.5	3261.3	3312.7	3640.0	3749.2	3717.5	3912.1	4041.2
Nicaragua	588.4	603.8	679.5	769.7	990.3	1180.8	1526.0	1603.5	1703.6
Costa Rica	3538.6	2886.2	3141.9	3364.2	3333.3	3415.3	3844.1	3941.5	3938.1
Panama	307.1	290.7	302.5	301.4	315.9	327.1	378.7	365.2	379.1

Source: U.S. Census Bureau, Foreign Trade Division.

Table 4.3 Costa Rica's Top Trade Partners: Exports, 2000–2008 (million U.S. dollars)

	2000	2001	2002	2003	2004	2005	2006	2007	2008
United States	3,056.7	2,504.8	2,650.4	2,834.1	2,783.1	2,806.9	3,161.5	3,287.8	3,359.0
China	12.7	13.8	33.7	88.9	163.3	244.7	558.3	848.2	680.0
Netherlands	394.9	275.2	311.6	360.7	331.6	449.0	502.6	462.2	490.1
Panama	129.0	142.7	144.8	165.8	184.0	207.2	267.6	327.2	411.4
Hong Kong	17.4	27.3	51.6	132.8	136.8	485.1	524.5	561.1	392.3
Nicaragua	179.1	163.3	166.0	184.8	220.1	263.8	290.5	354.0	378.0
Guatemala	193.4	211.4	236.4	256.8	279.0	290.6	331.7	362.0	359.3

Source: Ministry of Foreign Trade of Costa Rica (COMEX).

fundamentally different from that of its neighbors. Moreover Costa Rica's foreign trade is more diversified than that of its Central American neighbors. China is the country's second market for its exports (see Tables 4.2 and 4.3). In 2009, Costa Rica abandoned its historical relationship with Taiwan and established formal relations with the People's Republic of China. In exchange the Chinese will build an $84 million new National Soccer Stadium and has agreed to buy $300 million of Costa Rican bonds.

The CAFTA-DR debate polarized the country as never before. It coincided with that nation's last presidential election: Ottón Solís, the Citizen Action Party candidate ran on a fair trade platform against CAFTA-DR, while Nobel-Prize winner and former president Oscar Arias became the free trade standard bearer, winning by the narrowest margin of votes in Costa Rica's history. He was sworn in for his second presidency in May 2006.

Early in 2007, the National Assembly passed a measure establishing a national referendum on whether Costa Rica should enter CAFTA-DR. The country had never organized a referendum before and the legality of such a vote is not contemplated in the country's laws, so its constitutionality had first to be approved by Costa Rica's Supreme Court. Once that hurdle was overcome, the Supreme Electoral Tribunal set the date for the referendum for October 7, 2008. For ten months Costa Rican society debated passionately the pros and cons of adhering to CAFTA-DR. Even the U.S. Ambassador was part of it. An uninvited participant in the debate, he misleadingly suggested that there would be economic reprisals if the agreement were rejected. He was promptly disavowed by Nancy Pelosi and reprimanded by the Costa Rican electoral court and asked to refrain from intervening in Costa Rica's domestic affairs.[11]

The referendum was won by the pro CAFTA-DR sectors 52 percent to 48 percent thanks to the support of the urban and middle class votes (the rural sectors favored rejection). The agreement was subsequently ratified by the National Assembly with the required qualified two-thirds majority. Since the treaty contradicted various existing laws, it was necessary to modify them before CAFTA-DR could go into effect. Under the pact's terms, this should have been done by March 2008, but Costa Rica had to request two extensions, which were granted, until the end of the year.

Costa Rica joined the pact on January 1, 2009. However, several issues remain to be addressed concerning the privatization of insurance and telecommunications state monopolies.

According to the original timetable, liberalization in insurance would be achieved through a phased-in approach, with an initial limited opening at entry into force, an opening of the vast majority of the market by 2008, and a total opening by 2011. Costa Rica also agreed to the establishment of an independent insurance regulatory body, which required further legislative and regulatory reform. Since treaty ratification took considerably longer, the established periods had to be rescheduled.

Costa Rica made specific commitments to open its telecommunications market in three key areas and to establish a regulatory framework to foster effective market access and competition. Under the CAFTA-DR terms that anticipated timely agreement ratification, certain telecommunications market segments in Costa Rica were to have opened up gradually, beginning with private network services on January 2006; Internet services and wireless services were to have followed on January 1, 2007. However, since the CAFTA-DR did not enter into force with respect to Costa Rica by those dates, the regulatory framework has not been fully established and it is unlikely that it would be fully operational before 2010.[12]

As in the case of the North American Free Trade agreement, and despite the global economic crisis, CAFTA-DR is expected to bolster trade between the region and the United States in both directions and to increase foreign direct investment in the small Central American economies coming from the United States and also from foreign investors trying to better position themselves to enter the U.S. market. It will also certainly impact migration flows.

Migration and Remittances: The Engines of Transnationalization

Globalization has had a profound impact in the small countries of Central America and its vehicle has been emigration—and tourism in the case of Costa Rica. In 2000, according to the U.S. census, the foreign-born population of Central American origin amounted to 2 million people concentrated in the states of California, Florida, New York, New Jersey, and the greater District of Columbia area. Two-thirds of that number had come from El Salvador and Guatemala. However unofficial estimates calculate higher numbers. According to some, including undocumented or unauthorized migrants, there would be between 1.5 million and 2.5 Salvadorans, 1 to 1.5 million Guatemalans, and close to one million Hondurans.[13] It is very difficult to come by reliable estimates.

The same goes for remittances. According to official data, remittances constitute 10 percent of Guatemala's gross national product (GNP), close to 20 percent of El Salvador's, and around 15 percent of Honduras' but these figures do not take into account informal channels. According to the World Bank, underestimates could be as high as 5 percent for Guatemala and 15 percent for El Salvador. Yet, even according to official figures, remittances are more important sources of revenue than foreign direct investment and official development aid for El Salvador, Honduras, and Guatemala, despite the fact that the three countries are Millennium Challenge Account beneficiaries. Remittances generate more hard currency than coffee exports for Guatemala, El Salvador, and Nicaragua and are more important than banana exports for Honduras. Their growth has been short of miraculous. From 2000 to 2004 remittances to Guatemala tripled, and in the case of Honduras in 2006 they registered a 35 percent growth rate compared to the previous year. In 2008 remittances continued to grow, albeit at a slower pace. The change came in 2009. World Bank economists have projected that the monthly remittances to Central America from migrants in the United States would fall 10 to 15 percent in 2009, the first annual decline since the Bank began tracking the funds.

Assessments by development experts differ regarding the macroeconomic impact of remittances beyond the impressive balance of payment figures. An often-cited study by the United Nations Economic Commission for Latin America and the Caribbean (ECLAC) concluded that they did not seem to have much impact on the overall poverty statistics; however, the study also found that remittances did have a significant impact on households receiving remittances and enabled many recipients to escape poverty. The impact of remittances on indigence in the receiving households seems even more dramatic. ECLAC found that 64 percent of Salvadoran households receiving remittances were lifted out of extreme poverty. Corresponding figures for Guatemala (43 percent), Honduras (28 percent), and Nicaragua (27 percent), although smaller, are still impressive.[14]

Remittances have been evolving and put to work in innovative experiments. One of the most interesting initiatives started with the migrants themselves. Following the Mexican example, Central American migrants have formed hometown associations or HTAs. Members of these associations pool their financial resources and send money or goods back to their hometowns. These so-called "collective remittances" finance infrastructure and social projects, such as building small bridges, paving roads, remodeling churches and schools, or buying ambulances or fire trucks.

HTAs were very successful at mobilizing support for their countries after the 1996 peace agreements in Guatemala, and in raising money for crises such as Hurricane Mitch, the two 2001 earthquakes in El Salvador, and more recently have joined reconstruction efforts after hurricanes Stan, Rita, and Wilma that devastated the region in 2005.

Once more, following the Mexican government example, Central American governments have also taken initiatives to maximize the benefits from remittances. El

Salvador launched a $300,000 matching fund in 2003 to implement joint partnerships with HTAs. The fund serves as an incentive for HTAs to start and/or broaden development initiatives in their hometowns. Unlike in Mexico, where the state offers a three-to-one match, the Salvadoran government is offering only a one-to-one match with HTA money. For the time being, only 1 percent of all remittances to Central America come from HTAs. However, experts believe that, if managed correctly, such remittances could rise to between 3 and 5 percent in 10 years.

Another aspect of HTAs' impact in their members' hometowns is their increasing participation in local politics—very often the funded projects are implemented in collaboration with local authorities who are held accountable to the HTAs for the management of the resources.

One Guatemalan-American organization deeply concerned about migration policy's effects on Guatemalans has already demonstrated its influence at home. Founded in 1998, the National Coalition of Guatemalan Immigrants in the United States (CONGUATE) is working in Guatemala toward giving Guatemalans abroad the right to vote. The Salvadoran conference "Salvadorans in the World" (*"Salvadoreños en el Mundo"*), brings together a wide array of diaspora organizations. To date, conferences have been held in Los Angeles, Washington, DC, and Boston. The goal is to develop a common political platform. Thus far, the platform includes demanding the right to vote abroad and greater attention to their needs as investors and remitters.

Credit unions in El Salvador, Guatemala, Honduras, and Nicaragua were instrumental in the creation of the International Remittance Network (IRnet), which in collaboration with migrant services organizations lobbied successfully for lower remittance costs through raising customer awareness of remittance fees. Even the powerful private sector has become involved. Several banks in Central America have been able to raise relatively cheap and long-term financing from international capital markets via securitization of future remittance flows.

As remittances change the character of the region's financial sector, the governments are increasingly involved in encouraging and managing the flows of people and remittances. Migration has become an important policy concern that affects the design of state institutions and political rhetoric in the press and media.

In El Salvador, one example of the redesign of state institutions was the creation of the Directorate General of Attention for the Community Abroad, inaugurated under the 1999–2004 presidency of Francisco Flores with the stated goal of establishing an axis for development based on the potential of the Salvadoran community abroad. Another example of new institutions created to cultivate the Salvadoran diaspora was the creation in 2004 of a Vice Ministry of Foreign Affairs for Salvadorans Abroad. Today El Salvador has consular offices in sixteen U.S. cities (Argentina, Colombia and Brazil have seven, eight, and nine respectively). In addition to offering the customary consular services and providing information on Salvadorans living abroad, the consulates provide legal assistance regarding U.S. immigration laws and regulations. On the website of the Salvadoran Embassy to the United States, for example, detailed information is available about the different types of visa statuses for which Salvadorans are eligible and also on the array of nongovernmental and private organizations dedicated to facilitating migrant regularization or legalization.

As part of the ongoing campaign to renew channels of legalization, the Salvadoran government has successfully lobbied the U.S. government to expand and renew Temporary Protection Status for Salvadorans. TPS for Salvadorans, Hondurans, and Nicaraguans was extended until 2010. In 2006, an estimated 374,000 Central American lived in the United States under TPS.[15] While the Nicaraguans have powerful allies in Congress, particularly with the Florida delegation, El Salvador's participation in the "coalition of the willing" and its long military deployment in Iraq provided the Salvadoran government with unprecedented leverage vis-à-vis the Bush administration. TPS has not been extended for Guatemalans despite the hardships created by the 2005 hurricanes.

Guatemala has also made important strides in cultivating its diaspora. It has ten consulates in the United States servicing its nationals. Each one of these offers itinerant consular services in nearby cities, such as Homestead in Florida, serviced by the Guatemalan consulate in Miami. Among the important services they supply is issuing a consular identification card that provides undocumented migrants with a government ID that is accepted by some banks and other service providers in the United States. The Guatemalan government created a Deputy Ministry for Human Rights and Migrant Affairs. The Guatemalan Congress formed a Commission for Migrant Affairs, which regulates migration laws and tries to support migrants in their efforts at repatriation. Finally, the Office of the Human Rights Ombudsman signed an agreement with CONGUATE, the Guatemalan American migrant services organization, to monitor and protect migrant's rights. It also set up a modest fund of U.S.$50,000 to repatriate the remains of migrants who die in the United States when their families cannot afford the bill.

As the Central American governments expand their engagement with the diaspora, Central Americans in the United States have been trying to build a coalition of organizations with the powerful Mexican-American ones to bring together various diaspora organizations advocating for immigrant rights to lobby both in Central America and in the United States for immigration reform. Central American migrant associations' leaders lobbied hard to persuade the Central American negotiators and the U.S. Trade Representative (USTR) to include a migration clause in the CAFTA-DR text. They were of course unsuccessful and opted in the end to oppose the treaty. Ecotourism, not migration, has been Costa Rica's gateway to globalization; the country has become an attractive destination for nature lovers worldwide.

Cell phones are ubiquitous in Central America as are internet cafes; thanks to them, communication between those who left and those who stayed is constant. Daily flights link all major U.S. cities with Central American capitals, big cities like San Pedro Sula, and important tourist attractions such as Roatan island in Honduras or the city of Liberia near Costa Rica's Nicoya Gulf. Information from the U.S. Bureau of Transport Statistics shows that air traffic between the United States and Central America has increased exponentially in the last twenty years from a hundred thousand passengers to a million per year. Originally catering mainly to returning migrants, TACA, *Transportes Aéreos Centro Americanos,* the Salvadoran airline, has become a continental travel powerhouse.

Migrant workers have contributed significantly to reduce food prices in the United States. Where would Californian or Floridian fruit and vegetable growers be without Central American and Mexican workers? The same question pertains to North Carolina's poultry and meat packing industry or construction in Long Island. Migrant labor has kept U.S. middle-class homes clean, gardens trimmed, children supervised, and allowed millions of women in the United States to become full-time professionals. Since 2005 more than half of children born in the United States are Latinos, giving the country one of the healthier demographic profiles among developed societies.

To a large extent, migration has been a good thing for the receiving as well as sending countries. For Central America, unfortunately, it has also come with important dislocations: family separation, changing generational roles, and increased number of women heads of households. In many parts of the region, rural life is no longer based on agriculture, it is now based on remittances. Social networks across borders are stronger than between rural communities and capital cities. Perhaps, the most destructive link has been the one between migration and violence.

Central America Security Challenges

Central America faces numerous challenges, but public opinion routinely cites personal insecurity as its most important concern in the five countries, including Costa Rica and Nicaragua whose crime figures are well below those of the countries that form the Northern Triangle. El Salvador, Honduras, and Guatemala are among the most violent countries on earth. The murder rate in the three countries is well above 50 homicides per 100,000 inhabitants. An average of six people are murdered in Honduras (a country of 6 million) daily, twelve in El Salvador (5.7 million), and fourteen in Guatemala (with 12 millions). According to the Inter-American Human Rights Commission, with seventy homicides per 100,000 people, Guatemala has the highest murder rate in Latin America and one of the three highest in the world.[16]

The factors contributing to this violence epidemic are manifold: income inequality, enduring effects of the prolonged civil conflicts, large availability of weapons, families broken by migration, and repressive policies.[17] Contrary to generalized perceptions, only 30 percent of homicides are the product of gang violence. Organized crime and paramilitary structures account for most of the violence and the corruption that permeates all sectors of the mentioned countries' state apparatuses.

The infamous death squads were never fully dismantled during the peace processes, many went underground, while others incorporated former guerrilla combatants to form organized criminal networks involved in drug trafficking, money laundering, abductions for ransom, and car theft. Unlawful activities provide economic and logistical support to maintain networks and structures that can be utilized for political purposes, if needed. Unfortunately that seems to be the case in Guatemala, where human rights and environmental activists continuously receive death threats.[18]

After the 1996 U.S. immigration reform, the United States began deporting undocumented immigrants, many with criminal convictions, back to the region. Between 2000 and 2004 an estimated 20,000 convicted felons were sent back to Central America, the majority of them linked to the violent youth gangs established in Los Angeles by the young Central American refugees fleeing war in their countries during the two previous decades. Massive deportations resulted in the emergence of transnational youth gangs: the well-known *maras*, MS13, or "*mara salvatrucha*," and 18th Street or "Barrio 18." If the U.S. immigration policy favoring deportation of criminals contributed to the transnationalization of youth gangs, the repressive policies implemented by the governments of El Salvador, Guatemala, and Honduras were instrumental in creating linkages between the *maras* and organized crime through the penal system. It was in prison that the gang members got acquainted with organized crime strategies and, once out of prison or through their outside contacts, became foot soldiers of traffickers of all stripes.

Central American societies are the victims of a balloon effect. As Mexico cracks down on drug trafficking, new routes and transshipment sites are being set in Guatemala and El Salvador, disrupting the existing balance of power established by local criminals. Homicides bearing the distinctive trademarks of drug cartels have multiplied and important drug seizures have become routine in the five countries.

Organized crime undermines the structure of the state, democracy, the rule of law, and human rights. Overcoming the penetration of organized criminal networks in the state apparatus is a very difficult task much more than stopping drug traffickers or gang members. It is however an urgent task.

U.S.–Central America Military and Law Enforcement Cooperation

For several years U.S. authorities overlooked the impact that deportations were having in Central America but, when former deported felons were apprehended again in the United States, it was clear that the gang problem needed an integrated approach. In December 2004, the FBI created a special task force focusing on MS-13 and, in April 2005, it opened a liaison office in San Salvador to coordinate regional information-sharing and anti-gang efforts. Only recently, the gang task force introduced regulations allowing U.S. officials to provide information to Central American authorities about the criminal records of deportees. In the U.S. Department of Homeland Security, U.S. Immigration and Customs Enforcement (ICE) has created a national anti-gang initiative called "Operation Community Shield" that, in addition to arresting suspected gang members in the United States, works through offices in Central America to coordinate with foreign governments that are also experiencing gang problems.

On the preventive side, the U.S. Agency for International Development (USAID) worked with the Department of Justice's International Criminal Investigative

Training Assistance Program (ICITAP) to create community policing programs in 200 municipalities in El Salvador and implement a similar community crime prevention program in Villa Nueva, Guatemala.

Established in 1983 to provide training and logistical support to the Salvadoran Armed Forces and to the Contra rebels, the base at Palmerola continues to operate under the name Soto Cano Airbase as a joint venture between the U.S. and Honduran governments. It houses the Honduran Air Force Academy and the Joint Task Force Bravo (JTF-Bravo), which is 500 U.S. soldiers strong. The primary mission of JTF-Bravo is drug interdiction, but it has played a central role in disaster relief operations as well.

The U.S. Southern Command also operates a Forward Operating Location (FOL) in El Salvador, located at the international airport, to support aircraft and crews that monitor and intercept drug traffic. FOLs are not considered bases but staging airfields, owned and operated by host nations, in this case El Salvador. The other FOL host nation in the hemisphere is the Netherlands (Curaçao).

With Costa Rica, in 1999 the United States established a Joint Patrol Agreement to provide for increased intelligence sharing and coordination in counterdrug activities. It permits Costa Rican law enforcement personnel to embark on U.S. vessels as "ship riders" and authorizes U.S. vessels to pursue suspected traffickers in Costa Rican territorial waters. In exceptional "hot pursuit" situations, the agreement allows U.S. law enforcement vessels to pursue, stop, and secure a suspect vessel while awaiting the arrival of Costa Rican authorities.

After unsuccessful attempts to establish a training facility for Central American law enforcement agents (first in Panama, then in Costa Rica), the United States established in El Salvador the International Law Enforcement Academy (ILEA), which is also a U.S.-Salvadoran joint venture. Run by the Salvadoran Ministry of Government and the U.S. State Department, its instructors come from the United States; their salaries as well as most of the school's other expenses are covered by U.S. tax dollars. According to an ILEA estimate, by the end of 2007, the United States had spent at least $3.6 million on the academy and a $4 million headquarters is under construction.[19]

U.S.-Central American security cooperation will be further strengthened by the Merida Initiative announced by Presidents Calderón of Mexico and Bush in October 2007 and voted into law on June 30, 2008. Although Mexico will get the lion's share of the $1.6 billion three-year initiative, roughly a third of the whole amount will go to improve security in the seven Central American countries plus Haiti and the Dominican Republic.

Funds will support the Central American Fingerprinting Exploitation Initiative (CAFE) established to facilitate information-sharing about violent gang members and other criminals. They will also help develop an electronic travel document system to provide biometric and biographic information on persons being deported from the United States. Additionally funds will be directed to train and expand sensitive investigation police units dedicated to counter narcotics efforts. Other support will go towards improving maritime interdiction capabilities, port, airport, and border security and for providing technical assistance on firearms tracing, interdiction, and destruction. The initiative will also support ILEA's police training in community policing and community prevention programs as well as what has been labeled "rule of law" programs, such as improvement of court and prison management, prosecutorial capacity building, and the establishment of juvenile justice systems.[20]

Unlike U.S. cooperation with Nicaragua within the framework of the Millennium Challenge account, which has been suspended, U.S.-Nicaraguan cooperation continues regarding drug interdiction. The Nicaraguan navy periodically participates in joint training exercises with the U.S. Southern Command. The Ortega government signed its formal participation in the Merida initiative on May 15, 2009.

Scenarios for the Future

For better or for worse, the Central American republics are more integrated with the United States than ever before: demographically through migration, economically through remittances and *maquiladora* exports. Even Costa Rica, notwithstanding its more diversified economy, still depends heavily on American tourists, U.S. investments, and U.S. markets for its agricultural exports and its high value-added *maquiladora* products.

The global economic and financial crises are impacting Central American countries very harshly. Exports have tanked and remittances have shrunk, as has tourism. Economic growth is at a halt. Unlike other Latin American economies, those in Central America did not benefit from the commodity prices boom of the years prior to the burst of the U.S. housing market. Central America exports mainly assembled products from *maquiladoras*, non-traditional agricultural products such as fruits, vegetables, and flowers, and it continues to export coffee, bananas, and sugar, which are not the commodities that saw their prices soar. All Central American countries are net importers of oil. When the global economic crisis hit them, their economies had already been considerably weakened by oil prices. The slowdown of the U.S. economy will temper any gain that the CAFTA-DR agreement could have had. The Central America urgently awaits a fast U.S. economic recovery and the enactment of a comprehensive immigration reform with clear mechanisms for the incorporation of undocumented migrants into mainstream U.S. society. These two issues depend basically on domestic U.S. dynamics.

Politically, in the years ahead these already fragile states are going to be challenged to the core by rising levels of poverty, widespread violence, transnational criminal networks, and state corruption, not to mention the earthquakes and hurricanes that periodically hit the region.

Electoral democracy has taken hold in the region. Between 2000 and 2008 eight presidential elections took place in Central America. El Salvador recently elected the opposition candidate. Honduras will hold presidential elections by the end of 2009 and Costa Rica in February 2010. Unfortunately, a few black clouds have appeared in the horizon.

In Honduras, Manuel Zelaya, a rather conservative businessman, was elected in 2005 to succeed Ricardo Maduro, another rather conservative businessman but from a different party. Zelaya surprised friends and foes when he sought and obtained Honduran's membership to the Bolivarian Alternative for the Americas, Venezuela's project for regional integration (ALBA). He subsequently promoted a constitutional amendment to make reelection possible in order to seek a second term. Opposition to the reelection amendment was widespread. In June 2009, the Congress, the Supreme Court, and the armed forces deposed and exiled Zelaya, installing the president of Congress, who was from Zelaya's own Liberal Party, as interim Honduran president until the presidential election. All Latin American countries, the United States, and the European Union condemned the coup; the United States and the European Union cut some of their assistance to Honduras and imposed other sanctions. With Secretary of State Hillary Clinton's blessing, Costa Rican president Oscar Arias undertook a mediation to salvage Honduras' democratic institutions without much success. As in the past, trouble in a small Central American country spilled over to Washington DC. Florida Republican lawmakers and a U.S. Senator from South Carolina traveled to Tegucigalpa in support of the de facto government thus undermining the U.S. official position of not recognizing the de facto government.

While the ideological conflict plays itself out in the halls of power in Washington DC and on the streets of Tegucigalpa (after a month in Nicaragua, President Zelaya regained Tegucigalpa by car and took refuge at the Brazilian Embassy) and despite admonitions from the international community not to recognize the November 29 elections results unless President Zelaya is reinstated, the race for the Presidential Palace continued. Porfirio "Pepe" Lobo, a rancher, was elected president. Zelaya and Lobo agreed that Zelaya would go into exile in peace.

In 2006, Nobel Prize winner and former President Oscar Arias won the election by the narrowest of margins in a presidential contest. His challenger was not from the Social Christian Union Party, National Liberation Party's traditional rival since the 1950s, but rather a relative newcomer, Ottón Solís, former member of the National Liberation Party, who led the ticket of the Citizenship Action Party (PAC) on a staunch anti-CAFTA-DR platform. Solís had founded PAC to compete in the 2002 contest and surprised most observers by winning fourteen seats in the National Assembly and 22 percent of the popular vote. After 2006, the Christian Democrats all but disappeared; PAC won seventeen deputies at the National Assembly and 26 percent of the popular vote. In the 2010 Costa Rican presidential election, Laura Chinchilla (National Liberal Party) won the presidency.

In his third attempt to regain the presidency of Nicaragua, Daniel Ortega, was elected in 2006 with only 38 percent of the vote thanks to a split among the non-Sandinista parties. Although deserted by most of his Sandinista comrades and allied to former foes such as the Catholic Church and former Liberal Party president Arnoldo Alemán, Ortega tried to establish a new brand of "participative democracy" wrapped in a pro-poor, pro-Chávez, anti imperialist rhetoric. Upon election, Ortega declared Nicaragua's adherence to ALBA and was duly compensated by Chávez who arrived at his inauguration with multiple gifts. The bounty included preferential pricing on crude oil in an amount equal to about a third of Nicaragua's annual oil consumption, a refinery, the forgiveness of some $30 million in debt, new interest-free or low-interest loans of $20 million, and a nice sum for homes and healthcare. Like other ALBA members, Ortega is attempting to amend the Constitution to seek a consecutive second term in office, which would be his third.

In 2007, Guatemalans elected Alvaro Colom, the social democrat candidate. In 2009 in El Salvador, for the first time the candidate of the Farabundo Martí National Liberation Front (FMLN), Mauricio Funes, an independent left-of-center former journalist, was elected to the presidency, albeit without a legislative major-ity, putting an end to ARENA's twenty years in government. Funes reestablished full diplomatic relations with Cuba, but has identified President Lula of Brazil as his role model. His first international trip as president-elect was to Brazil. His wife is Brazilian and a former member of Lula's Workers' Party.

With the exception of El Salvador—probably not for long—all Central American countries participate either as full members (Nicaragua, Honduras, and Guatemala) or as observers (Costa Rica) in PetroCaribe. PetroCaribe S.A. is a Caribbean Basin oil cooperation scheme established by Venezuela, which allows its members to purchase oil on conditions of preferential payment. The alliance was launched in June 2005. The payment system allows for seventeen Caribbean and Central American nations to buy oil at market value but only a certain amount is needed up front; the remainder can be paid through a twenty-five year financing agreement at 1 percent interest.[21] Membership in PetroCaribe is a pragmatic choice, not an ideological one. Even Honduras and Nicaragua, the two Central American ALBA members have kept their CAFTA-DR and Merida Initiative par-ticipation.

In Port of Spain, at the Fifth Summit of the Americas, President Obama criticized his country's excessive reliance on military cooperation vis-à-vis the whole region, hinting towards more reliance on diplomacy and development cooperation. However, considering the many domestic and international problems that he needs to address, it is unlikely that the president will pay much attention to Latin America, let alone to Central America. The principal decision makers regarding the CAFTA-DR countries will probably be those whose job is precisely that of paying attention to the region at the State Department and the National Security Council.

Arturo Valenzuela is Obama's chosen U.S. Assistant Secretary for Western Hemispheric Affairs, a key player in U.S. Latin American relations. Valenzuela, an academic, has spent his career studying Latin American societies and political sys-tems. Although not a specialist in Central America, he understands that the small countries for all practical purposes constitute the U.S. southern border and need help to overcome the challenges of the next decade. Dan Restrepo at the National Security Council was the liaison to the Latino community and understands very well the deep linkages that most of its members maintain with their countries of ori-gin. He knows that, for U.S. migration policy to be effective, it must include com-prehensive domestic reforms and an international cooperation program with the sending countries.

Notes

1. In this chapter, by Central America I will mean the "historic five," but I will also refer to the countries of the Northern Triangle, the CA4, SICA, and CAFTA-DR. However I will not discuss the dynamics of the U.S.–Panama, the U.S.–DR, or the U.S.–Belize relationships.
2. Office of the United States representative, http://www.ustr.gov/_Development/ Preference_Programs/CBI/Section_Index.html.
3. Susan Gzesh, "Central Americans and Asylum Policy in the Reagan Era," *Migration Information Source*, http://www.migrationinformation.org/Feature/display.cfm?id=384#top.
4. Norma Stoltz Chinchilla and Nora Hamilton, "Central American Immigrants: Diverse Populations and Changing Communities," in *The Columbia History of Latinos in the U.S. since 1960*, ed. David G. Gutiérrez (New York: Columbia University Press, 2004), 210.
5. As reported by Salvadoran president Francisco Flores after his visit to Washington following his country's 2001 earthquakes. President Flores requested the United States to extend TPS status for Salvadorans, which President Bush granted.
6. http://www.census.gov/foreign-trade/balance/.
7. Principal donors were USAID, IDB, BCIE, ECLAC, and OAS. See Vincent McElhinny, "Update on the U.S.-Central American Free Trade Agreement (CAFTA): Implications of the Negotiations," http://www.interaction.org/idb, p.67.
8. Salomón Cohen (at the time Guatemalan lead negotiator) quoted by Vincent McElhinny, ibid.
9. Chapters 19 and 20 of the Agreement. http://www.ustr.gov/Trade_Agreements/ Bilateral/CAFTA/CAFTA-DR_Final_Texts/Section_Index.html.
10. Mary Jane Bolle, "DR-CAFTA Labor Rights Issues," *CRS. Report for Congress* http://fpc.state.gov/documents/organization/50152.pdf.
11. House Speaker Nancy Pelosi and Senate Majority Leader Harry Read in late September sent a letter to Costa Rica's Ambassador to the United States correcting Langsdale's false threats, http://www.alternet.org/workplace/64680/.
12. Mario Bermudez Vives, "Seguros y telecomunicaciones: aperturas se concretarán juntas," *El Financiero* (Costa Rica) May 11, 2009.
13. http://www.migrationinformation.org/DataHub/whosresults.cfm and Salomón Cohen, CAFTA: What Could It Mean for Migration? http://www.migrationinformation. org/feature/display.cfm?ID=388.
14. ECLAC, Social Panorama of Latin America 2005, http://www.eclac.cl/ cgi-bin/getProd.asp?xml=/publicaciones/xml/4/24054/P24054.xml&xsl=/dds/tpl-i/p9f. xsl&base=/tpl-i/top-bottom.xslt.
15. Megan Davy, *The Central American Foreign Born in the United States*, April 2006. http://www.migrationinformation.org/feature/display.cfm?ID=385.
16. Manuel Bermúdez, *Central America: Gang Violence and Anti Gangs Death Squads*, Inter Press Service, September 6, 2008. http://ipsnews.net/news.asp?idnews=30163.
17. Between 1960 and 1974 the homicide rate in El Salvador ranged between 23.6 and 32 per 100,000. After 1992, however, the homicide rates reached unprecedented levels of 138 per 100,000 in 1994–1995, which was attributed to the aftershocks of the civil war. See Roberto Steiner, "Criminalidad en El Salvador: diagnóstico y recomendaciones de política," San Salvador: FUSADES, February 1999.
18. See Amnesty International country report, 2008.
19. http://www.fletc.gov/training/programs/international-training-and-technical-assistance- itt/international-law-enforcement-academies/ilea-san-salvador.
20. Colleen W. Cook, Rebecca G. Rush, and Clare Ribando Seelke, "Merida Initiative: Proposed U.S. Anticrime and Counter Drug Assistance for Mexico and Central America," *CRS Report to Congress*, June 3, 2008. http://www.wilsoncenter.org/news/ docs/06.03.08%20CRS%20Report.pdf.
21. Petro Caribe has a special arrangement with local governments led by the Farabundo Martí National Liberation front (FMLN) to sell oil at preferential prices.

5 U.S.–Caribbean Relations

Modifying Traditional Hegemony and Sovereignty in the Caribbean

Anthony P. Maingot

The idea of a hegemonic system where "the strong do what they can and the weak suffer what they must,"[1] has not existed in the Caribbean for the past two decades.[2] One would have thought that the onslaught of the aggressive neo-Conservative ideology and its influence in the U.S. administration for the past eight years would have led it to reassert its hegemony in a region which has traditionally been America's "can do" region.[3] Surprisingly, this did not occur. Since the Spanish-American War and the opening of the Panama Canal in 1914, the dominance of the United States in the Caribbean has been such that one sophisticated historian can continue to argue that "[T]he United States practices almost total control in the Caribbean."[4] This was certainly the case not so long ago, when strategic considerations led to the militarization of the area through a ring of military bases, and one island in particular, Puerto Rico, served as a veritable regional fortress for the United States.[5] So long and so total was U.S. hegemony that terms such as "the Marines," "Banana Republics," "Dollar Diplomacy," "American Lake" all originated with U.S. action in the Caribbean. By the end of the twentieth century, however, virtually all U.S. bases had been closed. Defense is now controlled from the U.S. Southern Command (SouthCom) based in Miami with a limited number of "forward operating bases," i.e., planes based in civilian airports (viz. in Aruba and Curaçao, Netherlands Antilles), serving mostly counter drug trade functions. With the exception of relations with Cuba, the post-Cold War era witnessed the beginning of what can accurately be called an era of complex interdependence between the U.S. and the Caribbean. The more recent entry of Venezuela and, to a lesser degree, China as actors on the Caribbean's geopolitical scene has added complexity to the policy environment of these small states.

This complex interdependence goes well beyond purely economic and military relations to include both bilateral and multilateral relations on a continuum from cooperation to competition to open discord. In such a complex environment, both hegemonic inclinations and strident nationalist claims of sovereignty have been modified. This system has properly been called a "post-hegemonic" environment.[6] Consider the following active processes in the international relations of the region. First, the continuation of four critical pillars of U.S.-Caribbean interdependence: trade and investments, migration, remittances, and tourist flows. These are historical and deeply rooted in the perceptions and aspirations of Caribbean people. The

United States still stands relatively unchallenged in all four areas. Secondly, in order to facilitate the smoother operations of these critical processes, Caribbean states have modified one of the initial tenets of sovereign status: a strong sense of nationality based on unique citizenship. Today, they virtually all allow dual citizenship while the United States has largely ignored enforcing its principle of single citizenship. So common, and so functional, has this fact become that a Caribbean Community (CARICOM) prime minister recently lamented that the holders of U.S. and European Union (EU) passports have far greater freedom of travel and investment in CARICOM countries than do holders of CARICOM passports.[7] A third factor contributing to modifying both hegemony and sovereignty is the new environment of international organizations and regulations within which they all operate. As we shall see, small Caribbean nations have learned to use and leverage this international environment as a "multiplier" of their limited power.

This freedom of action on the part of small states does have limits, however. Two cases involving the state of Antigua/Barbuda will illustrate. When Antigua challenged the U.S. prohibition of internet (cyberspace) gambling, it used the World Trade Organization (WTO) as the court before which to argue its case. It won on the grounds that the U.S. prohibition violated international principles and agreements on free trade.[8] The fact that larger states allowed internet gambling and that the U.S. General Accounting Office found no definite evidence of a direct link between it and money laundering also helped Antigua make its case.[9] On the other hand, when Antigua attempted to use the WTO to challenge the Organization for Economic Co-operation and Development's (OECD) implementation of supervisory powers over off-shore financial businesses by its Financial Action Task Force, the WTO refused to act. Pointing to the attempts of a handful of powerful states to coerce "small countries," Antigua's Minister of Foreign Affairs, Sir Ronald Sanders, wondered how they could reject a role for the WTO, "a genuinely international body."[10] The OECD, he said pointedly, was an "economic," not an international body.[11] Whether this was true or not, the case illustrated the limits of sovereign action. Both state size and the realities of location in an archipelagic area do set limits as was recently recognized by two key studies.[12] There are other areas which the new global economy presents challenges to the small islands of the Caribbean.

1   While the Caribbean did receive privileged trade preferences through the Caribbean Basin Economic Recovery Act (CBERA) and the Caribbean Basin Trade Partnership Act (CBTPA) which provided opportunities for products not covered by the CBERA, the CBTPA expired on September 30, 2008. With the U.S. Congress showing greater reluctance to support trade concessions, the era of privileged trade protocols for Caribbean countries is rapidly coming to an end.

2   Even if well-intentioned U.S. Members of Congress, such as Charles Rangel of the powerful Ways and Means Committee, seek ways to promote trade with the Caribbean, there are private sector interests which think otherwise and are even more influential in Washington. The recent final ruling of the WTO that the EU preference program for Eastern Caribbean bananas was not in

compliance with the international trade rules and had "harmed American trade rights" represents the last nail in the coffin of the Caribbean banana industry. Caribbean islanders note that the United States does not grow or export any bananas, but that three powerful U.S. companies do: Chiquita Brands International, Del Monte Foods and Dole Food Company. Similarly, competition from the heavily subsidized sugar industry in Florida greatly restricts the market for Caribbean sugar.

3   While the European Union appears to want to assist its former colonies and both sides have made great strides regarding tariffs, taxes, and duties, the Caribbean is ill-prepared to confront the stringent phyto-sanitary conditions imposed by the EU and, indeed, even among themselves.

4   The U.S. "War on Terrorism" is widely perceived in the Caribbean as putting undue burdens on the foreign policies of these small nations. If it is true—as U.S. Navy Admiral James Stavridis, former Commandant of SouthCom stated—that "the specter of Islamist terrorist activity" is gaining traction in the Caribbean, it is equally true that these terrorists convert to Islam in U.S. jails and are then deported to the Caribbean.[13] These deportations respond to the laws and political climate in the United States, and the small nations of the Caribbean—wracked, as they all are, by rampant crime—are incapable of dealing with the fall-out. Let it be said, however, that it is much to the Admiral's credit that on another occasion he recognized the issue of deportees as a "significant and legitimate concern" for the islands.[14]

5   All the nations of that region with the exception of Venezuela and Trinidad/Tobago are energy dependent. This was recognized by the foreign ministers who met at the Organization of American States (OAS) General Assembly meeting in Panamá in 2007 when they highlighted the fact that "... energy is an essential resource for the sustainable development of peoples ... access to energy is of paramount importance. ..." This was hardly a new finding. In 1980, Mexico and Venezuela inaugurated what was called the "San José Accord," an oil facility geared to reducing the financial burden of energy costs for eleven Central American and Caribbean countries when the price of oil exceeds $15 per barrel. That Accord is today in frank decline for two reasons: [a] Mexico's declining production, and [b] President Hugo Chávez's promotion of his own energy aid, PetroCaribe which is far more generous.

In short, this *tour d'horizon* of the region reveals nation-states struggling to survive and develop in a world of ever-increasing energy costs, competition from lower-wage areas, demands to fight "terrorism" and reduced geopolitical leverage since the end of the Cold War. Under such circumstances, it is not reasonable to expect that any meaningful assistance, from the EU, the United States, Venezuela, or Cuba, will be rejected. In the context of a declining U.S. hegemonic presence, such circumstances provide opportunities to those who have the capacity to assist and who attach defined geopolitical designs to that assistance. Such is the case with the challenge presented by Venezuela's foreign policy.

The Venezuelan Challenge

Much of the world in late 2008 focused on the visit to Venezuela and other Caribbean states by Russian aircraft, naval vessels, and the Russian prime minister. Much more important for the Caribbean, however, has been Venezuela's use of petro-diplomacy. On the whole this diplomacy has been welcome in the region, but there are exceptions which illustrate the complexities of sovereign decision-making in archipelagic areas. Four case studies will illustrate.

Jamaica: The Pragmatic Borrower

Jamaica is heavily energy deficient: it imports 90 percent or more of its energy needs. This fact alone goes a long way in explaining the compulsion it felt to secure the steady flow of oil promised by PetroCaribe. Consider the following:

- In 2004, the year before signing the PetroCaribe Agreement, Jamaica spent over 60 percent of its export earnings on petroleum products. The price of a barrel of crude in 2004 was $34, bringing the cost to double what it had been in 2001.
- Using 1987 as a base year, the GDP of Jamaica grew by 20 percent, but energy consumption increased by 112 percent. Sixty percent of petroleum imports went to electricity generation, mining (i.e., bauxite, alumina), and manufacturing.
- Part of the agreement with Venezuela was to upgrade the island's PetroJam refinery by about 42 percent to 50,000 barrels per day.

The prime minister at the time, P.J. Patterson, summed up the global context facing his island and why the 23,500 barrels a day imported from Venezuela was so welcome:

> A new corridor has been created for us in the Caribbean to supply to Venezuela certain goods and services that may be affected by emerging trade policy including decisions of the WTO which are inimical to member states.[15]

As it turned out, and as we will note further on, fellow CARICOM member Trinidad/Tobago (T.T.) was not at all happy with Jamaica's cozying up to Venezuela. In early 2007 it announced that it was not going ahead with the previously arranged supply of liquid natural gas (LNG) to Jamaica and advised Jamaica to approach Venezuela on the possibility of obtaining natural gas supplies. On March 13, 2007, Jamaica signed a memorandum of understanding with Venezuela covering the supply of 150 million cubic feet of LNG per day.

Jamaicans reciprocated, showing their displeasure with T.T.'s actions. The Jamaican Manufacturers Association criticized the T.T. Government for reneging on the agreement, and for making it increasingly difficult to export Jamaican goods to that island despite the fact that T.T. had a U.S.$500 million favorable balance of trade with Jamaica.[16]

While Jamaica certainly benefited from the PetroCaribe deal and especially from the PetroCaribe Development Fund, in no way did it change the dynamics and orientation of Jamaican politics. In 2007 the Jamaican people voted out the People's National Party (PNP) which had signed PetroCaribe, replacing it with the more conservative Jamaica Labor Party (JLP). PetroCaribe was never an issue during the campaign. The new prime minister, Bruce Golding, kept the Agreement going as a purely "business" arrangement, proof that whatever geopolitical and ideological intentions President Chávez might have had have not materialized. Jamaica learned a painful lesson during the 1970s when Michael Manley made a sharp turn to the left to become part of a "correlation" of left forces in the region only to see the economy, and his political base, collapse. Jamaica's politics, and its foreign policies, are today geared towards a pragmatic search for solutions to its many domestic problems, and Cuban and Venezuelan aid is widely popular.[17]

Dominica—An Eager Participant

In February, 2007, two weeks before the CARICOM Heads of Government were to meet in Washington with President Bush, President Chávez visited Dominica and St. Vincent. In St. Vincent, he spelled out the plans for a new U.S.$200 million airport to be built with Venezuelan monies and Cuban labor. He took the occasion to declare, "Down with U.S. imperialism! Long live the people of the world!" An Associated Press journalist present noted that, "The crowd did not respond with applause to the Venezuelan leader's vitriolic statements."[18]

This author does not know what President Chávez said in Dominica, but given Prime Minister Roosevelt Skerrit's signing on to PetroCaribe, to being the first CARICOM member at that point to have joined the Bolivarian Alternative for the Americas (ALBA)[19] and his close ties with Cuba, there are those who are warning of an American "backlash" *à la* Grenada, 1983. Since Antigua and Barbuda and St. Vincent and the Grenadines have also joined ALBA, There is talk of "nations . . . expectantly entering into Venezuela's geopolitical orbit."[20] This is simplistic and alarmist to an extreme.

Dominica is one of the poorest islands in the Eastern Caribbean. This poverty has been aggravated by the decline of the banana industry. In 2006 Dominica's total tax revenue was U.S.$61.42 million, (EC$194 million), its expenditures, U.S.$101.12 million (EC$270 million). This budgetary short-fall has been the case for years. What economic opportunities does this island of 290 square miles and 65,000 people have to "balance its books," as the thrifty and conservative folk on the island tend to put it?[21] They are not sanguine that they will get a good deal from the United States Consider the following:

Dominicans know well that it was the U.S., protecting its banana companies based in Ecuador and Colombia, which brought the WTO suit against UK preferential prices for Eastern Caribbean bananas. This loss of market for their main product plus the losses wrought by the increasingly frequent hurricanes (damages from hurricane David were 20 percent of GDP), have left them with few options. They have been making a serious effort at developing ecotourism. But, unlike some of the other islands where an expanding tourist industry has compensated for the decline in agricultural exports, Dominica's volcanic, mountainous terrain (61 percent of the land is mountainous and forested), while ideal for eco-tourists, is not conducive to mass tourism. Additional deficiencies which hinder the establishment of mass tourism are a lack of white sandy beaches and an airport of easy access. None of this, of course, stops Venezuela from making Dominica the second country, after Cuba, where "Bolivarian social tourism" is promoted.[22] This politically driven exercise in subsidized group tours once a week is hardly what the island's economy needs or the tourist authorities wish to promote.

It is evident that the alternatives are few. This is why joining President Chávez's ALBA makes sense to even the most conservative Dominican sectors such as the Chamber of Commerce which voted in favor. The Dominica—Venezuela link is sustained by eleven cooperative programs, four of which were non-controversial, to wit:

1   Improvement of housing damaged by hurricane "David";
2   Paving mountain roads;
3   Upgrading the agricultural sector;
4   Increasing the number of university scholarships to 100.

On the other hand, the following proposals generated much opposition on the island:

1   The plan to build a U.S.$76 million refinery on the northeastern coast capable of refining the 10,000 barrels of Venezuelan crude to arrive under the PetroCaribe arrangement. Widespread public protests in March this year forced the Dominican Government to put the project on hold. The objections were three fold: (a) the project clashed with the nationally agreed plan to promote eco-tourism, (b) the deal was signed without any public consultation, and (c) the deal put at risk Dominica's pre-existing relations with other countries, i.e., the United States and Trinidad-Tobago.[23] A fuel storage and distribution plant was built and inaugurated by President Chávez in June, 2009. It is a modest affair, employing ten Dominicans.
2   Assistance to the Carib People. Less publicly controversial, but very much so among local intellectuals, is the donation of U.S.$4.5 million to build houses and schools in the Carib reservation. There can be no doubt that the Caribs need help with housing: 83 percent of the Caribs believe they live in "deplorable" circumstances.[24] The objections stem from the fear that the Venezuelan monies will dramatically alter the basis of Carib society: communal land holdings and cultivation. Whatever the objections, the infusion of Venezuelan monies was accepted on the grounds that it would have to be better than the official Dominican Government's recommendation that the solutions to the high levels of alcoholism and drug addiction in the reservation lie in "Prayers and Bible Study . . . creation of Godliness and brotherly love."[25]

In a sort of *quid pro quo*, Dominica has put on hold its dispute with Venezuela over the neighboring Islas Aves (Aves Rock in English) which Venezuela claims and which affects Dominica's territorial water claims. Dominica has a vibrant two-party system, a pragmatic foreign policy which takes into account its debts to T.T., Barbados, and its large migration to Martinique. The current government is clearly sympathetic and will make some concessions to the Chávez Bolivarian initiatives. That said, it is clear that in the parliamentary, two-party system which exists by popular choice, the government cannot formulate foreign policy without regard to the opinions of the opposition and to the built-in democratic safeguards and insistence on transparency and accountability.[26]

Trinidad/Tobago (T.T.): The Non-Participant

T.T.'s reservations with Venezuelan initiatives are not new. In fact, the present reservations regarding PetroCaribe bear resemblance to a heated controversy which broke out in the mid-1970s between T.T. and Venezuela.[27] To T.T.'s prime minister Eric Williams, a new threat was posed by what he regarded as Venezuela's improper designs on the Caribbean area generally and T.T. specifically. Two speeches made in 1975 give a picture of Williams's concern with Venezuelan moves and reveal much about intra-regional frictions which have little to do with U.S. actions.

In the first speech (May 1975) Williams attacked the notion that Venezuela was a Caribbean country ("I expect next to hear that Tierra del Fuego is") and pointed to "Venezuela's relations, territorial ambitions in respect of our area." The second speech was delivered to his party's convention on June 15, just two days before his trip to Cuba (and to the USSR, Romania and the United States, where he met with Henry Kissinger). In what amounts to one of the most scathing attacks by one Caribbean country on another during peacetime, Williams warned of Venezuela's "penetration" of the Caribbean, berated that country for its "belated recognition of its Caribbean identity," and chastised his CARICOM partners for falling for the new Venezuelan definition of the Caribbean (the "Caribbean basin") and leading a "Caribbean Pilgrimage to Caracas."

The sources of Williams's irritation with Venezuela were many, and some were certainly legitimate. For instance, contrary to the provisions of the CARICOM Charter, which called for multilateral trade with non-members, Venezuela was—as it is now—encouraging bilateral deals. This was especially the case in bauxite and oil, two markets which Williams had long wanted to dominate. But there were also differences regarding the law of the sea, objections to certain Venezuelan claims to nearly half of Guyana's territory and to islets in the Caribbean (viz. Islas Aves off Dominica) and to Venezuelan loans, tourism initiatives, and cultural "penetration" through scholarships. Williams expressed the fear that Caribbean and Latin American primary products were "jumping from the European and American frying pan into the South American fire" and that the net result would be the recognition of Venezuela as a "new 'financial centre' of the world."

Today, the issues might vary, and certainly the language is much more diplomatic, but there is no doubt that PetroCaribe represents, if not a threat, at least, serious competition to the oil-gas based economy of T.T. If one understands that 56 percent of product sales of T.T.'s PetroTrin refinery are in the Caribbean, one understands the perceived commercial threat. For instance, when Venezuela supplied St. Vincent with 7,200 10 kg liquefied propane gas (LPG) tanks as part of the PetroCaribe Agreement, this came at the expense of T.T.'s gas processors.

Beyond the more narrow commercial interests, however, there is the fact that T.T. has had its own "petro-diplomacy" in the region. T.T. perceives PetroCaribe, in conjunction with ALBA, as representing a challenge to its plans to be a major player in the Caribbean. The nature of T.T.'s arrangements differed from those of PetroCaribe in that they were a longer-term type of assistance: a rebate on purchases of oil which was deposited in a collective fund meant for developing the economies of CARICOM countries. It was never intended to be used as a "slush fund" for individual countries. T.T. had other major foreign policy initiatives:

- A cable carrying electricity to Grenada. Close ties with that island is a long-held plan of T.T. Additionally, there are large pockets of Grenadians in Trinidad who have considerable political clout.
- An Eastern Caribbean Gas Pipeline. This has involved T.T. in high-level talks with France since the plan includes the French islands of Martinique and Guadeloupe.
- A major liquefied natural gas (LNG) project in Jamaica.
- Forging a T.T.-led "Economic Union," occasionally spoken of as a "federation," with the islands of the Organization of Eastern Caribbean States (OECS). This despite the fact that on its face it is contrary to the stated goals and spirit of CARICOM regionalism and especially the region's much-discussed efforts at creating a CARICOM Single Market and Economy (CSME).

In order to carry out these monumental projects, T.T. will need foreign private investments (specifically excluded by PetroCaribe terms), the consent of the other islands (hardly in a position to wait that long), and an agreement with Venezuela on sharing the gas fields located in the Gulf of Paria. It all might look quite distant and improbable at this point but this does not stop that ambitious island from thinking big and resenting those who might rain on its parade.[28]

None of this, however, should be taken to mean that T.T. has strained relations with Venezuela. During a meeting in Caracas between T.T. prime minister Patrick Manning and President Chávez, it was announced that both countries had joint commissions studying the issue of oil and gas deposits in the narrow Gulf of Paria.[29] This continues a tradition of deft foreign policy initiatives, more akin to Brazil's *pragmatismo responsavel* than to the erstwhile U.S. propensity to a "with us or against us" approach.

It should be remembered that in 1972 T.T.'s prime minister Eric Williams led the move of the four independent Caribbean Free Trade Association (CARIFTA) states (Trinidad/Tobago, Jamaica, Barbados, and Guyana) to establish relations with Cuba. By 1993, all CARICOM states had diplomatic relations with Cuba and there is a CARICOM-Cuba Joint Commission which meets once a year to coordinate activities in a range of areas. These relations with Cuba serve T.T. well in cases where relations with Venezuela become difficult. It is certainly the case that T.T. has learned well the art of diplomatic triangulation but it is also true that the waning of U.S. hegemony has allowed the flowering of these diplomatic skills.

Barbados Responds Coolly

T.T. has found additional satisfaction in the fact that Barbados, generally considered the best governed of the CARICOM islands, has also refused to join PetroCaribe. Several reasons can be adjudged:

1   Barbados has always had close relationships with both T.T. and the United States and did not wish to affect that in any way.
2   The island is now one-third self-sufficient in oil and wishes to attract more foreign investments for exploration. In early May, 2008 Barbados opened the trading on rights to explore twenty-eight offshore "blocks" on which some thirty companies were expected to bid. When Venezuela claimed that two of these blocks were in its waters, a repeat of the T.T.-Venezuela disputes of the 1970s appeared to be in the making.[30] Nothing came of this however. In January 2009, Barbados awarded the first two of twenty exploration licenses for offshore "blocks" to an American company with major operations in T.T.[31] Venezuela seems to have put this claim on ice in the same way as it has put the territorial claim on a major part of Guyana on ice. The claims are not dismissed, they are simply put on Venezuela's geopolitical back-burner.
3   Barbados's economy is sustained by tourism and the financial services sector, hardly items propitious for a barter arrangement. With little in terms of native products to provide as exchange, the island was apprehensive about incurring heavy debts to repay any PetroCaribe loans. Barbadian eyes were on the Dominican Republic where, as of the fourth quarter of 2008, the issue of a heavy debt burden from PetroCaribe oil was agitating political opinions. Because of PetroCaribe's refusal to deal with private companies, the big issue was whether the government's buy-out of Shell's 50 percent of the island's only refinery (Refidomsa) in order to increase the flow of Venezuelan oil would pay off. Doubts about the state's managerial skills and its capacity to repay Venezuela are the main issues debated. Comparisons between how Barbados and the Dominican Republic arrived at their respective decisions regarding PetroCaribe reveal the sovereign independence of these small states as well as revealing why, despite the region's needs, President Chávez's geopolitical designs will not be so easily realized.

What the Barbados case demonstrates is how any country—no matter how small—arrives at its foreign policy decisions based on their overall political and economic systems and customs. Steady resoluteness has long been a cultural trait of Barbados and it has demonstrated this characteristic quite clearly in the case of PetroCaribe.[32]

Complicating this geopolitical picture of bilateral and multilateral relations in the Caribbean are the rapidly evolving relations with Cuba.

CARICOM—Cuban Relations

As already noted, the first English-speaking countries to establish diplomatic relations with Cuba were Jamaica, Guyana, Trinidad and Tobago, and Barbados in 1972. It was fundamentally a symbolic gesture intended to assert the sovereign independence of the newly minted nations. There were virtually no trade or other material interests involved. The context included the very evident pressures and hostilities on the part of the United States but hardly the kind of overbearing to which the Caribbean had been historically subject. This, in a way, gave the green light to other Caribbean countries to follow suit: St. Lucia and Grenada in 1979, St. Vincent in 1992, Belize in 1994, Antigua/Barbuda, Dominica, St. Kitts/Nevis after 1994. During the Cold War years, Cuba's involvement tended to be more party-to-party than state-to-state. In Jamaica the relations were with Michael Manley's People's National Party (PNP) and in Grenada with Maurice Bishop's New Jewel Movement (NJM). Predictably, when both parties were defeated, diplomatic relations came to an end (in 1982 and 1983, respectively). Jamaica restored relations in 1990 and Grenada in 1999.

Given this very recent and turbulent history of diplomatic relations, one has to note with no small amount of amazement the recent level of Cuban—Caribbean relations. Just as Jamaica has regular meetings with the United States on issues of illegal narcotics, people-smuggling, money-laundering and terrorism, so it has also with Cuba. Yet there is only a minimal increase in Cuban—Caribbean trade. What explains the increased prominence of recent Cuban—Caribbean relations?

The explanation lies in Cuba's use of soft power, specifically the delivery of educational and health services. Cuban exchanges and medical scholarships have expanded considerably since 2001–2002 (see Table 5.1). Dominica and Haiti are two specific cases which illustrate well the depth and breadth of Cuban technical/medical assistance in the Caribbean.

In 2004, the Dominica Guild of Cuban Graduates celebrated twenty-five years of Cuban scholarships. Prime Minister Roosevelt Skerrit—who, like Préval in Haiti and Prime Minister Patrick Manning of Trinidad and Tobago, goes to Cuba for his medical attention—noted that Cuba "has done more than any other to establish and strengthen the bonds of friendship and cooperation, so vitally necessary for the maintenance of regional cooperation and integration."[33] The Guild had two economists make an approximate calculation of the economic impact of the Cuban scholarship program: a total of U.S.$19 million to graduate fifty medical doctors from a six-year program. As of mid-2009, 320 Dominicans had graduated from Cuban universities, 102 were at the time studying in Cuba while thirty-six Cuban medical personnel were serving in Dominica.

Aside from the large number of CARICOM students in Cuba, in 2002 there were 1,192 Cuban doctors serving in those countries. According to *Granma*,[34] there are 36,578 Cuban doctors and health workers operating in eighty-one countries.

Table 5.1 Foreign Scholarships Offered by Cuba for Academic Year 2001/2002

Countries	MINPUH Tert. Level	Sec. Level	LASM	Prep.	MINTED	Centres	NISR INSPES	MINED Sec. Level	Pre-Univ.	Total
Antigua/Barbuda	30			5	53	1	8		0	97
Bahamas	69	3		0	82	0	0	3		157
Barbados	11			0	56	0	10	1		78
Belize	9	2	40	0	73	0	1	1		126
Dominica	63	3		3	212	6	2	1		290
Grenada	28			2	57	0	9	4		100
Guyana	11			4	31	0	5			51
Haiti	8	6	313	1	178	9	39			554
Jamaica	106	19		15	171	0	25	1	4	341
St. Kitts/Nevis	22			0	46	0	2			70
St. Lucia	71	1		9	165	2	6	1		255
St. Vincent/Grenadines	25			6	87	1		3		122
Suriname	3			0	11	0				14
Trinidad/Tobago	7			4	16	0	8			35
Total CARICOM	**463**	**34**	**353**	**49**	**1238**	**19**	**115**	**15**	**4**	**2290**

Legend:

Tert. Level = Tertiary Level

Sec. Level = Secondary Level
Prep. = Preparatory
Pre-Univ. = Pre-University

MINPUH = Ministry of Public Health

LASM = Latin American School of Medicine
MINTED = Ministry of Tertiary Education
NISR = National Institute for Sport and Recreation

INSPES = International School for Physical
    Education and Sport
MINED = Ministry of Education

Source: Norman Girvan, "Cuba, The Caribbean and the ACS: A Note," (Wilton Park, UK, Conference Paper, October 18–20, 2002).

Interestingly, and significant for the analysis presented here, this is just below the size of the present Cuban Army: 38,000.[35] Cuban officials claim that they are well-equipped to sustain this level of medical "internationalism."[36] It has a hemisphere high of six doctors per 1,000 population and they are all, in the strictest sense of the word, state employees. Starting in 1984 Cuba initiated the system of family medicine, with doctors and nurses living in the neighborhoods they serve. It is calculated that 30,000 (i.e., 45.6 percent of all doctors on the island) are now neighborhood doctors. Their fundamental mission is to practice "preventive medicine."[37]

Evidently, and logically, all this has had a dramatic impact on Cuban—CARICOM relations. It stretches even to energy-sufficient T.T. In December, 2008 the people of that island were surprised to learn that not only had their prime minister had a malignant kidney removed in Cuba, the complex surgery had been done with no charges of any kind. Soon a major newspaper was calling for the island to do something "reciprocal" for Cuba, the Minister of Health admitted that there were several Cuban doctors working in T.T. and that he had appealed to the Cubans for help in eradicating dengue-bearing mosquitoes on the island.[38] Cuba's foreign policy, once so feared, is today enormously popular.

Arguably the most dramatic case of the receding of U.S. hegemony, but also of sovereignty, is Haiti. No country in the Caribbean experienced a U.S. occupation as long as that in Haiti (1914–1934), and no country experienced such continued U.S. interventions, either military or through official agencies such as USAID and non-governmental agencies such as the National Endowment for Democracy or the Carter Center. The U.S. intervened to put an end to the Duvalier dynasty, to restore elected President Jean-Bertrand Aristide to office and then intervened to have him removed and exiled. It is because of this long and pervasive exercise of hegemonic dominance that the sovereign Haitian decision to engage Cuba at multiple levels so clearly reveals the changed geopolitical milieu in the region.

Again, it is Cuban soft power, backed by Venezuelan funds, which represents the main thrust of the new diplomacy. Haiti's desperate health situation explains the need for the Cuban presence. Even Dominica, the poorest of the Eastern Caribbean states, has much better health and economic standards than Haiti. Where life expectancy in Haiti in 2000 was 56 years, in Dominica it was 80, the same as in Cuba. Whereas in 2002 Haiti had 2.5 doctors per 10,000 inhabitants, Cuba had 59.6. But the presence of Cuban doctors in Haiti was only part of the exchange: there were 554 Haitians on scholarships in Cuba, 313 of whom were studying at the Latin American School of Medicine. This explains in part why the United States, which initially sent a platoon of Marines to Haiti after the forced departure of President Jean-Bertrand de Aristide in March 2004, made no demands for the removal of the Cuban medical teams. Even the French Government, eager to see the last of the Jean-Bertrand Aristide regime, was at pains to discuss the retention of the Cuban "Health Brigade."[39] There is nothing surprising about this given the presence in Haiti of 332 Cuban doctors and 193 "health assistants" who, according to President René Préval, operate in areas "where even Haitians dare not go"[40] Cuba's Minister of Foreign Affairs informed the Council of Ministers of the Association of Caribbean States on February 12, 2004, on a long list of achievements for the years

1999–2003, including educating 247 Haitian students at the Latin American Medical School in Cuba.

Most dramatic, perhaps, has been the Cuban participation in the fight against HIV-AIDS in Haiti. AIDS is the number one cause of all adult deaths in Haiti, the island with the highest incidence of AIDS in the hemisphere. Because AIDS is "generalized" and heterosexually transmitted, its legacies are decreasing life expectancies, leaving in its wake massive numbers of orphans as well as an epidemic of opportunistic ailments such as tuberculosis. Cuba, with the lowest incidence of HIV-AIDS in the hemisphere, brought to the Haitian campaign its considerable experience with domestically produced generic anti-retroviral drugs, screening of blood donations and public education.[41]

It is not yet clear just how much of a dent the Cuban intervention has made in this Haitian pandemic but the political payoff is evident. "In Haiti," said René Préval, "they say that after God, there are the Cuban doctors."[42] It is a plausible assumption that, since Préval initiated the Cuban-Haitian medical program during his first administration (1996–2001), this contributed substantially to his election to a second term in 2006.

In April 2006, Préval paid an official visit to Cuba and, as would be repeated time and again with other Caribbean missions, he was accompanied by sixty Haitians on scholarships to the Latin American School of Medicine and forty patients under the auspices of "Operation Miracle" going to Cuba's Pando Ferrer Ophthalmologic Institute.[43]

While all these activities reflect the absence of U.S. interference with Haitian decision-making, they do not in themselves tell the whole story of Haiti's dependence on two external actors, the United Nations and, through the UN, the United States. In both cases, Haiti has had to make major concessions in its sovereign control.

The United Nations is represented through the presence since 2004 of the 7,500 person strong UN Mission for the Stabilization of Haiti (MINUSTAH). Twenty nations are represented but the Brazilians—with one battalion of army troops—form the largest contingent and command the Mission. This explains why Brazilian president Luíz Inacio Lula da Silva has visited Haiti twice—once in 2004 and then in 2008. No high-level Cuban official has done so up to mid-2009.

The U.S. involvement came after the UN, instead of going the usual route of contracting a U.S.-based consultant on Haitian development, turned to one of the UK's foremost authorities on "fragile" states, Paul Collier. In his Report on Haiti, Collier addressed the same four instruments for lifting failing states out of their underdevelopment he had raised in his popular book, *The Bottom Billion*: aid, security, laws, and trade.[44] Collier noted that security was now in the hands of MINUSTAH, laws a sovereign matter, aid a concern for the multilateral agencies, but trade very much involved the United States.[45] Following the UN's endorsement of the Collier Report, the UN appointed former U.S. president Bill Clinton as Special Envoy to Haiti. Collier had argued that U.S. support could help lift Haiti "decisively out of fragility" for the following reasons: (1) the United States had already given Haiti more advantageous market access than it has given to any other country; Haiti needed U.S. help in accessing this market. (2) A significant part of that help can come from the Haitian diaspora in the United States, proportionately one of the largest in the world, which provides, he said, "a massive flow of remittances, a reservoir of skills, and powerful political lobby."

It is too early to determine whether this new multilateral approach with strong U.S. involvements will succeed. One is sobered by recollecting how many others have failed, yet cautiously optimistic by the changed geopolitical environment which allows concessions on sovereignty without hegemonic demands.

Conclusion

Jamaica is now governed by the Jamaica Labor Party, a party which has traditionally been hostile towards Cuba. Since early May, 2008, Jamaican society has been abuzz with the question: why did JLP prime minister Bruce Golding turn down two invitations to do the conventional and customary first visit to Washington but led a major governmental delegation to Cuba instead? No full explanation has been forthcoming but it was no surprise that the bilateral talks with Cuba would start with discussions on health care.[46] What does that case, and the analysis above, tell us about the modification of hegemony and sovereignty in the region? A quick review of some theory will help.

American theorizing in international relations has always alternated between "realists" who emphasize "hard" power, and "idealists" who argue in favor of using "soft" power. The former emphasizes military and economic power as deterrence, coercive diplomacy and threats of the use of force. Soft power emphasizes policies and diplomacy which engender admiration and attraction. The most influential voice in this reaction has been that of Joseph S. Nye, Jr.[47] At the risk of reducing excessively his wide-ranging ideas, this analysis derives the following theory of international dynamics from his work: The world today is characterized by an information revolution. This has created "virtual communities and networks" that cut across national boundaries, they are transnational. "Politics," says Nye, "become in part a competition for attractiveness, legitimacy and credibility."[48] From Nye's broad-gauged theory and the examples he cites to sustain it, we derive the following hypothesis:

> Given this political dynamic in a globalized information age, the relative importance of soft power will increase. Service providers will be the leading agents of soft power.

It is evident that on that score Cuba is doing very well. There is nothing to guarantee that this attraction will continue. What does sustain it is how poorly the United States is doing. As Joseph Nye has said, noting the recent U.S. penchant for using "hard power":

> We have been less successful in the areas of soft power, where our public diplomacy has been woefully inadequate and our neglect of allies and institutions has created a sense of illegitimacy that has squandered our attractiveness.[49]

What U.S. relations with Cuba, Venezuela, Trinidad/Tobago, Jamaica, Dominica, and Nicaragua demonstrate is that each country will react to these relations in its own way. This holds even as President Hugo Chávez attempts to use petro-politics to create a "Bolivarian" sphere of influence. Existing political cultures—even in the relatively new states—are not easily modified even in the face of the most attractive incentives. In the final analysis, it is the sophistication of Caribbean democrats which will be the main barrier to President Chávez's evident geopolitical designs. They frankly find President Chávez's "Socialism of the XXI Century" and strident anti-Americanism confusing and ultimately unconvincing.[50] "Socialism" still has an ominous ring in the Caribbean. The tragedy of Grenada, the assassinations in Suriname, the failure of Michael Manley to convince that a "humanistic" socialism was possible, all soured the region on that word.[51] Even the case of the Cuban economy, which engenders much sympathy and friendship throughout the region, is seen as an example of nationalistic determination in the face of the American onslaught, hardly as a shining model of economic development.

Finally, the most attractive and successful part of the "Bolivarian" initiative is the medical assistance. "Operación Milagro" must be ranked as one of the most generous and appreciated uses of "soft power" in the Greater Caribbean and perhaps Latin America. The problem for Chávez lies in the fact that even as he funds the initiative, those in the front lines are Cuban and they and their country get the credit for their good work. There are, of course, constant questions in the Caribbean press regarding the price of oil and Venezuela's long-term capacity to sustain this bountiful foreign policy.

Beyond oil and medical attention, it is also true that *Bolivarianismo,* Venezuela's general "soft power" program of material and ideological inducements, cannot compete with the attractions and "pull" of U.S. society mentioned above. The day large numbers of Caribbean people line up voluntarily and without financial inducements to secure visas to Venezuela or Cuba, one will be able to say that the direction of soft power "pull" has been fundamentally transformed. That moment appears nowhere in sight for the short or medium term.[52]

This is the main lesson learned: the modification of U.S. hegemony has allowed Venezuela and Cuba to use soft power in a wide-ranging fashion, and Caribbean states to challenge U.S. objections to certain initiatives such as, for instance, offshore banking and gambling. The sovereign determination of Caribbean governments to accept and respond to what are essentially anti-American initiatives such as ALBA, however, has limits. As the president of Haiti, the very pro-Cuban René Préval, has discovered, the limits are set by their peoples' political cultures and social preferences as well as the ongoing realities of trade, investment technology and, certainly not to be ignored, race and ethnic identifications and preferences. On this latter point it is worth noting that in May 2009 Antigua, now a member of ALBA, changed the name of its highest hill, "Boggy Peak," to "Mount Obama," part of a new "Mount Obama Monument and National Park," complete with a museum depicting the history of U.S.–Antigua relationships. That same month, Barbados changed the name of its Government Complex to the "Eric H. Holder, Jr. Municipal Complex" in honor of the new U.S. Attorney General whose father was born in Barbados. Such bonds of history are as solid and enduring as the coral rock of these islands. They give the United States a distinct advantage in this important game of geopolitical jockeying should they decide to engage it seriously.

Notes

1. This was Thucydides' definition of hegemony cited in Robert O. Keohane and Joseph Nye, *Power and Interdependence* (Boston: Little, Brown and Co., 1977), 42.
2. Judging from one of his very early essays, Abraham Lowenthal would argue that the weakening of U.S. hegemonic inclinations began much before the end of the Cold War. (See Abraham Lowenthal, "Ending the Hegemonic Presumption," *Foreign Affairs*, October, 1976.)
3. This author incorrectly anticipated a forceful U.S. response to a series of sovereign actions in the Caribbean based on the writings of many Neo-Conservatives who were in the George W. Bush administration. See "Ni el fin de las 'ideologias,' de la 'historia' o de las ansias imperiales: implicaciones del neo-conservatismo norteamericano." (Decimoseptima Lección inaugural, Año Academico 2004–2005, Universidad de Puerto Rico, Río Piedras, September 14, 2004.)
4. Juan R. Torruella, *Global Intrigues* (San Juan: Editorial de la Universidad de Puerto Rico, 1987), 165.
5. See, Humberto García Muñíz, *La estrategia de Estados Unidos y la militarización del Caribe* (Río Piedras: Instituto de Estudios del Caribe, 1988); Jorge Rodríguez Beruff, *Strategy as Politics: Puerto Rico on the Eve of the Second World War* (San Juan: La Editorial, Universidad de Puerto Rico, 2007).
6. The term, and the general argument, is from Robert O. Keohane, *After Hegemony: Cooperation and Discord in the World Political Economy* (Princeton, NJ: Princeton University Press, 1984).
7. *Trinidad Express*, "Caricom passport—a joke" (December 26, 2008).
8. Thirty-four states allow casino gambling, totaling a $27 billion take; another $60 billion are taken in from other forms of gambling. "Special Report," *The Economist* (October 2, 2004), 67–69.
9. See, GAO, *Internet Gambling: An Overview of the Issues* (Washington, DC: General Accounting Office, GAO–03–89, Dec. 2002).
10. UNITAR defines "small" states as having an upper limit of population of one million. There are 44 such independent states.
11. See *Antigua Sun* (October 10, 2003), 1.
12. Caribbean Secretariat, *Caribbean Trade and Investment Report, 2000* (Kingston, Jamaica: Ian Randle, 2000), 165–166. T.N. Srininvasan, *The Costs and Benefits of Being a Small Remote Island, Landlocked and Mini-state Economy* (Washington, DC: World Bank and IMF in cooperation with the Commonwealth Secretariat). What these studies do not mention is that limitations of size have not stopped Caribbean states from challenging Washington's continued opposition to both internet gambling and offshore secrecy jurisdictions. So intense is the Caribbean's pursuit of offshore jurisdictions that a Jamaican paper recently carried the headline "Offshore Jamaica vs. Offshore Trinidad—Let the Games Begin," *The (Jamaica) Gleaner*, August 24, 2008, 1.
13. Benedict Mander, "Bolivarian Bravado," *Financial Times*, November 28, 2008, 7; see, *New York Times*, December 17, 2008, 1; *Financial Times*, November 28, 2008, 4; Bloomberg Service, December 11, 2008; see *Alexander's Gas and Oil Connection* 6, No. 16 (August 28, 2001); see at www.Caribbean360.com.
14. See the piece by James Stavridis and Thomas Shannon in *The Miami Herald*, April 3, 2008.
15. See Statement to Parliament by the Most Hon. P.J. Patterson, July 13, 2005 at www.jis.gov.jm/special_sections/CARICOM.

16. *Jamaica Gleaner*, (March 20, 2007), 1.

17. See, for instance, Norman Girvan, "Alba, Petro-Caribe and CARICOM: Issues in a New Dynamic," in *Venezuela's Foreign Policy: The Role of Petro-Diplomacy*, ed. Ralph S. Clem and Anthony P. Maingot (Miami: Latin American and Caribbean Center, forthcoming).

18. See Duggie Joseph, "Chávez in St.Vincent calls for anti-imperialist unity," AP release February 17, 2007.

19. Antigua and Barbuda and St.Vincent and the Grenadines joined ALBA in June, 2009.

20. See Nikolas Kosloff, "Dominica: The Caribbean's Next 'Terror Island'?" www.coha.org (February 26, 2008).

21. On the conservative nature of Caribbean culture, see Anthony P. Maingot, "The Caribbean: The Structure of Modern-Conservative Societies," in any of the four editions of *Latin America: Its Problems and its Promise*, ed. Jan Knippers Black (Boulder, CO: Westview Press).

22. See Agencia Bolivariana de Noticias, March 14, 2008 at www.abn.info.ve/.

23. See "Freedom Party Slam's [Prime Minister] Skerrit's ALBA Agreement," *The Sun* (Roseau, Dominica: February 25, 2008), 17.

24. Lotell Williams, "Carib People Development Plan," February 20, 2003, 26. Caribs are also known as Kalinago people.

25. Ibid., 50. See further: *Ministry of Community Development, Heritage of the Kalinago People* (Roseau, Dominica: 2007).

26. Further on this in Anthony P. Maingot, "Citizenship and Parliamentary Politics in the English-Speaking Caribbean," in *The Contemporary Legacy to the Caribbean*, ed. Paul Sutton (London: Frank Cass, 1986), 120–140.

27. This section is taken from Anthony P. Maingot, *The United States and The Caribbean: Challenges of an Asymmetrical Relationship* (London: Macmillan and Boulder, CO: Westview Press, 1994), 131–132.

28. In November 2008, the Government of T.T. allocated TT\$500 million to host two international conferences in 2009, the Summit of the Americas in March and the Meeting of Heads of Government of the Commonwealth States in November. These were clearly, as the local newspaper editorialized, attempts to "position" the island on the international stage. (See Editorial, *The Trinidad Guardian*, December 27, 2008.)

29. See at www.politica.eluniversal.com/2007/03/20/pol.

30. See *The Daily Nation* (Barbados), June 18, 2008, 1.

31. See "Barbados issues license to drill for oil," dated January 19, 2009 at www.caribbeannetnews.com/news.

32. On this see Anthony P. Maingot, "The Paradoxical Origins of Barbados' Civic Culture," Presented to the Culture Change Institute, The Fletcher School of Law and Diplomacy, October 24, 2008.

33. Dominica Guild of Cuban Graduates, *25 Years of Cuban Scholarships*. (Roseau, 2004).

34. *Digital Granma Internacional* (April 1, 2008). *Granma* is the newspaper of Cuba's Communist Party.

35. See International Institute for Security Studies, *The Military Balance 2006*, ed. C. Langton (London: Routledge): 322.

36. One of the unexplored issues of the Cuba-Venezuela-Caribbean nexus is how much the Cuban state earns from this medical internationalism. Economist Carmelo Mesa-Lago estimates that in Venezuela, Cuban doctors are paid U.S.\$50 per month even as the Venezuelan Government pays Cuba U.S.\$ 18,376 per month for that doctor. (See interview, *El Nuevo Herald*, February 1, 2009, 23–A.)

37. A. Ramírez Márquez y G. Mesa Ridel, "El Proceso de Desarrollo del Sistema Nacional de Salud de Cuba," *Revista Bimestre Cubana* 16 (enero—junio, 2002), 152–161.

38. *Trinidad and Tobago Express*, December 27, 2008, 1.

39. Author's interview with Patrick Paoli, France's Under-Secretary of Caribbean Affairs, Miami, January 19, 2005. On France's growing impatience with Aristide, see *Rapport au*

Ministre des affaires étrangères, M. Dominique de Villepin du Comité independant de réflexion et de propositions sur les relations Franco-Haitiennes (Janvier, 2004). Régis Debray was one of the main authors of this report.

40. Cited in *Granma Internacional* (April 19, 2006).
41. "The Fight Against AIDS in Cuba and Haiti," *MEDIC Review 8* (March–April 2006): 26–30.
42. *Agence France Presse*, April 14, 2006.
43. See *FOCAL POINT*, March 2006.
44. See Paul Collier, *The Bottom Billion: Why the Poorest Countries Are Failing and What Can Be Done about It* (New York: Oxford University Press, 2007).
45. Paul Collier, "Haiti: From Natural Catastrophe to Economic Security. A Report for the Secretary-General of the United Nations." Department of Economics, Oxford University, January 2009.
46. *The Jamaica Gleaner*, May 3, 2008, 1.
47. Joseph S. Nye, Jr., *"Soft Power" The Means to Success in World Politics* (New York: Public Affairs, 2004).
48. Ibid., 31.
49. Ibid., 147.
50. Further on this in Anthony P. Maingot, "Responses to Venezuelan Petro-Politics in the Greater Caribbean: Lesson from a Comparison," in *Venezuelan Petro-Diplomacy: Hugo Chavez' Foreign Policy*, ed. Ralph S. Clem and Anthony P. Maingot (Gainesville: Universities of Florida Press, forthcoming).
51. On this point see Anthony P. Maingot, "The Difficult Road to Socialism in the English-Speaking Caribbean," in *Capitalism and the State in U.S.-Latin American Relations*, ed. Richard R. Fagen (Palo Alto, CA: Stanford University Press, 1979): 254–289; "Political Processes in the Caribbean, 1970s to 2000," in *UNESCO General History of the Caribbean*. Vol. V, ed. Bridget Brereton (London: Macmillan, 2004): 312–345.
52. It is interesting to analyze the reporting of the Barbadian press regarding their Prime Minister's visit to Cuba followed "hours afterward" with a visit to Denver, Colorado where Barack Obama accepted the nomination to run in the presidential elections of November 2008. Next to the sober reporting from Cuba, the reporting from Denver took on a decidedly upbeat tone with descriptions of the Prime Minister's "front row seats" with U.S. House Majority Whip James Clyburn, Oprah Winfrey and "other well-known stars." (See *The Nation*, August 29, 2008, 1.)

6 Argentina and the United States

A Distant Relationship

Roberto Russell

Introduction

U.S.–Argentine relations experienced significant changes in the second half of 2001. The main causes of this trend can be found in Argentina, although George W. Bush's government made important contributions to this departure from the path that had been followed during the 1990s. The political and financial crisis in Argentina, which began in December 2001, not only led to the fall of Fernando de la Rúa's government (1999–2001), but it also ended the foreign policy framework, developed and implemented during the years of Carlos Menem's presidency (1989–1999) that had promoted a strategy of bandwagoning with Washington.[1]

From this moment onwards, Argentina slowly abandoned this blueprint, establishing an ambiguous relationship with the United States combining, at times, noisy dissent with selective cooperation on certain key issues for Washington such as counter-terrorism and counter-narcotics as well as participation in peacekeeping operations. In any case, the events of 9/11 relegated Argentina to an even less important position than it had occupied in the Bush administration's already reduced Latin American agenda. The securitization of the U.S. agenda had only a limited effect on the somewhat distant Argentina and on bilateral relations primarily dominated by trade and finance issues. U.S. authorities did not lose any sleep over the domestic disturbances in Argentina nor Néstor and Cristina Kirchner's endless attacks on neoliberalism nor their close ties with Hugo Chávez's Venezuela. None of these were sufficient to generate a negative agenda that would draw more attention from Washington or alter the Bush administration's indifference toward Buenos Aires. For their part, the Kirchners felt that they could, for the most part, do without ties to an administration for which they felt little personal or ideological affinity. At the same time, this attitude permitted them to reap the political benefits of the dominant anti-American sentiment in Argentine society.[2] The mishaps and growing weakness of the Bush government only deepened mutual disaffection.

Thus, a pattern of "pragmatic cooperation" was established, with little and later no presidential dialogue, a certain coolness, low mutual expectations, outspoken differences and cooperation on issues of common interest. Within this framework, the Bush government was prepared to overlook a certain degree of rebelliousness, peppered with insults and accusations emanating from Buenos Aires. Always careful to avoid direct confrontation, the Kirchners criticized the unilateralism of the United States and its lack of interest in Latin America with their eyes firmly fixed on domestic politics rather than because of any genuine opposition. At a ministerial level, communication, with all its differences and agreements, was managed in a more discreet tone without any major upheavals. It was through these channels that the key issues of the bilateral relationship were discussed and where, upon reflection, there was a fair balance between agreements and discrepancies.

This chapter consists of three sections. In the first, the main issues that defined the U.S.–Argentine relationship from the crisis of 2001 until Néstor Kirchner took office on May 25, 2003 are outlined. This period of around 18 months prefigured the course and character of the bilateral relationship during Néstor Kirchner's presidency (2003–2007), which is the subject of the second section. In this part, the most relevant areas of the bilateral agenda are discussed to demonstrate the main hypothesis of this work: relations were characterized by a mutual pragmatism within a framework of unstable and distant coexistence. Buenos Aires' most notable public clashes with Washington with their sometimes excessive displays of intemperance, theatrical flourishes, and a certain hubris typical of Néstor Kirchner's style of governing were fundamentally a product of political or economic expediency at a domestic level. In short, differences were more practical in nature than ideological. Areas of agreements followed the same pattern. The final section comments on bilateral relations starting from the beginning of Cristina Fernández de Kirchner's government and provides some thoughts on its future now that Barack Obama has taken office as president of the United States.

The Transition Government of Eduardo Duhalde

The terrorist attacks of 9/11 in the United States coincided with the final throes of Fernando de la Rúa's administration. The government was paralyzed by its growing inability to govern the country and control the precarious economic situation that would conclude in its collapse as a result of the crisis of December 2001. Its immediate reaction to the 9/11 terrorist attacks adjusted to the parameters established by the Menem administration to conduct bilateral relations, although without the same conviction and, on occasions, with reluctance. The Argentine Minister of foreign affairs, Adalberto Rodriguez Giavarini, clearly defined the position of La Casa Rosada after pointing out that Argentina had also been the victim of serious terrorist attacks within its territory: "One cannot remain neutral or indifferent when faced with terrorism. Argentina is prepared to cooperate by all means at its disposal."[3] The extent of this commitment could never be put to the test, though, as the government entered its final throes.

Argentina's understanding and expression of solidarity with the United States after 9/11 were appreciated by the Bush administration but not reciprocated. Shortly after the attacks, U.S. treasury secretary Paul O'Neill admitted before the Senate Commission for Banking Affairs that: "One week ago, Argentina was top of our agenda, it is now no longer in this position, or at least not in the same way as before."[4] For Washington, a looming financial crisis of a distant neighbor was of little importance compared to the global challenge faced by the threat of transnational terrorism. Argentina's fate was sealed; its collapse would be inevitable. Besides, it was unlikely that it would have been treated very differently had 9/11 not taken place: the Bush administration was already intent on making an example of Argentina for its continuous failure to fulfill its commitments.

The main political consequence of the crisis was Peronism's return to power. In line with the provisions established in the Constitution for situations when the country finds itself leaderless, Eduardo Duhalde was elected president by a majority of both Houses of Congress with support from a strong Peronist-Radical coalition. He received 262 votes in favor, 21 against and 18 abstentions. Among other issues of great political importance, the failure of Fernando de la Rúa's government sparked a broad debate on the relative merits of the policies carried out in the 1990s, both at home and internationally. Those who still defended these policies considered that the close ties with Washington should be maintained, given the serious nature of the crisis and the extreme vulnerability of the country abroad. The involvement of the United States was seen as essential for gaining the support and understanding of what was perceived as a hostile world, particularly after the carnival atmosphere in which the Argentine Congress announced the default during the most uncertain days of the crisis. Others favored a more selective rapprochement with Washington rather than merely bandwagoning. Eduardo Duhalde's transition government (2002–2003) sought to navigate the path between these two options, but with considerable difficulty. Circumstances, however, gradually drew him to follow the second alternative.

Soon thereafter, the Bush administration effectively put the already weakened arguments of its strongest allies in Argentina to rest, giving weight to those that held the view that it does not pay to bandwagon with Washington, and even more that this strategy was one of the very causes of the Argentine tragedy at that moment. Showing a distant coldness, the Bush administration made the country a test case for its newly announced policy for emerging nations in financial crisis: the United States would not lend taxpayers' money to countries whose debt was unsustainable, nor would it bail out those who had made bad investments in high-risk economies in search of greater profits. This rather merciless position was communicated to Argentina through an unforgettable statement by Paul O'Neill that was interpreted, at the time, as an expression of imperial arrogance and indifference to the fate of the country: "It is not fair to use the money of American carpenters and plumbers to rescue banks and companies that have invested in high risk countries in order to make a quick buck. If they take the risk, they should bear the cost."[5]

It was only in late 2002 that the Bush administration softened its position and made concrete efforts to encourage Argentina and the International Monetary Fund (IMF) to compromise and reach a temporary agreement, departing from the tough negotiations that had already lasted for one long year.[6] This change was due to a pragmatic reading of the situation in Argentina: the State and Treasury Departments agreed that a failure to reach an agreement with the Fund could lead the ever-unpredictable Peronism to turn to more interventionist policies. Furthermore, the agreement was seen as a prerequisite for macroeconomic stability during the transition to a new government. In this context, the Duhalde administration did everything possible not to contradict Washington, keeping its vote condemning Cuba's human rights performance at the Annual Session of the UN Commission on Human Rights taking place in Geneva.[7] It also supported the military strategy of the incoming president of Colombia, Álvaro Uribe, for combating terrorism and, faced with Washington's growing hostility toward Saddam Hussein's regime in Iraq, the Duhalde government sought to find a balance that would satisfy domestic public opinion, strongly opposed to military intervention in Iraq, while at the same time avoiding snubbing the expectations and requirements of the Bush administration. The Duhalde administration's initial position was to consider the possibility of sending peacekeeping troops to Afghanistan and, once the war had ended, to Iraq also. However, this stance gradually shifted to a policy of non-participation in the war regardless of the circumstances (whether as a U.S.-led unilateral decision or one approved by the UN Security Council.) The Argentine government made several such U-turns although it always made sure not to distance itself from attitudes that could be read by the White House as too neutral. Therefore, it always put more emphasis on its criticism of the Baghdad regime and terrorist threats to international security rather than whether the decision to go to war should be approved by the Security Council. On balance, Washington looked upon the Argentine position favorably, given its tacit acceptance that the war was inevitable and its low level of criticism to what most of the world saw as a flagrant violation of the UN Charter.[8]

Emboldened by the first signs of economic recovery in Argentina, Duhalde's government began to voice its opposition to U.S. military intervention in Iraq towards the end of the administration, as it looked more toward the general elections in April 2003 than to its relationship with the United States. This same logic explains the change in Argentina's voting behavior from condemnation to abstention over the issue of human rights in Cuba that same year. Opposition to certain U.S. policies served Duhalde's two immediate political aims: first, to garner votes for his then heir apparent, Néstor Kirchner, with powerful arguments that resonated in post-crisis Argentina, and second, to distance himself from Carlos Menem who was in the process of attempting to win the presidency again and who supported keeping the vote condemning Cuba and accompanying the United States in Iraq.

The Bush administration chose to keep a low profile regarding Duhalde's later behavior and quietly awaited the outcome of the first round of elections in Argentina, where Carlos Menem and Néstor Kirchner won 24.36 percent and 22 percent of the vote respectively. Despite his triumph, the former president decided not to compete in the second round scheduled for May 18 to avoid a certain, crushing defeat. This cleared the way for Néstor Kirchner, a politician unfamiliar to most Argentines, who would achieve high levels of popular support and turn out to be one of the most powerful presidents in Argentine history. Everything remained to be seen; the Bush administration sent a junior delegation headed by the Secretary of Housing and Urban Development, Mel Martinez, to Néstor Kirchner's inauguration ceremony as a way of showing its differences with the outgoing government. At the same time, however, it sent goodwill messages that went beyond the usual decorum warranted for these types of occasions.

Kirchner's Government: Construction and Concentration of Power

At his inaugural address, Néstor Kirchner spoke of the start of a new era and a new way of connecting the country with the world. Still without the harsh tone of the months that would follow, his message offered a critical reading of the years that had preceded. The main target of his attacks was the policies of the Menem administration.

How Kirchner took office was reminiscent of the way both Carlos Menem, faced with hyperinflation, had taken over from Raúl Alfonsín, and how Alfonsín himself had come to power after the disasters and burdensome legacies of the military dictatorship that ruled Argentina between 1976 and 1983. History repeated itself with new actors and new, always negative, interpretations of the past.

For Néstor Kirchner, the "neoliberalism of the 1990s," market reforms and the foreign policy that had served it, were the main cause of Argentina's latest failure. In its place, he proposed a new and more balanced relationship between the state and the market with a greater emphasis on social issues (at a time when the levels of poverty and marginalization had reached heights that had never been seen before in Argentina's history).[9] Instead of an "automatic alignment" Kirchner proposed a relationship of "cooperation without cohabitation" with the United States (according to the blueprint chosen by his first foreign minister, Rafael Bielsa) in order to mark a clear distance from the "carnal relations" of the Menem era.[10]

As had been the case for Menem, the country's state of turbulence permitted Kirchner to gain access to special powers, approved by Congress, which afforded him a large degree of discretion in the exercise of his functions as president. From then on, he always found excuses to keep these "superpowers," which he used to govern until the end of his term, successfully transferring them to his successor, Cristina Fernández de Kirchner, his wife. Mindful of the fact that his government stood on weak foundations, he was forced to construct his own political space; he skillfully built a new party structure in the name of "cross-partisanship," which included the majority of Peronism and important sectors of other political groups; particularly the Alliance for a Republic of Equals (ARI), Radicalism, the Socialist Party and various left-wing groups. The Peronists, until then Duhaldistas and in the 1990s Menemistas, for the most part had no qualms in defecting to this renewed expression of Peronism: the Kirchnerist centre-left. The main effect of this process, in political terms, was the gradual concentration of power in the hands of the president, the establishment of a compliant Congress, and a weakened opposition that was rendered incapable of becoming an alternative to the incumbent government. Kirchner also partly changed the membership of the Supreme Court by appointing distinguished lawyers to replace the discredited Menemist judges. This measure stopped short of making the judiciary body completely independent from the increasingly powerful executive, although it proved to be one of Kirchner's most popular decisions, appreciated throughout the whole of Argentine society.

Kirchner pressured many judges and courts to take into account or even rule in favor of the whims or wishes of a small select circle surrounding him. As Menem had done in the 1990s, Kirchner perpetuated this same deep-rooted flaw of Argentine politics.

Besides his undeniable political skills, two other factors helped Kirchner to concentrate so much power in so little time. First, Argentine society called for a strong government after Fernando De la Rúa's brief and indecisive rule. The social protests during the crisis in 2001 under the slogan "*Que se vayan todos*" (translated roughly as "Get rid of all of them") included another less tangible and deeper desire that someone would take control of the country and put it back on the right track. This was an old practice in Argentina that used to end being resolved in the country's barracks. Second, an economic recovery was already emerging by the end of Duhalde's rule. In 2001 and 2002 Argentina's economy suffered negative growth of 4.4 percent and 10 9 percent respectively. From 2003 on, the figures were spectacularly reversed: the growth rates were 8.8 percent (2003), 9.0 percent (2004), 8.5 percent (2006) and 8.7 percent (2007).[11] The country kept trade and fiscal surpluses throughout this time.[12] Economic growth at "Chinese rates" and the virtuous combination of twin surpluses enabled Néstor Kirchner to galvanize forces, discipline the Peronist party and co-opt adversaries.[13] Discretionary use of the state's "pot" became a formidable political tool at the disposal of a president who was becoming increasingly powerful and even feared. As during Menem's first term, economic success and a shared sense that the nightmare of the crisis was being left behind led the bulk of the population to prefer governability and efficiency over the quality of and respect for democratic institutions. Argentina again experienced this century-old antagonism between these two sources of legitimacy with governability and efficiency winning over institutional quality this time.[14]

The president not only accumulated power, he also concentrated it in a manner that had been unheard of in the years since the restoration of democracy. Meticulous and obsessive, he involved himself in every last detail of government business, no matter how unimportant. In foreign policy, for example, showing extraordinary toughness, he oversaw the drafting of the precise conditions of the agreements reached with the International Monetary Fund paragraph by paragraph during 2003 and 2004.[15] Furthermore, to make things absolutely clear, he indicated from the outset that relations with both Brazil and the United States would be handled exclusively by him. Without missing a beat, he placed all contact with Venezuela and Bolivia in the hands of one of his oldest and most faithful supporters, the minister of planning, Julio De Vido.

During this process of power construction and consolidation, the president did not define a clear strategy on foreign policy beyond vague references to the need to maintain "serious, mature and rational" relations with the world and the importance of Latin American and regional integration (with an emphasis on MERCO-SUR).[16] The same could be said of the rest of his public policies: Kirchner was never a fan of large government plans or designs, which enabled him in true Peronist tradition to turn to the right or left according to changing circumstances. Behind the fiery and ideology-laden, at times primitive, rhetoric, lay a cast-iron pragmatism, hidden from the eyes of many observers that determined, above all, his relations, both good and bad with the rest of the world.

May 2003 to November 2005: A Tale of Pragmatism in Two Cities

Kirchner, still weak and preoccupied with the construction of his own personal power base, was careful not to criticize the Bush administration, whose role was considered crucial to the country's main foreign policy issue at the time: the renegotiation of the national debt with multilateral lending agencies and private creditors. Consequently, the Argentine government avoided any public questioning of the U.S. intervention in Iraq. Its criticisms were expressed in a vague manner against unilateral practices and in favor of a peaceful resolution to conflicts within the framework of the UN. This was a simple and effective device that was essential in order to save face in front of his nationalist and leftist supporters while at the same time avoiding directly attacking the Bush administration. The Argentine government preferred to level fierce criticism time and time again at the IMF, which it accused of being largely responsible for driving the country to ruin.

With all eyes in Washington turned to Iraq, any decision by Kirchner that could be construed as contrary to U.S. objectives or expectations in Latin America did little to unsettle the White House. As had been the case in the last months of Duhalde's rule, Argentine domestic political considerations got in the way of bilateral relations. In late October 2003, a joint military exercise involving all MERCOSUR members along with Bolivia, Chile, United States, and Peru was due to take place in the Argentine province of Mendoza. However, opposition from human rights activists and a Congress where Kirchner faced strong resistance, even from his own party, made him change his position three times over the decision to approve the operation. The basis of the controversy revolved around the U.S. requirement that its troops would have complete immunity from prosecution during their stay in Argentina.[17]

Kirchner was, at first, in favor of granting immunity to foreign troops involved in the operation, as had been requested by a bill sent to the Defense Committee of the Chamber of Deputies in the last days of Duhalde's presidency. The negative reaction of Congress to this request led Kirchner to propose a compromise to grant only "functional" immunity to the troops while they carried out their specific duties.[18] The response he received from leaders of the Peronist party in both houses of the legislature was that they would not to support this measure without an explicit and public request from the executive. Unwilling to pay the political costs or to support a wearing negotiation in Congress, particularly within his own ranks, Kirchner decided to suspend the operation, despite promises made by the Argentine foreign minister to Secretary of State Colin Powell that the exercise would not be cancelled.

Later on, the bilateral relationship was marked by other differences. For both domestic reasons and its own political convictions, in April 2004 the Argentine government upheld its vote of abstention regarding the condemnation of Cuba over human rights issues at the United Nations Human Rights Commission, ignoring the requests and subsequent criticisms of the then Assistant Secretary of Western

Hemisphere Affairs, Roger Noriega. Economic interests and a rejection of the nineties-style economic openness determined the government's position against the FTAA. Kirchner developed much of his political discourse and its promises of change in Argentina by criticizing liberal economic theory on the "trickle down effect" of free trade. He always maintained that hemispheric integration had no future so long as the asymmetries between the United States and Latin America were not taken into account in the negotiations and sufficient resources were not committed to reduce this gap. As one would expect, this vision, closer to the European experience of integration, was ignored by Washington, which interpreted it as a return to an antiquated form of state intervention in the economy.

Similarly, Kirchner's heterodox and neo-developmentalist orientation and the die-hard conservatism of the Bush administration could not but result in very different readings of the so-called "left turn" in Latin America, particularly with regard to the political situation in Bolivia and Venezuela. Kirchner never perceived Hugo Chávez or Evo Morales as a threat to democracy or regional security. Rather, he considered them the natural result of more democratic societies addressing the long-neglected claims for political and social inclusion. This idea was reflected in an oft-repeated phrase of the Kirchner married couple "that the presidents of the region today look more like its people." Thus, every time Hugo Chávez was portrayed by the United States to Kirchner as being a danger to democracy and stability in Latin America, the Argentine government's response was always the same: Venezuela has a legitimate president chosen by free and fair elections. The same line would be used later to define the government's position on the political process led by Evo Morales in Bolivia.

These tangible differences and Kirchner's occasional overreactions and excesses in his constant onslaught against "neoliberalism" and the Washington Consensus did not alter the main lines that guided the bilateral relationship at the time, namely, Argentina's need for U.S. support at the G-7 and multilateral lending agencies and Washington's desire to preserve the stability of the Southern Cone and hope that Argentina would return to the international financial system by respecting the rules of the game. With these objectives in mind, from the outset the Bush administration adopted a friendly and frank position with Kirchner's Argentina. Two weeks after the new government's inauguration, Colin Powell spent a few hours in Buenos Aires after attending a meeting of the OAS General Assembly in Santiago, Chile, to convey the U.S. support for the new government in Argentina and to express Washington's readiness to continue working with La Casa Rosada to facilitate its negotiations with the IMF. Powell deliberately avoided entering into any depth on issues that could expose differences between the two countries.[19]

Nestor Kirchner encountered the same warm and relaxed tone when invited by George W. Bush to his first official visit to Washington in July 2003. They were said to have "good chemistry" by the press of both countries, attributed to their common status as stubborn politicians considered outsiders to the political establishment in power, one from Texas and the other from Patagonia.[20] The U.S. president used the meeting to express his "firm and resolute support" to the Argentine government during the difficult process of restructuring the foreign debt, but left it clear that the ball was in the Kirchner's court. Bush succinctly stated his position: "Keep up the good work. If you help yourselves, you can count on our government's decisive support."[21] From this moment on, the United States lent crucial support in the arduous and endless negotiations between Argentina and the IMF and other multilateral lending agencies throughout 2003 and 2004. It played a moderating role between the more inflexible G-7 countries and the equally uncompromising Argentine government in order to facilitate and unblock stalled negotiations.

The support received from Washington led Kirchner's government to have mixed feelings with regard to the U.S. presidential elections of November 2004. His heart and ideology were closer to the Democrats than the neoconservatives in the White House. However, he never hid his concern that a change of ruling party could cool the favorable climate of understanding reached with Washington. In this context, news of Bush's victory was received in Buenos Aires with a mixture of relief and caution. With Bush remaining in the White House, Argentina would continue to receive U.S. support at the IMF and non-interference in the complex negotiations with private creditors, which had yet to be defined.[22]

The deal for these creditors' defaulted debt was agreed to in early March 2005 with the backing of 76 percent of bondholders.[23] Within little over three years of having declared the biggest ever national debt default, Argentina had negotiated the largest debt restructuring deal in global economic history. Washington was present throughout this process that allowed the Argentine government to draw a line under its worst ever crisis. The United States put on hold the fate of the 24 percent of bondholders who had not accepted the deal, only to raise it again with insistence after the first few days of euphoria over the success of the action had subsided.[24] In Buenos Aires, the government exploited this sense of satisfaction. Most of Argentina saw this experience as a recovery of its collective self-esteem. Kirchner felt that standing up to the powerful of the world pays dividends. He also knew that the success of the renegotiation would gain him votes in the legislative elections in October, which he awaited with great eagerness because he knew they could give him electoral legitimacy on top of the credibility already achieved in the exercise of power in his first two years in office.

Up until that point, relations remained cordial and stable. Both countries had their differences, but also found new issues that helped to nurture the positive agenda in the relationship. The United States was willing to maintain its support for Argentina, now in negotiations for its post-default agenda. For its part, the Argentine government received full acknowledgment from Washington for its role in the stabilization of South America and its participation in the UN peacekeeping operation in Haiti. Secretary of Defense Donald Rumsfeld emphasized these two points during his visit to Buenos Aires on March 22; so too did the new Secretary of State Condoleezza Rice in a meeting with Argentine Foreign Minister Rafael Bielsa, held in Washington at the end of the same month.[25] Both Rice and Rumsfeld praised Argentina for its role in supporting democracy in Bolivia during the most difficult moments of the Carlos Diego Mesa government (2003–2005) and the professionalism of the Argentine troops in Haiti, particularly with regard to their ability to relate to the local population.

Argentina's involvement in Haiti this time marked major differences from its participation on that island in the 1990s. After the coup d'état of September 30, 1991 against President Jean Bertrand Aristide, Argentina was the only Latin American country that participated in the embargo and naval blockade of the Caribbean country, which had been approved by the UN Security Council. More importantly, it was the only country in the region that joined the multinational force that the Security Council had authorized to intervene in Haiti to restore the deposed government.[26] This high-profile action by the Menem government was not only due to Argentina's close ties to Washington but it was also a significant part of a policy that made Argentina by far the largest contributor of peacekeeping troops from Latin America throughout the world. With this, Menem sought to strengthen the integration of the Argentine military in the democratic system and its commitment to UN collective security mechanisms. The United States rewarded this policy, awarding the category of major non- NATO ally to Argentina in January 1998—a status that no other country in the region has held to this day and that Kirchner has quietly upheld albeit without the same fanfare seen in the 1990s.

The 2003 crisis in Haiti saw Argentina adopt a very different position. The intervention required by the United Nations set off a broad domestic debate, which led the government to hesitate as to what action to take. Some government supporters and members of the opposition led by the Radicals and centre-left blocs opposed joining the mission, on the grounds of the principle of non- intervention and because they considered it tantamount to supporting the virtual coup d'état against Jean Bertrand Aristide backed by United States and France.[27] Meanwhile, Brazil, Chile, Paraguay and Uruguay had already sent troops to Haiti, with Brazil taking military command of the mission. The United States and France, both of which supported Argentina in the G-7, fully expected La Casa Rosada to participate in the peacekeeping operation. Furthermore, the Argentine Ministers of Economy, Defense, and Foreign Affairs all considered participation to be invaluable for their respective departmental interests. In particular, the Ministry of Defense saw the operation as a way to develop closer ties between the military and the government in addition to promoting cooperation with Brazil and Chile. Under this framework, the president was inclined to favor participation to avoid losing influence in Latin America and also to avoid snubbing France and United States. On May 8, 2004 Kirchner announced his decision and pressured Congress to authorize the sending of Argentine troops to Haiti.[28]

Few phrases sum up the Argentine vision of the bilateral relationship better than those expressed by the Foreign Minister Bielsa after George W. Bush's reelection:

> We've managed to establish a relationship with the United States where, on the one hand, we accept the relative indifference that we evoke from them and, on the other hand, we could get on in an atmosphere of mutual respect over insurmountable issues while at the same time maximizing the issues on which we agreed.[29]

Bielsa's words encapsulate the three major assumptions that guided foreign policy towards the United States during this period: the recognition that Buenos Aires had little significance for Washington, that 9/11 had accentuated this irrelevancy,[30] and that despite this fact, Argentina need not acquiesce in U.S. objectives or interests when they are not shared or when they work against the government's interests or objectives on domestic policy issues. These assumptions continued to guide foreign policy towards the United States for the following two years although Buenos Aires felt it needed Washington far less than before. The time had come for Argentina to weigh anchor.

From the Fourth Summit of the Americas until the End of Néstor Kirchner's Government: Between Indifference and Irrelevance

The October legislative elections gave Néstor Kirchner control of both houses of Congress, filling it with his own legislators and allies.[31] Strengthened by this success and the tailwinds provided by the rising world demand for food crops, which had sent prices soaring, the president now had the power and resources necessary to centralize decision-making even further and govern with yet greater discretion through the allocation of rewards and punishments. From his consolidated position as the one who called the shots, Kirchner made two decisions that would have a major impact on relations with the United States: to block the Bush administration's plan to re-launch the FTAA and to cancel all of Argentina's debt with the IMF.

The first battle took place at the Fourth Summit of the Americas held in Mar del Plata on November 4 and 5, 2005. In the weeks running up to the summit, Kirchner transmitted this tough message to the Argentine negotiators who had joined forces with Brazil and Venezuela to form a united front where no one would budge an inch: Argentina would maintain that, as long as the asymmetries between countries were not recognized and the agricultural subsidies and tariff barriers applied by developed nations were not removed, the conditions were not present to negotiate the FTAA. Nor was Buenos Aires willing to accept the argument put forward by Canada, Mexico, and Chile, which advised Argentina and Brazil to join the FTAA in order to redress the imbalances and contribute to greater democratization in the integration of the hemisphere.

Kirchner expressed this hard stance in his opening speech to the summit, where he again attacked the IMF. Citing economic indicators showing the accomplishments of Argentina's economy under his rule, he asserted that it was possible to achieve growth and distribute wealth in ways that were different, or even contrary, to those promoted by the Washington Consensus. To the surprise of Bush and most of the audience, he also railed against the United States. He accused Washington of having an "anachronistic view" of developing nations' problems and called on Bush to show more responsible leadership in Latin America by ending his support for policies that had "not only led to misery and poverty but also the fall of democratically elected governments."[32] He gave Hugo Chávez the green light to organize an event called the People's Summit III with the help of an entourage of his government's politicians and supporters in addition to many leftist groups, which attracted almost as many headlines as the summit itself. It was there that the verbose president of Venezuela theatrically announced the FTAA's demise.[33]

Of course, the Kirchner government was unwilling to go so far. Kirchner's criticisms sought to protect his neo-developmental model based on heterodox economics that were inconceivable in Washington. He considered that this model was under threat from those who defended the "one track" advance of free trade, as he put it, at the summit. Likewise, the parallel platform that he offered to Chávez in Mar del Plata was a way to express his distaste for the overbearing U.S. attitude: Washington had put the issue of regional trade on the summit's agenda, when the subject under discussion had been "fair working conditions" and "poverty reduction" in the Americas. He concluded that the Bush administration had imposed a debate to get the FTAA back on track without the domestic conditions required to make it effective and with a simplistic and outdated script for a Latin America increasingly heterogeneous in political terms and diverse in its economic interests. Most of the world saw the summit as a failure. There can be no doubt that it achieved only modest results.[34] For Kirchner, however, it was a clear victory; he had defended his position using his preferred confrontational style and had gained a high level of political support domestically. He seemed to care little that the event at Mar del Plata had put an end to any dialogue with Bush or that, later on, the State Department would lower the rating of the bilateral relationship from "excellent" to "positive."[35] Nor did Kirchner pay much attention to the deep discomfort that his attitude provoked after the summit amongst leading government and private circles in the United States.

Undoubtedly, Mar del Plata marked a turn for the worse for bilateral relations. Washington was left with a bitter taste, which would linger until the end of Kirchner's presidency. Thereafter, the Argentine president would be seen as politically unpredictable and unreliable. The summit even failed to strengthen ties between countries that had joined forces to oppose the "re-launch" of the FTAA. Nor did the summit breathe new life into the weakened MERCOSUR bloc. In terms of its relations with Brazil, Argentina was unable to capitalize on the useful role that it had played in Mar del Plata defending the interests of its main partner in Latin America. The fallout that occurred in Washington as a result of Kirchner's mistreatment of Bush hid the fact that Brazil's somewhat less combative stance was exactly the same as Argentina's opposition to the U.S.-led free trade project. Brazil had consistently opposed such initiatives for specific interests rather than because of ideology. After the summit, President Bush traveled to Brasilia where he was received in a relaxed and friendly atmosphere. Lula praised the dialogue between them as being without "clashes or confrontations."[36] Bush, meanwhile, acknowledged the international leadership role of Brazil and the strength of the bond between the two countries. Thus, Brazil was able to build its own agenda with Washington, without hiding its differences, while Argentina only accentuated its estrangement.

The summit agreed that the formal meetings to discuss hemispheric integration would be suspended pending the commitments arising from the Doha Round, putting things off yet again. As a result, free trade disappeared from the U.S.-Argentine trade agenda. Buenos Aires considered it dangerous and inappropriate. Besides reasons concerning its increasingly weakened and stalled strategy of continental integration, Washington was never particularly interested in Argentina's participation in the FTAA or in signing a bilateral free trade treaty.[37] The Southern Cone country ranks fortieth in U.S. global trade in goods and sixth in Latin America after Mexico, Venezuela, Brazil, Colombia, and Chile, respectively.[38] In 2007, Argentina made up 0.35 percent of U.S. exports and 0.26 percent of U.S. imports.[39] In contrast, the United States that year was the fifth largest market for Argentine exports (after Brazil, the European Union, China, and Chile, respectively)[40] and the third biggest market for its imports (after Brazil and the European Union).[41]

The historic trade imbalance between the two countries prompted the Kirchner government to emphasize two themes that have dominated the trade agenda between Argentina and the United States: the barriers that affect Argentina traditional export products such as meat, dairy, and fruit, and the frequent use of defensive trade measures (e.g. anti-dumping measures and countervailing duties on steel and honey). Due to the asymmetry of trade interests, the primary U.S. concern had been with how Argentina's politics influenced the business world. Since the 1990s, this had consisted of fears regarding government corruption and inadequate protection of intellectual property rights.[42] After Kirchner's rise to power, an emphasis was placed on certain heterodox elements in its economic policy (in particular, export taxes, price controls, tariffs for public services, massaging official statistics, and changes in the rules of the game).[43] Nevertheless, Argentina's economic recovery enabled the United States to regain its place as the main investor in the country, displacing Spain, which had been the star of the 1990s.[44] However, the total proportion of U.S. investment received in Argentina has been very small; in 2007, it made up only 0.4 percent of total U.S. investment in the world and only 3.9 percent in Latin America. In that same year, Mexico and Brazil attracted, respectively, 26.1 percent and 12.2 percent of total U.S. investments in the region. Argentine investment in the United States is negligible.

Now for the Fund

After the Fourth Summit of the Americas, Néstor Kirchner got ready to carry out an idea that he had been toying with since at least mid-2004: to get rid of the IMF once and for all.[45] The economic recovery and the high commodity prices of Argentine exports fanned the flames of his desires. Showing an accountant's patience and notable glee, he watched as the Central Bank accumulated more reserves day after day, far exceeding the limited amount of $9 billion it had held when he assumed office.

In late November 2005, he dismissed his Minister of Economy, Roberto Lavagna, and took personal control of economic policy in the same way as he had done with foreign policy when he took office. With Lavagna, he had maintained a far from easy relationship, although it had been perfectly useful in coping with the economic problems of the post-crisis and dealing with the negotiations for the defaulted debt.[46] However, there was no room for Lavagna in this new phase announced by Kirchner after his election victory. Lavagna expressed differences with the president over the handling of inflation, pricing policies, the management of public works, and how to conduct the relationship with the IMF. Moreover, he had wavered in his support during the election campaign and denounced the alleged corrupt practices of the minister closest to the president, Julio de Vido, both cardinal sins in the Kirchnerist universe.[47]

Without Lavagna and with an increasingly faceless and completely submissive cabinet, on December 15, 2005 Kirchner announced, in a festive atmosphere at La Casa Rosada, that Argentina would cancel its debt of $9.8 billion with IMF in a single payment using its Central Bank reserves, which totaled $27 billion at the time. In a curious turn of history, many of those who had excitedly welcomed the declaration of the default in 2001 now celebrated the final payment to the IMF. Argentina was following in Brazil's footsteps, which, also using its monetary reserves had announced two days before that it would pay off its total debt of $15.5 billion to the IMF.

Kirchner felt like he was walking on water. In one fell swoop, he had rid himself of both the IMF's overbearing tutelage, which had infuriated him like nothing else, and the Bush administration's role as facilitator for Argentina's negotiations with that entity. Most Argentines shared his delight, feeling that another step had been taken toward the recovery and reaffirmation of their collective national dignity. Kirchner certainly presented it this way in public, although he was careful to stress that the advance payment to the IMF should not be read as an act of rebellion or as a nationalist gesture intended to withdraw the country from the international financial system. The measure, he said on more than one occasion, was a necessary step for the country to gain autonomy to run its economic policy and be free from recommendations that would only have a negative impact on Argentina's booming economy. He also considered it imperative to curtail IMF lobbying of certain foreign and domestic groups that opposed specific government actions, e.g. refusal to reopen negotiations with the bondholders that had not entered into the previously negotiated deal or demands to raise the rates of public utilities. Finally, he stated that the battle was not over with the payment to the Fund. Argentina would continue to campaign in all international areas and forums so that the Fund would return to its original brief, established at its inception: to prevent crises and to foster development.

Consequently, financial issues were sidelined to a less grand position in the bilateral agenda; suffering the same fate that trade issues had. Now that there was no FTAA to oppose or IMF to demand reforms or provide help, the only important issues remaining were the unpaid debt to the Paris Club and the fate of U.S. bondholders who had not been included in the negotiated deal for the defaulted Argentine debt. The Bush administration forgot about Argentina, except occasionally to applaud certain measures its government took (such as La Casa Rosada's decision to actively back the investigation into the terrorist attack on the Asociación Mutual Israelita Argentina (AMIA) in Buenos Aires in July 1994), or to assess its role in the containment of political strife in Bolivia after Evo Morales took office,[48] or to request clarifications for its ties with Venezuela, a relationship which although suspect, was never considered dangerous by Washington.[49] The White House's initial wish for Néstor Kirchner to contain Hugo Chávez soon fell on deaf ears; the Argentine president would never have been comfortable in a role that was beyond him and that he considered futile anyway. Argentina's ties with Venezuela revolved around two issues that had little to do with ideology: business and finance. The two countries signed a number of economic and cooperation agreements between 2003 and 2008 which exceeded all previous bilateral agreements and provided an extraordinary opportunity for both legitimate and shady business dealings. For his part, Hugo Chávez's financial support was vital in an Argentina which had increasingly fewer external credit lines available.[50] Apart from these issues, Chavez's anti-imperialist rhetoric failed to resonate in Buenos Aires; Caracas's regional integration initiative, the Bolivarian Alternative for the Americas (ALBA), failed to impress as well. The Kirchner government's support of Venezuelan candidacy to become a full member of MERCOSUR was not "a matter of personal friendship or political cronyism."[51] Rather, it was considered essential for the productive, energetic, and social integration of the regional bloc to afford it greater autonomy vis-à-vis the rest of the world: two goals wholly consistent with the neo-developmentalist economic model that Kirchner promoted at home.

The Argentine government did not worry too much about the United States, except to scold it sporadically for some of its policies (e.g. its lack of interest in the problems of Latin America or the construction of the border wall over part of the frontier with Mexico, which Kirchner called a "disgrace") or to express its annoyance at Washington's neglect of Argentina. The most notorious example occurred in March 2007 when Kirchner offered Hugo Chávez a forum in Buenos Aires in retaliation for Bush's snub of Argentina during his presidential trip to Latin America, which included Brazil, Chile, and Uruguay in the Southern Cone. Kirchner made sure the forum was timed to coincide with Bush's arrival in Montevideo.[52]

The Argentine president's remarks, which have included grievances and some insults, have remained, by and large, the only expression of an erratic relationship marked by serious disagreements. In short, the Bush-Kirchner period would merely repeat the historical pattern of misunderstandings and opposition that, according to most authors, characterized Argentine–U.S. relations in the twentieth century, except for a temporary interruption during the 1990s.[53] Undoubtedly Argentine–U.S. relations deteriorated the most after the Mar del Plata. Dialogue broke down; mutual indifference accentuated personal and ideological differences, particularly on the Argentine side. The waning Bush administration had no time for Argentina, and Kirchner was devoting his energies to his succession in a context where the country's economy began to show its first signs of weakness, particularly with regard to inflation.

However, Argentina and United States did develop close cooperation at a lower level where there was a far greater coincidence of interests. I have mentioned Argentina's participation in the peacekeeping force sent to Haiti, which had been greatly appreciated by the Bush administration. Similarly, the two countries established a positive relationship based on common strategic interests regarding nuclear non-proliferation, counter-narcotics operations, and counter-terrorism. As a member of the Board of Governors of the International Atomic Energy Agency, Argentina has maintained a consistent and high-profile stance on issues related to non-proliferation in line with most of the positions adopted by the United States. For its part, the U.S. Drug Enforcement Administration (DEA) has worked closely with Argentine federal and provincial law enforcement agencies, prosecutors and judges, Ministry of Interior, and the Secretariat of Planning for the Prevention of Drug Addiction and Drug Trafficking (SEDRONAR) to improve coordination, cooperation, training, and exchanges.[54]

Having suffered two serious terrorist attacks on its soil, Argentina shares with the United States the painful experience and a genuine interest in combating international terrorism; this has resulted in various forms of collaboration. According to the State Department's annual terrorism report, Argentina "cooperates well with the United States at an operational level, and has addressed many of the legal and institutional weaknesses that previously hindered its counter-terrorism efforts."[55] In June 2007, the Argentine Congress passed key legislation criminalizing acts of terror, terrorism financing, and money laundering for the purpose of financing terrorism. This law has provided the legal foundation for Argentina's financial intelligence unit (the Financial Intelligence Unit, or FIU), Central Bank, and other regulatory and law enforcement bodies to investigate such crimes and prosecute them. Finally, along with the other two countries in the Tri-Border Area (Brazil and Paraguay), Argentina worked closely with the United States through the "3 +1 Group on Tri-Border Area Security." This Group was established in 2002 to serve as a mechanism for improving the capabilities of the three South American countries to address cross-border crime and thwart money laundering and potential terrorist financing activities.

Looking Ahead

The first year of President Cristina Fernández de Kirchner's government coincided with Bush's last and was marred by the so-called "valijagate" (suitcase scandal) and the financial crisis in the United States.[56] For Washington and a large part of Argentine society, the expectation that Cristina would offer a different style of government and a more coherent and open foreign policy was soon dashed. Valijagate was dismissed by Cristina as a "garbage operation" orchestrated by the U.S. intelligence services and so, within a few days of taking office, she buried any possibility of constructive dialogue with Washington. This occurred just as the State Department was looking to approach Argentina in order to provide the beleaguered bilateral relationship with a new lease of life and to ask the country to assume greater responsibilities in South America.[57]

Until the end of the Bush presidency, there were only a few sporadic and inconsequential meetings between the president and various ministers and an enthusiastic U.S. assistant secretary Thomas Shannon (official contact between Argentina and the United States was relegated by Washington to this level), who made great but ultimately fruitless efforts to improve relations. As had been the case under Kirchner, domestic policy took up most of the attention and efforts of the new government, which began to resemble a presidential marriage rather than one single president.[58] There was little room in La Casa Rosada for what happened in the United States or for what it did; interest perked up only when Washington announced that it would reestablish its Fourth Fleet under the Southern Command and, of course, when the U.S. financial crisis took hold.

In September 2008, Cristina Fernández de Kirchner referred to the financial crisis as the "jazz effect" in her address to the UN General Assembly, in reference to the fact that, originating from the heart of the world economy, the crisis would spread to other countries. Barely disguising her glee, she took the opportunity to criticize neo-liberalism:

> Throughout the duration of the Washington Consensus, all the countries of our region were told that the market solves everything, that the State was unnecessary and that those who supported state intervention were simply being nostalgic having failed to understand how the economy had evolved. However, we have just seen the most formidable example of state intervention along with massive fiscal and trade deficits in living memory precisely from the place where we were told that the state was not required.[59]

For the Kirchners, the crisis in the United States merely reinforced their own beliefs and policies: it now seemed that the powers that be were ready for change or, at least, prepared to listen to other points of view. A humble country at the periphery of the international system had shown itself to be at the forefront of how capitalism should be conducted and regulated. This rather grandiose assertion was expressed with a certain air of vindication directed at the developed world and those in Argentina who were increasingly questioning the Kirchners' understanding and management of the economy.

The message, however, resonated far less than in the years of economic prosperity. Before the U.S. financial crisis, Argentina's economy had already begun to falter with inflation reaching 30 percent a year, economic activity levels were beginning to slow down with a strong impact on job creation, and many Argentines had begun to resort to the old practice of taking their savings out of the country. Under pressure from a looming fiscal crisis, the government embarked on an exhausting conflict with the farm sector over export duties on agricultural products, especially soybeans, where it suffered its first major political defeat. The deadlock over the bill to increase the taxes on farmers was broken in dramatic fashion in the Senate on July 17, 2008, by the vote of the vice-president of Argentina who, as presiding officer in the Senate, cast the tie-breaking vote to reject the official position of the government to which he belonged. The government's confrontation with the farmers changed the mood in a society that is so prone to volatility. As in Menem's final years, the end of economic prosperity renewed the century-old antagonism between the two sources of legitimacy in Argentina previously mentioned, this time in favor of the institutional quality of democracy. In the space of a few months, the government had squandered the political capital it had brought to office on December 10, 2007 after winning the election with 45 percent of the vote and with a positive approval rating of over 55 percent. Moreover, the conflict exposed the fact that the real political boss of the government was not Cristina but Nestor Kirchner, who has overshadowed Cristina's presidency ever since.[60]

It is this different Argentina that was hit by the U.S. crisis and which was forced to begin constructing a new relationship with Washington. Barack Obama's arrival in office was considered by the Argentine government as providing an opportunity to open a new dialogue. Also it was felt that the arguments, long espoused by the Kirchners, on the role of government in the economy and the need to reform the multilateral lending agencies would now find a willing ear at the White House. Indeed, the "new era of capitalism" offered the perfect circumstances for Argentina to promote this position at the G-20 meeting in London (April 2009) and the V Summit of the Americas in Trinidad and Tobago (May 2009). In harmony with the tone of the meeting, the president of Argentina adopted a moderate and conciliatory stance, although she did not miss the opportunity to criticize past U.S. policy towards the region and to portray the Fourth Summit of Mar del Plata as the birth of a more balanced relationship in the Americas. She ended her speech by asserting that the crisis in the United States should be taken as a turning point for a new regional order based on "collaboration and cooperation rather than subordination."[61]

The new U.S. government responded to these first signs of rapprochement from Buenos Aires by passing up gestures of goodwill. In his first hundred days, Obama made it clear that Argentina was not among his priorities in Latin America; its partner in South America would be Brazil because of its relative power and the strategic link that Bush and Lula had established. Furthermore, the Obama administration demonstrated that the ideological affinity between the White House and La Casa Rosada was far more limited than the Kirchners could have imagined. In April 2009, U.S. treasury secretary Timothy Geithner presented a report on the global economy; its references to Argentina reported: "The government's formal response to the crisis has contributed to the political uncertainty, exacerbated the existing economic vulnerability and encouraging capital flight."[62] This view was shared down to the last comma by the bulk of the Argentine opposition who took away the government's majority in both houses of Congress in the mid-term elections of June 28, 2009 in which the Kirchners suffered a severe defeat: the government fell from 46 percent of the votes it had obtained in 2007 to only 26 percent.[63]

In their heyday, Nestor and Cristina Kirchner established a relationship with the United States tainted by one fundamental flaw: the vocal expression of differences in public, a style that has left a black mark on relations with Washington. This is the complete opposite to what countries such as Brazil, Chile, or Mexico have done. As a result, the relationship has lacked a general framework where dissent could be expressed, misunderstandings avoided, and cooperation, which also characterized bilateral relations, facilitated. In Washington, Bush is no longer around to be condemned or to be used for domestic policy purposes. Now there is a president willing to strengthen cooperation with Argentina on the basis of common interests and give more attention to what is happening in Latin America, as he expressed in

Trinidad and Tobago. Despite Argentina's relative loss of clout in the region, Washington recognizes the importance of the country and the role it can play in the defense of peace, democratic stability, and human rights as well as combating terrorism, organized crime, and the proliferation of weapons of mass destruction at a global level. In Buenos Aires, we will see a weakened government from now until the end of its term in December 2011, a situation that the Kirchners had not experienced and that raises questions about how they will behave. Still, it is highly unlikely that we will see a return to the noisy criticism of the United States of recent years. Argentina has numerous internal and external commitments ahead and it will need the help of the Inter-American Development Bank and even ask the IMF for credit from the new line of flexible loans launched to protect countries from the global crisis. In both organizations, U.S. opinions carry weight. Therefore, it is likely that the pragmatism seen in the first two years of Kirchner's government will return to relations with Washington, albeit in a context of decline rather than of power building. Domestic politics in Argentina will also be a key factor determining bilateral relations in a country that will remain until the end of Fernández de Kirchner's term of office as it continues looking at its navel and pierced by infighting.

Notes

1. See also Roberto Russell and Juan Gabriel Tokatlian, *El lugar de Brasil en la política exterior argentina* (Buenos Aires: Fondo de Cultura Económica, 2003): 45–59.
2. In 2007, the percentage of Argentines with a favorable view of the United States reached only 16 percent. Favorable views of other countries were as follows: Brazil (44 percent), Chile (55 percent) and Mexico and Venezuela (56 percent each). See "Global Unease With Major World Powers, Rising Environmental Concern in 47-Nation Survey," *Pew Global Attitudes*, www.pewglobal.org.
3. See declaration of Argentine Secretary of Foreign Affairs in Chamber of Deputies, http://www.mrecic.gov.ar/portal/prensa/comunicado.php?buscar=512. December 13, 2001.
4. Cited in María O'Donnell, "Las consecuencias económicas de los ataques," *La Nación*, September 21, 2001, 9.
5. "La llegada de Paul O'Neill" http://nuevamayoria.com/ES/ANALISIS/martini/020806.html.
6. The agreement, reached on January 25, 2003, only lasted eight months. By the same token, Argentina managed to postpone the $11,000 million payment due to the IMF and the $4,400 million due to the IDB and World Bank between January and August of the same year. The agreement included $5,112 million worth of maturities that had been rescheduled from 2002. Thus the final sum totaled $16,112 million.
7. Thereby maintaining the position held by the previous governments of Carlos Menem and Fernando de la Rúa while ignoring Congress where both Houses had approved a request to the Executive asking for the country to refrain from condemning Cuba. See "La Cámara Baja se sumó al reclamo del Senado" http://www.lainsignia.org/2000/enero/be_156.htm.
8. See Roberto Russell y Juan Gabriel Tokatlian, "La crisis en Argentina y las relaciones con Brasil y Estados Unidos: continuidad y cambio en las relaciones triangulares," *Análisis Político* 52 (September/December 2004): 9–14.
9. According to data from INDEC, in the first half of 2003 poverty reached 54 percent of the population with marginality indices rising to 27.7 percent. See *INDEC Permanent Household Survey* http://www.indec.mecon.ar.

10. See Rafael Bielsa: "No hay hostilidad con Estados Unidos," *Clarín*, May 23, 2003 http://www.clarin.com/diario/2003/05/23/p-00901.htm.
11. See "Preliminary Overview of the Economies of Latin America and the Caribbean 2008," *Economic Development Division, ECLAC.* http://www.eclac.org/cgi-bin/getProd.asp?xml=/publicaciones/xml/5/34845/P34845.xml&xsl=/de/tpl/p9f.xsl&base=/de/tpl/top-bottom.xsl.
12. Argentina's trade surplus was$16 billion in 2003, $12 billion in 2004, $1.7 billion in 2005, $12 billion in 2006, and $11 billion 2007. Source INDEC, www.indec.gov.ar. The fiscal surplus reached in billions of pesos, 8.6, 17.3, 19.7, 23.2, and 25.7 during the same period. Source: *Bureau of National Budget, Ministry of Finance, Ministry of Economy.* www.mecon.gov.ar.
13. The most notorious case was that of the many Radicals who joined the president and were renamed 'K Radicals,' the most prominent being Julio Cobos, whom Kirchner would later choose to run as the vice president on the ticket led by his wife in the presidential election of 2007.
14. See also Luis Alberto Romero, "Veinte años después: un primer balance" in *La historia reciente. Argentina en democracia*, ed. Marcos Novaro and Vicente Palermo (Buenos Aires: Edhasa, 2004), 281–282.
15. According to IMF officials, Kirchner participated in the negotiations as no other world leader had before, even attempting to incorporate his own wording in the literature for technical agreements. See Joaquín Morales Solá, "Al final, la Argentina no se cayó del mundo," September 11, 2003, *La Nación*, http://www.lanacion.com.ar/nota.asp?nota_id=526551.
16. Inauguration Speech of Néstor Kirchner as president of the Republic, May 25, 2003, *Presidential Speeches, Presidency of the Nation*, http://www.casarosada.gov.ar/index.php?option = com_content & task = discursosArchivo & Itemid = 120.
17. This is a routine request from the White House for their soldiers not to be tried under the law of the country where the operation would take place or to be answerable to the International Criminal Court for crimes committed abroad.
18. This immunity, limited to military personnel, included any crime committed in Argentina by a U.S. soldier, even outside a military exercise e.g. they could not be tried by local courts. For more details on changes in the position of the Argentine government, see Mariano Obarrio, "No se haría el ejercicio Águila III con EEUU," *La Nación*, October 4, 2003, https://www1.lanacion.com.ar/nota.asp?nota_id=532985, and Carlos Eichelbaum, "El gobierno apoya la inmunidad para las tropas de EEUU," *Clarín*, September 18, 2003, http://www.clarin.com/diario/2003/09/18/p-01402.htm.
19. For example, he avoided asking Argentina to send gendarmes for the reconstruction of Iraq, despite his government's expectations that Argentine security forces would join at this stage, and referred to the FTAA in a vague manner, merely stating U.S. interest in advancing hemispheric integration.
20. Fernando Cibeira, "Como dos amigos que vienen desde el Sur," *Pagina 12*, July 24, 2003, http://www.pagina12.com.ar/diario/elpais/1-23148-2003-07-24.html.
21. "Fuerte apoyo de Bush a Kirchner," *La Nación*, July 24, 2003, http://www.lanacion.com.ar/nota.asp?nota_id=513679.
22. See Roberto Russell, "¿Qué espera Argentina de un segundo mandato de Bush?" *Foreign Affairs en español* 5, no. 1 (2005): 34–39.
23. At the time of the declaration of the default, public debt amounted to $144.4 billion and the amount of interest was around $10 billion annually. "Datos Deuda Post Reestructuración," Secretaria de Finanzas, *Ministerio de Economía*, www.mecon.gov.ar. Of this amount $81.8 billion went into the restructuring plan. "Preguntas sobre la reapertura del Canje," *La Nación*, July 23, 2008. See also Presentación: Oferta de Canje—12 de enero de 2005, Information about the debt, Ministerio de Economía y Producción, http://www.argentinedebtinfo.gov.ar/esp_presen.htm.
24. Of the $81.8 billion defaulted Argentine bonds, 9.1 percent was in American hands—the

fourth country after Argentina itself, Italy, and Switzerland. "En el exterior esperan para ver qué hacer," *La Nación*, January 15, 2005, http://www2.lanacion.com.ar/nota. asp?nota_id=671405.

25. The same day that Rumsfeld visited Buenos Aires, the Argentine government gave its support to the controversial nomination of Paul Wolfowitz as president of the World Bank.

26. Deborah L. Norden and Roberto Russell, *The United States and Argentina. Changing Relations in a Changing World* (New York and London: Routledge, 2002): 105.

27. For more on this debate, see María Florencia Zárate, "La participación de Chile, Brasil y Argentina en las operaciones de mantenimiento de la paz en Haití. Entre las motivaciones nacionales y la cooperación regional." Degree thesis, University of Torcuato Di Tella, June 2005, 72/80, and Gilda Follietti "La participación argentina en Haití: el papel del Congreso," *Revista Fuerzas Armadas y Sociedad* 19, no. 1 (2005): 37–56.

28. The vote in the Senate was 40 in favor, and 19 against with no abstentions. Deputies recorded 136 votes in favor, 21 against and 13 abstentions.

29. Cited in Roberto Russell, "¿Qué espera Argentina de un segundo mandato de Bush?," *Foreign Affairs en Español* 5, no. 1 (2005): 36.

30. For a similar analysis, Diana Tussie, "Argentina y Estados Unidos, bajo el signo de la era K," in *Relaciones bilaterales entre Argentina y Estados Unidos. Pasado y Presente*, ed. Cynthia Arnson with Tamara P. Taraciuk (Washington, DC: Woodrow Wilson International Center for Scholars, 2004): 81–87.

31. The government won a majority in the Senate (41 senators). It did not win the 129 seats for an outright majority in the House of Representatives but it garnered enough votes from allies to win the majority. For final results, see Ministerio del Interior, http://www.mininterior.gov.ar/elecciones/2005/esc_def.asp.

32. Remarks by the president of the Argentine Republic, Néstor Kirchner at the inauguration of the IV Summit of the Americas, Mar del Plata, http://www.summit-americas.org/Documents%20for%20Argentina%20Summit%202005/IV%20Summit /Discursos/Discurso%20del%20presidente%20de%20la%20Rep%C3%BAblica%20A rgentina.pdf.

33. Despite this somewhat melodramatic death knell, the de facto demise of the FTAA had already occurred during the Eighth Trade Ministerial Meeting, held in Miami in November 2003 where the original project, structured on the basis of continent-wide consensus and the "single undertaking" was replaced by a "FTAA light" with vague commitments and less depth. After this meeting, the United States would focus on bilateral agreements or FTAs with small sets of countries.

34. See, among others, Juan Gabriel Tokatlian, "Una Cumbre bastante modesta," *La Nación*, 7 November 2005, http://www.lanacion.com.ar/nota.asp?nota_id=754160.

35. U.S.–Argentine Relations, Bureau of Public Affairs, U.S. Department of States, http://www.state.gov/r/pa/ei/bgn/26516.htm.

36. See Eleonora Gosman, "Tras la Cumbre, Bush elogió a Brasil y resaltó su liderazgo," *Clarín*, November 7, 2005, http://www.clarin.com/diario/2005/11/07/elpais/p-00301.htm.

37. See Mark Falcoff, "Argentina y Estados Unidos: Retorno al desencuentro histórico," in *Relaciones bilaterales entre Argentina y Estados Unidos. Pasado y Presente*, ed. Cynthia Arnson with Tamara P. Taraciuk (Washington, DC: Woodrow Wilson International Center for Scholars, 2004): 77–79.

38. *U.S. Trade Balance, by Partner Country 2008, United States International Trade Commission*, http://dataweb.usitc.gov/scripts/cy_m3_run.asp.

39. Since the 2001 crisis, bilateral trade enjoyed sustained growth with favorable balances for Argentina up to 2005. Since 2006, the trade balance returned to its historic pattern with a surplus in favor of the United States, due to its role as an important supplier of industrial goods, which Argentina has been unable to compensate for with its exports of raw materials, energy, agriculture, and manufacturing.

40. *Centro de Economía Internacional en base a Indec,* http://cei.mrecic.gov.ar/estadisticas/mercosur/cuadro14.xls.
41. Ibid.
42. Washington has questioned the protection afforded by Argentina for intellectual property rights on its territory. The U.S. Office of the Special Trade Representative (USTR) has included Argentina in the annual U.S. Priority Watch List under the "Special 301" statute.
43. See U.S. Department of State, 2008 Investment Climate Statement-Argentina, Openness to Foreign Investment www.state.gov/e/eeb/ifd/2008/101776.htm. The report cites the World Bank "Doing Business 2007 Report," which ranks Argentina 109th out of 178 countries in terms of the ease of conducting business.
44. U.S. investment has been directed mainly at the oil and gas, electricity, communications sectors, and construction industry.
45. See Horacio Verbitsky, "El mal Rato" and "El rescate," *Página 12,* August 8 and December 5, 2004, http://www.pagina12.com.ar/diario/elpais/1-39335-2004-08-08. html, http://www.pagina12.com.ar/diario/elpais/1-44469-2004-12-05.html.
46. Lavagna had been the leading figure in Duhalde's cabinet. As Kirchner's minister for the economy, he played a key role in the country's external financial negotiations with the IMF and private creditors. Moreover, Kirchner had announced during the election campaign in 2003 that he would keep Lavagna in office, something he did to win more votes by capitalizing on Lavagna's achievements in abating the crisis and initiating Argentina's economic recovery.
47. See Gustavo Bazzan, "Kirchner abrió una nueva etapa: echó a Lavagna y lo reemplazó por Felisa Miceli," *Clarín,* September 29, 2005.
48. Because of the historical ties between Bolivia and Argentina and the personal political history of many of its staff members, Néstor Kirchner's government had more weight and political clout than that of the Lula administration in cooperating with various political and social actors to maintain the democratic stability of its neighbor. In addition, he played an important role in reducing the severity of the dispute between Brazil and Bolivia created after Evo Morales's government's decision to nationalize gas production in May 2006.
49. The Bush administration especially welcomed the decision of the Kirchner government to order the capture of eight senior officials from Iran who were alleged to have been involved in the bombing of the AMIA. These include the former president of Iran, Ali Rafsanjani, and the former ambassador to Buenos Aires Hadi Soleimanpour.
50. Since May 2005, through the direct allocation of public debt bonds, Venezuela became the main source of external financial support for the Argentine government. By August 2008, Venezuelan purchases of Argentine bonds amounted to $9.2 billion. See "Del FMI a Chávez," *La Nación,* August 31, 2008,http://www.lanacion.com.ar/nota.asp?nota_id =1044947&high=bonos%20venezuela and "La deuda supera los fondos," *La Nación,* August 31, 2008, http://www.lanacion.com.ar/nota.asp?nota_id=1044923& high=bonos%20venezuela.
51. I refer to terms used by Cristina Fernández de Kirchner to explain the reasons for the incorporation of Venezuela in MERCOSUR. See Message of the President's Office, Cristina Fernández de Kirchner to the Legislative Assembly, March 1, 2008, http://www.casarosada.gov.ar/index.php?option=com_content&task=view&id=1741. For more on this see "Chacho Álvarez impulsa la integración de Venezuela al MERCOSUR," *Terra,* July 19, 2007, http://www.ve.terra.com/imprime/0,,OI1769185-EI9837,00.html.
52. This space, which turned out to be a soccer stadium filled with his supporters and anti-imperialist slogans, was used by Chávez to repudiate Bush's trip.
53. For more on this historic pattern, see Joseph S. Tulchin, *Argentina and the United States. A Conflicted Relationship* (Boston: Twayne Publishers, 1990).

54. See International Narcotics Control Strategy Report, U.S. Dep. of State, vol. 1. *Drug and Chemical Control*, March 2008, 103–106.

55. Country Reports on Terrorism, 2007, U.S. Dep. of State Publication. Office of the Coordination for Counterterrorism, April 2008, 148.

56. The so-called "valijagate" refers to a scandal that unfolded in August 2008 at the airport in Buenos Aires when a Venezuelan citizen attempted to enter the country with a suitcase full of around $800,000 in cash. The passenger arrived on an airplane chartered by the Argentine state energy company (Enarsa) on which five Argentines and two Venezuelans linked to Enarsa and PDVSA, Venezuela's state oil company, were traveling. In December 2008, prosecutors in the U.S. State of Florida, who were investigating alleged Venezuelan agents, claimed that the money in the suitcase was for Cristina Fernández de Kirchner's campaign. Hugo Chávez and Cristina Fernández both rejected the accusation, declaring it part of a U.S. intelligence services operation to create divisions between Argentina and Venezuela.

57. See Ana Barón, "Los Estados Unidos esperan que, con Cristina, la Argentina vuelva a la escena internacional," *Clarín*, December 12, 2007.

58. See Beatriz Sarlo, "El doble cuerpo presidencial," *La Nación*, November 11, 2008, 21.

59. President Cristina Fernández de Kirchner before the UN General Assembly, September 23, 2008, http://www.casarosada.gov.ar/index.php?option=com_content&task=view&id=5017&Itemid=66.

60. See "Cristina Kirchner logró superar la barrera del 45 por ciento," *La Nación*, November 13, 2007, http://www.lanacion.com.ar/nota.asp?nota_id=961731.

61. See Cristina Fernández's speech at the opening of the 5th Summit of the Americas, April 17, 2009, http://www.casarosada.gov.ar/index.php?option=com_content&task=view&id=5825.

62. The document adds, ". . . the farmers' strike depressed consumption and business confidence and contributed to growing uncertainty about the government's ability to maintain the boom after six years of economic expansion." *La Nación. Economía y Negocios*, April 17, 2009.

63. Official results of the Argentine legislative election 2009, Ministry of Interior, http://www.elecciones2009.gov.ar/Telegramas/paginaspdf/if_top.htm and *La Nación*, Buenos Aires, http://www.lanacion.com.ar/especiales/elecciones-legislativas-2009/resultados.asp.

7 Brazil–U.S. Relations

Getting Better All the Time*

Mônica Hirst

United States–Brazil relations are facing a period of change which could reshape the contents and implications of bilateral understandings in the following decades. Although it is true that this process may find explanations in the history of this bilateral tie, it is equally important to put it into the context of the transformations of the international system, U.S. foreign policy since September 2001, and Brazil's recent steps forward in regional and global politics. Also, notwithstanding the evidence of a particularly positive chemistry established immediately at the level of presidential diplomacy between Presidents Obama and Lula, positive signs had already been observed during the late years of the Bush administration.

In fact, and contrary to initial expectations, in recent times U.S.–Brazil relations became more substantial, with constructive outcomes for both sides. In the late period of the Bush and Lula governments, a new stage was inaugurated, replacing previous misunderstandings with an optimistic pragmatic relationship based upon concrete interests. According to the interpretations shared within Brazilian official circles, a stage of maturity has been finally reached, launching a strategic dialogue between Brasilia and Washington.[1]

From a historical perspective, U.S.–Brazil relations have gone through different phases, oscillating from "good" to "cool" without ever breaking out into open hostility. Five different historical phases can be traced: "unwritten alliance" (1889–1940); "automatic alignment" (1942–1974); "autonomy" (1975–1990); "adjustment" (1990–2002); "affirmative relations" (2002–2008).[2] Although U.S.–Brazil relations have always been dominated by an intergovernmental agenda, in the recent decades non-governmental actors have expanded noticeably their presence especially motivated by inter-democratic connections. Besides a diversified set of economic, political and cultural interests, societal organizations and networks—particularly those dealing with environmental and human rights issues—are part of a lively bilateral interaction.

In the regional context, U.S.–Brazil ties feature a unique profile. Even though Brazil has faced competitive edges in the past with other countries in the Americas—such as Mexico and Argentina—it has preserved, for good or ill, a distinct agenda with the U.S. State-to-state political relations between the United

* I thank Jazmin Sierra for her assistance.

States and Brazil have primarily aimed for prudent coexistence, collaboration on specifics, and minimal collision. In world affairs, the United States and Brazil have always maintained their discrepancies; Brazilian foreign policy has insisted upon an autonomous worldview. While in regional politics both countries have increased communication and coordination in different political-institutional crisis situations, differences have persisted in trade and security matters.

This chapter will be structured in four sections plus a set of concluding remarks. The first section addresses the regional and global context of Brazil–U.S. relations under the Bush and Lula governments. The second explains the main elements of Brazilian foreign policy under Lula, highlighting the country's expanding role in global affairs. The third contextualizes the economic and the political dimension of bilateral relations, which combines the most relevant regional and global negotiations undertaken since the early twenty-first century. Finally, the conclusion addresses the challenges and most probable outcomes of U.S.–Brazil relations in the near future.

The Regional-Global Context

The deterioration of U.S.–Latin American relations during the Bush administration is one of many indicators of the disastrous consequences of the miscalculations of American unilateralism. While the region has traditionally played a marginal part in Washington's strategic policies, it did contribute to highlight the blunders of U.S. foreign policy during the Bush administration.[3] In fact, throughout the region, there was a renewed skepticism and political contestation regarding the U.S. approach to neo-liberal globalization and its post 9–11 security priorities, thereby widening the reach of anti-Americanism in domestic political polarization. At the time, American liberal segments involved in the previous inter-American rapprochement of the 1990s criticized the effects of the securitization of hemispheric policy promoted by the White House and regretted the lack of a "constructive regional commitment."[4]

For some, the "indiscipline" of Latin American governments, especially those in the Andean area, was a sign of a leadership crisis, the inadequate use of coercive measures, and the costly consequences of wrong strategic priorities, unsupportive of U.S. priorities focused on the war against terror. At the same time, the irrelevance of South America to the White House—with the exception of Colombia—manifested in the official strategic documents broadly diffused in 2002—marginalized the region even more with regards to Washington's new priorities.

In this context, Brazil built its affirmative policy towards the United States. The priorities of the post 9–11 American policy had an immediate negative impact on relations with Brazil because from the start Brasilia rejected the global fight against terrorism and made clear its limited willingness to participate in an anti-terrorist crusade led by the White House. While Brazil maintained a low-key position *vis-à-vis* the Bush administrations security obsessions, U.S. neglect towards the region opened a new space of maneuver for Brazil in regional and global politics. A win-win situation slowly took shape; Brazil became useful for U.S. interests in hemispheric affairs, while at the same time it fostered its autonomous international aspirations, which did not involve friction and misunderstanding with Washington, as had occurred in the past.

Brazil's International Affairs under Lula

In recent years, Brazil has put forward a more ambitious foreign policy with the aim of expanding the country's presence in global economic negotiations, multilateral institutions and regimes, and in regional affairs.[5] Since the inauguration of the Lula administration, Brazilian foreign affairs have expanded in order to project the country as a global political and economic player. Presidential diplomacy has been linked to an active foreign policy concerned simultaneously with the expansion of ties with the industrialized economies and the emergent South. Relations have been reshaped with the United States and the European Union (EU); ties have deepened with China, India, and South Africa, together with a renewed South-South multilateralism and unprecedented activity in South America. A diversified set of "external fronts" has led to an expanded participation in global politics and economic forums, even though Brazil still faces the constraints imposed by the structural asymmetries of the international system.

Increased involvement in global matters has not prevented nationalistic stances from becoming more visible in the formulation of foreign policy priorities of the Lula government. From an institutional standpoint the Foreign Ministry—known as the Itamaraty—remains the main state agency in charge of Brazil's international affairs, whether these are related to political, security, economic, bilateral, regional, or multilateral, agendas. This imposes a statist profile on external negotiations and the options in economic, political, and security policies. Yet, diplomatic activity has also become more specialized, given the diversity and complexity of Brazil's international agenda; it is also subject to greater societal and political pressures in a context of intense inter-bureaucratic competition and the deepening of democracy.

In international security, Brazil has been developing since the mid-1990s a positive agenda regarding adherence to international non-proliferation regimes.[6] Brazil has become an active supporter of enhanced multilateral initiatives, particularly the expanded role of the United Nations (UN) in world politics, and it has increased its own participation and responsibilities.[7] For Brazil, the reinforcement of the juridical and parliamentary structure of the UN System has become a permanent demand, making explicit to the international community its ambition to be one of the new permanent members of the UN Security Council, if the number of seats were to increase.[8] Besides being part of the so-called G4, the other countries sharing the same aspirations—Germany, Japan, and India—Brazil has also become a participant in various emerging power coalitions such as BRIC (Brazil, Russia, India, China) and IBSA (India, Brazil, South Africa).[9]

Brazil has become an active player in global trade negotiations, more so since the creation of the World Trade Organization (WTO).[10] Brazilian foreign trade policy should be understood in the context of the macroeconomic changes the country underwent in the early 1990s. Since then, Brazil has steadily advanced towards free market economics; it has been liberalizing its economy but it has not given up its industrial development strategies. In the last fifteen years, as Brazil became increasingly exposed to global financial turmoil and speculative monetary attacks, the country struggled to preserve room for maneuver when handling critical situations. The continuity of Brazil's economic stability involved until very recently recurrent monitoring and endorsement from the IMF and the World Bank. Brazilian economic policies improved the domestic environment for private transnational capital, and improved economic performance became an important incentive for the growth and diversification of foreign investment. Measures facilitating investments from abroad in financial, telecommunications, and transportation sectors led to a major expansion in flows coming from different OECD countries.

Besides its involvement in numerous WTO trade disputes, Brazil has been an active player in the international community regarding the review of rules of the multilateral trade system. The country has concentrated its attention on two main subjects in multilateral trade negotiations: ending the subsidies for agriculture, which is particularly aimed at the European Union and the United States, and seeking flexibility in meeting demands regarding new issues on the agenda. After the fiasco at the 2000 Third Ministerial WTO meeting in Seattle and the failed attempt made in 2001 at Doha, a consensus for a new round of global trade negotiations was finally reached at the Cancún Ministerial in 2003. Since then, Brazil assumed a leading role—together with India and Argentina-in the creation of the G20, a group of WTO member states concerned with the distortion of trade practices for agricultural goods, the uneven conditions of market access, and the dramatic problems of food security.[11]

Last but not least, regional affairs—and particularly South America—have assumed unprecedented importance for Brazil. During the 1990s, Brazil's regional policy gave priority to regional integration and particularly to the establishment of MERCOSUR.[12] During the presidency of Fernando Henrique Cardoso, ties with the Andean countries were developed either as part of MERCOSUR's interregional negotiations, such as those pursued with the Andean Community of Nations (CAN), or as a reflection of specific bilateral interests. Slowly Brazil's identity as a Latin American country was gradually replaced by that of a South American power; support grew for the idea that Brazil should expand its responsibility to maintain regional political stability by means of stronger democratic institutions and values. During Lula's government, bilateral ties with Argentina have been deepened even more, as the rivalry of previous times was supplanted by a "strategic partnership" which combines asymmetric interdependency with a close political coordination in regional affairs. Besides acting jointly in specific turbulent situations, such as Bolivia's in 2003, 2004, and 2008, Argentine-Brazilian coordination, with the support of Venezuela, led to the creation of the Union of South American Nations (UNASUR) in 2005.[13]

As Brazil dramatically expanded its economic and political presence in the area, new challenges have emerged. Acknowledgement on the part of its South American partners of its role as a regional leader has been held back by a combination of structural asymmetries, enduring misperceptions, and political differences.

Furthermore, lack of domestic support among business, political, and intellectual sectors has contributed to a slowdown of Brazil's regional leadership. The difficulties for Brazil in South American regional politics were aggravated by the spread of ideological polarizations posed by Venezuela's government; Lula's government dealt with this challenge with a large dose of pragmatism but the Venezuelan challenge also fostered discussion in Brazil regarding the political pros and cons of Brazil's higher regional profile.

Fitting Relations with the United States into the Broader Picture

When it came to power, the Lula administration faced the necessity to commit to economic policies that would maintain the same macroeconomic fundamentals of the Cardoso government. Thus, signs of continuity were more important than those of change regarding Brazil's economic and foreign policy. The Lula government would downplay and prove wrong the alarms generated by Lula's own rise, given his biography as a leftist union leader—worries that had spread in the Washington establishment and Wall Street about the unwelcome beginning of an era of presumed anti-Americanism in Brasilia.[14] Therefore, the first effort of the Lula government concentrated on dispelling such worries. It was a priority to eliminate the apprehensions that Lula's political party would lead to a radical government, impregnated by an ideology that would question the values defended by the business community and the American government. Once this mission had been accomplished, the new Brazilian government became concerned with maintaining a fluid communication between both governments, with the objective of assuring an inter-presidential dialogue that would identify common interests in the economic, political, and even security areas.

The Economic Front

Through 2003, the (mis)understanding over the Free Trade Agreement of the Americas/Área de Libre Comercio de las Américas (FTAA/ALCA) negotiation process became the most relevant and sensitive bilateral matter between the Lula and Bush administrations. This was an unwanted legacy—especially after the approval of the U.S. Farm Bill, which generated generous domestic subsidies—that the Lula administration had to cope with in the context of its affirmative foreign policy. The fact that Brazil shared the co-presidency of the negotiations with the United States conferred on it high visibility and political responsibility. The first decision was to accept January 2005 as the date of implementation of the agreement. For this to be possible, trade negotiations between the United States and MERCOSUR would have to reach a positive conclusion. It was crucial to develop a consensus with its intra-MERCOSUR partners—especially Argentina—on issues such as: industrial and agricultural goods, services, intellectual property, government procurement, and agricultural subsidies.[15] Consolidating ties with the Argentine government, as agreed to in the Buenos Aires Consensus (October 2003), contributed to smoothing out problems generated by MERCOSUR's chronic ineffectiveness since the late 1990s.[16] The decrease in intra-MERCOSUR trade together with growing political difficulties among its members added to the differences regarding negotiations with the United States. While both Brazil and Argentina had lost interest in reaching an accord with Washington, Uruguay and Paraguay remained clearly in favor of moving ahead.

In this context, domestic actors in Brazil sought a radicalization of the stance against the FTAA. As many domestic opponents voiced their firm disapproval, the politicization process involving trade unions, business sectors, political leaders, and diplomats revived nationalist sentiments similar to the campaigns of earlier times.[17] The social and economic discontent evident in domestic Brazilian politics regarding the pro-liberal economic policies of the Lula administration facilitated a policy change. The administration found it to its advantage to toughen its bargaining position with regard to FTAA negotiations. Nevertheless this tactic met its limits as Brazilian diplomacy realized the costs of walking out of hemispheric negotiations.

Also, the dialogue between the Brazilian government and the local business sector turned out to be quite complex as a series of intra- and inter-ministerial disagreements regarding hemispheric negotiations unfolded. There was an apparent link between the controversy about the FTAA and the feud between neo-developmentalist and liberal orthodox economic policy approaches. At the same time, the pressures of the Bush government, and its "divide and rule" tactics in the Latin American realm, suggested the possibility of U.S. coercive actions against Argentina and Brazil, hinting at a link between monetary-financial and trade negotiations.

In the sub-regional spheres, Brazil had to deal with the consequences of MERCOSUR's imperfections and delays that impeded its consolidation as a customs union. Brazilian diplomacy tolerated and was occasionally an "accomplice" of such setbacks. This political process came on top of a legacy of prior under-accomplishment regarding sub-regional economic integration. As a result, the MERCOSUR's bargaining power in hemispheric trade negotiations was curtailed. In reality, the gap between the MERCOSUR's discourse and the reality turned the advantages obtained at the initial stage of the FTAA negotiations into a missed opportunity. The MERCOSUR accomplished almost nothing, notwithstanding that it had managed at the start of the talks to ensure that there would be no zero-sum gaming and that the commercial sub-regional agreements already in effect would not be sacrificed with the development of a hemispheric accord.

In February 2003, the United States announced that it would partition its negotiation offers, differentiating its proposals according to lists of products with varying tariff reduction schedules—one each for the Caribbean (85 percent), Central America (64 percent), the Andean countries (68 percent), and MERCOSUR (50 percent). Brazil and its partners considered it an adverse initiative. Furthermore, a differentiated calendar of deadlines led to a tangle of negotiations and pressures, stimulating competition among the countries in the region, strengthening U.S. bargaining power, and promoting a *de facto* burial of the "most favored nation" principle in intra-hemispheric trade practices.

Another source of U.S.–Brazilian discord was the treatment of trade items in the WTO and FTAA agendas; the United States considered that the agricultural subsidies and the rules of origin (antidumping and export credits) should be addressed within the scope of global negotiations. This strategy, however, led to unfavorable outcomes at the WTO Cancún Meeting (September 2003) whose effect would be to postpone the Doha Round and deepen the North–South divide within and outside the hemisphere. In this context, U.S.–Brazil commercial disputes ran their everyday course at the WTO; since the creation of the WTO, Brazil filed two of its ten demands against the United States during the Lula administration while the Bush administration filed four against Brazil.[18]

The Lula government acknowledged the political cost of abandoning the hemispheric negotiation table but, given the unease caused by the reformulated U.S. tariff reduction offer to the MERCOSUR countries, the whole package had to be rethought. This led to a Plan B, a "light" FTAA (called *Alquinha*, in Portuguese, from ALCA plus an ending meaning "small"). "Damage control" became the Brazilian foreign ministry priority, which meant that the only deals to be signed were those that would cause fewer costs to the country. The aim was to prevent the United States from resorting to its "something for nothing" tactic, common in the history of its trade negotiations with Brazil.[19] However, the agenda change did not diminish the level of tension or contain the escalation of disagreements between Brasilia and Washington in the ministerial meetings that took place in 2003 and 2004. Each time it seemed harder to keep both delegations seated at the bargaining table.

On the American side, the tripartite pressure articulated by the United States Trade Representative (USTR), the Department of Commerce, and the Treasury Department reloaded the guns of coercive diplomacy: links were suggested between the success of the FTAA negotiations and the continuity of IMF loans to the various countries. In 2003, the interest groups that represented the U.S. industrial and agricultural sectors were strengthened through the protectionist measures enacted in the U.S. Trade Promotion Act; the labor unions and environmentalist organizations joined them, once they left behind the illusion that the Lula administration would adopt a more flexible stance with regards to the inclusion of labor and environmental protection clauses in trade negotiations. In fact, when the Democratic Party obtained the majority in the U.S. Congress in the November 2006 elections, the approval of free trade treaties with the Latin American countries became more difficult and divisive, as evident in the bare approval of the accord with the Central American countries (CAFTA) and the postponement of the ratification of a free trade agreement with Colombia.[20]

In Washington, the dominant perception was that Brazil had become the main obstacle for the success of hemispheric trade negotiations. While the Brazilian government was absolutely aware that the country's domestic market represented the main attraction for the U.S. government in the FTAA-MERCOSUR talks, the American officials knew it was easier to press for Brazil's trade liberalization within the framework of regional negotiations. On the Brazilian side, expanding its access to the American market constituted a permanent interest for the country's exports.

Table 7.1 Brazil's Trade with the United States (U.S.$)

Year	Exports	Percentage of Total Exports	Imports	Percentage of Total Imports
1990	7,594,263,027	24.17	4,160,683,895	20.14
1991	6,264,436,712	19.81	4,687,570,150	22.28
1992	6,932,757,328	19.37	4,538,666,763	22.08
1993	7,843,335,397	20.34	5,062,251,046	20.04
1994	8,816,241,304	20.25	6,674,390,616	20.18
1995	8,682,812,161	18.67	10,519,498,419	21.05
1996	9,182,584,604	19.23	11,818,422,203	22.15
1997	9,274,987,124	17.51	13,706,094,568	22.94
1998	9,747,316,066	19.06	13,514,742,008	23.4
1999	10,675,124,224	22.23	11,741,047,942	23.81
2000	13,189,576,929	23.93	12,899,226,083	23.1
2001	14,208,572,954	24.38	12,905,492,013	23.21
2002	15,377,822,589	25.44	10,287,452,316	21.78
2003	16,728,079,047	22.85	9,569,454,702	19.8
2004	20,099,235,400	20.79	11,357,061,637	18.07
2005	22,539,731,875	19.02	12,666,508,176	17.21
2006	24,524,748,523	17.8	14,657,479,678	16.05
2007	25,065,048,412	15.6	18,722,266,348	15.52

Source: Ministerio do Desenvolvimento, Industria e Comercio, Intercambio Comercial Brasileiro Estados Unidos (1987–2007 figures).

But Brazil's efforts to expand trade with other big economies, such as Russia, China, and India, and deepen the link with Latin America, were showing results. Even though the United States still represented a significant destination for Brazilian exports, its relative importance was not the same as at the start of the FTAA negotiations. In 2002, the United States absorbed 25 percent of Brazilian exports—of which 75 percent corresponded to industrial products of great aggregate value and technological content—and was responsible for 42 percent of the country's trade surplus. (See Table 7.1.) In 2005, the American market absorbed 19 percent, in 2006 17 percent, and in 2007 15 percent of Brazilian exports.[21] (See Table 7.2.) Relative importance had decreased on reciprocal bases. For U.S. foreign investments, Brazil dropped from the 9th and 10th rank in the 1990's to the 18th rank in 2005–2007.[22]

Table 7.2 Brazil's Annual Net Foreign Direct Investment (FDI) from Latin America and the Caribbean

By Country of Origin	1997	2006
United States	29%	20%
Holland	10%	16%
Spain	4%	7%
France	8%	3%
Portugal	5%	1%
Others	45%	53%

Source: Central Bank of Brazil.

After three years, the impossibility of harmonizing differences, the fragmentation of hemispheric negotiations, and the expiration of the agreed deadline for the conclusion of the accord led to a literal implosion of the FTAA talks in a context of intense polarization. Meanwhile, anti-FTAA stances had assumed a symbolic significance for neo-populist South American leaders such as Hugo Chávez, Evo Morales, Rafael Correa, and Nestor Kirchner. The social consequences of the neo-liberal policies implemented in Latin America in the 1990s fueled a radical anti-American discourse, making clear the precarious political conditions in the region for signing a FTAA with the Bush administration. Even if it were true that Brazil had contributed decisively to obstructing the negotiation process, its performance was always led by substantive and concrete reservations in contrast to the ideological objections flagged by other Latin American countries.

In this context, the collapse of the FTAA in the IV Summit of the Americas (2005) had a symbolic impact that went beyond the negotiation agenda for a free trade area in the hemisphere. Brazil was able to detach itself from a project that, besides always carrying a high degree of domestic disapproval, had prevented the Lula government from creating its own agenda with the United States.

In this sense, it is symptomatic that, on the day after (literally) the Mar del Plata Summit, the United States and Brazil announced their intention of constructing an encompassing bilateral agenda. Almost immediately the bitter flavor of ten years of frustrated trade negotiations was replaced by a positive agenda of common interests, in which cooperation in bio-fuels took center stage.[23]

Brazil has accomplished much with regard to bio-fuels. During the oil crises of 1973 and 1979, Brazil had launched Proalcool, a government program to stimulate the production of fuels based on sugar cane. It has been highly successful; Brazil has become the second largest producer of ethanol, representing 37 percent of the world's market.[24] Private interests have also become active in this sector; private domestic investments in the sugar cane industry are estimated at 14.6 billion dollars for the 2008–2013 period.[25] Above all, the Brazilian government views ethanol production as an important element of its international status.[26] Brazil's Petrobras plans to increase the production of ethanol destined for exports and the government has launched partnerships in the Caribbean, Africa, and Asia to transmit its know-how on bio-fuels.[27]

The 2006 negotiation of a U.S.-Brazil memorandum of understanding on this topic committed both countries to collaborate in research and development as well as more widely in order to define universal technical standards.[28] According to the Brazilian authorities, the identification of this area of common interest played a key role in expanding the range of bilateral convergence and paved the road for assigning a strategic meaning to the dialogue between Washington and Brasilia.

In 2008, in the context of the global economic crisis, these understandings between Washington and Brasilia facilitated the dialogue between both countries. The United States fully acknowledged Brazil as an emerging power, with a say within the G24, when for the first time OECD partners realized it would be necessary to expand the inner circle of decisions and commitments to overcome the major difficulties posed by the financial disaster shared by all.

The Political Front

As guarantees were offered in the economic area, the Bush government revealed new expectations with regards to Brazil, particularly related to its moderately pitched performance and intervention in situations of turbulence (Bolivia), radicalization (Venezuela), or institutional collapse (Haiti). The Lula government responded positively to the expectations of the White House but nonetheless maintained its own room for maneuver. Hence, U.S.–Brazil relations regarding international and regional politics followed a similar pattern to the one observed in economic matters. After a period of distance and silence, a new wave of positive inter-ministerial and presidential talks took place. An initial stage of disagreements was replaced by one of relative calm; the main points of divergence, although still present, seemed no longer to represent an impediment to identify areas of coincidence.

The differences between the United States and Brazil in global politics deepened after September 11, 2001. Brazil avoided full-scale alignment with U.S. security policies while in its own way supporting the U.S.-led war against terrorism.[29] The Lula administration has tried to maintain a balanced position in dealing with Islamist terrorism and Middle East matters. On the one hand, it aimed to enlarge its visibility with the Arab countries, as was the case with the initiative of a 2005 Summit of South American-Arab Countries when Brazil refused to invite the United States as an observer. On the other, Brazil declined to adopt a flexible approach towards terrorism, which might have justified the use of violence as legitimate to resist foreign occupation, as many Arab countries claimed. Brazilian diplomacy also made a special effort to express a view regarding the Israeli-Palestinian conflict, which in 2008 had led to a major humanitarian crisis in the Gaza area. Together with its IBSA colleagues, Brazil gave even greater support to the Palestinian cause in recent years. The White House acknowledged to a certain degree Brazil's aspiration to expand its presence as a mediator when it invited President Lula to participate as an observer in the 2007 Annapolis summit on the Middle East.[30]

By trying to trace its own course of action, Brazil at no point endorsed U.S. unilateralism; on the contrary, it reinforced its support for multilateralism to deal with crisis situations in international politics and security. Lula's administration did not support the White House actions in Iraq, it was frustrated with the United States' non-cooperative policy towards the Kyoto Protocol, and maintained clear differences regarding U.S. pressure for the adherence to the additional protocol of the nuclear nonproliferation treaty. Nevertheless, commonalities were shared with respect to UN peace missions (particularly in Haiti) and the two countries coincided often in their votes at the UN Security Council when Brazil had the chance to occupy a non-permanent seat in 2004–2005.[31] This convergence with Washington was reflected in various issues facing the United Nations. Between 2003 and 2007, Brazil and the United States coincided in 70–80 percent of their votes in the General Assembly, with more votes in common in the human rights area than over disarmament. (See Table 7.3.) However, the Brazilian government became especially

Table 7.3 UN Voting Coincidence

	2000	2001	2002	2003	2004	2005	2006	2007
All Consensus Resolutions	86.7%	84.6%	81.8%	78.8%	79.6%	75.3%	73.3%	70.2%
Important Consensus Resolutions	83.3%	72.0%	74.2%	75.0%	75%	62.8%	61.9%	66.7%
Arms Control	68.4%	50.0%	42.3%	26.1%	8.7%	28.1%	26.8%	3.3%
Human Rights	50.0%	27.3%	40.0%	31.6%	38.9%	26.3%	13.3%	21.1%
Middle East	10.0%	28.6%	39.3%	12.5%	5.6%	5.9%	4.5%	0.0%

	2004	2005
Identical Votes	58	69
Opposite Votes	2	0
Abstentions	1	1
Voting Coincidence	96.7%	100%

Source: UN Yearbook.

disappointed when the Bush administration refused its support for the UN Security Council reform, even though this had been the result principally of the lack of agreement between the five permanent members rather than a U.S. position against any particularly candidate country.

Since 2003, the U.S. government has reiterated the special appreciation for the Brazilian intervention in Haiti under United Nations auspices and the decision of the Lula government to assume the military command of the MINUSTAH—the peace mission sent to that country.[32] The outstanding joint participation of Argentina, Brazil, and Chile gave this mission an emblematic meaning as a sub-regional cooperation initiative in post-conflict situations. From the perspective of Brazilian foreign policy, it became imperative to differentiate the actions in Haiti from other examples of foreign intervention propelled by imperialist motivations. Hence, from the start Brazil has emphasized that it assumed the military command of the MINUSTAH to to preclude the presence or control of "others" in or over Haiti.[33] But the premises of the international policy of the Lula government did not prevent this Brazilian presence from being useful for the United States, given how difficult it would have been for the United States to intervene in Haiti while engaged in wars in Afghanistan and Iraq. This aspect has led some to argue that a de facto U.S. military overstretching led third countries to serve its own strategic interests.[34] From the Brazilian side, the participation in MINUSTAH has been perceived as a way to avert other undesirable foreign intervention. Also, Brazil has voiced the urgent need for substantial U.S. economic and humanitarian assistance aid to Haiti.

In the first years of the twenty-first century, South America faced a new phase of political instability, particularly in the Andean area, which led to institutional breakdowns, massive popular protests, political violence, and local turmoil accompanied by strong anti-American sentiments.[35] Regional and sub-regional instruments and regimes—such as MERCOSUR, the Andean Community, the Rio Group, and the Organization of American States (OAS)—were incapable of preventing or containing these developments, which were both a cause and a consequence of the deepening of political fragmentation within the region. In general, domestic actors did not abandon democratic institutions, yet the intra-regional interpretations and alignments from these domestic developments led to growing international ideological polarization. Washington was unable to deal easily with this reality, categorizing some of these processes as "radical populism" and regarding them as an emerging threat for the inter-American environment.[36]

Washington and Brasilia did not share the same premises when addressing conflict-zone areas, such as Colombia, or politically uncertain contexts, such as Bolivia and Venezuela. Yet, the Bush administration increasingly recognized the necessity of maintaining an open channel of communication with Brazil to deal with the regional political agenda, particularly where democratic institutions faced risks to their own continuity. For Brazilian foreign policy, this represented the challenge of carrying forward its regional policy and simultaneously avoiding collision with Washington. A first benign experience was the coordination between the two countries with regards to the crisis in Venezuela at the beginning of 2003. For the first time, the United States accepted to participate inter pares in a diplomatic regional initiative.[37] Also for the first time, Brazil assumed a leading role in the conduct of such an initiative, denominated "The Group of Friends of Venezuela," which also included the OAS Secretary General, Mexico, Chile, Colombia, Spain, and Portugal. Its main objective was to promote the dialogue between the government of Hugo Chávez and the opposition groups, seeking a political solution that would not violate democratic principles. Although the results were modest, the presence of Brazil and the United States added to the mediating OAS impulse and helped to prevent the deterioration of the Venezuelan political situation.

But Brasilia and Washington maintained their differences with regards to other turbulent realities in the region, especially when these affected strategic American interests. Conflicting perceptions in the case of the war in Colombia were constant, even more when the White House clung to the idea that its presence in that country was part of its military and political action to fight terrorism. Washington expected Brazilian policy toward the Colombian war to adjust to its security priorities. Inversely, the Lula administration pretended to contribute—alongside the UN and other multilateral regional institutions—to a peace-making dialogue between all the parties in conflict. Also, the Brazilian government has always been quite defensive towards Plan Colombia, and perceived its renewal in 2006 as both a threat to its sovereignty, given the increased U.S. military presence close to Brazil's Amazon borders, and stimuli to the expansion of the Revolutionary Armed Forces of Colombia (FARC) activities in the area, now connected with Brazilian drug trafficking organizations. Brasilia also regretted the impact of the dispute between the Uribe and Chávez governments, encouraged by the White House, as it seriously damaged the regional political environment and impeded the development of a South American Community envisaged by Lula and his international advisory team.[38]

The role of Brazil in Bolivia became another recurrent issue of dialogue between Washington and Brasilia, in the context of the chronic institutional crisis of that country.[39] Washington and Brasilia communicated much more effectively with regard to turbulence in Bolivia. Two major differences explain this: (1) to Washington's eyes, there were no key security interests, unlike in Colombia; (2) the local complexities in the Bolivian political crisis along with the limited U.S. government understanding and interest led mainly just to misunderstanding and disdain. The White House's only concern with Bolivia was its ties to Venezuela, and Brazil's entrance into scene was perceived as a way to moderate this.

In this context, the participation of Brasilia in the political and economic life of Bolivia, as a consequence of its new energy interests and investments in natural gas, and its determination to carry forward actions to maximize the conditions for Bolivia's democratic governability, were gradually recognized by the White House as positive and useful. Brazil became a crucial stabilizing force, especially in the context of internal polarizations that led to subsequent ideological confrontations where the banner of anti-Americanism was permanently waved. But the United States closely watched the Brazilian insistence on finding political solutions that avoided securitized interpretations and, while it accepted them as the best options, it remained worried until the end of the Bush administration. The close political relations and ideological affinities between the Morales and Chávez governments, and the substantial economic support from Caracas to La Paz, were always a source of suspicion for Washington. This led to the continuation of longstanding covert actions, which, in turn, were a permanent source of unease for Brasilia.[40]

All in all, Washington's leadership crisis in the region, accompanied by a lack of interest and political energy to deal with the "turbulent peripheries," contributed to Brazil assuming its condition of regional power. The South American policy of the Lula government added to a new economic presence in the entire region and allowed a positive association between Brazilian aspirations and U.S. needs. Naturally, this "game of conveniences" will have to be re-configured with the new American administration. Brazil has proven that it has the intention of advancing in the next years to construct its South American leadership, with the expectation of advancing its international presence. This determination will be less costly and risky for the country the less its negative impact on its relation with the United States.

Conclusion

An overview of U.S.–Brazilian relations under the governments of Bush and Lula shows that, rather than a reality of fragmented interactions, this relationship became a complex and dynamic process that included a great diversity of issues and actors as well as governmental and non-governmental interests. In the near future, cooperation initiatives between both countries may follow an irregular and uncertain course.

The first signals of the Obama administration have been quite generous and open regarding Brazil's role as regional leader. But the asymmetric power structure will be an undeniable limitation in the development of a partnership between both countries, and its "strategic" implications will always be deeper for Brazil. This has always been the case with respect to recent U.S.-Colombia negotiations regarding U.S. use of Colombian military bases.

Yesterday and today economic and political agendas generate a cyclical movement between expectations and frustrations. In Brazil, these cycles accompany visions over the potential of the country that tie the notion of its specificity with the idea of its future. When this type of vision is associated to its relationship with the United States, an expectation is created over Washington's recognition of the Brazilian status in the Latin American and global spheres. At present, Brazil is experiencing a process of international upgrading, which undoubtedly has positive effects on its relationship with the United States.

The frame of convergence observed between the Lula and Bush governments has smoothly been passed on to the new administration in Washington. From a comparative diachronic perspective, commonalities exist between the present times of bilateral relations and those in the mid 1970s. One can observe a certain revival of the idea that a "special relationship" between Brazil and the United States should take place without any kind of bandwagon foreign policy on the part of Brazil. What is different is that today a closer cooperation with the United States fits without greater difficulty in the frame of the affirmative principles and the domestic democratic context that inspire the foreign policy of the Lula government.[41]

As the first Latin American president to visit Obama, Lula has given clear signs of the role he wishes his country to play in inter-American as well as global affairs in the years to come. In both cases it will be important to ensure an expansive bilateral agenda, triggered by the development of the bio-diesel and clean energy cooperation structure. But there seems to be room for much more.

With regard to the inter-American agenda, political matters tend to dominate as the free trade negotiations have been buried or frozen—depending upon the country—ever since the Democratic Party won control of the U.S. Congress. Brazil for sure is the country in the region least affected by this outcome, even though bilateral trade constraints do affect the access of Brazilian exports to the U.S. market, particularly steel industry products. But on the whole, the FTAA was a costly option for the Brazilian government, as made clear all through the ten-year negotiation process.

There is a juicy agenda where Brazil wishes to act as a mediator capable of pulling strings to de-ideologize the dialogue between the United States and Bolivia, Venezuela, and Cuba. Indeed, Cuban affairs are likely to become a new issue on the Brazil-U.S. agenda. Lula's government has invested politically and economically in Cuba in the last years. Brazilian investments have increased in the island—as well as in other parts of the Caribbean – and there has been a special interest in building partnership in bio-fuel projects with the Cubans. In political terms, Brazilian diplomacy has been playing an active role in the re-incorporation of the Havana regime in the Latin American community, as was observed in the regional consensus-building when Cuba was accepted as member of the Rio Group at the 2008 annual meeting in Bahia. Fraternal relations with the Castro brothers has not impeded Lula from persuading the Cuban regime to assume a less defensive position with regard to democratization; in the same vein, it has urged the Obama administration to moderate the use of coercive politics and lift the U.S. embargo against Cuba. This was one of the points highlighted by the Brazilian stances during the April 2009 Summit of the Americas in Trinidad and Tobago.

While the Obama administration has addressed the region in positive and constructive terms, it seems that Latin America will continue to play a marginal role in the big picture of U.S. interests. In fact, regions matter more for emerging powers—Brazil, India, South Africa—than for those that are well established in the international system. It will be Brazil's aim to build up such leadership in non-competitive terms with the United States. It would be less costly and risky if this trajectory could avoid having a negative impact on Brazil's relationship with the United States, and it could also become a new incentive for both countries to identify common interests. Also, if Washington wishes Brazil to do well as an emerging power, it will support it as a regional power. But this does not mean that as a regional power Brazil can turn its presence in the region into leadership. Brazil will have to move cautiously in the region; its involvement in local crises, together with growing trade and investment activities with its South American neighbors, has not implied automatic acknowledgement of regional leadership. The question is: If Brazil does not succeed in gaining support and acknowledgment from its neighbors, will the United States become more hesitant to recognize its role as a regional power?

The fact that the bilateral agenda is not loaded with intermestic issues—such as immigration and drug trafficking—helps to keep the relationship on a track that depends more upon creativity than in previously contaminated agendas. In this case, common global interests may play a major part in the future of bilateral relations. Shared, complementary and/or critical constructive perspectives on climate change, peace building and maintenance, and the international financial crisis are some of the areas where the diplomatic stances of both countries encourage them to travel together on the same roads ahead.

Notes

1. Antonio de Aguiar Patriota, "O Brasil e a política externa dos EUA," *Política Externa* 17, no. 1 (June–August 2008).
2. Each phase has been briefly presented in: Mônica Hirst, *The United States and Brazil. A Long Road of Unmet Expectations* (New York: Routledge, 2004). Translated version published in Brazil: *Brasil-Estados Unidos: desencontros e afinidades* (Rio de Janeiro: FGV Editora, 2009).
3. Joseph Nye, "The Decline of America's Soft Power," *Foreign Affairs* 83, no. 3 (May/June 2004). Stanley Hoffmann, "The Foreign Policy the US Needs," *The New York Review of Books* 53, no. 13 (August 10, 2006). Julia Sweig, *Friendly Fire. Losing Friends and Making Enemies in the Anti-American Century* (New York: Public Affairs, 2006).
4. Arturo Valenzuela, "Democracy and Trade: US Foreign Policy Towards Latin America," Madrid: Real Instituto Elcano, 2004.
5. See: Mônica Hirst and Maria Regina Soares de Lima, "Brazil as an Intermediate State and Regional Power: Action, Choice and Responsibilities," *International Affairs* 82, no. 1: 21–24. Andrew Hurrell, "Lula's Brazil: A Rising Power, but Going Where?," *Current History* 107, no. 706 (February 2008). Maria Regina Soares de Lima, "Liderazgo regional

en América del Sur, ¿tiene Brasil un papel a jugar?," in *América Latina: Integración o Fragmentación*, ed. Ricardo Lagos (Buenos Aires: Edhasa, 2008). Sean W. Burgues "Without Sticks or Carrots: Brazilian Leadership in South America During the Cardoso Era, 1992–2003," *Bulletin of Latin American Research* 25, no. 1 (2004): 23–42.

6. In 1994, Brazil joined the Missile Technology Control Regime (MTCR) and in 1997 it ratified the Nuclear Non-Proliferation Treaty (NPT).

7. Brazil participated in the UN Observer Missions in El Salvador (ONUSAL) and Mozambique (ONUMOZ) and in the UN Mission in Angola (UNAVEM) where it sent 1,300 soldiers, the largest military force it has sent abroad since World War II. Brazil also contributed police forces to the 1999 UN peace operation in East Timor and has assumed the military leadership of the UN mission to Haiti (MINUSTAH), initiated in 2004.

8. Brazil's pro-active diplomacy allowed its election as a non-permanent member of the UN Security Council (UNSC) five times in the post-cold war era: in 1989–1990, 1993–1994, 1998–1999, 2003–2004 and 2009–2011.

9. The BRIC countries are intermediate powers, considered as pivotal emerging markets that share similar regional and global capacities and a basic internal cohesion conducive to effective state action. The IBSA initiative was launched in 2003 as a trilateral forum to articulate interests and positions based upon common interests.

10. Brazil's use of contingency measures increased, as did its participation in multilateral consultations and panel reviews. Brazil has been a WTO member since its creation in January 1995. Between then and April 2009, Brazil has been involved in 87 disputes: 24 as a complainant, 14 as a respondent, and 49 as a third party. See: WTO, "Dispute cases involving Brazil." Available on-line at: http://www.wto.org/english/thewto_e/countries_e/brazil_e.htm (accessed May 20, 2009).

11. The G20 members are: Argentina, Australia, Brazil, Canada, China, EU, France, Germany, India, Indonesia, Italy, Japan, Mexico, Russia, Saudi Arabia, South Africa, South Korea, Turkey, the United Kingdom, and the United States.

12. MERCOSUR (Common Market of the South) is an inter-governmental trading bloc created by the Asunción Treaty in 1991 that aims to become a Custom Union. It includes Argentina, Brazil, Paraguay, Uruguay, and Venezuela (whose membership is yet to be approved by the Brazilian Congress). Bolivia, Chile, Colombia, Ecuador, and Peru are associate members.

13. UNASUR, the Union of South American Nations, was created in 2005.

14. Joseph Stiglitz argues that at present leftist governments—of a social-democrat orientation—are favorable to the principles of a market economy. Joseph Stiglitz, "Si quieren crecer giren a la izquierda," *El Pais* (September 7, 2008).

15. Argentina's foreign policy in the 1990s maintained a close link with the United States. In contraposition, the presidency of Nestor Kirchner strongly questioned the FTAA negotiations.

16. The Buenos Aires Consensus was signed during a state visit by Lula to Argentina in October 2003.

17. The most important campaign took place in the 1950s when the question of oil nationalization during the second Getúlio Vargas administration became a major issue in domestic and foreign policy. See Mônica Hirst, *Brasil-Estados Unidos: desencontros e afinidades* (Rio de Janeiro: FGV Editora, 2009).

18. World Trade Organization, "Disputes by Country." Available on-line at: http://www.wto.org/english/tratop_e/dispu_e/dispu_by_country_e.htm (accessed: September 3, 2008).

19. Marcelo de Paiva Abreu, an outstanding Brazilian international trade analyst, expressed a negative perspective over Brazil's leeway in the FTAA negotiation process. See Marcelo de Paiva Abreu, Op Ed, *Estado de Sao Paulo* (February 16, 2003).

20. The CAFTA was signed in May 2004.

21. Ministério do Desenvolvimento, Indústria e Comércio Exterior do Brasil, Intercâmbio

comercial brasileiro—países e blocos econômicos, "Intercâmbio Comercial Brasileiro-Estados Unidos" (accessed: September 3, 2008).

22. Bureau of Economic Analysis, International Economic Accounts, U.S. Direct Investment Abroad: Balance of Payments and Direct Investment Position Data, "Position on a historical-cost basis" (accessed: September 9, 2007).

23. Brazil and the United States lead the production of ethanol with a combined output of 89 percent of the world's market. See: Renewable Fuels Association, "Statistics." Available on-line at: http://www.ethanolrfa.org/industry/statistics/#E (accessed May 20, 2009).

24. Renewable Fuels Association, "Statistics." Available on-line at: http://www.ethanol-rfa.org/industry/statistics/#E (accessed May 20, 2009).

25. Woodrow Wilson International Center for Scholars, Brazil Institute Special Report, "The Global Dynamics of Biofuels," April 2007, Issue no. 3.

26. Lula Da Silva, "Building on the B in BRIC," *The Economist* (November 19, 2008).

27. Petrobras, "Exportation." Available on-line at: http://www2.petrobras.com.br/atua-caointernacional/petrobrasmagazine_old/pm52/eng/etanol_3.html (accessed May 20, 2009). Woodrow Wilson International Center for Scholars, Brazil Institute Special Report, "The Global Dynamics of Biofuels," April 2007, Issue no. 3.

28. U.S. House of Representatives, Foreign Affairs Subcommittee on the Western Hemisphere, "Hearing on U.S.—Brazil Relations" (September 19, 2007): 29.

29. The U.S. government has become particularly concerned with the need to improve intelligence and police control in the triple-border area between the cities of Puerto Iguazú (Argentina), Ciudad del Este (Paraguay), and Foz do Iguaçu (Brazil), which the U.S. Federal Bureau of Investigation (FBI) considers a sanctuary for Islamic terrorists. Combined counter-drug efforts have become intense between Brazil and its MERCO-SUR partners in accordance with a Triple Border Security Plan launched in 1998, followed by agreements facilitating extradition and joint police operations. Special attention has also been given to the presence of money laundering, illegal arms, and drug trafficking activities in the area. Rex Hudson, "Terrorist and Organized Crime Groups in the Tri-border Area of South America," *Federal Research Division* (July 2003).

30. Lula Da Silva's foreign policy has sought to expand its relations with the Arab world, and he was the first Brazilian president to travel to the region.According to him, the "invitation for Brazil to participate in the Annapolis Peace Conference in the United States is proof that the country is increasingly regarded as a relevant interlocutor in the region." Joel Santos Guimarães, "For President Lula, Arab countries are key partners," *ASPA* (July 18, 2008).

31. U.S. Department of State, Bureau of International Organization Affairs, *Voting Practices in the United Nations,* 2004 and 2005, "Security Council."

32. The MINUSTAH is the UN's fifth mission in Haiti with the objective of re-establishing institutional order and democracy in the country. Three elements guide its action: the maintenance of order and security, the encouragement of political dialogue with the aim of a national reconciliation, and the promotion of economic and social development. Besides its military command of the mission, Brazil has sent an annual average of 1,200 troops to Haiti since 2003.

33. This idea was expressed by Celso Amorim: "Brazil accepted sending troops and assumed the military command of MINUSTAH above all because it is an operation decided by the Security Council, the only legitimate institution for determining the presence of foreign troops in a sovereign country." Governo Brasileiro, Ministério das Relações Exteriores Discurso do Ministro das Relações Exteriores, "Embaixador Celso Amorim, na sessão de abertura da Reunião Internacional de Alto Nível sobre o Haiti," May 23, 2006.

34. Juan Gabriel Tokatlian, "Haití: una intervención equivocada," *Observatório Politico Sul-Americano* 8 (Julho 2005).

35. Examples include Argentina (2001), Bolivia (2003, 2005), Ecuador (2000, 2005), Haiti (2004), Paraguay (1999), Peru (2000), and Venezuela (2002).

36. In June 2005, Latin American countries refused a U.S. plan to establish a permanent committee of the Organization of American States (OAS) to monitor the exercise of democracy in the hemisphere. See Joel Brinkley, "US Proposal in the OAS Draws Fire as an Attack on Venezuela," *New York Times* (May 22, 2005).
37. Renata Miranda and Denise Chrispim Marin, "Tensão com Chávez aproximou EUA e Lula," *O Estado de São Paulo* (May 7, 2008).
38. Marco Aurélio Garcia, the president's advisor for international affairs, is the main architect of Lula's regional policy.
39. Three stages characterized the Bolivian crisis of 2002–2006: (I) After the presidential victory of Gonzalo Sánchez de Lozada, a protest cycle commenced in opposition to his energy policy and the social costs of his economic program, concluding with his resignation in January 2005. (II) The rise of the vice president Carlos Mesa generated a new protest cycle led by mobilizations in two departments in the west of the country (III) The election of Evo Morales as president, followed by the implementation of an energy policy that nationalized the natural gas resources of the country and the call of a Constitutional Assembly. This led to the rise of a new protest cycle with regards to the autonomy of the departments of Santa Cruz, Panda, and Tarija.
40. Interviews of the author with Lula government officials.
41. "Informação para o Sr. Presidente," *AAS .Despachos com o Presidente*, no. 61/99 (1976).

8 Chile and the United States 2000–2009

From Elusive Friendship to Cooperative Friendship

Claudia F. Fuentes Julio* and Francisco Rojas Aravena

Introduction

The relationship between Chile and the United States has certain historical peculiarities that make it unique in the inter-American context. During the nineteenth century, Chile had been an important rival of the United States for control of the South Pacific. Even during the first part of the twentieth century, when Chile maintained a "status quo" position in international affairs, significant disagreements arose between the two countries every time the United States tried to alter hemispheric policies according to its interests. Chilean foreign policy options at the time, beyond the leanings of the government that happened to be in power, were marked by significant levels of conflict in the bilateral relationship. After Cuba, Chile experienced the longest period of tension with the United States in the previous century, from 1969 to 1989.[1] This situation was analyzed in the mid 1980s by academics such as Heraldo Muñoz and Carlos Portales who described relations between Chile and the United States as an "elusive friendship" where conflict had historically prevailed over cooperation, especially during the final third of the past century.[2]

This chapter suggests that, unlike previous patterns of interaction between them, the current relationship between Chile and the United States is marked by cooperation more than conflict. The meeting in June 2009 between President Barack Obama and President Michelle Bachelet[3] is one of the best examples of the new state of affairs in the bilateral relationship. The Chilean president was the second Latin American leader to visit Obama in an official capacity after Brazil's president Inacio Lula Da Silva, signaling the importance that the new U.S. administration has given to its relationship with Chile within the current Latin American context. The friendly character of the dialogue between the presidents and the mutual agenda discussed at this meeting—ranging from evaluating the results of the Free Trade Agreement to signing an accord on energy policy[4]—are a good sign of the type engagement between these two countries. As stated by President Obama: "I think the relationship that we have with Chile—which, by the way, does not fall in line with U.S. foreign policy on every single issue—but it's a respectful policy. Chile is an important partner. I think that's the model that we want: partnership."[5]

* I dedicate this chapter to the memory of my colleague and good friend, Claudia Castañeda, who passed away during its writing.

The idea of a partnership between both nations was not an original statement from President Obama. In a previous visit of the Chilean president to the United States, she already characterized the relationship as a partnership in the following manner:

> Let me begin by assuring the United States that it can count on Chile as a reliable partner, not an unconditional ally, but certainly an open and frank one, a country that attaches great importance to multilateralism and international law, the principle of consensual solutions to international controversies, and the exhaustion of diplomacy in response to crisis. This partnership with the United States goes beyond any administration in particular, and therefore Chile is ready to collaborate with the new president and his team.[6]

The statements from both presidents reflect the excellent conditions of current bilateral relations and also highlight the historic emergence of a new cooperative relationship, one founded on mutual respect and important common interests.

The nature of the bilateral relationship became evident in the summer of 2003, when one of the more salient events in Chile–U.S. relations took place: the Chilean Delegation to the United Nations Security Council rejected a draft resolution sanctioning a White House proposal for intervention in Iraq. Could a small country like Chile refuse a request by the United States? What consequences would this have on the Free Trade Agreement (FTA) which was being negotiated at the time? How would ties between the two countries be affected? The answers to these questions were much simpler than the Chilean political elite believed at the moment.[7] Not only did Chile sign a FTA with the United States within a few months, but during the following years the relationship deepened to the point where both countries referred to each other as important allies within the hemisphere.[8]

How can the outcome of this impasse be understood? How can a cooperative bilateral agenda that includes a significant degree of international autonomy for Chile be explained? How is it possible for Chile to be characterized as a partner of the United States despite some levels of political disagreement? This chapter addresses these questions and reviews Chile–United States relations from the 1990s to the present. We analyze the bilateral agenda since the return to democracy in Chile and pay special attention to changes and continuities following the events of September 11, 2001.

Early in the present century, the bilateral relationship is defined by the following elements:

1 Chile is not highly dependent on the United States. This is the result of Chile's trade and economic strategy and market diversification plus low levels of strategic dependency (security). This provides Chile with a higher degree of flexibility in its decision-making process.
2 Since the 1990s, converging interests have been observed on three key issues: trade openness, democracy, and security. Chile is seen as a good example of an internal democratization process combined with economic openness, a "model" that the United States is interested in promoting and exporting to the

rest of Latin America. One of the most important components of the agenda during this time was the signing of a Free Trade Agreement, the first between the United States and a developing nation. Converging values and interests gave rise to a number of common practices and a set of institutions for the two countries that have granted greater stability to bilateral relations.

3   Chile is seen as an ally of the United States that enjoys a broad level of independence in making foreign and domestic policy decisions. This opens the door for Chile to act with greater credibility at the international and regional levels. The United States sees this behavior as an asset because it then has an ally with credibility in a region that appears, to the White House, to be undergoing turmoil.

Such factors have produced a unique situation in the history of Chile–United States relations: *a cooperative friendship.* This is different from earlier periods of time, which were permeated by severe tension and ideological confrontation or characterized by an "elusive friendship." Currently, both nations have not only "come in from the cold"[9] but have also grown closer, sharing a common agenda that respects differences and encourages the convergence of initiatives. Such is the opinion of Chile's main political leaders and those in charge of foreign policy. They emphasize the remarkable confluence of interests between the two countries. This conclusion, according to the Chilean minister of foreign affairs Mariano Fernández, is shared by the U.S. Department of State, which has indicated that "relations between both countries are better now than at any other previous moment in history."[10]

This work is divided into three sections. The first describes the principles and objectives of Chilean foreign policy to put the relationship with the United States into context. Some elements of U.S. foreign policy are included, particularly those that pertain to the two George W. Bush administrations. The second section describes milestones in the relationship from 2000 onwards, including Chile's membership in the United Nations Security Council prior to the Iraq war in 2003. The type of relationship between the two countries is analyzed to understand why during this period a relationship based on friendship, cooperation, and mutual respect was achieved. In the third section of this work, the two countries' common agenda is evaluated, along with a description of the institutional mechanisms that shape it. Special attention is given to trade openness, democracy, and security. A number of new themes that emerged in 2005, such as education, energy, and technology, are also considered. Finally, the chapter presents some conclusions on Chile–United States relations and highlights the prospects for strengthening a mutual agenda in the future.

Chile and United States Foreign Policy

Chile's International Strategy since 1990

Since the return to democracy in 1990, Concertación por la Democracia (CPD) governments made international reinsertion a policy priority,[11] followed by a concrete agenda to consolidate Chile's position within the international community.[12] By way of platform goals and mainly through the actions of the four CPD governments,[13] a coherent foreign policy focused on three main themes can be observed: strengthening trade (open regionalism), multilateralism and the promotion of peace, and Chile's integration in Latin America.

The policy of internationalizing the Chilean economy during the 1990s or of open regionalism was one of the greatest innovations in Chilean foreign policy in recent decades and became the main component of the Chilean strategy to open up to the world. Economic insertion sought to consolidate and expand export markets to boost Chilean presence in trade and foreign investment. This was achieved by signing bilateral agreements and not through the unilateral opening that had taken place under the military regime.[14]

Chile currently has a network of signed free trade agreements (FTAs) with 56 countries. These FTAs cover different regions of the world, such as Canada, Mexico, Central America (six countries), the European Union (27 countries), the United States, South Korea, the European Trade Association (4 countries), China, Singapore, New Zealand, Brunei Darussalam (P4), and Japan, representing over 60 percent of the world's population. Seven out of every ten pesos of Chilean wealth come from foreign trade.[15] Chile also enjoys highly diversified trade. The percentages are almost equally divided between U.S., Latin American, and Asian markets.

Chile has purposely expanded into new markets. Asia, and in particular China, has grown increasingly important as a market for Chile since the Free Trade Agreement came into force in 2006. The FTA, first of its kind between China and a Latin American country, generated an important increase of exports to China during 2007 due the international rise of the price of cooper. The increased number of exports to China made this country the first destination of Chilean exports worldwide, superseding for the first time the trade partnership with the United States (Table 8.1).China also plays an important role in helping Chile to maintain a favorable trade surplus. In 2008, more than half of the total net dollars that Chile received due to international trade came from the exchange with China[16].

Chilean trade strategy is not based on a purely state-devised formula. Chilean entrepreneurs worked with the Ministry of Foreign Affairs to finalize international trade agreements and build consensus and obtain ratification at home. This public–private relationship has been key in negotiating the agreements. In many cases,

Table 8.1 Chile's Main Trade Partners, 1997–2008

1997	2000	2004	2008
USA 19%	USA 18%	USA 15%	China 15.6%
Japan 11%	Argentina 10%	China 10%	USA 14.5%
Argentina 7.5%	Japan 9.3%	Argentina 8.5%	Brazil 8.6%
Brazil 6.3%	Brazil 6.6%	Japan 8.4%	Japan 8.4%
South Korea 4.5%	China 5.4%	Brazil 7.8%	Argentina 5.1%
China 3.6%	South Korea 3.8%	South Korea 4.6%	South Korea 4.6%

Source: Data from the Chilean National Customs Service (2008). Trade in millions of U.S. dollars.

it was the entrepreneurs who fostered trade and investment before the treaties had been signed.

Participation in the multilateral system has been historically a central aspect of Chile's insertion into the world.[17] Thus, one main objective of the first CPD governments was to boost Chile's presence in international fora, an objective that was pursued even further by the Ricardo Lagos administration.

> We have said that we are an intermediate country in a complex world in which the types of association and relationships are increasingly diverse, and where cooperation is indispensable if we are to fulfill international obligations, maintain peace and achieve the common good. In the international arena, this country must be in a position not only to seize opportunities but also to face responsibilities.[18]

Peace and international security, defense of human rights, free trade, and social development are some of the issues promoted by Chile at the global level. Chile has focused its efforts on strengthening diverse multilateral settings for the purpose of conflict prevention and the resolution of international disputes.

A key theme in Chilean foreign activities is the preservation of peace and heightening international security, while simultaneously adhering to the concept of human security as a focus of its foreign policy. During the 1990s, Chile started participating in peacekeeping operations: Iraq-Kuwait (1991), Cambodia (1992), Iraq (1996), Bosnia-Herzegovina (1997), East Timor (2000), and Cyprus (2003). In 2004, Chile decided to actively participate in the Multinational Force for Haiti and later in the United Nations Stabilization Mission in Haiti (MINUSTAH). Chile is also active in various UN bodies, with the goal of building international regimes. In fact, since the return to democracy, Chile has been elected twice to a non-permanent seat on the UN Security Council, in spite of a domestic debate on the possible political costs associated with such a decision. Moreover, a recurrent theme in Chilean foreign policy has been the inclusion of democratic clauses in association agreements or in coordinating positions on human rights issues with OAS, MERCOSUR, the Río Group, and even the European Union.

Given Chilean efforts to promote global initiatives, and in spite of a number of convergences with the U.S. agenda, there are also differences in the multilateral arena. For instance, Chile has strongly urged that the UN Framework Convention on Climate Change and the Kyoto Protocol be signed by every country, calling on industrialized countries to step up their efforts to mitigate greenhouse gas emissions and contribute technology and financing to help developing countries face this phenomenon. Unlike the United States, in 2001 Chile ratified the Ottawa Convention on humanitarian de-mining, a central element of its international security policy in line with its participation in the Human Security Network. In addition, even though Chile has not yet ratified the Rome Treaty establishing the International Criminal Court (ICC), this is a priority of the country's diplomats—Chile was one of the first signatories—and it is expected to be approved by the Chilean Congress in spite of disagreement with the White House.

The third key component of Chilean policy is to integrate with the region.[19] Chile has important economic and commercial interests in the subcontinent, which have been promoted through various economic and trade agreements with almost all Latin American countries. During 2008, total Chilean exports to Latin America amounted to U.S.$13 billion, representing an increase of 21.3 percent compared to 2007. This increase is 16.7 percent higher than growth in exports to the entire world. MERCOSUR is Chile's main export market.[20]

Furthermore, Chilean investment abroad is primarily concentrated within the region. Argentina and Peru are the main recipients of Chilean capital flows. So, in spite of having signed trade agreements with various countries at the global level, Chile has important economic ties with the region. Besides the trade agreements between Chile and other countries in the Americas, relevant political initiatives have also been promoted, such as coordination on UN Security Council issues as well as democracy promotion and peacekeeping operations. The "open regionalism" strategy has strongly prioritized the Latin American region.

A substantial part of the Chilean foreign policy agenda for the region deals with neighborhood issues. One of the most salient initiatives in Chilean history and foreign policy in the 1990s was to settle border disputes with Argentina, which eventually led to a strategic relationship between them. Relations with Peru and Bolivia, however, have moved at a slower pace because of the territorial claims by Bolivia and a maritime limits dispute with Peru. Two different rhythms are in play: the problems that exist with Argentina are those of a relationship that progresses in terms of economic and political interdependence, while past issues with Chile's neighbors to the north determine the future agenda on integration, preempting deeper economic and political relations between them and Chile.[21]

Chile–USA in the 1990s: Building Trust

Within the framework of the three foreign policy areas described above, Chile tried to restore its relations with the United States in the early 1990s. Good ties with Washington would help Chile's international reputation, as it attempted its reinsertion into the world after seventeen years of military rule.[22] President Patricio Aylwin was the first Chilean leader to have visited the United States since 1962. Relations became stronger during the subsequent Eduardo Frei administration, a period marked not only by a number of presidential summits but also by the establishment of a Political Consultations System that added an institutional foundation to relations.

The bilateral relationship revolved around the promotion of democracy and trade, which tracked nicely with President William Clinton's agenda. President Frei's address to the U.S. Congress states it clearly:

> My presence here symbolizes a new era of friendship with the people of the United States. We want to leave fears and distrust behind . . . we are neither an economic nor a military power but we want to be a part of the history that is being born. Allies in the solution that is being born. Partners in furthering freedom. Brothers in the promotion of peace and democracy.[23]

In addition to strengthening political-diplomatic ties, the Chilean strategy later turned to improving trade links with the United States. As part of its trade openness strategy, signing a Free Trade Agreement with the United States meant access to the world's largest economy, which represents close to 22 percent of world GDP—a country with an annual per capita income of U.S.$35,400 and a market 148 times the size of the Chilean market.[24] For more than twelve years, Chile–U.S. relations were centered around the negotiations over this agreement, which was signed in June 2003. From the U.S. standpoint, the agreement opened the way for similar negotiations with other developing countries. Chile was a good example of sound economics and political stability in a democracy. During his 1998 visit to Chile, President Clinton underscored the importance of the FTA:

> We want and will resolutely pursue a free trade agreement that includes our two nations and will not be satisfied until we have achieved that objective. Chile and the United States should be full partners in the twenty-first century. We should also fully associate ourselves with the democracies of our regions with similar aspirations.[25]

Finally, progress was also made on the security and defense agenda. In 1991, the United States repealed the Kennedy Amendment, which had prohibited the sale of arms to Chile, and for the first time a civilian Chilean minister of defense visited Washington . The trip paved the way for developing a common agenda in the areas of military training and educational exchanges. That same year, the Armed Forces of Chile participated in "Joint Forces-Chile 21" and "UNITAS XXXII," their first joint military training exercises with U.S. forces.

United States Foreign Policy towards Chile

Even though U.S. policies in Latin America had become more bilateral, this did not result in specialized individual policies for each country, with the exception of "crisis" cases. The Bush administration was known for its "radical unilateralism," which led to increased rejection of its central policies throughout the world: the war against terrorism and the invasion of Iraq.[26]

Global changes and the aftermath of 9/11 led the United States to lower even further its priorities for Latin America and the attention it paid to the region. Within the global framework, Latin America had little relevance. In the traditional "intervention/forget" pattern, this "forget" portion of the cycle was long. As a result, the region enjoyed a higher degree of autonomy and developed more independent foreign policies. Geographical proximity, however, has a big impact on many countries in the region. In those cases, special attention must be paid to migration and border safety issues. However, Chile, so distant from the U.S. border, does not rank high on the agenda as a threat in migration and drug trafficking issues.

In this context, we note three features of the Chile-U.S. agenda in the 1990s:

First, *common interests*. This agenda promoted the triad of free trade, democracy, and security. Chile wanted to reassert itself internationally as a democratic country, respectful of human rights, while simultaneously formulating a domestic growth platform based on a trade openness strategy. It wanted to be recognized as a "serious" country in the region and the world with well-grounded policies in areas essential in achieving national development and regional and global stability. A good relationship with the United States would allow Chile to realize these goals. From the U.S. standpoint, Chile was seen as a "good student"—i.e., responsible— in the region, helping to advance its three-pronged agenda at the regional and international levels.

Second, *flexibility in Chilean foreign policy.* One of Chile's goals was to strengthen its international insertion in markets and multilateral fora. The relationship with the United States was a key part of this global strategy within the broader framework of connecting with Latin America and other regions.

Third, *an international environment that allowed a cooperative relationship to be built.* In the early 1990s, the bilateral relationship developed against the background of the end of the Cold War and subsequent U.S. supremacy, making it possible to develop a more cooperative agenda with Latin America in general and Chile in particular.

Chile and the United States since 9/11

The new millennium looked promising for U.S.–Latin America relations. President Bush expressed his intention, shortly after his inauguration, to place a higher priority on inter-American relations. The terrorist attacks in New York, Washington, and Pennsylvania, however, forced a realignment of priorities and a change in U.S. strategy for the region and the world.

Relations between the United States and Chile since 2001 can be divided into three periods. From 2001 to 2003, the relationship freezes. The United States was addressing important changes in its international policy and Chile had no priority on that agenda. As a result, a low intensity bilateral relationship is observed. The next stage, from 2003 to 2005, is characterized by both freezing and readjustment. This coincides with Chile's decision to reject the U.S. invasion of Iraq (2003) and the consequences of this decision. In the third stage, beginning in late 2005, the bilateral relationship is reactivated. An agenda is formulated based on mutual cooperation that includes the traditional themes of democracy, trade, and security. A new agenda is also created that focuses more heavily on education and energy, as well as relations with other countries in the region.

Chile's refusal to side with the United States in the Iraq case marked the agenda during this time-period and it constitutes a major turning point for the bilateral relationship. Contrary to expectations, this decision prompted a series of positive responses from the United States and a change in its perception of Chile and the role that it could play in Latin America.

Towards the end of February 2003, Chile and Mexico were non-permanent members of the UN Security Council.[27] In a coordinated move, both made it known that a decision regarding Iraq should comply with UN requirements and that it was up to the superpowers to reach such an agreement. Chile proposed that additional time be allowed for new inspections to be carried out and to give Iraq the opportunity to provide the international community with additional information. On March 17, however, the Chilean Ministry of Foreign Affairs received a "non-paper" from the United States stating that Washington would not seek a new resolution since the time for continued inspections had ended. The document expressed the "hope that you will instruct your United Nations delegation to work with us, not against us, to face the challenges that await us."[28] This left Chile in the uncomfortable and unavoidable position of having to make a final decision on the issue.

The signals coming from the White House calling for Chilean support were strong and direct. As early as January 2003, the U.S. national security advisor, Condoleezza Rice, had called the minister secretary general of the Government of Chile, Heraldo Muñoz, to tell him: "We would like our friends to be on our side in this. Of course, when the time comes to vote in the Security Council, abstention will not be good enough . . . all is at stake here."[29] In addition, Otto Reich, the person in charge of hemispheric affairs for the U.S. government, indicated while visiting Chile that "we want to hear Chile's opinion through its president. President Bush has spoken with him, but it is always good to come personally and consult with friends." At that time, the United States was receiving positive reports about Chilean support in the Security Council and did not consider the possible refusal of a country that had been such a good political and commercial partner. The Bush administration seemed to have perceived Chile as a sure vote for the United States, without considering the fact that Chile had a long tradition of defending international law. Chile faced a serious dilemma.

The Chilean decision was complicated because it meant putting the principles of multilateralism and peace promotion before specific economic and commercial interests vis-à-vis the United States. It seemed that the entire relationship built during the 1990s was crumbling. Washington was also sending messages suggesting that this situation could endanger the signing of the Free Trade Agreement, which had been under negotiation since the early 1990s. Without a doubt, Chile's refusal to support the use of force in Iraq would threaten the agreement, a cornerstone of Chile–U.S. relations during the previous decade. According to media speculation, a Chilean vote against the United States would elicit "a moment of revenge."[30] This view gained strength after Robert Zoellick, the U.S. trade representative, became one of the first American officials to criticize the Chilean position on Iraq. Zoellick stated that there was no firm date to sign the FTA, adding that the Bush administration was disappointed by the Chilean position. "We worked very closely with our Chilean partners. We expected their support at a moment that we considered important."[31]

On the domestic side, polls showed that over 80 percent of the Chilean population opposed the war.[32] Such an overwhelming consensus afforded the Chilean government an opportunity to expand its support base as long as it acted accordingly at the international level. As Joaquín Fermandois observed, there was a return to the old anti-Americanism among Chilean criticisms of the war and it became part of the political debate in Chile while the matter was being discussed by the United Nations. Among the Concertación political parties there was a clear trend in favor of opposing the war, while only a portion of the right-wing conveyed the need to support the United States.

Another element had to be considered when examining U.S. arguments for the war. The Chilean Ministry of Foreign Affairs was not convinced by the evidence supplied by the United States to back up the assertion that the Iraqi government possessed weapons of mass destruction. Chile also did not agree with the idea of intervening for the purpose of deposing the Hussein regime to impose a democratic political system on a country and region in turmoil. In the end, given this lack of certainty regarding the reasons behind the U.S. intervention in Iraq, Chilean support would amount to "almost automatic alignment"[33] with the White House. This was viewed with concern by the Chilean government, which wanted to show the international community, and particularly the region, a certain level of autonomy and flexibility in foreign policy decision making.

The failure of UN negotiations led Chile to issue a declaration reaffirming its interests:

> Chile, inspired by the principles that permanently guide its foreign policy, has made every effort to achieve a diplomatic solution to reach the common goal of disarming Iraq. The proposals made by our country last Friday were made with that constructive purpose in mind. We believed that there was still room for reaching an agreement and avoiding the use of force, the last resource available to the UN Security Council.[34]

In the end, Chile opted for a course of action that was consistent and coherent with its diplomatic tradition: to favor multilateral policy, search for agreements within the United Nations framework, and the peaceful resolution of conflict. Even though this presented the very real risk of throwing away more than ten years of Free Trade Agreement negotiations, the political costs of limiting Chile's autonomy in the international arena were considered even higher by Chilean policymakers. Chile's reasoning indicated that, in the middle and long term, its interests were better served by reasserting the primacy of multilateralism and international law.

The White House promptly expressed its disappointment with Chile's and Mexico's decisions on Iraq. Chile was sent to the "distant friends" list. In spite of the obvious discontent of U.S. authorities, the most direct impact of the decision was a delay in signing the Free Trade Agreement. Yet, only a few months later, on June 6, 2003, the FTA was signed and the United States reiterated its willingness to formalize such an instrument with a friendly country like Chile. In terms of the FTA, Chile did not pay a cost for opposing the invasion of Iraq. U.S. ambassador to Chile, Paul Simons, agrees with this interpretation, indicating that the impact of the Chilean refusal was minimal and that progress continued on an agenda that "was being drafted since the 1990s."

The Chilean decision, however, did have other consequences for bilateral relations with the United States. As confirmed by Chilean academics and politicians interviewed for this article, there was a medium-term effect: a change in the U.S. perception of Chile. The White House no longer saw Chile as an unconditional ally, as was the case before the UN Security Council episode, but as a friendly country possessing a degree of autonomy in international decisions, and therefore, with a higher level of credibility both regionally and globally. As a result, the Iraq issue opened the door to a realization by the United States that Chile could play an important role in relations with other Latin American countries. Ambassador Carlos Appelgren, head of the Directorate for North America of the Ministry of Foreign Affairs of Chile, indicated that:

> Chile showed the United States that in terms of relations with Latin America, it was more convenient to have an ally who shared the principles of democracy and political and economic freedoms, yet one which simultaneously maintained its independence and therefore enjoyed credibility in the region. An unconditional ally cannot play a role in the region.

This opinion is shared by the undersecretary for war of the Ministry of Defense of Chile, Gonzalo García, who believes that Chile can play a positive role in bringing opinions together without being an instrument of U.S. policy.

This shift in the U.S. perception stemming, in part, from the Iraq episode, created a space for increased exchanges and cooperation between the two countries. Not only did the traditional agenda move forward, but new themes found their way onto it. In the end, the post 9/11 consequences in the medium-term were not a distancing of relations, as was the case with other Latin American countries. Not long after the Security Council incident, the intensity of Chile–U.S. relations increased, based not only on common interests but also on recognition of the possibilities and limits that the liaison could have in regional affairs. In sum, the relationship became more firmly grounded and featured opportunities for enhanced cooperation.

Main Topics on the Chile-United States Agenda

From the year 2000 onward, the major themes continued to be trade openness, security, and democracy. Twelve years of trade negotiations had come to an end when the Free Trade Agreement was signed, causing the trade relationship to deepen greatly. In addition, advances were made on security issues but, unlike in a majority of Latin American countries, these focused more on traditional security issues, including military training and education, joint exercises, and scientific cooperation on defense. There was no turn towards a "securitization" of the agenda in those areas linked to the fight against terrorism, transnational issues (drug trafficking, migration, etc.), or the use of the military in police tasks. With respect to democracy, Chile has been especially interested in strengthening democracy in Latin America, which the United States viewed positively as a formula for interacting with the region.

Since mid-2000s, the Chile-U.S. agenda has become stronger and been expanded to include less traditional topics. These include programs on education, science and technology, as well as energy, which has been an especially salient topic. For Chile, these new topics are particularly relevant because they hold a preferential place in national development and contribute to a more diverse and intensive agenda that is effective not only at the state level but also brings new actors into the bilateral relationship.

Apart from the common political interests that have encouraged positive bilateral relations, the mutual agenda has been strengthened by the creation of a set of common institutions. One current characteristic of the bilateral relationship has been the establishment of permanent mechanisms for dialogue, cooperation, and conflict resolution. The result is a set of institutions that provide a solid structure for common practices, reinforcing mutual trust and implementation of the agreements. According to Ambassador Simons, creating permanent institutions at the bilateral level is what distinguishes relations with Chile and sets them apart from those that the United States maintains with the rest of the Latin America. "The confidence in Chilean institutions and the creation of common mechanisms," according to Simons, has allowed a solid relationship to be built. U.S. vice president, Joseph Biden, during his recent visit to Chile was emphatic: "your institutions are institutions that the institutions in the United States enjoy working with. They are, they know, are equals and share mutual respect."[35]

Table 8.2 Institutional Mechanisms between Chile and United States

Topics	Institutions/ mechanisms	
Presidential Summits (various issues)	Patricio Aylwin	George H. W. Bush
	Eduardo Frei	Bill Clinton
	Ricardo Lagos	George W. Bush
	Michelle Bachelet	Barack Obama
Foreign Relations	Political-Strategic Committee	
Security and Defense	Defense Advisory Committee (CCD)	
	Political and Strategic Affairs Advisory Committee (CCAPE)	
Trade	Free Trade Commission, which oversees the following:	
	The Sanitary and Phytosanitary Committee	
	Working Group on Agricultural Trade	
	Government Procurement Committee	
	Financial Services Committee	
	Committee on Technical Barriers to Trade	
	Environmental Affairs Council	
	Committee on Temporary Entry	
	Committee on Trade in Goods	
	Labor Affairs Council	
Education, Science and Technology	Mixed Commission on Science and Technology	
	Chile-California Plan (cooperation on education, agricultural, energy and environmental issues)	
	Equal Opportunities Scholarship Program	
Others	Inter-Congressional Friendship Group	
	Chambers of Commerce (AMCHAM)	

Table set up by the authors. Information from www.minrel.cl, www.direcon.cl.

As demonstrated in Table 8.2, every topic on the bilateral agenda has a corresponding institutional mechanism. Since the 1990s, the presidential summits mechanism has paved the way for other institutions in the economic and social realms. This can be seen, beginning in 2004, with the creation of the Free Trade Commission and its committees, as well as with the establishment in 2006 of a series of commissions on education, science, and technology. Moreover, in 2006 committees on security and defense issues began to meet again on a periodic basis. Thus, relations between Chile and the United States became tighter at the institutional level, which has made it possible to maintain a solid relationship regardless of which administration is in power in either country.

Cooperation and Convergence: Trade Openness, Security and Democracy

Free Trade Agreement and Trade Openness

Within the Chilean strategy of trade openness, the treaty with the United States is of special significance. It symbolized greater and broader access by its products to the largest and most stable economy, which led the way toward the "new economy." Chile was able to rely on clear and permanent rules for the trade of goods and services and for investments, making it easier for Chileans doing business with United States to make decisions, while stimulating a greater level of U.S. investment in Chile.[36] From the U.S. point of view, as stated by President Bush when requesting FTA approval in July 2003, the agreement "will enhance prosperity in the United States and Chile, serve the interests of expanding U.S. commerce, and advance our overall national interest."[37] Additionally, the agreement was seen as a formula for expanding this type of treaty within Latin America. Bush stated this quite eloquently:

> The U.S.-Chile FTA is the first United States Free Trade agreement with a Latin American country. We hope that the FTA will add momentum to Chile's continued implementation of the free market open economies policies that have made Chile a model for its Latin American neighbors. This agreement will also encourage other countries in the Western Hemisphere to follow Chile's path, furthering our efforts to establish a Free Trade Area of the Americas.[38]

The treaty created a solid free trade zone between both countries. Most analysts concluded that it was an equitable and integral agreement that incorporated most aspects of the relationship, such as the trade in goods, government procurement, the promotion and protection of foreign investments, cross-border services and intellectual property rights protection. Furthermore, it addressed topics related to the environment and labor, which had been gaining relevance on the international trade agenda.

The Free Trade Agreement entered into force on January 1, 2004, and the results have been positive. According to the Chilean Directorate for International

Economic Relations (DIRECON), during the first five years of the Chile-U.S. FTA trade has grown by 155 percent. During 2007, exports totaled U.S.$8.7 billion, showing an increase of 135.9 percent over the last year before the FTA entered into effect, representing an average annual growth rate of 21.8 percent for the period 2004–2007.[39] Imports from the United States grew during the first four years of the FTA by 183 percent. The United States is the number one individual supplier of goods and services purchased abroad by Chile. Moreover, Chile's export structure to the United States is focused mainly on industrial products. The U.S. market is the number one individual destination for these types of Chilean exports, increasing the value added to Chilean exports and encouraging further industrial growth.

Security and Defense

The positive state of relations between Chile and the United States on security-related issues is centered primarily around topics on the defense agenda. There is good reason why the Pentagon has qualified Chile as a priority partner in its regional defense strategy. The U.S. secretary of defense, Robert Gates, is clear when defining the relationship with Chile:

> Our bilateral defense relationship with Chile is strong because it is driven by our shared values of democracy, market economy and a commitment to social justice and human rights . . . These values strengthen our countries and results in better governments, growing economies, lowering poverty rates and more effective defense against today's challenges and threats.[40]

The United States, therefore, sees Chile as a model it can work with to expand its political vision and it uses the security and defense agenda as a formula for achieving this objective.

From the Chilean point of view, it is important to strengthen defense ties because the United States is the primary military power in the world and for two other reasons as well. First, the United States is a guarantor to the Treaty of Ancón, which set borders with Peru in 1929. Within the context of Peru's demand to modify maritime limits with Chile, a positive relationship with the United States can be important if difficulties arise. In fact, in January 2008 the Peruvian government presented its case on maritime limits to the International Court of Justice and, in March 2009, it stated its position and entered its arguments before the Court. Chile has until 2010 to enter its arguments in response to the demand.

The second reason is access to American materiel. Following the repeal of the Kennedy amendment banning the sale of arms to Chile, the country bought a number of F16 fighter aircraft in 2002. Even though Chile does not depend exclusively on American weapons, having widened its sources (Holland), it is important to establish closer links with the United States on issues such as training and military education as well as research and development.

Relations based on defense issues experienced a resurgence following the renewal of annual meetings of the Defense Advisory Committee and the Political and Strategic Affairs Advisory Committee in 2006. They had been suspended in 2003.

Since 2006, the parties have developed a promising defense program that was implemented thanks to a series of official visits by the Chilean minister of defense to the United States and by the U.S. secretary of defense to Chile. This defense program focuses on three priorities.[41]

First, global political initiatives. This is centered around participation in or support for multilateral initiatives such as the Global Initiative to Combat Nuclear Terrorism. Moreover, one area with the greatest degree of convergence is Chile's participation in the peacekeeping operation in Haiti (MINUSTAH). The United States considers this an important contribution to peace in the hemisphere. "The United States is especially grateful for Chile's effort in Haiti. Your leadership and bond with the Haitian people has fostered stability and created space for institutions," declared U.S. defense secretary Gates.[42]

Second is the subject of inter-operability. One of the proposed goals is to improve the level of military exercises between the United States and Chile. Although joint exercises have been carried out since the 1990s, the level of exchange should deepen to develop new practices between both armies and to share knowledge regarding modernization of the military.

Third, increase the amount of exchanges in science and technology and education. Also since 2006, there have been a number of memoranda of understanding on information exchange related to research and development, exchanges involving scientists and military engineers, as well as sharing new technologies. With respect to educational issues, there has also been an increase in the number of exchanges between military academies and educational institutions in both countries. For example, at the beginning of 2009, an agreement was signed between the state of Texas and Chile on a wide-ranging military cooperation program. By way of the State Partnership Program of the Texas National Guard, the State of Texas will make available its 23 thousand men and women, including soldiers in the Army National Guard and officials in the Air National Guard, for various exchange activities related to human capacity building, education and training, as well as civilian skills to be shared with Chile.

Finally, relations between the United States and Chile on broader security issues such as drug trafficking or antiterrorism are very limited. Chile does not receive U.S. assistance in these areas beyond a minimum amount of exchanges and training on police matters and judicial reforms. Unlike many other countries in the region, the United States has not fostered this type of assistance because these problems occur at such a low rate within Chilean territory. Moreover, Chilean civilian and military leaders have insisted on separating the security and defense agenda into different spheres of action. Certainly, security issues on the agendas of many Latin American countries, and U.S. support for them, is an aspect that concerns Chilean political actors and the Chilean armed forces.

Democracy

Since the 1990s, relations between the United States and Chile have been based on Chile's recognition of the need to preserve and strengthen its democratic government. In contrast with what took place during the 1960s and 1970s, when both countries had conflicting views about the best way to generate political and economic development, the reestablishment of democracy in Chile played a major role in bringing both countries closer together. As noted, Chile needed the United States to help with recognition of its democratic credentials at the international level in the "West." The United States not only joined in the spirit of democracy that re-emerged within the Hemisphere at the beginning of the 1990s, but also simultaneously turned toward trade openness and economic reform.

At the beginning of 2000, the situation was less auspicious with respect to democratic progress, at least within the region. Although Latin America shows substantial advances in terms of electoral democracy, the quality of democracy leaves much to be desired in a majority of countries within the region. Moreover, many Latin American countries have political systems with low levels of credibility and face economic and social problems that democratically elected governments have been unable to resolve. The result is recurrent institutional crises and the search for less than democratic solutions to these problems. In these circumstances, democratic governability in the region has become an important goal of Chilean foreign policy and a growing concern for the United States.

This explains why the Chilean Foreign Policy Book (2008) stresses that the "principal objective of foreign policy with respect to the United States is deepening bilateral actions via policies and actions that are centered around our commitment to Latin America."[43] Certainly the United States wants to be able to count on an ally in resolving crises in Latin America, especially considering the fact that relations with certain governments in the region were very tense at the end of the Bush administration. Chile's participation, together with other Latin American nations, in the UN peace-keeping operation in Haiti (MINUSTAH) embodies the search for cooperative resolutions to institutional crises in the region. Within this same context, Chile worked with the United States and other Latin American countries to reach agreement on the Inter-American Democratic Charter of the Organization of American States—one of the primary mechanisms for preventing conflict and institutional crises in the region—which was signed in September 2001.

Nevertheless, it is not very clear what type of initiatives Chile wants or could foster with the United States to strengthen the democratic agenda in the region. The United States may believe that Chile can play a positive role on this subject within the region, promoting an agenda much nearer to its political and trade interests. The resolution of regional crises can, on the one hand, bring the positions of Chile and the United States closer, but on the other, it may generate differences between them because of dissimilar views on each case. Cuba is the most obvious example. One of the greatest future tasks for the bilateral relationship will be to find a way to advance bilateral relations in accord with the challenges that face the entire Latin American region.

The New Agenda

At the beginning of the Bachelet administration, work was being carried out not only on the traditional triad of issues for both countries but important developments began on matters linked to the social and economic agendas. These include education, cooperation on science and technology, the environment, energy, etc. This section describes the work being done on education and energy as an example of how the new bilateral agenda has developed.

Education

Educational exchanges and cooperation is one area where significant advances have been made at the bilateral level. One general objective of the Chilean government has been to make it possible for Chilean students to study in developed countries via scholarships. One of the star joint Chile-U.S. programs in the area of education is an agreement reached in 2007 that set up the "Equal Opportunities" scholarship program. This agreement states that each year 100 Chilean students can begin doctoral studies in U.S. universities with scholarships financed by the Chilean government. The U.S. government has brought together more than 50 universities, including some of the most prestigious institutions in the country, ranked among the best in the world, to join in this initiative. In the medium term, this agreement also promotes exchange programs and internships for professors and academics, development of joint scientific research projects, and working together to develop doctoral programs.[44]

Energy

Both Chile and the United States have defined energy security as a key issue for national development. From the Chilean standpoint, problems with the energy supply are a constant source of public concern due primarily to dependence on imported energy sources. Dependence on international markets has raised economic and supply problems for Chile. In December 2004, Argentina began to restrict exports of natural gas to Chile. This forced Chilean authorities to reconsider energy policies, which were based on cooperation with neighbors, primarily Argentina. Today, Chile seeks to diversify its energy matrix and create incentives for generating energy through non-traditional sources.[45] For the United States, energy security is essential, given the steep fluctuations in the price of oil. The Obama administration will emphasize collaboration on energy-related investments with a number of Latin American countries.[46]

The U.S. ambassador to Chile, Paul Simons, an expert on this topic, has contributed to the formation of a dynamic bilateral agenda on energy. Bilateral cooperation on energy consists of four areas of work:[47] (a) Energy efficiency, to which end bilateral cooperation programs on good practices are being developed. (b) Cooperation on producing renewable energies, such as solar energy, bio-fuels, etc. (c) Exploring nuclear energy to expand the Chilean energy matrix. The United States has organized visits by experts on nuclear matters to Chile. (d) Strengthening energy planning and design international public policies on this issue.

Conclusions

Relations between Chile and the United States are currently enjoying one of the best moments in history. In spite of changes to U.S. foreign policy following the 2001 terrorist attacks, making it more unilateral in nature and more focused on international security, the bilateral relationship between Chile and the United States has followed a different path. One of the most noteworthy characteristics of the current relationship is a vision shared by both Chilean and U.S. political actors on common values and goals, thus encouraging the search for areas of convergence in bilateral relations as well as regionally and internationally.

The relationship between these two countries has deepened, built on an agenda that has been continuously developed since the 1990s and includes trade openness, democracy, and security. Yet, issues specifically related to the post 9/11 agenda have not been incorporated, such as the fight against terrorism and its links with drug trafficking, topics that do shape relations with other Latin American countries. The Chilean-U.S. agenda has grown over the past three years to include social and economic development areas and aims to strengthen issues such as education and cooperation in energy. Even though differences exist between Chile and the United States on global initiatives, it is quite likely that there will be more harmony in the coming years as the Obama administration turns towards an international policy that stresses greater multilateralism.

Reasons for the positive state of relations between both countries can be summarized into four points. First, both countries share a set of common values on how to build a democratic society given similar economic systems. Unlike previous periods in history, today Chile and the United States share a similar vision on the domestic development models used by both countries and how they are linked to the foreign policy objectives that have been pursued since 1990.

Second, common interests paved the way for a complex institutional framework and common practices that have significantly strengthened bilateral relations. Institutions have made it possible to develop a dialogue and concrete instances of cooperation between both countries. The latter provides stability to the relationship and eases the resolution of conflicts when necessary.

Third, Chilean foreign policy favors a model of multiple insertions in the international arena. Diversifying its markets allowed Chile to enjoy more autonomy in its international decisions. It has made it possible to have more independence in its relations with the United States, proven by Chile's experience in the United Nations Security Council. In spite of being a small country on the international stage, this flexibility and autonomy have allowed Chile to position itself as a more significant actor when dealing with the main world power.

Fourth, the United States sees in Chile a political and economic development model that it would like to "export" to the rest of the region. U.S. interest is not based on Chile's predominance in military or economic matters (such as Brazil, for example), but rather on how Chile can project a political model to the rest of Latin America, show leadership, and bring about consensus in the region. Chile is seen by the United States as "part of the solution and not part of the problem"[48] in the region and, to a lesser extent, at the international level. For its part, Chile has demonstrated its intention to deepen bilateral relations with the United States within the context of its interests in Latin America. Therefore, one of the main themes for the future is whether positive relations between Chile and the United States can be turned into a focal point for synergy and greater consensus within the region. For this to happen, both countries, together with the rest of Latin America, will have to work on a common vision for facing the immediate challenges that confront the region.

Bachelet's meeting with Obama in the White House reflects a move in such direction. It reiterates the intention of the new U.S. administration to follow a strategy in which increasing the ties with Chile is seen as a formula to build bridges with the rest of the region and it also recognizes that this country possess important political leadership and negotiation capacity among Latin American countries. The dialogue between the presidents was fundamentally centered on how to engage in a better hemispheric dialogue to respond more effectively to political and economic crisis in the region.[49] In Obama's words:

> I look to President Bachelet for good advice and good counsel in terms of how the United States can continue to build a strong relationship with all of Latin America. And I think the good progress that we began to make at the Summit of the Americas can be built on with some very concrete steps in the months and years to come. We consider Chile to be one of our most important partners in that process. And so I expect that in the months to come we'll be working very closely together.[50]

For now, U.S–Chile relations are in very good standing and with even better prospects for the future. The bilateral agenda has expanded and strengthened in the past years, and the relationship is extending its frontiers to build a new partnership in the context of strengthening inter-American relations. The political momentum is optimal for such a new engagement. President Obama has significant political capital in Latin America. This will help him gain the region's trust as long as the United States once again upholds international law, multilateralism, and international institutions. Within this context, Chile can be a privileged partner of the United States within Latin America.

Interviews

Appelgren, Carlos. Director for North America, Central American and the Caribbean. Chilean Ministry of Foreign Affairs.

Cheyre, Juan Emilio. Director, Center for International Studies, Catholic University of Chile.

Fermandois, Joaquín. Professor, History Department, Catholic University of Chile.

García, Jaime. War Department, Chilean Ministry of Defense.

Muñoz, Heraldo. Chilean Ambassador to the United Nations

Simons, Paul. United States Ambassador to Chile.

Notes

1. David Mares and Francisco Rojas Aravena, *Coming in from the Cold: The United States and Chile* (New York: Routledge, 2001); Paul E. Sigmund, *The Overthrow of Allende and the Politics of Chile, 1964–1976* (Pittsburgh: University of Pittsburgh Press, 1977); Joaquin Fermandois, *Chile y el Mundo 1970–1973: La Política Exterior del Gobierno de la Unidad Popular y el Sistema Internacional* (Santiago: Universidad Católica, 1985).
2. Heraldo Muñoz and Carlos Portales, *Una Amistad Esquiva: Las Relaciones de Estados Unidos y Chile* (Santiago: Pehuén, 1987).
3. For details see "Remarks by President Obama and President Bachelet of Chile after Meeting," The White House—Office of the Press Secretary, June 23, 2009.
4. The presidents discussed a broad agenda including commerce and the impact of the financial crisis, science and technology, health, and the impact of the avian flu. They also signed a Memorandum of Cooperation in Energy Technologies.
5. "Chile's Bachelet Meets with Obama in Washington," *The Santiago Times*, Wednesday, June 24, 2009. More U.S. press coverage on the visit: ABC news, June 23, 2009; *Los Angeles Times*, June 23; *Americas Quarterly*, June 29. For a perspective from Chile on this topic see: *La Tercera*, Reportajes, June 28, 2009. http://www.latercera.com.
6. Michelle Bachelet, speech at the Council of Foreign Relations, 2008. http://www.cfr.org/publication/17372/conversation_with_michelle_bachelet.html?br eadcrumb=%2Fissue%2F104%2Frule_of_law.
7. Joaquin Fermandois, "Chile y la Guerra en Irak 2003," *Bicentenario. Revista de Historia de Chile y América* 17, N01 (2008).
8. Claudio Fuentes S., "La apuesta por el 'Poder Blando': Política exterior de la concerta-ción," in *El Gobierno de Ricardo Lagos: La Nueva Vía Chilena al Socialismo,* ed. Robert Funk (Santiago de Chile: Antartica, 2008).
9. David Mares and Francisco Rojas Aravena, *Coming in from the Cold.*
10. Mariano Fernández, "Chilean-US relationships are in good shape," in *Visions from Finis Terrae. Chilean Voices in the United States,* ed. Pablo Arriarán (Washington, DC: Inter-American Dialogue, 2008), 16.
11. Francisco Rojas Aravena, *La reinserción internacional de Chile. La política exterior del gobierno democrático marzo-diciembre 1990* (Santiago: FLACSO-Chile, 1991). Francisco Rojas Aravena, *De la reinserción a los acuerdos. La política exterior chilena en 1991* (Santiago: FLACSO-Chile, 1992).
12. On Chilean foreign policy during the Concertación governments see: Claudia Fuentes J. and Claudio Fuentes S., "Las Relaciones Exteriores del Chile Democrático," in *Chile: Política y Modernización Democrática,* ed. Manuel Alcántara Sáez and Leticia M. Ruiz Rodríguez (Barcelona: Bellaterra, 2006).
13. This refers to the governments of Patricio Aylwin (1990–1994), Eduardo Frei (1994–2000), Ricardo Lagos (2000–2006) and Michelle Bachelet (2006–2010).
14. For an excellent analysis of Chilean foreign relations during the military government see Heraldo Muñoz, *Las Relaciones Exteriores del Gobierno Militar Chileno* (Santiago: Editorial Ornitorrinco, 1986).
15. Ministry of Foreign Affairs of Chile, *Principios y Prioridades de la Política Exterior de Chile* (Santiago de Chile: Government de Chile, 2008).
16. Ministerio de Relaciones Exteriores de Chile, DIRECON, "Relaciones Económicas entre Chile y China: Evaluación a tres años del TLC," October 2009. http://cms.chileinfo.com/documentos/EVAL_3_AGNOS_TLC_CHINA.pdf.
17. Alberto van Klaveren, "Inserción Internacional de Chile," in *Chile en los noventa,* ed. Cristian Toloza and Eugenio Lahera (Santiago: Presidencia de la República/Dolmen, 1998).
18. José Miguel Insulza, *Ensayos sobre Política Exterior de Chile* (Santiago de Chile: Editorial los Andes, 1998), 61.

19. Claudia Fuentes J. and Claudio Fuentes S., "¡¡Good bye! América Latina?" *Revista de Sociología,* School of Social Sciences, University of Chile (2004): 37–52.
20. DIRECON, "Comercio Exterior de Chile. Cuarto Trimestre de 2008," February 2009.
21. Claudia Fuentes J. and Claudio Fuentes, "Las Relaciones Exteriores del Chile Democrático."
22. David Mares and Francisco Rojas Aravena, *Coming in from the Cold,* 15–24.
23. David Mares and Francisco Rojas Aravena, *Coming in from the Cold,* 18.
24. Osvaldo Rosales, "Chile-U.S Free Trade Agreement: lessons and best practices," DIRECON,
    http://www.direcon.cl/documentos/TLC%20EEUU/ChileUS%20Free%20Trade%20
    Agreement%20lessons%20and.pdf.
25. David Mares and Francisco Rojas Aravena, *Coming in from the Cold,* 19.
26. Francisco Rojas Aravena, "Unilateralismo Radical y América Latina," in *Bajo la mirada del halcón. Estados Unidos–América Latina post 11/9/2001,* ed. Claudio Fuentes (Buenos Aires: Biblos/FLACSO Chile, 2004), 9–18.
27. The section on Chile's participation in the United Nations Security Council is based on interviews with Heraldo Muñoz and Juan Gabriel Valdés. However, the final content is the responsibility of the authors.
28. Joaquín Fermandois, "Chile y la Guerra de Irak 2003," *Bicentenario. Revista de Historia de Chile y América* 17, No. 1 (2008): 46.
29. Heraldo Muñoz, *Una Guerra Solitaria. La Historia Secreta de EE.UU. en Irak, la polémica en la ONU y el papel de Chile* (Santiago de Chile: Randolph House Mondadori, 2005), 19.
30. Heraldo Muñoz, *Una Guerra Solitaria.*
31. Heraldo Muñoz, *Una Guerra Solitaria,* 145.
32. Joaquín Fermandois, "Chile y la Guerra de Irak 2003."
33. Joaquín Fermandois, "Chile y la Guerra de Irak 2003," 71.
34. Cited in Claudio Fuentes S., "La apuesta por el 'Poder Blando': Política exterior de la concertación," in *El Gobierno de Ricardo Lagos: La Nueva vía Chilena al Socialismo, ed.* Robert Funk. (Santiago de Chile: Antartica, 2008).
35. Vice President Joseph Biden's remarks to the media at La Moneda, United States Embassy in Chile, http://chile.usembassy.gov/OpenNews/asp/pagDefault.asp?arg InstanciaId=2&argNoticiaId=4500&argEdicionId=41.
36. Osvaldo Rosales, "Chile-U.S Free Trade Agreement: lessons and best practices."
37. George W. Bush, "The United States-Chile Free Trade Agreement," message from the president of the United States transmitting a draft of proposed legislation and supporting documents to implement the United States-Chile Free Trade Agreement (FTA), pursuant to 19 U.S.C. 3805(a)(1)(A) and (B). (Washington: U.S. Government Printing Office, 2003).
38. George W. Bush, "The United States-Chile Free Trade Agreement."
39. DIRECON, "Relación económica entre Chile y Estados Unidos. Evaluación a cinco años del TLC," December 2008. http://cms.chileinfo.com/documentos/EVALUA-CION_5_anios_TLC_EE_UU.pdf.
40. Robert Gates, "US-Chile sign information sharing agreements," news articles from the U.S. Department of State. http://www.defenselink.mil/news/newsarticle.aspx?id= 49504.
41. A significant portion of this section was based on information gathered during an interview with the undersecretary of war for Chile, Gonzalo García.
42. Robert Gates, "U.S. to strengthen relationship with Chile," news articles from the U.S. Department of State. http://www.defenselink.mil/news/newsarticle.aspx?id=47689.
43. Ministry of Foreign Affairs of Chile, *Principios y Prioridades de la Política Exterior de Chile* (Santiago de Chile: Government of Chile, 2008), 54.
44. More information about this program can be found on the Fulbright Chile website: www.fulbright.cl.
45. Oscar Landerretche, "Energy and Cooperation in Latin America: A Challenge to

Chilean Policy Making" in *Visions from Finis Terrae. Chilean Voices in the United States,* ed. Pablo Arriarán (Washington, DC: Inter-American Dialogue, 2008), 16.

46. Abraham Lowenthal et al., *The Obama Administration and the Americas. Agenda for Change* (Washington, DC: Brookings Institution Press, 2009).

47. Interview with Paul Simons, United States Ambassador to Chile

48. Interview with Heraldo Muñoz, Chilean Ambassador to the United Nations.

49. The military coup in Honduras (June 2009) and the immediate reaction from Latin American countries, the United States, and regional organizations (OAS, Rio Group, UNASUR, SICA, MERCOSUR, CAN) calling for the reestablishment of democracy in the context of the Inter-American Charter is a good example of hemispheric coincidences on the importance of respecting democratic norms and not allowing military coups in the hemisphere. To see all the declarations and official documents about the crisis in Honduras see: www.flacso.org.

50. "Remarks by President Obama and President Bachelet of Chile after Meeting," The White House-Office of the Press Secretary, June 23, 2009.

9 Colombia and the United States

Strategic Partners or Uncertain Allies?

Cynthia J. Arnson and Arlene B. Tickner[1]

Introduction

Between the end of the Cold War and the close of the first decade of the new millennium, Colombia—Latin America's third largest country and oldest electoral democracy—came to occupy a central place in U.S. foreign policy. By 2000, Colombia was the third largest recipient of U.S. foreign aid worldwide, surpassed only by Israel and Egypt.[2] Between fiscal years 2000 and 2008, U.S. economic and military aid exceeded $6 billion.[3] For several years the U.S. embassy in Bogotá hosted the largest U.S. diplomatic mission in the world, until overtaken by Baghdad in the years following the 2003 U.S. military invasion. At a 2009 White House ceremony scarcely seven days before leaving office, President George W. Bush bestowed on Colombian president Álvaro Uribe the Presidential Medal of Freedom, the highest U.S. civilian honor. The award was given, said Bush, "in recognition of exemplary achievement, and to convey the utmost esteem of the people and the president of the United States."[4]

Why has Colombia been so important to the United States? The simplest explanation has to do with illegal narcotics. In the decades following President Richard Nixon's coining of the phrase, the "war on drugs" to oppose the legalization of marijuana,[5] Colombia's role as a provider of cocaine and heroin to meet voracious U.S. demand expanded dramatically. Between 1995 and 1999, coca cultivation in Colombia more than doubled, making the country the world's largest producer of coca and source for over three-fourths of the world's cocaine supply. By the year 2000, 80 to 90 percent of the cocaine and 62 percent of the heroin consumed in the United States came from Colombia.[6]

But the narrative of the drug trade tells only part of the story. As the twentieth century came to a close, the chronic weakness of the Colombian state—characterized largely by its absence from vast expanses of the national territory—had brought the country to what many analysts in and outside Colombia feared was the brink of state collapse. The country's chronic political violence worsened as illegal armed actors—guerrillas as well as paramilitaries—grew exponentially in size and territorial presence, largely by sucking resources from the drug trade. Guerrilla groups staged ever-more effective military attacks on the armed forces in remote rural areas and achieved virtual control over the major coca-growing areas in southern Colombia. Paramilitary groups similarly filled the vacuum left by an absent state, attacking the guerrillas and massacring civilians presumed sympathetic to them. Colombia's human rights and humanitarian crisis became one of the worst in the entire world Strengthening the state in its capacity to confront armed violence became—in addition to drugs—the principal issue in U.S.–Colombian relations.

The deteriorating situation in Colombia in the mid- to late 1990s and the growing intersection between the armed conflict and the drug issue became the backdrop for an ambitious and unprecedented deepening of the bilateral relationship. The rubric for this expansion was Plan Colombia, unveiled in 1999 and billed as a comprehensive strategy to combat narcotics, foster peace and human rights, build democracy, and further economic recovery and development.[7]

Over the next decade, the relative emphasis accorded to each of these objectives by Washington and Bogotá varied, as did the central justification for U.S. assistance, which was eventually subsumed in both capitals as part of the war on terrorism. Contrary to common misperception, only part of the shift in policy objectives corresponded to the change of presidents in the United States from Bill Clinton to George W. Bush in 2001, and in Colombia from Andrés Pastrana to Álvaro Uribe in 2002. Furthermore, the transformation in U.S. global foreign policy priorities following the terrorist attacks of September 11, 2001, did not dramatically affect its policy toward Colombia until internal developments there—the collapse of a four-year peace process between the Colombian government and the largest guerrilla group, the Revolutionary Armed Forces of Colombia (FARC)—drove a re-ordering of both countries' priorities. This switch took place in the waning months of Pastrana's presidency, and more than a year after Bush took office.

As much as both countries have emphasized partnership, the relationship has been highly asymmetrical. This is due to the leverage inherent in yearly U.S. aid packages in the hundreds of millions of dollars and their importance in Colombia's overall security strategy. In the context of the Colombian government's persistent quest for a free trade agreement (FTA) with the United States, the asymmetry has been rooted in the vastly different sizes of the two economies and the relative importance of each country as a trading partner for the other.

And yet, it would be a mistake to say that bilateral relations have simply been a reflection of U.S. interests and goals, and that Colombia has passively accepted them. The two countries' initial visions of Plan Colombia differed sharply. And while Bogotá accepted the primacy of the U.S. anti-narcotics agenda, it did so in order to secure sorely needed support from Washington to combat state weakness, while also maintaining efforts to negotiate peace with the guerrillas. The Colombian government's active courting of its U.S. counterpart to become more involved in the country's internal conflict also suggests a larger degree of agency than is normally recognized. Colombia further demonstrated a degree of independence from the United States over the issue of Cuba. At the same time that the Bush administration was attempting to deepen the isolation of the Cuban government, Colombian officials were meeting in Havana in several rounds of negotiations with the National Liberation Army (ELN). The Colombian government also accepted Cuba's good offices in quietly mediating a number of skirmishes with neighboring Venezuela, headed by President Hugo Chávez.[8]

Notably, neither the United States nor the Colombian government has been able to pursue its objectives free of domestic constraints or partisan considerations. The power of the U.S. Congress in particular frustrated the ratification of the FTA sought by both Presidents Bush and Uribe. Their close personal affinity, and the Uribe government's initial failure to see Republican control of the U.S. executive and legislative branches as a transitory phenomenon, cost Colombia dearly when the Democratic Party won control of both houses of Congress in November 2006. Similarly, Colombia's open embrace of and support for the U.S. war on terror contributed to its isolation from other countries of the hemisphere, where governments of the Left as well as public opinion throughout the region became deeply critical of the Bush administration's foreign policy, especially the war in Iraq. (Colombia was the only South American country to endorse the war in Iraq, but notably, did not join several Central American and Caribbean countries in sending small contingents of troops.)[9] Colombia's regional isolation reached its apogee in 2008, when the country's armed forces staged a cross-border attack against a FARC camp inside Ecuadorian territory. At a subsequent meeting of the Organization of American States, member countries—with the exception of the United States and Colombia—rejected the Colombian action but fell short of a full-blown condemnation.

This chapter traces the evolution of relations between Colombia and the United States since the mid-1990s. It shows that, a decade after the advent of Plan Colombia, some goals have been advanced while others have been thwarted. The Uribe government has succeeded in vastly improving the country's security situation, achieving more effective control of the countryside, demobilizing thousands of paramilitary fighters as well as insurgents, and delivering a series of punishing defeats to the guerrillas. Key indicators of violence—kidnappings, murders, disappearances—have also declined dramatically.[10] These positive trends have been embraced by the Colombian public and are reflected in Uribe's consistently high approval ratings and his re-election as president in 2006 by a solid 62 percent majority.

At the same time, however, the "war against drugs" has resulted in marked failure. The principal benchmark established in Plan Colombia of reducing drug cultivation by 50 percent over a period of six years was not met. According to the State Department's annual *International Narcotics Control Strategy Report*, drug cultivation in 2007 was slightly higher than it had been in 2000. Even the more generous picture offered by the United Nations Office on Drugs and Crime's *Colombia Coca Cultivation Survey* suggested that coca levels in 2008 were similar to those reported in 2004 and 2006 (see Table 9.1).

Moreover, a series of domestic scandals in Colombia—related to illegal surveillance by state authorities, links between members of the political elite and the paramilitaries, extrajudicial killings committed by the Colombian army, and President Uribe's controversial bid for a third term—suggest that the goal of democratic state strengthening has been met only partially. Finally, the kind of strategic partnership that would have been symbolized by the ratification of a U.S.-Colombian free trade agreement had not yet materialized as of this writing in early 2010.

The Core of the Relationship: Illegal Narcotics

Since the advent of the 1989 Andean Initiative during the administration of President George H. W. Bush, drugs appeared to be the only issue in Colombia that directly affected U.S. interests.[11] The emphasis on counternarcotics crowded other issues off the bilateral agenda, leading to cyclical attempts by Bogotá to "denarcotize" its relations with Washington.[12]

Notwithstanding Colombia's willingness to collaborate with the United States on the drug issue, the costs to Colombian society were substantial. In the late 1980s, Colombian drug cartels waged a campaign of terror and violence to prevent their extradition to the United States. Then-President César Gaviria (1990–1994) focused his administration's drug policy on domestic objectives instead of those set by Washington, deeming that narco-terrorism,[13] and not the drug traffic, was the principal threat to the country's democracy.[14] As a consequence, the Colombian government adopted measures to combat this specific facet of the problem, including a plea-bargaining system that entailed reduced sentences for those accused of drug-related crimes in exchange for their surrender. Under significant pressure from the drug traffickers themselves, the 1991 Constitutional Assembly voted to prohibit the extradition of Colombian nationals.

The mid-1992 escape from prison of Medellín Cartel leader Pablo Escobar—ultimately hunted down and killed in December 1993—and the luxurious prison conditions that he enjoyed led to increasing U.S. apprehension over the effectiveness of Colombia's drug strategy.[15] U.S. dismay grew when the country's prosecutor general began stating publicly that legalization might be an alternative to a failed drug suppression strategy, and when Colombia's Constitutional Court approved a measure to legalize personal consumption of certain illicit substances.[16]

As U.S.–Colombian differences over counter-drug strategy increased, another issue—human rights—began to occupy a significant place in the relationship. Reporting in 1990 from the U.S. Embassy in Bogotá, for example, detailed allegations of the Colombian army's involvement in a series of "grievous human rights violations," including the grisly execution of 11 detainees "by cutting off the limbs and heads of the still living victims with a chain saw." The Embassy cable, based on investigations and charges filed by the Colombian office of the inspector general (Procuraduría), detailed cases of the torture of labor union activists, the dressing up of murdered civilians in military uniforms in order to present them as guerrillas killed in combat,[17] indiscriminate aerial bombings in rural areas, the intimidation of civilian government investigators working on human rights cases, and the participation of army officers and enlisted men in paramilitary operations. The army had been "extremely reluctant" to discipline officers and enlisted men for specific abuses, the embassy concluded, and "many army officers continue to discount virtually all allegations of military abuses as part of a leftist inspired plot to discredit the military as an institution."[18]

The U.S. Congress took an ever-increasing role in demanding improvements in human rights and accountability as a condition of U.S. assistance. The effort began timidly in 1993 when, pushed by human rights groups, the Congress adopted a series of largely procedural measures to require greater scrutiny of military aid provided to the Colombian armed forces in the context of the war on drugs.[19] In subsequent years, Congress tied U.S. military training to the human rights conduct of Colombian officers, and required the State Department to report on Colombian efforts to sever ties between military officers and the paramilitaries and to end impunity. Congressional scrutiny of Colombia's human rights record, backed by an active human rights lobby in Washington, achieved its fullest—and most contentious—expression in the debate over labor rights in the context of the proposed U.S.-Colombia free trade agreement.

If the Gaviria government's growing independence on drug issues produced rifts in the bilateral relation, Ernesto Samper's inauguration as president in August 1994 soon put it in the deep freeze. Before Samper even took office, allegations surfaced that his presidential campaign had received $6 million dollars from the Cali drug cartel.[20] Washington's initial stance toward the incoming Colombian government was cool but pragmatic. But as speculation grew concerning Samper's level of awareness and involvement in the campaign scandal, U.S. officials began referring to Colombia as a "narco-democracy" and a "narco-state" and the policy toward the Colombian president became openly hostile.[21] In June 1996, the U.S. government revoked Samper's visa and direct contacts with the Colombian executive branch ceased altogether. In both 1996 and 1997, the Clinton administration invoked a provision of U.S. law to "decertify" Colombia as a partner in the drug war. Although the decertification contained the threat of economic sanctions, they were never fully applied.[22]

U.S. isolation of the Colombian president and its strategy of coercive diplomacy eroded Samper's domestic as well as international credibility. Other governments joined the United States in viewing Colombia as a pariah state, with significant political costs for the country's foreign policy. During his entire presidency, Samper received only two official visits by foreign heads of state—from Venezuela and Ecuador. Meanwhile, ten of Samper's twelve trips abroad were taken in his capacity as president of the Non-Aligned Movement, not as president of Colombia.

While the bilateral relationship was still deeply strained, General Barry McCaffrey, director of the White House Office of National Drug Control Policy, tacitly acknowledged U.S. government concern with Colombia's worsening situation by traveling to Bogotá in October 1997 to meet with President Samper. His visit, which was criticized publicly by U.S. ambassador to Colombia Myles Frechette, sent the message that the U.S. interest in counternarcotics transcended other political considerations. This message was reinforced by an active group of "drug war hawks" in the U.S. Congress, primarily, but not exclusively, from the Republican Party, who were active boosters of the Colombian police's counternarcotics efforts.[23] Indeed, from the early 1990s onward, the Colombian and U.S. governments had directed most U.S. anti-narcotics assistance to the National Police rather than the armed forces, due to a combination of the military's overall ineffectiveness in the drug war and its lack of interest in diverting attention from the principal strategic objective of combating the guerrillas.

Throughout the Samper years, the National Police and the office of the prosecutor general maintained close working relations with the U.S. government on counternarcotics issues. In a pattern that would continue and deepen during the subsequent presidencies of Andrés Pastrana (1998–2002) and Álvaro Uribe (2002–present), the Colombian police, the armed forces, and to a much lesser degree, the prosecutor general's office became key players in the Colombian foreign policy process. Given the absence of effective policy coordination mechanisms within the Ministry of Foreign Relations, each of these institutions achieved a lot of room to maneuver in establishing direct relations with counterparts and constituencies within the U.S. executive branch and Congress and often acted independently of the Colombian executive.[24]

The Samper Legacy

General McCaffrey's concerns were well-placed. The structure of Andean drug production had begun to change dramatically in the mid-1990s, when successful coca suppression efforts in Peru and Bolivia began to push coca cultivation northward, into southern Colombia.[25] Between 1991 and 1999, Colombia's share of hectares devoted to coca cultivation in the Andean region rose from 18 percent to 67 percent. One province alone, Putumayo, accounted for half the coca grown in Colombia and was effectively controlled by the guerrillas.[26] An additional opportunity for violent armed actors to benefit from the drug trade was linked to the Colombian government's successful dismantling of the Medellín and Cali cartels in the mid-1990s. The power vacuum was rapidly filled not only by micro-cartels (*cartelitos*), but also by paramilitary groups and the FARC.[27] The paramilitaries stepped into the void left by their former cartel bosses, winning control over trafficking operations that offered a crucial source of income for their rapidly expanding movement.[28]

The security implications of these shifts were profound. From late 1996 onward, the FARC inflicted a series of humiliating defeats on the Colombian army, taking hundreds of soldiers hostage, routing elite units, and attacking or destroying counter-drug bases. By November 1997, the situation appeared so grim that the U.S. Defense Intelligence Agency (DIA) predicted that the guerrillas could defeat the Colombian government in five years unless the armed forces were restructured.[29]

Within this milieu of domestic crisis and institutional weakness, Colombia held presidential elections in 1998. Andrés Pastrana ran on a platform that centered on ending the country's armed conflict by negotiating with the country's two main guerrilla organizations, the FARC and the National Liberation Army (ELN). During the campaign and subsequently as president-elect, Pastrana steadfastly challenged the wisdom of U.S. counternarcotics policies. Although acknowledging that drugs were a key component of U.S.–Colombian relations, he insisted that they had dominated the agenda for too long and that they should be replaced by more important issues such as trade.[30]

On June 8, 1998, at a speech in downtown Bogotá's military-owned Hotel Tequendama, Pastrana unveiled his plan for achieving peace. Illicit crop cultivation was portrayed as a social problem that needed to be addressed through a type of "Marshall Plan" for Colombia.[31] Pastrana's reference to the massive post-World War II effort to rebuild Europe was not accidental. In choosing this wording, Pastrana's team hoped to engage foreign support for its reconstruction project. The new government's foreign policy strategy, aptly named "Diplomacy for Peace," intended to do just that, by seeking out cooperation from multiple international sources, including the United States, Europe, Japan, as well as multilateral donor institutions such as the United Nations and Inter-American Development Bank.[32]

From the U.S. perspective, Pastrana´s election offered a welcome opportunity for reinstating the bilateral relationship in the wake of the disastrous Samper years. Yet the next several years would witness significant tension and disagreement over how to move beyond counternarcotics in order to address the multiple and inter-related factors involved in the country's security and governance crisis. Declassified U.S. documents indicate persistent U.S. pressures on Colombia prior to the September 1999 unveiling of Plan Colombia, not only to develop a strategy to confront the crisis but also to accept the primacy of counternarcotics in its resolution.

The Origins of Plan Colombia

During Pastrana's first official visit to the White House in late October 1998, Clinton pledged to support the new government's signature policy initiative—a peace process with guerrilla groups, most notably the FARC.[33] But in the months prior to Pastrana's visit, Colombia had been, in the words of a former National Security Council official, "the focus of a protracted, vigorous debate within the U.S. government." On one side were "those favoring full-fledged counterinsurgency assistance to Colombia" to combat the FARC and ELN, and on the other were "those seeking to engage the new Colombian government without engaging the Colombian military." The debate ended in an "enlightened compromise" in which broadened U.S. assistance would be subject to the new government's "development of a coherent national plan" to address the country's various social problems.[34] Reflecting the emerging consensus, Deputy Secretary of State Strobe Talbott wrote the U.S. embassy in Bogotá in September 1998 that, while the Clinton administration agreed that "our bilateral relationship should be broadened," the U.S. government could "only do so in the context of increased counternarcotics cooperation." What was needed in Colombia was "the development of an integrated national counternarcotics strategy."[35]

In responding to pressure from Washington, Pastrana refined the approach laid out in his pre-inauguration Marshall Plan speech but continued to emphasize counternarcotics an instrument of his broader peace initiative. In October 1998, he announced "an integrated drug policy for peace," with alternative development identified as the first of six objectives.[36] Colombian officials indicated to U.S. diplomats that "eradication will now complement alternative development, not the other way around." According to the U.S. embassy, Pastrana's strategy "includes, but by no means emphasizes, military and police roles."[37]

Close Pastrana advisers sustain that the president recognized that breaking guerrilla control of coca-growing regions in southern Colombia was critical: illegal drugs threatened Colombian national security because they fueled the armed conflict, and the state was incapable of confronting these dual problems on its own. In Pastrana's view, the state had been weakened because the government lacked control over the national territory, and because de facto powers in many parts of the country blocked the successful execution of counternarcotics operations by the National Police. But Colombian officials worked under the assumption that drug-related military aid from the United States could be harnessed in favor of other objectives. This view was echoed in Pastrana's own assertions that Colombia needed professional and modern armed forces in order to bolster the state, and that it was up to the FARC whether or not the military would be used to make peace or war.[38] At the same time—and unlike Uribe, his successor—Pastrana saw military strengthening as proceeding in tandem with peace and development initiatives, not as the prerequisite upon which other goals depended.

One year after Pastrana took office, the peace talks had failed to advance, and their critics in and outside of Colombia mounted.[39] More importantly, in the view of Washington, was that Colombia continued to lack a viable strategy for dealing with the "rapidly deteriorating situation."[40] Undersecretary of State Thomas Pickering traveled to Bogotá in August 1999, followed by a team led by Assistant Secretary for International Narcotics and Law Enforcement Rand Beers at the end of the month. Pickering told Pastrana that the U.S. government was prepared to offer Colombia additional assistance if the government

> could quickly deliver a plan that addressed all the elements of the Colombian crisis: narcotrafficking and the weakness of the military and judicial system; Colombia's economic crisis; the country's social and human rights problems, especially in the rural areas where drug production and the guerrillas flourish; and the faltering peace process, which is widely seen as a failure, both in and outside Colombia.

Beers and his delegation, meanwhile, met with senior government officials to suggest that, while "this must be a Colombian strategy," it would be "most useful in responding to numerous constituencies in Colombia and Washington."[41]

Within the Pastrana administration, officials understood that counternarcotics—deemed crucial to combat the FARC's stronghold in southern Colombia—and the government's Marshall Plan, which envisioned the reconstruction of war-damaged infrastructure, alternative development, and humanitarian assistance, hinged largely upon support by the United States. Therefore, the government decided to articulate the two, separately conceived programs under one umbrella, thereby combining a wide-range of issues considered crucial to the Pastrana government's peace effort, including economic recovery, judicial sector reform, social development, democratization, and human rights. Colombian Peace

Commissioner Víctor G. Ricardo, however, was opposed to this umbrella strategy, arguing that it would derail the peace process with the FARC altogether.[42]

Officially, Pastrana unveiled Plan Colombia, or the "Plan for Peace, Prosperity and the Strengthening of the State," at the United Nations General Assembly meeting in New York on September 21, 1999.[43] The ready availability of the text—in English—occasioned much speculation as to whether the plan had been devised in Washington or Bogotá.

While U.S. officials took pains to credit the Colombian government with authorship of Plan Colombia, behind closed doors U.S. officials made no secret of their involvement. A September 1999 Department of Defense (DOD) memorandum indicated that DOD "actively participated in the development of both the content of the plan and the planning process itself, but it is important that the final product enjoy Colombian ownership in order to win Colombian commitment."[44] The U.S. aid package to support Plan Colombia reflected DOD's heavy hand. When finally presented to the U.S. Congress, some 80 percent of the $1.6 billion request was for military and police purposes, including the purchase of 30 Blackhawk and 33 Huey helicopters, the training of two additional special army antinarcotics battalions, and other support for drug interdiction and eradication efforts. The amounts for alternative development and for programs to reform the judicial system, protect human rights, and promote the peace process were large by Colombian standards, but dwarfed by the military component.

The identification of Plan Colombia with U.S. goals and counternarcotics strategy scared other international donors away from a major commitment, for many years undermining Colombia's effort to multilateralize its strategy to include European countries in particular.[45]

The Changing U.S. Role in Colombia

The change in U.S. administrations from Bill Clinton to George W. Bush in January 2001 did not initially occasion a shift in policy toward Colombia. As General Colin Powell was briefed to be incoming secretary of state, "there was extensive discussion of CN/CI [counternarcotics/counterinsurgency] questions, with no changes to the current operational processes."[46] Even after the September 11, 2001, terrorist attacks on the United States, policy toward Colombia underwent only minor modification. In his first foreign aid request to Congress in February 2002, President Bush asked for $98 million in military assistance to train and equip Colombian troops to protect the Caño Limón–Coveñas oil pipeline, frequently targeted by the guerrillas. This was the first time in over a decade that U.S military aid was to be used in support of a limited mission other than counternarcotics, but fell far short of full-blown aid for the Colombian army's fight against the guerrillas.

The catalyst for a significant change in priorities came with the collapse of the peace process in February 2002. Although the talks had faltered almost from the beginning, the Pastrana government had maintained a carefully worded but increasingly harsh discourse aimed at keeping the hope of a negotiated settlement alive. "The FARC are the only ones who can decide how they want the international community to define them," Pastrana had declared to the UN General Assembly in September 2001, ". . . as terrorists, as drug traffickers, or as a guerrilla organization seeking a political solution to the armed conflict."[47] Then, following the FARC hijacking of a civilian airplane and the kidnapping of a Colombian senator in February 2002, Pastrana ended the process. He declared in a televised address, ". . . no one can doubt that, between politics and terrorism, the FARC chose terrorism."[48]

Within weeks of the breakdown of peace talks, the Bush administration asked the U.S. Congress for authority to use aid previously appropriated for antinarcotics for counterterrorism purposes in Colombia.[49] The Colombian government, too, began to actively and publicly push the idea that the country's armed conflict constituted the major terrorist threat in the Western hemisphere.[50] By August 2002, Congress approved the Bush administration request, making hundreds of dollars in previously approved military aid available to prosecute the counterinsurgency war.

The move towards an enlarged counterterrorist as well as counterdrug alliance in U.S.–Colombian relations had important regional consequences. In its 2002 counternarcotics budget, the Bush administration had already jettisoned Plan Colombia in favor of a broader Andean Regional Initiative aimed at addressing the "spillover" of its Colombian strategy in neighboring countries. However, the portrayal of the Colombian armed conflict as an instance of terrorism also led Washington and Bogotá to put increased pressure upon Colombia's neighbors to support, at least indirectly, the Colombian counterterrorist effort. This tendency accelerated following President Álvaro Uribe's inauguration in August 2002. These two facets of U.S. strategy in the Andes were met with a tepid and sometimes even hostile reception. As will be discussed subsequently, the increased influence of U.S. anti-terrorism policy on sub-regional agendas and cooperation and the expanding bilateral alliance added fire to already complicated relations between Colombia and its immediate neighbors.[51]

Tough on Terrorism

The election of Álvaro Uribe as president in May 2002 signaled a profound shift in Colombian domestic politics. Uribe won a resounding victory by promising a more robust effort to combat the guerrillas. His hard-line message of restoring security resonated with a national public fed up with guerrilla violence and cynical about the FARC's interest in peace.[52]

Upon taking office Uribe set out to delineate and execute a "democratic defense and security policy" (hereafter, DSP) that stressed the link between security and democracy.[53] Its basic premise was that state weakness, in combination with the fragility of Colombia's democratic institutions, had created permissive conditions for the growth of armed actors and the drug traffic, and that a necessary precondition for guaranteeing the rule of law was the strengthening of state control over the national territory. While similar in key aspects to the Pastrana government's diagnosis of the country's crisis—which was also rooted in state weakness—the strategy set forth by Uribe could not have been more different. Although the strengthening and professionalization of the Colombian armed forces commenced during the Pastrana years (largely due to U.S. assistance provided through Plan Colombia), government policy had privileged the peace talks in the absence of a comprehensive policy for achieving military control over the national territory.[54] One of the main lessons learned from this botched experience was that Colombia needed a full-blown security and defense strategy, with clear objectives and benchmarks, if the state was to consolidate its territorial control, extend the rule of law, and subsequently pursue economic and social development. DSP sought to fill this void.[55]

The initial measures adopted by the Uribe administration included a plan to expand, professionalize and modernize the armed forces; the application of a "war tax" on the wealthiest Colombians to be able to fund this effort; the intensification of the "drug war"; the creation of rehabilitation and consolidation zones under military control; the inauguration of local informant networks; the recruitment of rural soldiers; the bolstering of a highway security program; and the adoption of an anti-terrorist statute that was ultimately declared unconstitutional. All of these were viewed as key components of a three-step strategy to "clear" specific areas of illegal actors, "hold" military control over them, and finally, "consolidate" the state's presence via civilian authority and the rule of law.[56]

President Uribe parted company with the past even more dramatically by declaring an all out war against illegal armed actors, in particular the FARC, and by framing the Colombian crisis as an instance of terrorism and not an armed conflict.[57] His strongly worded anti-terrorist discourse resonated much better in the White House than Pastrana's talk of peace. In addition to a new shared goal—terrorism—the personal empathy that existed between Presidents Uribe and Bush in terms of a "get tough," "wild West," "anything goes" leadership style buttressed the bilateral relationship even more. And by asking Luis Alberto Moreno—Pastrana's ambassador in Washington and a key player in the approval of Plan Colombia by the U.S. Congress—to stay on, the Colombian government assured the continuity and experience with Capitol Hill needed to adjust the military aid and cooperation agreements already in place through Plan Colombia to its specific policy needs.[58]

Uribe's DSP, and especially, the dual "war on terrorism and drugs," became the cornerstone of Colombian politics in general, including its international relations. To the extent that a "special" relationship with the United States was seen to further the ends set forth by this policy, strengthening and deepening Bogotá's ties with Washington became the government's key foreign policy objective.[59] As a result of a perceived coincidence of interests between the two countries, coupled with a U.S. willingness to commit significant resources, the United States became much more deeply involved in the country's internal conflict. This was mainly through the transfer of new practices—combat techniques, intelligence gathering, resource management, and troop organization—that became crucial to changing the balance of power with the FARC.[60] To the degree that fighting terrorism overrode all other goals, Colombia's relations with the rest of the world also became determined by this single, narrow lens, with only limited results.[61]

Within a year of Uribe's taking office, in no small measure due to stepped-up U.S. support, Colombia's internal security situation began to improve. With the inception of Plan Patriota in June 2003, designed to drive the FARC out of strategic areas under its control, the armed forces recovered an offensive capacity. The goal of establishing a police presence in all the country's 1,099 municipalities was achieved in 2004. Key indicators of violence (homicides, kidnappings, and massacres, in particular) dropped; attacks against the civilian population decreased; and in 2002 and 2003, coca cultivation was reduced by 15 percent (only to start rising again the following year).[62]

The reduction in massacres and homicides overall was due to another major facet of President Uribe's "clear and hold" security strategy—opening talks with the paramilitaries. In July 2003, the government and the principal paramilitary umbrella organization, the Autodefensas Unidas de Colombia (AUC), signed the Santa Fe de Ralito Agreement, whereby the AUC agreed to demobilize its forces gradually and lay down its weapons by the end of 2005. Formal talks began in May 2004 and—in sharp contrast to the absence of international monitors in the *despeje* accorded earlier to the FARC—the Colombian government invited an Organization of American States mission to verify the process. By 2006, more than 31,000 paramilitary combatants had been demobilized, although many independent observers considered that the actual number of paramilitary fighters was far below the official figure.[63] To facilitate demobilization, Uribe introduced a Justice and Peace Law by which paramilitary leaders would be afforded reduced sentences in exchange for a confession of their crimes, asset forfeiture, and reparations to victims. An initial draft law proposed by Uribe was rejected by the Colombian Congress and provoked over a year of intense debate; a revised bill passed after the Uribe administration agreed to strengthen a number of important sanctions. Colombia's Constitutional Court subsequently struck down a number of important provisions, deeming them too lenient and contrary to the principle of justice.[64]

While the Bush administration officially supported the paramilitary demobilization, it was concerned by the number of AUC leaders for which the United States had already issued extradition requests, or who had been formally designated by the U.S. Treasury Department as drug trafficking kingpins.[65] Uribe ordered the arrest of paramilitary leaders in August 2006, following evidence that paramilitary compliance with the Justice and Peace Law was wavering. Nearly two years later, as evidence mounted that the paramilitaries continued to direct illegal activities from prison, the Colombian president extradited thirteen AUC leaders to the United States.[66] Although celebrated by the Bush administration, Colombian and international human rights organizations expressed dismay, as it appeared that paramilitary leaders would be prosecuted for drug trafficking but not for their numerous atrocities. Details of paramilitary crimes, their links to high-ranking members of the military. and their collusion with the political establishment—some of which they had begun to confess—would be lost with the transfer to U.S. jails.[67]

The extradition of the AUC's leadership reflected the extent to which the Uribe government had made extradition a key instrument in the "war on drugs." Although historically one of the thorniest issues in U.S.–Colombian relations, it became widely embraced: between August 2002 and July 2009, Uribe extradited over 900 Colombians to the United States, more than all previous governments combined. The numbers included not only drug king-pins such as those from the AUC, but also several high-ranking members of the FARC as well as mid-level peripheral traffickers.[68] The number of extraditions did not mask, however, the dismal results of efforts to eradicate coca. Despite the massive aerial eradication of coca crops—fumigation had increased 58 per cent since 2003—coca cultivation remained stubbornly high. According to the U.S. Government Accountability Office, the production of coca and cocaine was higher in 2006 than in 2000, the year Plan Colombia began (see Table 9.1). Heroin and poppy production, however, had declined.[69]

Colombian security gains, meanwhile, continued on a solid path. In keeping with U.S. demands that Plan Colombia undergo gradual nationalization (as contemplated in the original agreement), the Uribe government presented its Plan Colombia Consolidation Phase strategy (PCCP) in early 2006.[70] The PCCP contemplated the gradual phasing out of resources from international donors such as the United States as the Colombian government developed the capacity to assume program costs itself. The strategy was rooted in a new and evolving doctrine that envisioned an integrated effort, combining military, police, judicial, and economic development programs that would in principle allow Colombia to move beyond the territorial "holding" stage and consolidate the rule of law. "The strongest thing you can do to the FARC," said a senior Colombian defense official, "is to retake areas key to them and to the country and establish permanent control."[71] The seed for the "integrated action" doctrine was planted in early 2004, when the Southern Command proposed that counternarcotics and counterterrorism efforts be coordinated between the different Colombian and U.S. agencies involved in order to maximize results.[72] The Colombian Defense Ministry and President Uribe looked favorably upon this idea and adopted it as their own. The result, in 2006, was the creation of the Coordination Center for Integrated Action (CCAI), comprised of nearly 20 Colombian ministries and supporting agencies and representatives of the United States; the CCAI was located within the Colombian presidency's Social Action office under the supervision of its director. By mid-2008, promising civilian-military "fusion centers" were up and running and employing the CCAI's phased strategy in the broad regions of the Macarena and in Montes de María, formerly under FARC control. These fusion centers appeared the model that the Uribe government hoped to deploy throughout Colombia during the consolidation phase of the war.[73]

The roll-back of the FARC achieved notable visibility on March 1, 2008, with the bombing of a FARC camp in Ecuador that killed a senior member of the FARC secretariat, Raúl Reyes. The raid also netted three laptop computers allegedly containing extensive information on FARC support networks, financing, and international contacts, including members of the Venezuelan and Ecuadorian governments.[74] Only one week after the raid, another member of the FARC secretariat, Iván Ríos, was murdered by a member of his own security detail. And at the close of the month, word leaked that the FARC's historic leader, Manuel Marulanda, had died of natural causes. Adding to these FARC losses was a dramatic and bloodless rescue by the Colombian military of Colombia's most famous hostage held by the FARC,

Table 9.1 Coca Cultivation and Potential Cocaine Production in Colombia, 2000–2008 (in hectares and metric tons)

	2000	2001	2002	2003	2004	2005	2006	2007	2008
Coca Cultivation UNODC	163,000	145,000	102,000	86,000	80,000	86,000	78,000	99,000	81,000
Coca Cultivation U.S. State Department	136,000	170,000	145,000	114,000	114,000	144,000	157,000	157,000	N/A
Cocaine Production UNODC	695	617	580	550	640	640	610	600	430
Cocaine Production U.S. State Department	530	700	585	445	415	525	550	535	N/A

Sources: UN Office on Drugs and Crime (UNODC), Colombia Coca Cultivation Survey, June 2009; UN World Drug Report 2008; U.S. State Department, International Narcotics Control Strategy Report, 2009.

former presidential candidate Ingrid Betancourt. After years in captivity, Betancourt was rescued along with three U.S. defense contractors and a group of Colombian soldiers. The impeccably executed mission, Operación Jaque, constituted a major psychological victory for the Uribe government and, in the view of the Colombian armed forces, the accumulation of victories in 2008 represented a "point of no return" in the war against the FARC.[75] In both the Ecuador bombing and in Operación Jaque, U.S.-provided military intelligence and training was a key factor.[76]

Trouble in the Neighborhood

The Reyes bombing brought sub-regional tensions to a boiling point. Colombia had had uneasy relations with Ecuador and Venezuela for years pre-dating the Uribe government, mainly due to the regional effects of the Colombian armed conflict and counter-drug efforts and the opposition of the Venezuelan and Ecuadorian governments to the increased U.S. military presence stemming from Plan Colombia. Both countries (along with neighboring Brazil, Panama, and Peru) had adopted varying degrees of border militarization to contain and limit the spill-over effects of the Colombian conflict, whether measured in terms of refugee flows, the growing presence of armed groups (guerrillas as well as paramilitaries) in border areas, the environmental and public health effects of aerial fumigation, or simply the "balloon effect," by which successful counternarcotics operations in Colombia would cause cultivation and production to move elsewhere.[77] At the same time, the Colombian government decried what it viewed as neighboring countries' tolerance of a FARC presence in their territory, a subject of behind-the-scenes diplomacy and repeated warnings to Ecuador, Venezuela, Brazil, Argentina, and Bolivia, in particular during the Uribe years.[78] Generalized disdain for the anti-terrorist alliance between the Bush and Uribe administrations, and Uribe's conviction that Presidents Chávez and Correa were FARC allies, played off each other in cyclical episodes of mutual recrimination, conflict, and diplomatic rupture.[79]

What the Colombians considered the extraordinary military success of the March 2008 raid into Ecuador was soon followed by diplomatic fiasco. At a meeting of the Rio Group in the Dominican Republic days later, Uribe was forced to offer a half-hearted apology and the assembled heads of state "reject[ed] this violation of the territorial integrity of Ecuador."[80] At a subsequent meeting of the Organization of American States, member countries adopted a resolution calling for measures to reestablish calm in the sub-region, but also criticizing the incident as a violation of sovereignty. The United States was the sole country to support Colombia's effort to exclude this censure.

Armed with information found on the confiscated laptops in Raúl Reyes's camp, the Uribe government went on a diplomatic offensive to demonstrate the links established by foreign governments (especially Correa and Chávez) and domestic opponents with the FARC. In mid-2009, the Colombian government also leaked information connecting the Chávez government to four AT4 Swedish-made rocket launchers sold to the Venezuelan army in the 1980s and subsequently found at a

FARC camp in July 2008.[81] Simultaneously, the Colombian government engaged in quiet efforts to convince neighbors such as Brazil to permit Colombian troops to enter their territory in hot pursuit of FARC units. The July 2009 revelations in the Colombian media[82] about secret negotiations between Colombia and the United States to allow U.S. access to seven military bases in Colombia sparked controversy in Colombia and added further to regional tensions, undermining the progress the Uribe administration had made in courting allies of Latin America's social democratic left. Brazil, Chile, and Uruguay, among others, condemned the U.S. proposal and what it signaled about U.S. military intentions, once again putting Uribe on the defensive and making common cause among Chávez, Correa, and more moderate left governments in the region. Reports in Washington about Venezuela's growing role as a transit point for cocaine leaving Colombia—given the Chávez government's reluctance to cooperate with U.S. counternarcotics programs[83]—further entangled the rifts between Washington and Caracas with the Colombian government's mounting concerns over collusion with the FARC in the immediate neighborhood.

Free Trade: An Uphill Battle

For the most part, the dynamic surrounding the negotiation of a U.S.-Colombia free trade agreement unfolded independently of the debate over Plan Colombia, involving different sets of actors in both countries and overlapping but distinct objectives. During the Uribe years, however, the goals of combating narco-terrorism and deepening Colombia's insertion in the international economy via an FTA with the United States became entwined as never before. This was true not only because Uribe and members of his administration saw closer integration with the U.S. market and, hence, attractiveness to foreign investment as an essential pillar of the democratic security policy; just as important, U.S. approval of an FTA took on profound symbolic value as a stamp of approval and expression of confidence in Colombia as a U.S. ally in the wars against drugs and terrorism.

Colombia's interest in an FTA with the United States had been long-standing. Since the mid-1980s the expansion of trade and investment relations and the promotion of economic integration had served as two pillars of the country's international economic policy. However, despite efforts at bilateral and multilateral integration, Colombia's economy remained relatively closed: by 2002, the Uribe administration's first year, foreign trade accounted for only 30 percent of Colombia's GDP, one of the lowest rates in the region.[84] Agriculture, in particular, continued to enjoy high levels of protection, due in part to the political influence of the country's rural sector. Also of growing concern to Colombian government officials was the country's excessive dependence on the Venezuelan market, given President Hugo Chávez's strident anti-capitalist rhetoric and erratic behavior toward Colombia. (See Table 9.2.) Indeed, some 86–90 percent of products sold to Venezuela—Colombia's second largest trading partner—were manufactured goods. Trade between the two countries dropped as tensions over U.S. access to Colombian military bases came to a boil in mid-2009.[85]

Table 9.2 Colombian Trade Relations with the United States and Venezuela, 1995–2008 (thousands of U.S. dollars)

	1995	2000	2001	2002	2003	2004	2005	2006	2007	2008
Total Exports	13,883,541	11,757,004	12,820,623	12,690,450	13,880,613	16,744,848	21,204,164	26,162,440	32,897,045	36,668,841
Exports to US	3,526,566	6,524,140	5,255,029	5,163,662	5,779,441	6,611,138	8,479,657	9,650,252	10,373,300	14,052,729
	(34.6%)	(49.6%)	(42.6%)	(43.1%)	(44%)	(39.4%)	(40%)	(39.6%)	(34.6%)	(37.3%)
Exports to Venezuela	966,993	1,307,591	1,741,961	1,127,184	691,165	1,627,053	2,097,591	2,701,734	5,210,332	6,091,560
	(9.5%)	(9.9%)	(14.1%)	(9.4%)	(5.3%)	(9.7%)	(9.9%)	(11.1%)	(17.4%)	(16.2%)
Total Imports	10,201,064	13,158,401	12,329,896	11,975,424	13,128,524	16,788,328	21,190,439	24,390,975	29,991,332	37,625,882
Imports from US	4,669,846	3,878,114	4,413,899	4,020,070	4,081,181	4,838,092	6,005,625	6,919,658	8,568,977	11,436,952
	(33.6%)	(33%)	(34.4%)	(31.7%)	(29.4%)	(28.9%)	(28.3%)	(26.4%)	(26%)	(28.8%)
Imports from Venezuela	944,948	1,387,248	792,693	788,056	727,417	1,081,798	1,219,124	1,497,616	1,365,956	1,198,107
	(10%)	(8%)	(6.2%)	(6.2%)	(5.2%)	(6.5%)	(5.7%)	(5.7%)	(4.2%)	(3%)

Source: Colombian Ministry of Trade, Industry and Tourism, http://www.mincomercio.gov.co, Section "Estadísticas e informes," "Comercio exterior de Colombia."

Notwithstanding Colombian efforts to diversify its economic relations, the United States market has played a dominant role in the Colombian economy. In 2008 it accounted for 37 percent of Colombia's exports (some 80–86 percent of which consisted of raw materials) and supplied 29 percent of the country's imports.[86] U.S. approval of the Andean Trade Preference Act (ATPA) in 1991, designed to assist drug-producing nations in the Andean region to diversify their export base, reinforced this tendency, as did the ATPA's amended and renewed version, the Andean Trade Preference and Drug Enforcement Act (ATPDEA), enacted in 2002.

Despite the benefits of duty-free access to the U.S. market for over 90 percent of Colombian exports, economic and trade officials in that country viewed the ATPDEA as inherently limited in fostering economic growth. Because the benefits were transitory in nature, they had little impact on Colombia's ability to attract long-term foreign investment from U.S. and other sources. The need for periodic renewals also created uncertainty, opening Colombia up to scrutiny by the U.S. executive branch and Congress in ways that threatened to further "narcotize" the bilateral relationship.[87] Nonetheless, architects of Colombia's commercial policy saw the ATPDEA as an important building block toward the eventual negotiation of an FTA with the United States, much as the Group of Three (G-3) experience with Mexico and Venezuela in the early 1990s had served to acquire the negotiation experience and domestic standards to reach this goal.[88]

For close to a decade, Colombia's interest in an FTA with the United States was forced to take a back seat to the effort to create a Free Trade Area of the Americas (FTAA), a hemisphere-wide trade pact promoted by the Clinton administration and endorsed by regional leaders at the first Summit of the Americas in Miami in 1994. By 2003, the bleak horizon for the FTAA—its ultimate demise did not come until two years later in Mar del Plata—created an opening for Latin American countries to seek bilateral or sub-regional trade pacts. Following the lead of Chile and Central America, the Colombian government began to aggressively seek out a trade deal. During a May 2003 state visit to the White House, Uribe presented a formal request to President Bush for a U.S.-Colombia FTA, but the U.S. preference for negotiating an Andes-wide agreement with ATPDEA beneficiaries Colombia, Peru, and Ecuador prevailed. (Bolivia, the fourth ATPDEA beneficiary, participated as an observer.) Peru and Colombia ultimately went their own ways, concluding agreements with the United States in December 2005 and November 2006, respectively.[89]

According to Colombian officials involved in the talks, representatives of the United States Trade Representative (USTR) made clear that the FTA negotiations would be strictly trade-based—that is, they would not be affected by counter-drug considerations—and that previously negotiated agreements between the United States and other Latin American countries would be the baseline for an accord. However, during several rounds of conversations the Colombian negotiating team attempted to test these markers, making the case, for example, for ongoing protection of certain agricultural products such as rice which were important to the government's rural counter-guerrilla and counter-drug strategy. In an indication of the marked asymmetry of the negotiations, members of the U.S. team rejected Colombian appeals to a "special relationship" between Bogotá and Washington, insisting instead that by obtaining preferential and permanent access to the U.S. market, Colombia was receiving benefit enough.[90]

Unlike other foreign policy issues, including Plan Colombia, on which public debate in Colombia had been scant or non-existent, the FTA with the United States sparked fierce opposition. The negotiation process had been widely publicized in the media, and criticism came from different business sectors that had benefited from high levels of protection, as well as from legislators, labor unions, academics, NGOs, and indigenous groups. The Colombian government engaged its critics via the detailed public presentation of the results of each round of negotiations, at times to the consternation of U.S. officials, and through constitutionally mandated national consultations on the provisions of the accord. In the view of government negotiators, the process of "selling" the pact to diverse constituencies—in effect, a second, internal negotiation following the negotiation with the United States— served to enhance Colombian democracy by fostering broad participation and dialogue.[91] Yet opponents of the FTA claim that public consultations were a mere formality: critics of the agreement were marginalized, excluded, or, at times, coopted, and dissenting views within Colombia had little or no impact upon the negotiation process itself.[92] After what Colombian officials described as an arduous process that lasted several months—a characterization perhaps exaggerated given that the majority of seats in the legislature were held by members of the *uribista* coalition—the Colombian Congress approved the FTA in June 2007.

In the United States, the context for the FTA debate could not have been more inhospitable. Less than three weeks before the Bush and Uribe administrations signed the trade pact, mid-term U.S. elections had returned both houses of Congress to Democratic control. As economic insecurity spread through the United States, free trade agreements became a campaign issue. Candidates blamed them for taking jobs from American workers, and in a short period of time, they came to serve as a proxy for a U.S. debate over the costs and benefits of globalization as well as the economic policies of the Bush administration.[93]

Over the course of President Bush's two terms in office, trade issues became increasingly partisan and attracted ever-shrinking margins of support in the U.S. Congress. Even with Republicans in charge on Capitol Hill, for example, a renewal in 2001 of presidential "fast track" authority to negotiate trade agreements squeaked by with only one vote. The Central American Free Trade Agreement (CAFTA) passed the House in July 2005 by a mere two votes. (Notably, Barack Obama and Hillary Clinton, both senators at the time, voted against it). According to Republican as well as Democratic staff members, the White House and the Republican leadership of the key committees overseeing trade routinely froze Democrats out of the discussions over key trade issues.[94] The fact that Colombian officials felt emboldened by Uribe's privileged relationship with Bush also led the Colombian negotiating team to do a particularly poor job of engaging with the Democrats. One consequence of this lack of bipartisan consultation was that the Colombia FTA was presented to Congress without side agreements covering labor and environmental protections.[95] These side agreements, which had been corner-stones of both CAFTA and the North American Free Trade Agreement (NAFTA) negotiated over a decade earlier, had been crucial to Democratic support.

Once the Democrats regained control of Congress, the White House was forced to negotiate a bipartisan "New Trade Policy for America." A set of principles agreed to in May 2007 contained new labor and environmental standards and called for more effective U.S. programs to assist workers in industries adversely affected by trade. These provisions applied to the pending free trade agreements with Colombia, Peru, and Panama. As a result of these changes, the Uribe administration was forced to resubmit the new protocols to the Colombian Congress, which approved them in August 2007. Although the amendments were acceptable in principle, senior Colombian officials saw them as part of a "very imperialist attitude" on the part of the United States.[96]

House Democratic leaders, meanwhile, agreed to apply the "New Trade Policy" negotiated with the Bush administration to pending trade agreements with Peru and Panama, but they exempted Colombia. As explained by the House leadership:

> There is widespread concern in Congress about the level of violence in Colombia, the impunity, the lack of investigations and prosecutions, and the role of the paramilitary. Issues of this nature cannot solely be resolved through language in a trade agreement . . . Consequently, we cannot support the Colombia FTA at this time.[97]

The question of labor rights thus moved front and center in the FTA debate.

Sorting out the various and competing truths regarding respect for labor rights in Colombia is beyond the scope of this chapter. On the one hand are the claims of U.S. and Colombian human rights and labor rights groups: that Colombia was "the most dangerous place in the world to be a trade unionist"; that the rate of impunity for the 2,685 killings of trade unionists between 1986 and 2008 was 97 percent (similar to the rate of impunity for all crimes in Colombia); that even if one took at face value the Uribe administration's claim that killings had declined between 2001 and 2007 (following which they actually rose in 2008), over 470 union members had been killed since Uribe took office in 2002; and that Colombian workers faced daily challenges to their ability to organize and bargain collectively.[98] Just as important in this view was that the Uribe government's steps to protect trade unionists and investigate past abuses had only come about as a result of pressure from the U.S. Congress, while Uribe himself remained deeply suspicious of—if not openly hostile to—the human rights movement in Colombia and abroad.[99]

Supporters of the FTA marshaled a different set of arguments: that the Uribe government had established a special prosecutor's unit to look into cases of violence against trade unionists and had negotiated the 200 priority cases with the unions themselves; that assassinations of trade unionists had fallen dramatically since Uribe took office; that the government had established special protection programs for union members; and that more people were convicted for the murder of trade unionists in 2007 than in the entire three previous years. Deeply frustrating to

Colombian officials was the refusal of congressional Democrats to articulate benchmarks for how much progress in Colombia would be sufficient in order for the FTA to garner support. Equally troubling was a conviction widely held in Colombia as well as in other parts of Latin America that the U.S. emphasis on labor rights was a thin smokescreen for blatant—and growing—U.S. protectionism. The "Buy American" provisions of the huge domestic stimulus package approved by Congress in early 2009 only reinforced those suspicions.

The waning months of 2008 and early 2009 did little to advance the FTA's prospects. A number of domestic scandals in Colombia dominated media attention both there and in the United States and continued to cast doubt internationally on Uribe's credibility on human rights issues. "Para-gate" (*parapolítica*), which erupted in November 2006 when the Colombian Supreme Court began investigating allegations that elected officials had supported and funded paramilitary violence, revealed a shocking level of collusion between the country's political and economic elite and the paramilitaries. By mid-2009, 81 Members of Congress—nearly a third of the Colombian House of Representatives—were under investigation. Of the 41 legislators that had been formally accused and jailed, 35 hailed from political parties belonging to President Uribe's coalition.[100]

In late 2005, Jorge Noguera, a close Uribe ally and former director of the Departamento Administrativo de Seguridad (DAS), had also been accused of close collaboration with the paramilitaries while holding public office.[101] But the DAS scandal did not end there. In addition to the paramilitaries having infiltrated the agency, in early 2009 it was learned that it had been conducting illegal wiretapping and surveillance, not only of members of the political opposition but also of journalists, scholars, civil society leaders, and Supreme Court justices involved in the para-gate investigations.[102]

A long-standing practice by the Colombian army of assassinating young male civilians and presenting them afterwards as guerrillas killed in combat also exploded into the headlines at the end of 2008. Twenty-seven high-ranking members of the armed forces—including three generals—thought to be directly or indirectly involved in the incidents were fired immediately, and 1,000 investigations were underway by May 2009 in the attorney general's office. Nonetheless, the Colombian government has been reluctant to admit that the "false positives" constituted a long-standing practice within the armed forces for at least several decades. In a fact-finding mission to Colombia in June 2009, the UN special rapporteur on extrajudicial executions, Philip Alston, sustained the contrary and criticized the government's failure to examine why this practice had emerged and the extent to which it penetrated the armed forces.[103]

Compounding mistrust of Uribe among Democrats even further, the Colombian president did little to dispel impressions of his partisan leanings during the 2008 U.S. presidential campaign. Although Republican candidate John McCain was the only candidate to visit Colombia during the campaign, he was personally welcomed by President Uribe himself. Several months later, during the UN General Assembly meeting in New York, Uribe appeared at a public event with Republican candidate for vice president, Sarah Palin. Uribe's closeness with President Bush was affirmed again by the January 2009 White House ceremony in which he received the presidential Medal of Honor.

Five months after Barack Obama took office, the Colombian government was successful in securing a state visit with the new president. The June 2009 invitation confirmed that Colombia continued to be an important U.S. partner regardless of partisan considerations. Nevertheless, the ensuing joint press conference by Obama and Uribe was remarkable as much for what wasn't said as for what was. The words "terrorism" and "narco-terrorism" were not uttered once by either president. Nor was there the slightest hint about the still-secret negotiations to formalize U.S. access to Colombian military bases. Uribe emphasized issues of social cohesion and the steps the Colombian government was taking to address the most recent scandal at the DAS. Obama was visibly non-committal about a timetable for approval of the FTA ("We've got a lot on our plates, if you haven't noticed," he quipped). While acknowledging steps the government had taken to improve labor and human rights, he emphasized bipartisan concern "that the human rights issues in Colombia get resolved." Finally, Obama expressed less-than-subtle opposition to President Uribe's bid for a third term. It was a matter for Colombians to decide, he acknowledged, but then made reference to President George Washington, part of whose greatness lay in knowing when to step aside and return to civilian life.[104]

Conclusions

We began this chapter by asking why Colombia became so important to the United States (and vice versa) and why—their intensity notwithstanding—bilateral relations have fallen short of a full-blown strategic partnership, as suggested by the failure to approve the FTA. An easy answer is that the change in government in Washington from Bush to Obama, and of party control of the Congress from Republicans to Democrats, led to shifts in U.S.–Colombian relations, primarily due to the different interests and objectives of the new occupants of the White House and U.S. Capitol. Indeed, it would be fair to say that since 2007, issues such as human rights, impunity, and the "softer" side of Plan Colombia represented by its socio-economic agenda have achieved greater salience in the bilateral relationship. This U.S. partisan realignment accounts not only for the stalling of the FTA but also the gradual redirection of U.S. aid away from military spending and toward a greater emphasis on social and economic assistance.

Yet this picture is incomplete. Alongside the apparent cooling of relations between President Uribe and the Democratic White House and Congress, military cooperation between the two countries proceeded unimpaired; by mid-2009, it appeared to stand on the verge of even greater deepening. At issue was a bilateral accord to allow U.S. troops the use of seven military bases in Colombia for both counternarcotics and counterterrorism purposes, which both governments insist represented nothing more than the formalization of a long-standing relationship. At one level, the ongoing military cooperation reflects a bipartisan consensus over the legitimacy of combating narco-trafficking as well as the FARC insurgency. But at another level, the continuity stems from the fact that U.S.–Colombian relations have evolved along distinct tracks, involving separate and even somewhat autonomous bureaucracies with institutional ties and long-standing interests that transcend political considerations.

Furthermore, although the Obama administration has attempted to distance itself from the policies of George W. Bush, rebuild regional trust through an explicit emphasis on multilateralism, and work closely with left-of-center governments in Brazil and Chile, Colombia continues to be, if not the "only game in town," certainly a major player in terms of many key U.S. foreign policy objectives, including counternarcotics and counterterrorism.

Overall, the most impressive and concrete achievements of U.S.-Colombian cooperation have been in the realm of security, especially when measured in terms of reductions in the FARC's strength and the number of casualties and voluntary demobilizations. Although definitively "winning" the war against the guerrillas and terrorism appears a long way off,[105] the dramatic reductions in the FARC's offensive capacity is undeniable. Nevertheless, the fact that Uribe's Democratic Security Policy has privileged "solutions of force" also means that other aspects of a more inclusive security agenda were postponed.

Undoubtedly, successful counterinsurgency has paved the way for certain aspects of state-building—significant reductions in indicators of violence (with the exception of forced displacement), increased state presence and greater state authority—and the Colombian government, in tandem with the United States, has deployed a model for consolidating these gains with corresponding social and economic programs in key areas of the national territory. Although representatives from both countries rarely acknowledged this publicly at the time, a Pentagon official involved in Plan Colombia's creation stated retrospectively that: "It wasn't really first and foremost a counternarcotics program at all ... It was mostly a political stabilization program."[106] Many years later, in 2009, U.S. ambassador to Colombia William Brownfield claimed that Plan Colombia "has been the most successful nation-building exercise that the United States has associated itself with perhaps over the last 25–30 years."[107]

However necessary the issue of military strengthening has been to state building overall, other aspects of government policy did little to advance democratic consolidation or the rule of law. Paramilitary penetration of the political class, the economy, and the justice system in many regions of Colombia continues to threaten and even undermine the advances in the security arena. Although most paramilitary leaders are either dead or in prison, many mid-level former AUC members have filled the void to form new criminal organizations (such as the Aguilas Negras), that continue to threaten the civilian population with violence. While institutional strengthening, particularly in the judicial sector, has occurred, the scandals represented by DAS wiretapping and the army's "false positives" show how democracy itself can suffer with the primacy accorded to national security. President Uribe's stubborn bid for a third term constitutes yet another challenge to democratic strengthening, diverting executive and legislative attention from other more important economic and social reform efforts and eroding checks and balances envisioned in Colombia's 1991 Constitution.

The negative balance sheet with respect to one of Plan Colombia's central goals—the reduction of narcotics production and trafficking—suggests the need for a more profound shift in counterdrug strategy. A prominent commission of ex-Latin American presidents, including former Colombian president César Gaviria, has explicitly called for decriminalization, and countries such as Mexico, Brazil, and Argentina moved to adopt measures to decriminalize the possession of illegal drugs for personal use. Some U.S.-based policy organizations also called on the Obama administration to consider an alternative roadmap for combating illegal narcotics. That strategic leap—the kind that would fundamentally alter demand reduction strategies in the largest consumer countries—is unlikely to be taken any time soon. This suggests that, even if Colombia succeeds in the "Colombianization" of its own internal struggles, U.S.–Colombian relations will be continued to be defined in large measure by their lowest common denominator.

Finally, the Colombian government only belatedly adjusted the use of the anti-terrorism component of its Democratic Security Policy as the central driver of Colombian foreign policy. As military advances against the FARC pushed the guerrillas further into border regions, cooperation with the country's Andean neighbors became more essential than ever. In that regard, the 2008 strike into Ecuador and the 2009 outcry over U.S. access to Colombian military bases raised key issues of sovereignty that added to Colombia's isolation, as did its close identification with U.S. interests. At the same time, regional leaders such as Brazil, Chile, and Argentina worked hard to prevent both the base issue and Andean tensions, particularly between Colombia and Venezuela, from tearing apart the nascent Union of South American Nations (UNASUR). When South American heads of state met under UNASUR's auspices in August 2009 amidst broiling controversy over the U.S. bases issue, the final declaration reflected an effort to satisfy Colombian as well as South American concerns. The communiqué reaffirmed a commitment to strengthen cooperation against terrorism and international organized crime and repudiated the presence or actions of "armed groups outside the law." The declaration also affirmed that "foreign military forces" could not be used to threaten the sovereignty or integrity of any South American country.[108]

In addition, as drug trafficking and organized crime surged in Mexico in 2008–2009, the Uribe administration forged powerful connections to the Mexican government of President Felipe Calderón. The common threat of drug-related violence allowed Colombia to step partially out of its regional isolation with offers of political and technical advice as well as military training. Colombia's relations with a new conservative government in Panama also improved, and the prospects that 2009 and 2010 elections in Chile and Brazil, respectively, could shift those countries further toward the center or center-right holds out the possibility that current differences between Colombia and important South American neighbors might diminish. Nevertheless, the immediate Andean neighborhood will continue to pose the greatest challenges. There, Colombia's ability to distinguish its security and foreign policy interests from those of the United States may well hold the key to successful diplomacy.

Notes

1. The authors wish to thank Camilo Zambrano, Latin American Program intern and Carolina Peña, M.A. student, Universidad de los Andes, for their research assistance. They are also grateful to Michael L. Evans of the National Security Archive in Washington, DC, and to Winifred Tate of Colby College for facilitating access to declassified U.S. documents regarding Colombia.
2. Curt Tarnoff and Larry Nowels, "Foreign Aid: An Introductory Overview of U.S. Programs and Policies" (Congressional Research Service, April 6, 2001), 12. Colombia fell to ninth place by fiscal year 2008, trailing Israel, Afghanistan, Egypt, Jordan, Pakistan, Iraq, Kenya, and South Africa.
3. Clare Ribando Seelke and June S. Beittel, "Colombia: Issues for Congress" (Congressional Research Service, January 12, 2009), 22. The figure does not include classified intelligence support.
4. The White House, Office of the Press Secretary, "President Bush Honors Presidential Medal of Freedom Recipients" (January 13, 2009), 1. Uribe received the medal along with two former prime ministers, Tony Blair of the UK, and John Howard of Australia. Other foreign leaders to have been so honored include Nelson Mandela of South Africa, Václav Havel of Czechoslovakia, and Ellen Johnson Sirleaf of Liberia.
5. Myles Frechette, "Uncle Sam's Unfinished Business in the Neighborhood: The War on Drugs—Colombia, a Case Study," unpublished mimeo (June 2007), 3.
6. Report to the Committee on Foreign Relations and the Committee on Appropriations of the Senate, and the Committee on International Relations and the Committee on Appropriations of the House of Representatives, in compliance with Section 3202 of the Military Construction Authorization Act of 2000, "Report on US Policy and Strategy Regarding Counternarcotics Assistance for Colombia and Neighboring Countries," mimeograph, September 18, 2000, 2; U.S. General Accounting Office, *Drug Control: Narcotics Threat from Colombia Continues to Grow*, GAO/NSIAD-99–136 (Washington, DC: U.S. General Accounting Office, June 1999), 10; USAID/Colombia, "FY 2000 – FY 2005 Strategic Plan" (Bogotá: July 2000), 2.
7. Office of the President of the Republic, "Plan Colombia. Plan for Peace, Prosperity and the Strengthening of the State" (October 1999).
8. In December 2004, Colombian guerrilla leader Rodrigo Granda was captured in Venezuela by Colombian forces. He was brought secretly to Cucutá, on the other side of the border, where Colombian government officials then insisted that he had been apprehended. A bilateral crisis regarding the incident erupted in January 2005. Cuban president Fidel Castro's mediation was crucial to resolving the impasse between the Uribe and Chávez governments; intermediation in similar episodes of tension continued until Fidel Castro left power in 2006. See "Las 72 horas en las que Fidel Castro ayudó a resolver la crisis," *El Tiempo*, January 29, 2005, http://www.eltiempo.com/archivo/documento/MAM-1695212; and "Las lecciones que dejó el caso Granda," *El Tiempo*, November 26, 2007, http://www.eltiempo.com/archivo/documento/MAM-2743068.
9. The simplest explanation for why Uribe decided not to commit troops is probably also the most plausible: to have done so would have sparked domestic opposition over a decision to divert the Colombian armed forces from its own internal armed conflict.
10. Nevertheless, other indicators, such as forced displacement, remain extremely high.
11. See Cynthia J. Arnson, "The Peace Process in Colombia and U.S. Policy," in *Peace, Democracy, and Human Rights in Colombia*, ed. Christopher Welna and Gustavo Gallón (Notre Dame: University of Notre Dame Press, 2007), 149. For background on the origins and evolution of the drug war, see *Drugs and Democracy in Latin America: The Impact of U.S. Policy*, ed. Coletta Youngers and Eileen Rosin (Boulder, CO: Lynne Rienner Publishers, 2005).

12. See Juan Gabriel Tokatlian, *Drogas, dilemas y dogmas* (Bogotá: TM Editores-CEI, 1995); Bruce M. Bagley, "Drug Trafficking, Political Violence and U.S. Policy in Colombia in the 1990s," unpublished mimeo (January 5, 2001); and Russell Crandall, *Driven by Drugs: United States Policy toward Colombia* (Boulder, CO: Lynne Rienner Publishers, 2002) for three comprehensive analyses of the role of drugs in U.S.–Colombian relations.

13. The term "narcoterrorism" is a problematic one. It was originally used by the Colombian government to refer to the campaign of terror waged by drug-trafficking cartels between the mid 1980s and early 1990s to exert pressure on the Colombian state and thus avoid extradition to the United States. During this period, the cartels committed over a dozen high-level assassinations of their outspoken opponents, including Justice Minister Rodrigo Lara Bonilla, and four presidential candidates, among them the Liberal Party candidate Luis Carlos Galán. The routine bombings in Colombia's major cities also spread fear among the Colombian population as a whole. Another word, used by the Colombian armed forces and made popular in the 1980s by then-U.S. ambassador to Colombia, Lewis Tambs, was that of "narcoguerrillas"; the term was coined following the discovery of a sophisticated drug laboratory in Caquetá Department, under FARC control. By the mid1990s, as evidence of FARC participation in the cultivation and processing stages of the drug production chain grew, the word "narcoguerrillas" slowly began to find its way into both Colombian and U.S. official jargon. Nevertheless, not until the terrorist attacks of 9/11 and the Pastrana government's decision to end its peace process with the FARC did the term "narcoterrorism" resurface in its current guise. Today, it is widely used to refer to the fact that the guerrillas, who are now officially classified in the United States and Europe as terrorists, are involved in the illicit narcotics trade. The principal paramilitary organization, the Autodefensas Unidas de Colombia (AUC), has also been designated a foreign terrorist organization, and the paramilitaries are much more deeply involved in drug trafficking—as suggested by the high numbers of their ranks who have been extradited to the United States. Paramilitaries, however, are rarely referred to with the same label. Singling out one group of illegal armed actors—the FARC—as "narcoterrorists" has had important political implications in the Colombian context. It has clouded the extremely complex relationship between drug trafficking and multiple actors in the armed conflict. Just as important, it has served to strip the armed conflict of any of its political dimensions and thus justify a purely military response to the guerrillas.

14. Tatiana Matthiesen, *El arte político de conciliar. El tema de las drogas en las relaciones entre Colombia y Estados Unidos, 1986–1994* (Bogotá: FESCOL-CEREC-Fedesarrollo, 2000), 259.

15. See Mark Bowden, *Killing Pablo* (New York: Atlantic Monthly Press, 2001).

16. Juan Gabriel Tokatlian, "La polémica sobre la legalización de las drogas en Colombia, el Presidente Samper y los Estados Unidos," *Latin American Research Review* 35, no. 1 (2000): 68.

17. This long-standing practice on the part of the Colombian armed forces exploded into the 2008–2009 scandal over the so-called "false positives" during Uribe's second term.

18. Declassified cable, AmEmbassy, Bogotá to SecState WashDC, "Human Rights in Colombia—Widespread Allegations of Abuses by the Army," July 27, 1990, 1–16. The massacres in Trujillo, Valle, of which the chainsaw episode was but one of many horrific abuses between 1988 and 1994, were documented by the Historical Memory Division of Colombia's National Commission on Reparation and Reconciliation (CNRR). See CNRR, Área de Memoria Histórica, *Trujillo: Una tragedia que no cesa* (Bogotá: Editorial Planeta, 2008).

19. After the General Accounting Office reported that neither the Colombian nor U.S. governments had established adequate "end-use monitoring" mechanisms to prevent the diversion of U.S. equipment from counternarcotics to counterinsurgency purposes, the Congress required the administration to inform four congressional committees

before providing economic or military assistance and gave the committees informal authority to block the aid.

20. The day after the second round of elections, Andrés Pastrana, the Conservative Party candidate, released an audiotape in which Cali Cartel leaders Gilberto and Miguel Rodríguez Orejuela were overheard offering money to the Samper campaign.

21. Arlene B. Tickner, "U.S. Foreign Policy in Colombia: Bizarre Side Effects of the 'War on Drugs'," in *Peace, Democracy, and Human Rights in Colombia*, ed. Christopher Welna and Gustavo Gallón (Notre Dame: University of Notre Dame Press, 2007), 316–318. In the July 2000 USAID/Colombia Strategic Plan, U.S. Ambassador to Colombia Curtis Kammen referred to the "narco-corrupted ex-President Ernesto Samper," op. cit., ii, see note 6 above.

22. According to the U.S. ambassador to Colombia at the time, Myles Frechette, Mexico's cooperation in the war on drugs was weaker than Colombia's, but Mexico was not decertified. Frechette, op. cit., 2007, 4.

23. A prominent member of this group was Rep. Dennis Hastert (R-Ill.), who served as Speaker of the House from 1999 to 2006.

24. Arlene B. Tickner, "Colombia: U.S. Subordinate, Autonomous Actor, or Something in-Between," in *Latin American and Caribbean Foreign Policy*, ed. Frank O. Mora and Jeanne A.K. Hey (Boulder, CO: Rowman and Littlefield, 2003), 179.

25. The reductions in coca cultivation in Peru and Bolivia and the increase in Colombia are outlined in a May 1998 declassified State Department document. See SecState WashDC to AmEmbassy Bogotá, "Colombia '98 Counternarcotics Initiative," May 2, 1998, 1–24.

26. Cited in Cynthia J. Arnson, "The Peace Process in Colombia and U.S. Policy," op. cit., 150. See also, U.S. General Accounting Office, *Drug Control: Narcotics Threat from Colombia Continues to Grow*, op. cit., 6.

27. Self-described as *autodefensas* (self-defense groups), the paramilitaries grew in tandem with the expansion of the drug trade in Colombia during the 1980s. Although paramilitary groups had been authorized by the state in the 1960s, this new phase of paramilitary activity was financed by the Medellin and Cali cartels and wealthy land-owners in order to defend their land-holdings from the guerrillas. Eventually, the paramilitaries evolved into independent organizations with offensive strategies and autonomous political aspirations. In 1997, the United Self-Defense Force of Colombia (AUC) was created as an umbrella organization to join disparate paramilitary groups operating throughout Colombia. It was under the AUC umbrella that paramilitaries entered into a negotiation process with the Uribe government in 2003 that led to their demobilization.

28. See Mauricio Romero, *Paramilitares y autodefensas 1982–2003* (Bogotá: Alfaguara, 2004).

29. Douglas Farah, "Colombian Rebels Seen Winning War," *Washington Post* (April 10, 1998): A17, quoted in Cynthia J. Arnson, "Introduction," in *The Peace Process in Colombia and U.S. Policy* (Washington, DC: Woodrow Wilson International Center for Scholars, Latin American Program, 2000): 8. For a discussion of the origins of this crisis, see also Michael Shifter, "Colombia on the Brink: There Goes the Neighborhood," *Foreign Affairs* 78, no. 4, (July–August 1999).

30. Cathleen Farrell, "Setting the Next Agenda," *Time* (July 6, 1998): 26–27.

31. Diana Jean Schemo, "Coca Growers in Colombia Scorn New President's 'Marshall Plan'," *New York Times* (August 20, 1998), http://www.nytimes.com/1998/08/20/world/coca-growers-in-colombia.

32. Rodrigo Pardo, "Relaciones internacionales y proceso de paz," *Colombia Internacional* (January–April, 2001): 36.

33. The administration's view that a negotiated settlement was possible and desirable was a direct consequence of the end of the Central American wars, and over a period of several years, the Clinton administration took a number of important steps to advance

the prospects for successful negotiations. This included authorizing secret meetings by mid-level State Department officials with members of the FARC leadership in Costa Rica. See Cynthia J. Arnson, "The Peace Process in Colombia and U.S. Policy," in *Peace, Democracy, and Human Rights in Colombia,* ed. Christopher Welna and Gustavo Gallón (Notre Dame: University of Notre Dame Press, 2007), 140–147.

34. Chappell Lawson, "Engaging Colombia: U.S. Policy Toward the Pastrana Administration," mimeographed, September 21, 1998, 1.

35. "Various Colombian government agencies involved in the drug war seem to act almost independently," Talbott wrote. "There does not seem to be an overall national strategy to provide a framework for these efforts." SecState WashDC to AmEmbassy Bogotá, "Counternarcotics Priorities for the Pastrana Government," September 29, 1998, 1–7.

36. The other five objectives were supply reduction, judicial strengthening, demand reduction, environmental protection, and international cooperation. Alternative development was sub-divided into community and human development programs at the local level, as well as socio-economic programs to assist migrant populations.

37. AmEmbassy Bogotá to SecState, WashDC, "Colombian Counternarcotics Strategy," October 23, 1998, 1–10.

38. Author interview with Jaime Ruiz, former director of the Colombian National Planning Department, Bogotá, and a key adviser to President Pastrana, Bogotá, June 4, 2009. Ruiz argued that it was clear to the Pastrana government from the start that Plan Colombia was not a viable counternarcotics strategy at all but rather, a means of assuring U.S. support for its wider state building project.

39. During the approximately 1,100 days that talks lasted, negotiations were frozen on six different occasions for reasons related to either FARC demands, paramilitary actions, acts of violence committed by the FARC, and controversy in Colombia and abroad over the management and periodic renewal of a Switzerland-sized demilitarized zone (the *zona de despeje*) created by the government in order to hold the talks. See Cynthia J. Arnson and Teresa Whitfield, "Third Parties and Intractable Conflicts: The Case of Colombia," in *Grasping the Nettle: Analyzing Cases of Intractable Conflict,* ed. Chester A. Crocker, Fen Osler Hampson, and Pamela Aall (Washington, DC: United States Institute of Peace, 2005), 231–268.

40. Action Memorandum, INL-Rand Beers to The Secretary, "Presidential Determination Regarding Drawdown under Section 506(a)(2) of the FAA to Furnish Counternarcotics Assistance for Colombia, Peru, Ecuador, and Panama," September 14, 1999, 1–7.

41. AmEmbassy Bogotá to SecState WashDC, "Visit of the Strategy Subgroup on CN [Counternarcotics], Military Reform and Judicial Cooperation," September 1, 1999, 1–7.

42. Author interview with Jaime Ruiz, op. cit. Pastrana ultimately decided that the policy laid out in Plan Colombia in no way contradicted the peace talks. But in response to FARC accusations that the government had betrayed them, National Planning Director Jaime Ruiz held several meetings with guerrilla negotiators in order to present the plan in more detail and to clarify Pastrana's intentions.

43. See Office of the President of the Republic, "Plan Colombia. Plan for Peace, Prosperity and the Strengthening of the State" (October 1999): 9.

44. Department of Defense, Coordinator for Drug Enforcement Policy and Support, "Memorandum for Under Secretary of Defense for Policy, 'Read-ahead for September 24, 1999 Principal's Committee Meeting on Colombia—Information Memorandum'," September 22, 1999, 1–6.

45. European countries and the European Union eventually expanded their assistance, focusing on development, conflict resolution, and human rights projects.

46. Memorandum from Colombia Initiative Task Force (CITF) James Mack to OSD/SOLIC Mr. Brian Sheridan et. al., "CIIG [Colombia Implementation Group] Meeting, Thursday, January 4, 2001 at 9:00 am," January 3, 2001, 4.

47. Presidencia de la República, "El mes en la Casa de Nariño" (Bogotá: Imprenta Nacional de Colombia, noviembre de 2001), 43.

48. Televised statement of President Andrés Pastrana, Bogotá, February 20, 2002. When talks ended, it became clear that the FARC had used the zone to hide kidnap victims, conduct arms transactions, and organize military attacks on neighboring areas. Soon after the collapse of the FARC process, on-again, off-again talks with the smaller ELN, held in Havana, adjourned without reaching agreement, leaving Pastrana with nothing to show for his massive political investment in the peace process.

49. The relevant language from the Fiscal Year 2002 supplemental aid request stipulated that "the term 'counter-drug activities' … shall be deemed to include activities in support of the government of Colombia's unified campaign against narcotics trafficking, terrorist activities, and other threats to its national security." All of Colombia's three major armed groups—the FARC, ELN, and AUC—were on the official U.S. list of terrorist organizations, for acts including kidnapping, targeted assassinations, and massacres aimed at Colombia's civilian population along with a small number of U.S. citizens. The FARC and ELN had been designated terrorist organizations in 1997. On September 10, 2001, the State Department added the AUC to the list, responding in part to criticism that the United States exercised a double standard by condemning terrorism by left-wing guerrillas while ignoring that by right-wing paramilitaries.

50. Luis Alberto Moreno, "Aiding Colombia's War on Terrorism," *New York Times* (May 3, 2002): 23A.

51. For a more detailed analysis of the role of U.S. policy in Colombia in larger Andean security dynamics, see Ann C. Mason and Arlene B. Tickner, "A Transregional Security Cartography of the Andes," in *State and Society in Conflict: Comparative Perspectives on Andean Crises*, ed. Paul W. Drake and Eric Hershberg (Pittsburgh: University of Pittsburgh Press, 2006), 89–92.

52. During Pastrana's four years in office, the conflict widened substantially, leaving over 40 percent of Colombian territory in the hands of the FARC, AUC, or ELN, according to U.S. Defense Department estimates. Testimony of Assistant Secretary of Defense Peter Rodman before the House Committee on International Relations, Subcommittee on the Western Hemisphere, April 11, 2002, mimeographed transcript, 2.

53. Presidencia de la República and Ministerio de Defensa Nacional, "Política de defensa y seguridad democrática" (June 2003, http://www.mindefensa.gov.go.2003), 12. See also, Julia E. Sweig, "What Kind of War for Colombia?" *Foreign Affairs* 81, no. 5 (September–October 2002): 122–141; and Ann Mason, "Colombia's Democratic Security Agenda: Public Order in the Security Tripod," *Security Dialogue* 34, no. 4 (2003): 391–409.

54. For an incisive analysis of Colombian security and defense policy during the Pastrana government and the early years of the Uribe government, see Francisco Leal Buitrago, *La inseguridad de la seguridad* (Bogotá: Editorial Planeta, 2006).

55. Author interview with Colombian Ministry of Defense official, April 22, 2009.

56. Ibid.

57. This portrayal of the war in Colombia was disconcerting to both the international and national human rights community, and to the European Union and the United Nations High Commissioner for Human Rights, basically because it conveyed, in principle at least, immunity to international humanitarian law, while also denying the political and social origins of the Colombian conflict.

58. In his August 7, 2002 inaugural speech, Uribe announced that Moreno would stay on as ambassador to the United States, highlighting the importance attributed by the new government to relations with Washington.

59. See Arlene B. Tickner, "Intervención por invitación: Claves de la política exterior colombiana y de sus debilidades principales," *Colombia Internacional* 65 (January–June 2007): 90–111; and Sandra Borda Guzmán, "La internacionalización del conflicto armado después del 11 de septiembre," *Colombia Internacional* (January–June 2007): 66–89.

60. This argument is made by Francisco Leal Buitrago, op. cit. (2006).
61. For example, during the early Uribe years Colombian diplomacy focused on exerting pressure on Latin American neighbors, the European Union and the United Nations to declare the FARC a terrorist organization. Although these efforts succeeded in the case of the latter two, the Colombian president's staunch anti-terrorist discourse was never well received.
62. U.S. Department of State, *International Narcotics Drug Control Strategy Report 2002* (March 2002 and March 2003).
63. For a critique of the demobilization process, see Human Rights Watch, *Smoke and Mirrors. Colombia's Demobilization of Paramilitary Groups* (July 31, 2005).
64. See Cynthia J. Arnson, Jaime Bermúdez, Father Darío Echeverri, et al., "Colombia's Peace Processes: Multiple Negotiations, Multiple Actors," *Latin American Program Special Report*, December 2006, 1–5.
65. See Cynthia J. Arnson, ed., *The Peace Process in Colombia with the Autodefensas Unidas de Colombia-AUC* (Washington, DC: Latin American Program Reports on the Americas, No. 13, 2005). Throughout the peace talks and the demobilization and reinsertion process, and with the consent of the U.S. government, President Uribe froze all extradition requests, using them as a threatened "stick" to enforce paramilitary compliance with the accords. "Uribe amenaza con retirar beneficios a AUC," *Semana* (August 14, 2006), http://www.semana.com/noticias-on-line/uribe-amenaza-retirar-beneficios-auc/96453.aspx.
66. Juan Forero, "Colombia Sends 13 Paramilitary Leaders to U.S.," *Washington Post* (May 14, 2008), http://www.washingtonpost.com/wp-dyn/content/article/2008/05/13/AR2008051300800.html.
67. See Human Rights Watch, *Breaking the Grip?* (November 17, 2008), for one such opinion.
68. Juan Forero, "U.S. Criticized for Extraditing Minor Colombian Drug Suspects," *Washington Post* (July 31, 2009), http://www.washingtonpost.com/wp-dyn/content/article/2009/07/30/AR2009073003808.html.
69. U.S. Government Accountability Office, *Plan Colombia* (Washington, DC: GAO, October 2008, GAO-9–71), 18.
70. Report to Congress, U.S. Assistance Programs in Colombia and Plans to Transfer Responsibility to Colombia, Submitted to the Congress by the Secretary of State Pursuant to House Report 109–952 Accompanying the Foreign Operations, Export, Financing and Related Programs Appropriations Act, 2006 (P.L. 109–12), March 2006.
71. Author interview, Bogotá, April 22, 2009.
72. Gabriel Marcella, *Affairs of State: The Interagency and National Security* (Strategic Studies Institute, U.S. Army War College, December 2008), 433–436.
73. Juan Manuel Santos, Ministro de Defensa Nacional, "Consolidación de la Seguridad Democrática. Un esfuerzo con decisión y resultados," Julio 2006–Mayo 2009. See also, Peter DeShazo, Johanna Mendelson Forman, and Phillip McLean, *Countering Threats to Security and Stability in a Failing State* (Washington, DC: Center for Strategic and International Studies, September 2009): 26–33.
74. The computer files reportedly revealed that the government of President Hugo Chávez had provided weapons, military support, and financial assistance to the FARC, that Ecuadorian president Rafael Correa had received FARC donations to his 2006 campaign, that high-ranking members from both countries' governments sustained close contacts with the guerrillas, and that the FARC had extensive diplomatic relations with likeminded actors in both Latin America and Europe. Chávez and Correa denounced the allegations as fabrications. In May 2008, Interpol issued a finding that the computer files had not been tampered with since they were seized, but did not certify the veracity of the information contained in them, a task reserved for the Colombian Supreme Court and General Prosecutor's Office. See Clare Ribando Seelke and June S. Beittel, op. cit., 7–8; Semana, "Las principales revelaciones del computador de 'Raúl Reyes,'"

Semana (March 3, 2008), http://www.semana.com/wf_InfoArticulo.aspx?IdArt= 109912; and Cambio, "La diplomacia de las FARC," *Cambio* (June 11, 2008), http://www.cambio.com.co/portadacambio/831/5346592-pag-3_3.html.

75. Defense Minister Juan Manuel Santos, Address commemorating the 100th anniversary of the *Escuela Superior de Guerra*, Bogotá, April 20, 2009.

76. El Espectador, "Operación Jaque 'fue una maniobra norteamericana'." *El Espectador* (April 2, 2009), http://www.elespectador.com/articulo133216-operacion-jaque-fue-una-maniobra-norteamericana. A Discovery Channel documentary, released on June 19, 2009, also confirms that the United States played a key role, especially in the covert rescue mission.

77. For more in-depth discussion of the roots of Andean tension, see César Montúfar and Teresa Whitfield, eds., *Turbulencia en los Andes y Plan Colombia* (Quito: Centro Andino de Estudios Internacionales, Universidad Andina Simón Bolívar-Corporación Editora Nacional, 2003; International Crisis Group, "Colombia and its Neighbours. The Tentacles of Instability" (ICG Latin American Report, no. 3 (April 8, 2003)); International Crisis Group, "Colombia's Borders: The Weak Link in Uribe's Security Policy," ICG Latin American Report, no. 9 (September 23, 2004)); and Grupo de Trabajo en Seguridad Andina, *Integración, seguridad y conflictos en la subregión andina* (Quito: Proyecto de Seguridad Regional, Fundación Friedrich Ebert-ILDIS, 2007).

78. See the article by Colombian senator and former defense minister Marta Lucía Ramírez, "Colombia: Foreign Policy, Economy and the Conflict," *Diplomacy, Strategy and Politics* 9 (January–March 2009): 69–90.

79. On several occasions before the Angostura, Ecuador bombing, both Venezuela and Ecuador had withdrawn their ambassadors from Bogotá in response to rifts with the Uribe government. However, not until the bombing did Ecuador break diplomatic relations with Colombia completely.

80. "Declaración de los Jefes de Estado y de Gobierno del Grupo de Río sobre los acontecimientos recientes entre Ecuador y Colombia," Santo Domingo, República Dominicana (March 7, 2008).

81. Simon Romero, "Venezuela Still Aids Colombia Rebels, New Material Shows," *New York Times* (August 3, 2009), http://www.nytimes.com/2009/08/03/world/americas/03venez.html?ref=americas. Chávez denied the accusations publicly.

82. The secret negotiations were revealed by *Cambio* magazine in its cover story, no. 835, July 2–8, 2009. According to both this report and information subsequently made public by the Colombian government, the agreement with the United States includes counternarcotics as well as counterterrorism activities. U.S. officials emphasize that the bilateral discussions to conclude what is known as a Status of Forces Agreement stretched back several years and had little to do with the Ecuadorian government's refusal to extend an agreement for U.S. operations at the Forward Operating Location in Manta, Ecuador.

83. United States Government General Accounting Office, Report to the Ranking Member, Committee on Foreign Relations, U.S. Senate, *Drug Control: U.S. Counternarcotics Cooperation with Venezuela Has Declined,* GAO-09–8016 (Washington, DC: GAO, July 2009).

84. Jorge H. Botero, "Prólogo: inserción de Colombia en la economía global, 2002–2006," in *1001 Batallas,* book manuscript (2009), 1–6. Botero was Colombia's minister of trade, industry, and tourism during Uribe's first term; as such, he played a key role in the negotiations. The authors are grateful for his willingness to share the manuscript prior to its publication.

85. Infolatam, "Las exportaciones de Colombia a Venezuela cayeron un 28,8 por ciento en julio," Bogotá, September 3, 2009.

86. M. Angeles Villareal, "The Proposed U.S.-Colombia Free Trade Agreement: Economic and Political Implications," July 27, 2009, CRS/RL34470, pp. 11–12; for annual

bilateral trade figures, see also Proexport, http://www.proexport.gov.co/VBeContent/NewsDetail.asp?ID=4282&IDCompany=16.

87. Jorge H. Botero (2009), 6.

88. Authors' interview, Hernando José Gómez, Colombia's chief FTA negotiator, and Javier Gamboa, lead negotiator for intellectual property, Bogotá, April 21, 2009.

89. The regional talks opened in May 2004. When no regional consensus could be forged after more than a dozen rounds of negotiations, Peru split from the group, concluding a bilateral agreement with the United States in December 2005. The U.S.-Colombia FTA was signed in November 2006. Ecuador dropped out of the negotiations in 2007 following the inauguration of President Rafael Correa, elected on a staunch, anti-neo-liberal platform.

90. Botero, p. 9. See also, Jorge Reinel Pulecio, "La estrategia Uribe de negociación del TLC," *Colombia Internacional* 61 (January–June 2005): 20.

91. Author interview with Jorge H. Botero, former Colombian minister of trade, industry, and tourism, April 8, 2009. See also Laura Cristsina Silva, "El proceso de negociación del TLC entre Colombia y Estados Unidos," *Colombia Internacional* 65 (January–June 2007): 112–133, for a detailed account of the government's two-level strategy.

92. Jorge Reinel Pulecio, op. cit. (2005): 12–32.

93. For example, thirty-nine of the forty-two new House Democrats elected in November 2006 claimed that they owed their victories to having taken a strong stand against the Bush administration's trade agenda. See I.M. (Mac) Destler, "American Trade Politics in 2007: Building Bipartisan Compromise" (Washington, DC: Peterson Institute for International Economics, May 2007): 1–3; Sandra Polaski, "U.S. Living Standards in an Era of Globalization" (Washington, DC: Carnegie Endowment for International Peace, July 2007); Robin Toner, "A New Populism Spurs Democrats on the Economy," *New York Times*, July 16, 2007: A1; and Robert Reich, "Structural Problems or Cyclical Downturn?" *Berkeley Review of Latin American Studies* (Spring 2009): 22–26.

94. See Cynthia J. Arnson, "La agonía de Álvaro Uribe," *Foreign Affairs en Español* 7, no. 4 (2007): 51–60.

95. Colombian negotiators viewed these side agreements as unnecessary, claiming that CAFTA's provisions had been taken as the basis of the negotiations and that Colombian domestic law already contained such protections.

96. Author interview, Jorge H. Botero, Washington, DC, April 8, 2009.

97. Speaker Nancy Pelosi, Press Release, "Pelosi, Hoyer, Rangel, and Levin Statement on Trade," June 29, 2007, 2.

98. For a summary of arguments by Medellín's Escuela Nacional Sindical and the AFL-CIO, along with the views of the FTA's supporters, see http://www.wilsoncenter.org/index.cfm?topic_id=1425&categoryid=34F7C805-A083-ABCF-C2F3CB646928E11E&fuseaction=topics.events_item_topics&event_id=397573. See also the letter from Human Rights Watch director Kenneth Roth to President Álvaro Uribe Vélez, May 2, 2007: 1–3; Juan Forero, "Unionists' Murders Cloud Prospects for Colombia Trade Pact," *Washington Post*, April 10, 2009, A9; and Clare Ribando Seelke and June S. Beittel, op. cit., 26–27.

99. Uribe's long-standing rift with Human Rights Watch/Americas director, José Miguel Vivanco, in which he accused Vivanco of being a FARC apologist and accomplice, is illustrative of a dangerous tendency to stigmatize human rights groups by publicly associating them with guerrillas or terrorists.

100. The "Observatory of the Armed Conflict," run by the Corporación Nuevo Arcoiris, maintains the most up-to-date statistics on para-gate. See the corporation's website at http://www.nuevoarcoiris.org.co/sac/.

101. The DAS is the Colombian equivalent of the FBI and reports directly to the president. Among the allegations against Noguera was that he had passed to paramilitary organizations the names of trade unionists to be assassinated. See Cynthia J. Arnson, op. cit. (2007).

102. See the February 23, 2009 edition of *Semana* magazine, which originally reported the story, http://www.semana.com/noticias-nacion/das-sigue-grabando/120991.aspx.
103. United Nations Press Release, Statement by Professor Philip Alston, UN Special Rapporteur on Extrajudicial Executions, Mission to Colombia, June 8–18, 2009.
104. The White House, Office of the Press Secretary, "Remarks by President Obama and President Uribe of Colombia in Joint Press Availability," June 29, 2009, 1–7.
105. The nexus between insurgency and the drug trade is a critical factor in the intractability of the Colombian conflict.
106. Ben Wallace-Wells, "How America Lost the War on Drugs," *Rolling Stone* 1041 (December 13, 2007), http://www.rollingstone.com/politics/story/17438347/how_america_lost_the_war_on_drugs/: 7.
107. "Colombia to Aid U.S. in Taliban Fight," CBS Evening News (July 27, 2009), http//www.cbsnews.com/stories/2009/07/27/eveningnews/main5192173.stml.
108. Final Declaration, "Reunión Extraordinaria de Jefas y Jefes de Estado y de Gobierno de la UNASUR," Bariloche, Argentina, August 28, 2009.

10 The United States and Peru in the 2000s

Cynthia McClintock and Fabián Vallas

Introduction

The first decade of the new millennium was a time of unprecedented bilateral cooperation between the United States and Peru. The George W. Bush administration (2001–2009) and the governments of Alejandro Toledo (2001–2006) and Alan García (2006–2011) held similar views on economic development, the "war on drugs" and security, and democracy, and worked together quite closely on these key issues in the bilateral agenda.[1] The highlight of bilateral cooperation was a U.S.-Peru Free Trade Agreement (FTA), approved by the U.S. Congress in 2007; while Colombia and Panama were also seeking a FTA with the United States during this period, only Peru achieved the agreement.

Although during the 1990s the bilateral relationship between the United States and Peru had also been cooperative on free-market reform, the "war on drugs," and security (which had been extremely important first amid the threat from the Shining Path guerrillas and then the outbreak of war between Peru and Ecuador), the relationship had been strained by the authoritarian abuses of Peru's president Alberto Fujimori (1990–2000). The William J. Clinton administration was displeased by these abuses but feared the loss of cooperation in other fronts on the bilateral agenda and did not steadfastly condemn them. This was particularly the case because under Fujimori's predecessor (ironically, the same Alan García), U.S.–Peruvian relations had been acrimonious, especially over the issue of Peru's debt service. Indeed, U.S.–Peruvian relations had been fraught with tension for decades; at the height of the Cold War, Peru had purchased considerable Soviet military equipment and had nationalized major U.S. companies.

The robust bilateral cooperation of the new millennium stood out not only with respect to the recent history of U.S.–Peruvian relations but also with respect to the trends in the Andean region. In the middle of the first decade of the new millennium, as oil prices skyrocketed, Venezuelan president Hugo Chávez proclaimed a "Bolivarian Revolution," and provided considerable support to allies in the region. In December 2005, Evo Morales was elected president of Bolivia; Bolivia became a member of ALBA (Alternativa Bolivariana para las Américas), which had been launched by Venezuela and Cuba. In November 2006, Rafael Correa was elected president of Ecuador; Correa opposed a free trade agreement with the United States and joined ALBA in 2009. Upon Chávez's criticism of the planned Peru-U.S. FTA, Venezuela withdrew from the CAN (Andean Community of Nations) in 2006. Even though Colombia remained a steadfast U.S. ally, the regional context was challenging for the United States and its partnership with Peru was of relatively greater value.

However, cooperation between the United States and Peru is clouded by the question of its sustainability. Cooperation may not be sustained for several reasons. First, cooperation may not be perceived as advantageous by a majority of Peruvians and a candidate unfriendly to the United States could be elected in 2011. Although Peru's economic growth was robust for seven years and the country's middle and upper classes benefited considerably, lower-strata Peruvians—who live disproportionately in the country's highland and jungle areas—continued to feel left out of the gains. In part as a result, Toledo's approval rating was below 20 percent for most of his administration and during 2008 and early 2009 García's rating ranged between 20 percent and 35 percent.[2] A fiery Chávez ally, Ollanta Humala, who was only five points behind García in the 2006 runoff and won easily throughout Peru's hinterlands, is among the frontrunners for the 2011 election.

Also, cooperation may not be sustained because of a perception that the United States is no longer hegemonic in Latin America and that Peru need not try so hard to win U.S. approval. Among Peru's middle and upper classes, a new vision of the global order is emerging, in which Peru—growing economically and relatively stable politically— is a hub for Pacific-coast countries and not without power in its own right. Whereas during the latter half of the twentieth century most Peruvian elites perceived the United States as Peru's key ally, unrivalled in importance, in the new millennium these Peruvians were inclined to perceive the United States as a power in decline. By contrast, Asian nations, and in particular China, were perceived as rising powers and it was anticipated that Peru would increasingly partner with Asia's Pacific-coast countries.

Peru's Post-2000 Governments: Key Actors and Perspectives

Since the flight of President Alberto Fujimori in November 2000 and the interim government of Valentín Paniagua, free and fair elections have yielded legitimate Peruvian presidents, first Toledo and then García. However, both Toledo and García failed to enjoy strong popular support, arguably at least in part because both had campaigned to the center-left but governed at the center-right. It is possible that the weakness of the two presidents at home helped them in their negotiations with the United States—in other words, they could argue that their pro-U.S. policies hurt them in some sectors of Peruvian opinion and accordingly additional U.S. support was necessary.

The Paniagua Government

On November 22, 2000, Paniagua, a widely-respected veteran leader of the Acción Popular (Popular Action) party, was inaugurated president of Peru. Fujimori, who less than four months earlier had been inaugurated to a third consecutive presidential term, and his spymaster Vladimiro Montesinos were engulfed in corruption and human-rights scandals and Fujimori's political coalition had collapsed; Montesinos had gone into hiding. The opposition had won control of Peru's Congress and had elected Paniagua as its president. Fearing prosecution, Fujimori had fled Peru for the safety of Japan; as both of Fujimori's vice-presidents had resigned, Paniagua was next in line for the presidency.

The primary responsibility of Paniagua's government was to clean up Peru's political, judicial, and other institutions so that free and fair elections could be held in April 2001—which it did, to considerable acclaim in both Peru and the United States The government began judicial procedures against numerous figures who had been complicit with the Fujimori regime and worked to capture Montesinos in Venezuela.

The Toledo Government

As the key victim of Fujimori's and Montesinos's fraud during the 2000 elections, Toledo, the candidate of the Perú Posible party, was well positioned for the 2001 contest. In the event, he won the first round with 37 percent of the valid vote and the runoff with 53 percent.

Although Toledo was disturbed by the U.S. government's toleration of the 2000 electoral fraud, Toledo knows and likes the United States and shares its core economic and political values.[3] With the help of U.S. Peace Corps volunteers, Toledo had secured a fellowship for undergraduate study at the University of San Francisco in 1965 and had remained in the United States for decades, completing his B.A. and his Ph.D. at Stanford University. At Stanford, he had met his Belgian-born wife, the anthropologist Eliane Karp, and at the end of his presidency they both took positions at Stanford.

Toledo's economic and foreign-policy teams were led by political independents who were highly respected in both Peru and the United States. His first prime minister was Roberto Dañino, an international lawyer; his second was Beatriz Merino, a World Bank economist and the first woman to serve in this position; and his third was Pedro-Pablo Kuczynski, an international businessman. The government's foreign policy team was led first by Diego García-Sayan, an international lawyer specializing on human-rights issues, and then by Alan Wagner, who had served as foreign minister during García's first government. Peru's ambassadors to the United States included Wagner, Dañino, and Eduardo Ferrero, a very able scholar and lawyer.

The García Government

During Alan García's first government (1985–1990), which coincided with the severe debt crisis in the region, he was at odds with the United States. At only 35 years of age, he was elected as the candidate of APRA (Alianza Popular Revolucionaria Americana, American Popular Revolutionary Alliance), a party that vilified Peru's oligarchy and was perceived as leftist and populist. In García's inaugural address, he called the United States "the richest, most imperialist country on earth," and said that Peru would pay only 10 percent of its export earnings for the servicing of its debt. García harbored grand illusions of leading an alliance of Latin American nations against debt payment.

Ultimately, García's first government was widely considered catastrophic. García was disdained as unprincipled, rash, and hot-tempered; the most notorious example was his sudden attempt to nationalize Peru's private banks in 1987. His government's fiscal policies led to quadruple-digit inflation, food shortages, and the worst economic crisis in Peru's history. At the same time, the economic debacle fanned the flames of the Shining Path insurgency, which expanded into Lima. Serious human-rights violations were common. Still, García should be credited with the establishment of the GEIN (Grupo Especial de Inteligencia, Special Intelligence Group), which ultimately captured the Shining Path's leader, Abimael Guzmán, in 1992.

Despite García's first government, he remained a brilliant political strategist and a spellbinding orator, and Fujimori feared his appeal. During the 1992 *autogolpe* (self-coup), Fujimori ordered García's arrest, but the former president escaped and spent most of the next eight years in Paris. After Fujimori's flight from Peru, García returned and finished second to Toledo in the 2001 elections.

In the 2006 elections, García came from behind to squeak past the center-right candidate, Lourdes Flores of the Unidad Nacional (National Unity), to secure a place in the runoff against the first-round winner, Humala. Slightly darker-skinned, Humala was a former lieutenant colonel in Peru's army and his core base of support was in the military. Humala had caught Peruvians' attention in October 2000 when he had led what appeared to be an uprising against the scandal-ridden Fujimori government. Especially in the early months of the campaign, Humala's discourse was highly critical of Peru's traditional white elites and also of Chile. (In the 1879–1883 War of the Pacific, Peru and Bolivia lost to Chile, and geopolitical tensions have endured.) Humala was the founder of his political party, the Partido Nacionalista Peruano (Peruvian Nationalist Party, PNP).

García won the runoff by five percentage points. In the runoff, he moved rightwards to capture voters who had favored Flores or Fujimori's party in the first round. Also, García was helped by Peruvians' nationalist backlash against Hugo Chávez's blatant support for Humala and Chávez's public insults of both Toledo and García.[4] However, there was a deep regional divide. While García won handily in Lima and the relatively prosperous coastal area, Humala won all but two departments in the interior; he averaged 75 percent of the vote in the departments of Peru's most impoverished region, the southern highlands.[5] In recent polls for the 2011 elections, this pattern continues; Humala is ahead by large margins in numerous departments of the interior.[6]

As under Toledo, key cabinet ministers under García were respected at home and abroad and a considerable number were political independents. His first (and third) minister of the economy, Luis Carranza, had worked with Pedro-Pablo Kuczynski and had strong links with the international financial community; this was also the case with his second minister, Luis Valdivieso. García's foreign minister, José Antonio García Belaunde, was an experienced professional; his minister of international trade and tourism, Mercedes Aráoz, was less well-known at the time of her appointment but rapidly won excellent reviews for her work on the Peru-U.S. FTA.

Given García's first government, his current staunchly pro-market and pro-American positions are surprising, and there has been considerable speculation about the reasons for García's ideological conversion. The interpretation advanced by García himself is that he was young and inexperienced at the time of his first government. Another interpretation is that, whereas in the mid- to late 1980s the Latin American political arena was open for an active critic of the debt crisis, in the new millennium the space on the region's left was occupied by Chávez, and García could better make a mark on the right. For their part, critics of García take the interpretation of opportunism one step further, emphasizing García's current close friendships with some of Peru's wealthiest businessmen.

The Bilateral Agenda: Free-Market Reform and the Peru-U.S. Free Trade Agreement

During the 1970s and 1980s, Peru's governments were largely skeptical of the free market, but the Fujimori government implemented free-market reforms that were widely perceived as successful and they have endured.[7] As globalization took hold, there emerged a vision of Peru as a key Latin American hub for trade and investment among the countries of the Pacific, including the United States, Colombia, and Chile but also China and other Asian countries. Especially at a time when Bolivia and Ecuador were becoming less open to trade and investment, many Peruvians were excited that Peru could be a market-friendly alternative. Yet, as the final section of this chapter will elaborate further, it was not clear that, as of the 2011 elections, a majority of Peruvians would believe that pro-U.S. market policies were in their interest—especially if the global financial crisis continued.

Negotiations for the Peru-U.S. Trade Promotion Agreement (PTPA) began in 2004. Negotiated by U.S. Trade Representative Susan Schwab and the Toledo government's Pablo de la Flor, the PTPA stipulated that 80 percent of U.S. consumer and industrial products and 67 percent of U.S. agricultural products would immediately enter Peru duty-free. The remaining tariffs would be phased out over ten years. (As of 2006, Peru's tariff on U.S. goods averaged between 5 percent and 25 percent, but the tariff on some products, such as rice, was as high as 52 percent.[8]) The PTPA assured that Peru would have permanent preferential access to the U.S. market; since 1991, Peru had enjoyed preferential access through first the Andean Trade Preferences Act (ATPA) and then its successor the Andean Trade Promotion and Drug Eradication Act (ATPDEA), but these were temporary and had to be reauthorized periodically by the U.S. Congress.

The PTPA was approved by Peru's Congress by 79 votes to 14, with 7 abstentions, on June 28, 2006 (the final month of Toledo's presidency). In nationwide public-opinion polls in December 2007, approval was at 66 percent and disapproval at 25 percent; 33 percent considered the PTPA the García government's principal achievement.[9] There were peaceful protests against the PTPA supported by Humala, but they were not massive.[10]

Approval in the U.S. Congress was more difficult. In November 2006, the Democratic Party, which had become critical of free trade agreements—in particular of the weakness of their provisions for labor and the environment—gained a majority. Some Democratic leaders may have wanted to show that they were not knee-jerk opponents of FTAs by supporting at least one of the pending agreements and may have chosen the Peru agreement as the best of the lot; in particular, in contrast to Colombia, Peru's current human-rights record was satisfactory. However, other Democratic leaders were very concerned with the specifics of the labor and environmental provisions and worked with both Peru and the Bush administration to try to assure the strength of these provisions. In contrast to Colombia's Álvaro Uribe, both Toledo and García met not only with Republicans but also with Democrats. In particular, Toledo became friendly with Rep. Charles Rangel (D-N.Y.), who became Chairman of the Ways and Means Committee in the U.S. House of Representatives. In his meetings in Washington, García emphasized APRA's history as a pro-labor party as well as his own personal commitment to workers' rights and the reduction of poverty.[11]

For its part, the Bush administration was opposed to labor and environmental provisions; but on May 10, 2007 a compromise agreement was forged between the House Democrats and the administration.[12] Subsequently, House Democrats were able to achieve what they considered almost a model FTA, with the provisions that they had long sought for these agreements.

Still, the García government had to persuade Democrats that these provisions would be implemented in Peru. In mid-2007, Rep. Rangel and Rep. Sander Levin (D-Mich., chairman of the Trade Subcommittee of the U.S. House) visited Peru to observe the government's work on the pact first-hand, and they concluded that the Peruvian FTA team was serious and responsible.[13] Among the steps taken by the García government was an increase in the number of inspectors of labor conditions and the establishment of a ministry for the environment.[14]

Finally, the PTPA was approved in the U.S. House of Representatives on November 8, 2007 by 285 votes to 132 and on December 4, 2007 in the U.S. Senate by 77 votes to 18. U.S. congressional support for the pact was larger than for any previous trade agreement. Almost one-half of all Democrats in the U.S. House voted in favor of the PTPA; six more Democrats voted for the PTPA than had voted for NAFTA in 1993 and 35 more than had voted for the U.S.-Chile FTA in 2003.[15]

Still, it was stipulated in the November 2007 vote that President Bush was not to certify the PTPA until Peru had further strengthened its protections for labor and the environment as well as for intellectual property rights and patents on medicines. In June 2008, the García government issued 102 legislative decrees, ostensibly to this end, but some of these decrees were declared unconstitutional and others, such as a new forestry law that would facilitate the sale of forest land, appeared antithetical to the goals of the FTA.[16] Rangel and Levin were especially worried about the high incidence of "subcontracting" in Peru, which was a strategy to circumvent workers' rights, and as late as January 2009 they raised the issue with the U.S. executive branch.[17]

As the date for President Bush's departure loomed, the García government rushed to secure the U.S. president's certification for the implementation of the PTPA. The García government devised new labor, forestry, and intellectual-property bills that were approved on January 13 in Peru's Congress by 61 votes to 31.[18] However, it was not clear that these bills would bring Peru into line with the stipulated standards; Rangel, Levin, the AFL-CIO and other important U.S. organizations called for a delay. But, on January 16, Bush certified Peru's fulfillment of the stipulations and the PTPA went into effect on February 1, 2009.[19]

As of the writing of this chapter, the PTPA has been in force for only a few months and accordingly its effects on bilateral investment and trade cannot yet be assessed. However, in recent years both investment and trade have increased dramatically, and it appears likely that merely the negotiations for the PTPA drew attention to Peru as an attractive commercial partner—to such facts as Peru's ranking number one in Latin America in 2007 on the indices "Protecting Investors" and "Government Readiness for Private Investment."[20] Another factor in the increase was strong global demand and high prices for many of Peru's products. Since 2001, Peru has been Latin America's top producer of gold, silver, zinc, tin, and lead, and the second-top producer of copper; these minerals compose approximately half of Peru's exports and their prices have skyrocketed, attracting investment.[21] Non-traditional agricultural exports have also soared; Peru is the top world exporter of asparagus and paprika.

For these reasons, the inflow of foreign direct investment (FDI) to Peru more than tripled. During 2007–2008, FDI inflow averaged about $4.7 billion annually (approximately 4 percent of total FDI inflow to Latin America), whereas in 1998–2002 it had averaged only $1.5 billion annually (roughly 2 percent of total FDI inflow to Latin America).[22] The sectors with the largest FDI stock as of 2008 were, in order, telecommunications, mining, industry, finance, and energy; between 2000 and 2008, the largest increase in FDI stock was in mining.[23]

Foreign investors in Peru are diverse. As of June 2008, Spain held the largest percentage of FDI stock (22 percent), the United Kingdom officially the second largest (20 percent, but this figure was inflated due to the lack of a distinction between head offices and subsidiaries abroad), and the United States the third largest (16 percent).[24] Other important investors, with more than 5 percent of FDI stock each, were the Netherlands, Chile, and Panama.[25] Chile's investments are in large retail stores, airlines, housing, and infrastructure and are accordingly much more visible to Peruvians than most other countries' investments in mining and energy (which are in remote areas). Investors with between 2 percent and 5 percent of FDI stock were Mexico and Brazil (which recently invested $1 billion in roads that will link Brazil to Peru's coast).[26]

Since 2000, while Spain's FDI stock has declined, British and U.S. stock has increased considerably.[27] Spain made its largest investment in Peru in 1994 when it purchased Peru's telephone company and most of its FDI stock remains in telecommunications. By contrast, between 2000 and mid-2008, U.S. stock increased 28 percent and British stock 57 percent.[28] The largest recent U.S. projects were Camisea gas (a total $3.7 billion investment) and Cerro Verde copper mine ($800 million).[29] The United States is also home to Newmont Mining Company, which has a 51 percent share in Peru's Yanacocha mine, South America's largest gold mine.[30] Currently, U.S.-based Hunt Oil is the lead company in the Peru LNG hydrocarbons project, a $4 billion project that includes companies from Spain, Japan, and South Korea.[31] With the implementation of the PTPA, the Peruvian government was estimating U.S. investment to average $1.8 billion during 2009–2010.[32]

China was not an important investor in Peru; as of mid-2008, it had less than 1 percent of Peru's FDI stock.[33] However, at this time China is purchasing the rights to invest in various mining projects and appeared likely to have a significant share within about two years.[34] One major project, the Toromocho copper mine in the central highlands in which China is expected to invest about $2 billion, is scheduled to begin production in 2011.[35]

Also, between 2000 and 2007, the value of Peru's trade approximately quadrupled (see Tables 10.1 and 10.2). Preliminary figures for 2008 indicated another jump in Peru's exports, to about $32 billion, and also in imports, to roughly $28 billion.[36] The United States has been Peru's principal trading partner for decades and remained so in 2007, but its relative importance has been declining. The U.S. share of Peru's exports was 37 percent in 1980, 35 percent in 1985, and, as Table 10.1 shows, 27 percent in 2000 and 19 percent in 2007.[37] Although for most of the twentieth century Peru's trade with China was negligible (0.5 percent in 1980 and 1.7 percent in 1985), China was Peru's second largest trading partner in 2007 (see Tables 10.1 and 10.2).

Table 10.1 Peru's Exports: Value (in billions of U.S. dollars) and Key Partners, 2000–2007

	2000		2007	
	Amount	Percentage	Amount	Percentage
Total	$6.7	100%	$27.6	100%
United States	$1.8	27%	$5.2	19%
China	$0.4	7%	$3.0	11%

Source: Richard Webb and Graciela Fernández Baca, *Perú en Números 2008* (Lima: Cuánto, 2008), 1193–1197, and Richard Webb and Graciela Fernández Baca, *Perú en Números 2002* (Lima: Cuánto, 2002), 1192 and 1209.

Table 10.2 Peru's Imports: Value (in billions of U.S. dollars) and Key Partners, 2000–2007

	2000		2007	
	Amount	Percentage	Amount	Percentage
Total	$6.8	100%	$20.4	100%
United States	$1.6	24%	$3.6	18%
China	$.3	4%	$2.5	12%

Source: Webb and Fernández Baca, *Perú en Números 2008*, 1193–1197, and Webb and Fernández Baca, *Perú en Números 2002*, 1209.

Following the United States and China on the list of largest purchasers of Peru's exports in 2007 were: Switzerland, 8 percent; Japan, 8 percent; Chile, 6 percent; Canada, 6 percent; Brazil, 3.5 percent; Spain, 3.5 percent; Germany, 3.4 percent; and South Korea, 3 percent.[38] (If the European Union is counted as one bloc, however, its share of Peru's exports have been larger than China's, with 18 percent.[39]) As China's share of Peru's trade has increased, the shares not only of the United States but also the United Kingdom, Mexico, and several other Latin American nations have declined.[40]

Remittances were also increasingly important for Peru. In 2008, remittances reached $2.4 billion (about 2.2 percent of GDP), versus $718 million (1.3 percent of GDP) in 2000; approximately half these remittances were from the United States.[41]

In this context of dramatic increases in investment and trade, Peru's economy grew robustly; as of December 2008, it had expanded for 88 consecutive months, a record without precedent.[42] Between 2002 and 2008, annual GDP growth averaged 7.4 percent (vs. 4.6 percent in Latin America overall), while inflation was negligible.[43] For 2002–2008, Peru vied with Panama for the accolade of the Latin American country with the highest growth rate.[44]

It is likely that Peru's FTA with the United States enhanced its international image and facilitated various achievements in the global arena. For Peru, 2008 was the "year of the summits"; in May, Peru hosted the summit of the ALC-UE (Latin American and Caribbean and European Union) and, in November, the summit of APEC (Asia-Pacific Economic Cooperation, which was established in 1989 and includes 21 nations from Asia, Australia, Latin America, and North America). Also, Peru was dramatically increasing its trade partnerships around the world. As of early 2009, FTAs between Peru and not only the United States but also China, Chile, Canada, Singapore, and the European Free Trade Association (including Iceland, Lichtenstein, Norway, and Switzerland) were in force. As of late 2009, a FTA with South Korea was almost complete and a FTA with Japan was likely in 2010; negotiations were underway with Mexico and the European Union. The successful summits and the FTAs were factors in rising approval ratings for President García in late 2008 and early 2009.[45]

Despite many Peruvians' excitement about the country's new globalized economy, its ultimate effects are likely to be mixed. As will be elaborated below, social and economic divisions in Peru are very deep. If the outcomes of other FTAs between the United States and Latin American nations hold in Peru, the PTPA is likely to continue to enhance investment and trade, but many of Peru's agricultural products will face severe competition from highly subsidized U.S. wheat, corn, and other foodstuffs. In other words, Peru's most disadvantaged group, its highland farmers, is precisely the group likely to be hurt by the PTPA. Also, as will be discussed further below, despite the benefits to Peru's economy as a whole from increased investment, the development of mines and other extractive enterprises, most of which are in remote highlands and jungle areas, has often provoked intense conflict with impoverished contiguous communities that perceive damage to the environment.[46] Although both the Toledo and García governments tried to channel some funds from the enterprises to the contiguous communities (through a tax called the *canon*), implementation has been difficult. It should also be noted that, due to ATPA and ATPDEA, Peru has enjoyed access to U.S. markets for years, but fuller U.S. access to the Peruvian market is new; for the first time in many years, in 2008 the value of Peru's imports from the United States was greater than its exports and this trend could accelerate in 2009.[47]

Further, while FTAs aligned Peru with the United States, China, and other Asian and European economies, they divided the Andean nations as a whole. As mentioned above, upon the negotiations for the PTPA, Venezuela withdrew from the CAN, and both Chávez and Morales criticized Peru's and Colombia's enthusiasm for FTAs with the United States. Accordingly, Andean integration processes were halted amid the polarization between Peru and Colombia on the one hand and Venezuela and Bolivia on the other.

The Bilateral Agenda: Drug-Trafficking and Security

For decades, Peru has been a priority theater in the "war on drugs." Since 2000, cooperation between the United States and Peru in the "war on drugs" has been considerable. Yet, the "war" is from being won; given the demand for drugs in the United States and Europe and the profits in the industry, supply (and, concomitantly, violent organized crime) is virtually certain to persist. While both Toledo and García endorsed the "war," opposition leaders such as Humala have not.[48]

From the 1970s through the mid-1990s, Peru was the world's top producer of coca and since the mid-1990s it has been the world's second-largest producer after Colombia. As in Colombia, the challenge in Peru was not only narcotics control but also an insurgency hugely strengthened by revenues from drug-trafficking. Until the mid-1990s, the Peruvian and U.S. governments clashed frequently about the appropriateness of forced eradication of coca; Peru feared that military force fanned the flames of the insurgency and argued for greater economic assistance for the cultivation of alternative crops.[49] In approximately 1995, however, Peru and the United States agreed to the initiation of a policy called "air bridge denial"—shooting down traffickers' planes flying between Peru and Colombia; this policy coincided with major changes in the coca industry. As a result, coca cultivation in Peru declined dramatically, from about 115,000 hectares in 1995 to roughly 32,000 hectares in 2000 (see Table 10.3). At the same time, Peru's key insurgency, the Shining Path, was decimated in the wake of the capture of its leader, Abimael Guzmán, in 1992.

However, in April 2001, "air bridge denial" was suspended after a U.S. missionaries' plane was shot down and a U.S. missionary and her daughter were killed. President Toledo repeatedly asked that "air bridge denial" be resumed with enhanced safeguards, but this did not happen; it was ultimately revealed that the April 2001 tragic error was not an aberration but that pilots' violations of legal procedures had been common.[50] At the same time, military initiatives against coca were increasing in Colombia; historically, pressure on one region or nation has led to the displacement of production to another, in what is called the "balloon effect," and accordingly the stage was set for the shift of production back to Peru.

In contrast to the pre-1995 period, Presidents Toledo and García cooperated closely with the United States. One likely reason was both governments' desire to please the United States amid the negotiations for the PTPA. (For example, just before García's March 2007 visit to the United States, he ordered the bombardment of a large number of cocaine labs and clandestine airports.[51])

For the most part, both governments endorsed the prioritization of repression ("sticks") over alternative development ("carrots"). Although in recent years the United States has provided almost as much social and economic aid as military and police aid in its narcotics-control budget, Peru's agency for social and economic programs, DEVIDA (National Commission for Development and Life without Drugs), has not acted as the lead agency; it has not coordinated effectively with other institutions either in Lima or in the coca-producing areas.[52] Also in contrast to the pre-1995 period, both Peruvian governments considered counternarcotics policy to be largely synonymous with counterinsurgency policy; this change was in part a reflection of the change in the Shining Path insurgency, which in the wake of Guzmán's capture had lost its ideological bearings and approximated a "narcoterrorist" organization.[53]

To the applause of the Bush administration, the Toledo and García governments undertook large-scale efforts to reduce the supply of cocaine. Since 2000, the number of hectares of coca eradicated in Peru has steadily increased— to an average of 11,000 hectares in 2007–2008 from approximately 6,200 hectares in 2000 (see Table 10.3). The García government destroyed record numbers of cocaine laboratories (1,225 in 2008) and, in part through improved interdiction at airports, seized record amounts of chemical inputs (850,000 kilos in 2007) as well as of cocaine itself (almost 28 metric tons in 2008).[54] Further, Peru was trying harder to enforce laws

Table 10.3 Control of Coca and Coca Leaf in Peru, 1995–2007

	Number of hectares eradicated	Number of hectares in coca	Labs destroyed	Potential coca leaf harvest (metric tons, MT)
1995	0	115,300	0	N.A.
1996	1,259	94,400	14	N.A.
1997	3,462	68,800	18	N.A.
1998	7,825	51,000	N.A.	N.A.
1999	14,733	34,700	51	41,000
2000	6,206	31,700	97	42,000
2001	6,436	32,100	72	42,500
2002	7,134	34,700	238	49,000
2003	7,022	29,250	964	41,000
2004	7,605	27,500	821	48,800
2005	8,966	34,000	1,126	56,300
2006	10,137	42,000	724	50,000
2007	11,057	36,000	650	67,645
2008	10,143	TBD	1,225	TBD

Source: For 1999–2008, International Narcotics Control Strategy Report, at www.state.gov/p/inl/rls/ nrcrpt/2009/vol 1/116523.htm, and for previous years Cynthia McClintock and Fabián Vallas, *The United States and Peru: Cooperation at a Cost* (New York: Routledge, 2003), 115.

against money laundering.[55] The U.S. Office of National Drug Control Policy was laudatory: "Peru has made a valuable contribution to the efforts to control drugs in the region. President Alan García has clearly shown his commitment to cooperation on this issue. For the third consecutive year, Peru surpassed its goal of the eradication of more than 10,000 hectares of coca."[56]

Yet, the "war on drugs" was not being won. Despite the eradication of increasing amounts of coca, the potential harvest of coca leaf in Peru in 2007 was 60 percent greater than in 1999 (see Table 10.3). As in other nations, cultivation was becoming more efficient (more cocaine was being produced from smaller amounts of land) and moving to yet more remote areas. Aware of these problems, the U.S. government was rewarding the García government for its political will. It should also be pointed out that the estimates of the number of hectares in coca cultivation made by the U.S. Department of State were often considerably lower than those made by the United Nations.[57]

The U.S. government was also pleased that, like the Mexican government of Felipe Calderón, in August 2008 the García government launched a military campaign, called Operation Excellence, against the drug-trafficking Shining Path remnants in the Apurímac-Ene River Valley (VRAE).[58] Currently, the VRAE produces a little more than half of Peru's coca.[59] To date, however, the offensive has not been considered successful. The military's strategy and combat readiness have been questioned; the number of Shining Path cadres and the sophistication of their weapons have been greater than what the government expected.[60] The Shining Path has ambushed army patrols, attacked a police base, and brought down an army helicopter. Between August 2008 and August 2009, at least 37 soldiers, police, and civilians were killed by the Shining Path, more than double the number killed during the five previous years combined.[61] Fears of Shining Path resurgence have been mounting.

U.S.-Peruvian military cooperation included the installation of about 100 U.S. soldiers in Ayacucho in mid-2008, for what was said to be a humanitarian mission called "Operation New Horizons." Skeptical Peruvians speculated that the United States hoped to establish a military base in Ayacucho that could replace its base in Manta, Ecuador, which it was due to lose. Amid popular disgruntlement, however, the U.S. soldiers withdrew.

A different, but potentially threatening, security issue is the increasing tension between Peru and Chile. As noted above, during the 2006 presidential campaign, Humala was very critical of Chile; since Peru's devastating loss to Chile in the War of the Pacific, Peru's military in particular has reviled its Chilean counterpart. More recently, Chile's investments in Peru have provoked resentments. In late 2008 at a party, General Edwin Donayre, Peru's army commander, derided Chile; Donayre retired from the military, but his insults resonated among a surprising number of Peruvians. A key current issue is the demarcation of the maritime border; approximately 37,900 square miles of Pacific Ocean are in dispute. Chile argues that the border was determined by two bilateral treaties in the 1950s, but Peru declares that it was not. In March 2009, the García government presented its case against Chile to the International Court of Justice at the Hague. Although Peru and Chile are bound by robust economic and people-to-people relationships, it is likely that the International Court's decision will ignite nationalist passions that could be exploited by politicians. In 2009, about 38 percent of Lima residents considered armed conflict with Chile "probable" or "very probable."[62]

The U.S. government has worked toward confidence-building measures between the two militaries, but the issue is not a U.S. priority. Worse from Peru's perspective, overriding a 20-year ban on the sale of high-tech weapons to Latin America, at the turn of the century the United States authorized the sale of F-16 combat aircraft to Chile; even prior to this sale, Chile's military capabilities were vastly superior to Peru's, and Chile has continued to make much larger military purchases than Peru.

The Bilateral Agenda: Democracy and Human Rights

During the Fujimori government, Peru and the United States were often at odds on issues of democracy and human rights.[63] In particular, in April 1992, President Fujimori, with the strong support of Peru's military, executed an *autogolpe*, suspending parts of the constitution, dissolving the Congress, arresting journalists and APRA political leaders, and trying to capture Alan García. The George W. Bush administration and the Organization of American States (OAS) were dismayed; ultimately, amid intense negotiations, the Fujimori government promised a return to constitutional rule and the international community resumed its support for Peru. During this period also, when the Shining Path was strong, the government's human-rights abuses disturbed sectors of the U.S. government. Further, in July 2000, amid considerable controversy within the Clinton administration and the OAS, Fujimori was inaugurated for a third presidential term, despite machinations to allow the third term and the rigging of the election.

By contrast, since the inauguration of President Paniagua in November 2000, there have not been significant tensions between Peru and the United States on issues of democracy and human rights. As mentioned above, both Peru's 2001 and 2006 elections were free and fair; without an insurgency threat, there has not been a pattern of human-rights violations. At times, the García government has been hostile towards non-governmental organizations (NGOs) and has pushed for legislative restrictions, but NGOs have rallied and the restrictions were not seriously implemented.

For its part, the Toledo government sought to place Peru at the forefront of the effort to defend democracy in the hemisphere. In 2001, Peru was the key catalyst of the Inter-American Democratic Charter, which was signed by Latin America's foreign ministers and U.S. Secretary of State Colin Powell at an OAS General Assembly meeting in Lima on September 11. Whereas previously OAS action was triggered only by a "sudden or irregular interruption" of democracy (such as a military coup), it was now authorized more broadly, in the case of "an unconstitutional alteration of the constitutional regime."

As the Paniagua government sought to track down Montesinos, the United States provided considerable support. The Federal Bureau of Investigation (FBI) secured information that was pivotal to the capture of Montesinos in a hide-out in Venezuela in June 2001. Also, authorities in the United States and elsewhere helped to track down illegal Montesinos bank accounts; about $180 million has been returned to Peru.[64] Montesinos has been tried and convicted on several counts and is likely to remain in jail in Peru for the foreseeable future.

Further, in a landmark trial, Fujimori was held accountable. After his flight from Peru in November 2000, Fujimori had claimed Japanese citizenship and settled in Japan; there was no extradition treaty between Peru and Japan and the former president had enjoyed a safe haven. However, apparently hoping to advance his own or his party's presidential campaign, Fujimori left Japan for Chile in November 2005. To his shock, he was immediately arrested and then in 2007 extradited to Peru to face charges of human-rights violations and corruption. On April 7, 2009, Fujimori became the first former Latin American president to be convicted in his own country for the indirect perpetration of human-rights violations; he was sentenced to twenty-five years in jail. Fujimori appealed the decision but it appeared very likely to stand. In April 2009, 73 percent of Lima residents believed that the trial was an important opportunity for justice; 67 percent, that the justices had been impartial; and 64 percent, that Fujimori was guilty.[65] In September 2009, Fujimori pled guilty to the corruption charges.

With respect to Fujimori's trial, the United States has been rather passive. Upon the requests of the Toledo government, the Bush administration released thousands of documents from the U.S. Department of State, several of which were advantageous to the Peruvian state's prosecution; but documents from the Central Intelligence Agency and the U.S. Department of Defense, virtually certain to contain pertinent information as well, remained classified.[66] After the 2009 verdict, which given the exemplary nature of the trial appeared likely to have international repercussions, a U.S. acknowledgement would have been welcome, but the Barack Obama administration was silent.

Will Cooperation between the United States and Peru Be Sustained?

The current cooperation between the United States and Peru may not be sustained. The most important issue for future cooperation is the capacity of the García government to convince lower-strata Peruvians that they are sharing in the benefits of the free-market model and concomitantly to boost the chances of victory of a market-friendly president in 2011. A second key factor (not unrelated to the first) is the capacity of the Barack Obama administration to restore global respect for the United States and check the decline in U.S. economic and political power.

Trends in Living Standards in Peru

Despite the recent outstanding economic growth in Peru cited above, many Peruvians have been dissatisfied. They do not believe that their lots have improved much, if at all.

Both the Toledo and García governments argued that they were trying to improve living standards and that they succeeded to at least some degree. Indeed, according to official figures (which were questioned), the percentage of the population in poverty fell twenty points: from 55 percent in 2001 to 44 percent in 2006, 40 percent in 2007, and 35 percent in 2008.[67] On various indicators, Peru was faring better than its neighbors. For example, recent declines in infant mortality were greater than in Colombia or Ecuador, and a higher percentage of the relevant age group was enrolled in secondary school.[68] Also, Peru's Gini index of inequality was at 49.6 in 2006, a slight decline from 2003 and a better figure than that of its neighbors.[69]

Yet, many Peruvians were frustrated. In the 2007 Latinobarometer survey, Peruvians were skeptical about their economic well-being. Only 21 percent of Peruvians, versus 31 percent of Latin Americans overall, believed that the economic situation of their country would be "a little better" or "much better" over the next year and only 8 percent of Peruvians, versus 21 percent of Latin Americans overall, considered the distribution of income in their country to be "fair" or "very fair."[70] Also, 72 percent of Peruvians, versus 46 percent of Latin Americans overall, were dissatisfied with basic social services.[71]

In part, dissatisfaction was a result of the enormous differences in living standards across Peru's regions. For example, in 2007, the poverty rate was 19 percent in Lima but 73 percent in the rural highlands.[72] In 2005, chronic malnutrition was suffered by 7 percent of children under five in Lima but 43 percent in the highlands, which was the same rate as in Burkina Faso and Mali.[73] The long-standing poverty of Peru's highlands relative to Lima has been attributed by Peru's highlanders, who are overwhelmingly of indigenous descent, to the exploitation of their natural resources, and concomitant devastation of agricultural land, for the benefit of the country's coastal elites.

In recent years, as international mining, energy, and logging companies have gained large swathes of land in Peru's mountains and jungles, these beliefs have resurged. In June 2009, tensions exploded in the northern-jungle town of Bagua. For fifty-five days, indigenous groups blocked roads and waterways to protest government decrees that they feared would facilitate the takeover of their lands; the police were sent to re-take the area by force. In the ensuing clash, twenty-four police officers and at least ten protesters were killed; the indigenous association put the toll at more than forty protesters.[74] The García government exacerbated tensions by blaming the protest on agitation by Chávez allies and by denigrating the native groups and arguing that their actions threatened the PTPA. Ultimately, the decrees were repealed.

Further, even middle-strata Peruvians on the coast were disappointed by the stagnation of their salaries. Whereas between 1994 and 2000 the nationwide real minimum wage more than doubled, between 2001 and 2008 it increased only about 12 percent.[75] In private businesses with more than ten workers in Lima, between 2000 and 2007 salaries increased by at most 5 percent.[76] In the public sector (where the government has power over salary levels), the trend is the same: if the average salary is indexed at 100 in 1994, it stood at 126 in 2001 and 128 in 2008.[77] By the author's calculation, in an area near Trujillo that is at the center of the asparagus boom, salaries have barely improved since the late 1960s.

Evolving Perceptions of Power in the Hemisphere

A second issue is the growing suspicion in Peru that the power of the United States is declining but that the power of Asia, and in particular China, is rising. Further, perhaps for the first time, Peru is now perceived to have a degree of power in its own right.

Despite the cooperation between the United States and Peru during this period, U.S. economic assistance to Peru did not increase dramatically; although there was considerable year-to-year variation, total economic aid provided under the auspices of USAID was approximately $200,000 per year in the late 1990s versus $250,000 per year between 2001 and 2006; about 70 percent of the aid was allocated for narcotics control.[78]

Among virtually all sectors of Peruvian society, there was derision of President Bush; the war in Iraq was universally condemned and Bush was considered incompetent. Even though Bush was the first sitting U.S. president to visit Peru, and even though he visited twice, the visits were very short and, in part for security reasons, Bush was not able to reach out to Peruvians. In a November 2008 survey by the Universidad Católica, Lima residents were asked to rate world leaders on a scale of 100, in which 100 was the most favorable rating, 50 was exactly neutral, and 0 the most unfavorable; Bush was rated at 42, only two points higher than Cuba's Raúl Castro, while Brazil's Lula Da Silva topped the list with 62 and Spain's José Luis Rodríguez Zapatero was next at 57.[79] In this survey, the United States was considered the country most trusted to maintain world peace—but also the country that was least trusted to maintain world peace.[80] In a University of Lima October 2008 survey, Barack Obama was the U.S. presidential candidate preferred by 86 percent of respondents, versus 10 percent for John McCain.[81]

In December 2008, as Peruvians became concerned about the implications of the global financial crisis for their own welfare, they correctly perceived that the crisis originated in the United States[82] During 2009, most Peruvians believed that Peru was weathering the crisis better than most countries in the region—precisely because its economy was not linked only to the United States but rather to multiple commercial partners.

In the latter years of the first decade of the new millennium, Peruvians' interest was shifting from the United States to Asian countries, in particular China. In June 2005, Toledo made a six-day state visit to China and in March 2008 García made a four-day state visit; García was particularly effusive in his praise of China. The FTA between Peru and China was negotiated in record time and went into force in March 2009, and as mentioned above FTAs with Singapore, South Korea, and Japan were at various stages of completion. Even though Bush attended the November APEC meeting, media coverage focused heavily on President Hu Jintao. Peru's foremost newsweekly *Caretas* featured large photos of Hu Jintao with García on its first page and only a smaller one of Bush on the next page; in its end-of-the-year "Imágenes 2008" issue, there were two large photos of an embrace between Hu Jintao and García at APEC in its first two pages but no photos of Bush.[83] Said one analyst: "The US has almost fallen off the map. All anybody is talking about now is China."[84]

Items in the November 2008 survey by the Universidad Católica are indicative of these trends. On the same scale as mentioned above, but with respect to nations, Peruvians gave China their top rating, 67, and Japan their second-top, 66; China and Japan were followed by Spain, Brazil, and Canada, with the United States in seventh place at 60.[85] Both China and the United States were perceived as business partners ("*socios*") by 42 percent of respondents and as "friends" by 41 percent; Argentina and Brazil topped the list of "friends" and Chile the list of "rivals."[86]

Also, especially among Peru's middle and upper strata, there is for the first time in decades—indeed, perhaps in the country's history—nascent national pride. In the Catholic University survey, 69 percent of respondents believed that Peru had more importance in the international arena now than ten years ago.[87] Peru has achieved international recognition for its archeological treasures; in 2007, in a global popularity contest, Machu Picchu was selected as one of the "new seven wonders of the world." (Both the Toledo and García governments fought Yale University for the return of artifacts that explorer Hiram Bingham took from Machu Picchu to Yale.) In this context, tourism has skyrocketed; in 2007, there were 1.5 million foreign tourists to Peru (including about 370,000 from the United States) versus 217,000 foreign tourists (including 43,000 from the United States) in 1992.[88]

Unusually but rather happily, a primary source of Peru's new pride is its cuisine—in particular, its tasty mix of diverse ethnic culinary traditions. Peru's top chef, Gastón Acurio, was featured on the list of 100 people of the year in Iberoamérica in Spain's *El País*.[89] In an article directed to attendees of the APEC summit, Gustavo Gorriti, one of Peru's top journalists, whose customary themes are political violence, human rights, and democracy, commented:

> We are a nation that is now experiencing a gastronomic florescence. And, without vanity, we can affirm that in few places in the world does one eat as well as in this country. . . . Our cuisine is great because it is mestizo—Andean, coastal, Amazonian, Iberian, African, Chinese, Japanese, Italian, finding its identity in its fusion that surpasses its individual elements. This is our strength and our future as a nation as well: the recognition of our brilliant mestizaje and the fascinating hues that the fusion of bloodlines achieves in a new and superior culture.[90]

Conclusion

Between 2001 and 2009, cooperation between the United States and Peru was robust. In Lima and on the country's coast, a good number of Peruvians were excited about the PTPA and were not opposed to military actions in the "war on drugs." For the first time in Peru's history, the nation simultaneously enjoyed economic growth, political peace, and one-person-one-vote democracy; increasingly optimistic and confident about their country, Peruvians cooperated with the

United States but at the same time reached out to build new partnerships with China, Brazil, and many other nations around the globe.

Yet, amid these achievements, it was not clear that Peru's deep socio-economic divides were being bridged. In the country's highlands and jungles, many Peruvians remained frustrated and political movements in these areas were critical of the PTPA and the "war on drugs." Only when Peru's majorities are convinced that they are sharing in the country's gains can the cooperation between the United States and Peru be considered likely to be sustained for the foreseeable future.

Notes

1. Among the U.S. officials making such an assessment in authors' interviews were Van S. Wunder, Counselor for Public Affairs, U.S. Embassy in Peru, September 12, 2008, Washington, DC; Judy Lao, Desk Officer for Peru, Office of South America, International Trade Administration, U.S. Dept. of Commerce, November 20, 2008; Dorothy M. Ngutter, Desk Officer for Peru, U.S. Dept. of State, December 12, 2008; Kevin Whitaker, Director, Office of Andean Affairs, U.S. Dept. of State, January 16, 2009, discussion at the Center for Strategic and International Studies, Washington, DC. Among Peruvian officials and analysts were the Peruvian ambassador to the United States, Felipe Ortiz de Zevallos, "Peru on the Global Stage," presentation at George Washington University, October 15, 2008, and Carlos Basombrío, "The Outlook for Chile and Peru," presentation at the Inter-American Dialogue, May 20, 2009.
2. "Curvas Contradictorias," *Caretas* 2059 (December 23, 2008):18–19.
3. Author's interview with Alejandro Toledo, November 18, 2008, in Washington, DC.
4. Cynthia McClintock, "An Unlikely Comeback in Peru," *Journal of Democracy* 17, no. 4 (October 2006): 95–109.
5. www.onpe.gob.pe, accessed August 2, 2006.
6. ConsultAndes, "*Peru Key Indicators 08-405*," (December 21–28, 2008): 2.
7. Cynthia McClintock and Fabián Vallas, *The United States and Peru: Cooperation at a Cost* (New York: Routledge, 2003): 91–110.
8. Leon Tramel, "The U.S.-Peru Trade Promotion Agreement," Hearing of the U.S. Senate Committee on Finance, U.S. Senate (June 29, 2006): 3.
9. "El 66% de los peruanos está en favor del TLC con los Estados Unidos," *El Comercio* (December 16, 2007): A8.
10. "Toledo signs FTA with US," *Latin American Andean Group Report* (July 2006): 5.
11. Alan García, "Free Trade Inside Peru," at the Institute for International Economics, Washington, DC, October 10, 2006; and author's interview with Stanley Gacek of the AFL-CIO on García's presentation at AFL-CIO offices, December 3, 2008.
12. A valuable source on the politics of the U.S.-Peru FTA is the newsletter *Inside Trade*.
13. Among other commentators, U.S. ambassador to Peru Michael McKinley, in his presentation at the Council of the Americas, October 16, 2007, in Washington, DC.
14. *Resumen Semanal* (March 21–27, 2008).
15. Peter Hakim, "Gaining Congressional Consideration and Approval of the Colombia-U.S. FTA," Paper at the Inter-American Dialogue, www.thedialogue.org (January 2008): 1.
16. Ibid.
17. Brian Scheid, "Bush Unlikely to Announce Full Implementation of U.S.-Peru FTA," *Inside Trade* (November 21, 2008): 1–3.
18. "Odisea TLC," *Caretas* (January 22, 2009): 28.
19. Will Petrik, "Ramming the Matter Home: Peru-U.S. FTA Rushed, Diluted, and Finagled," March 19, 2009, at www.coha.org/2009/01.

20. ProInversión, "Investment Opportunities in Peru," April 2008, PowerPoint presentation. Indices are from *Doing Business* and the World Economic Forum. Available at www.proinversion.gob.pe, accessed May 2, 2008.

21. ProInversión, "Investment Opportunities in Peru," April 2008; Economist Intelligence Unit, *Country Profile Peru 2008*: 45.

22. Economic Commission for Latin America and the Caribbean, "Foreign Investment in Latin America and the Caribbean 2007," *CEPAL News* XXVIII, No. 5 (May 2008): 3 and XXIV, No. 5 (May 2009): 3.

23. Richard Webb and Graciela Fernández Baca, *Perú en Números 2008* (Lima: Cuánto, 2008): 1248; their data are from the state agency ProInversión.

24. Ibid., 1248–1250.

25. Ibid., 1248–1250. The holdings of the Netherlands and Panama are probably also exaggerated because ProInversión does not distinguish between head offices and subsidiaries abroad.

26. Ibid., 1248–1250.

27. Ibid., 1248–1250.

28. Ibid., 1248–1250.

29. The Economist Intelligence Unit, *Country Profile: Peru 2008*, 37.

30. www.yanacocha.com.pe, accessed January 5, 2009.

31. ConsultAndes S.A., "Sector Report: Battling the Financial Storm" (December 2008), 5.

32. http://www.americaeconomia.com/343309-Peru-inversiones-de-EEUU-sumarian-U.S.$2000M.note.aspx.

33. Webb and Fernández Baca, *Perú en Números 2008*, 1248.

34. ConsultAndes, S.A., *Monthly Political Analysis* (April 2009): 6–7.

35. Ibid.

36. Author's calculation from the Economist Intelligence Unit, *Country Report: Peru* (April 2009): 9.

37. Figures for 1980 and 1985 from Richard Webb and Graciela Fernández Baca (eds.) *Peru en Números 1992* (Lima: Cuánto, 1992), 1021; for 2000 and 2007, see Table 9.1.

38. Ibid.

39. Webb and Fernández Baca, *Perú en Números 2008*, 1193–1197.

40. Ibid., and Richard Webb and Graciela Fernández Baca, *Perú en Números 2002* (Lima: Cuánto, 2002), 1192 and 1209.

41. Data from the Banco Central de Reserva del Perú, available at www.bcrp.gob.pe/docs/Publicaciones/Presentaciones-Discursos/2009/Presentación-05-2009.pdf, accessed May 25, 2009.

42. ConsultAndes, *Peru Key Indicators* 8, no. 404 (December 14–21, 2008): 6.

43. Webb and Fernández Baca, *Perú en Números 2008*, 181 (for 2003–2008) and Webb and Fernández Baca, *Perú en Números 2006*, 160 for the 2002 figure. Figures for 2008 were preliminary.

44. Figures for all Latin American nations for 2000–2009 are available at the World Economic Outlook Database, www.imf.org/external/pubs/ft/weo/2008/01/weodata/index.aspx. Accessed August 5, 2009. Figures for 2008 were preliminary.

45. Alvaro Henzler, "U.S.-Peru FTA: Impact and Perspectives," PowerPoint presentation at the George Washington University, October 2008, slide number 18. Public opinion polls were by Apoyo.

46. An excellent brief discussion is "Peru: To the Barricades," *The Economist* (December 6, 2008): 51–52.

47. Ibid., and Ambassador Felipe Ortiz de Zevallos, "Peru on the Global Stage," presentation at the George Washington University, October 15, 2008.

48. Humala has called for the legalization of some coca-leaf products and has rejected a role for the military in counternarcotics operations. See "Peru wins plaudits for anti-drug efforts," *Latin American Andean Group Report* 3, no. 3 (March 2009): 15 and "Humala absolved of murder charges," *Latin American Weekly Report* 9, no. 18 (May 7, 2009): 11.

49. McClintock and Vallas, *The United States and Peru*, 111–122.

50. Joby Warwick, "CIA Withheld Details on Downing, IG Says," *Washington Post* (November 21, 2008): A8.

51. "Ordena bombardear pozas de maceración," *Perú 21* (April 3, 2007), at http://peru21.pe/impresa/noticia/ordena-bombardear-pozas-maceracion/2007-04-03/53321.

52. Figures on social and economic aid vs. military and police aid from Just the Facts, at www.justf.org (accessed May 12, 2009); in 2004–2007, social and economic aid was about $55 million annually and military and police aid about $58 million. On the problems of DEVIDA, see Ricardo Soberón Garrido, "Situación del Narcotráfico en el Perú, Las Políticas Antidrogas y La Geopolítica Regional," Programa de Cooperación en Seguridad Regional Documento 23, Fundación Friedrich Ebert Stiftung (August 2008): 4–5.

53. Soberón, "Situación del Narcotráfico," 3–5; Simon Romero, "Cocaine Trade Helps Rebels Reignite War in Peru," *New York Times* (March 18, 2009): A1 and A10. Indeed, this description is not controversial.

54. Ibid.

55. "Embajador norteamericano destaca logros en lucha antidrogas," *El Comercio* (April 13, 2008), at http://www.elcomercio.com.pe/ediciononline/HTML/2008-04-13/embajador-norteamericano-destaca-logros-lucha-antidrogas.html.

56. See the statement at: http://www.whitehousedrugpolicy.gov/publications/policy/ndcs08sp/chap3.html.

57. For example, the 2009 International Narcotics Control Strategy Report indicated 36,000 hectares, but the United Nations 53,700 (see www.unodc.org/documents/crop-monitoring/Andean_report_2008.pdf, accessed May 24, 2009). The United Nations data are those used by DEVIDA and are widely considered to be less affected by politics than the U.S. data.

58. The 2008 International Narcotics Control Strategy Report, accessed on January 5, 2009, includes accolades for Peru's efforts to extend the state into remote areas.

59. Soberón Garrido, "Situación del Narcotráfico," 2.

60. "Sendero inflicts heavy losses on army," *Latin American Andean Group Report* 9, no. 4 (April 2009): 5.

61. Ibid., and death-toll figures for subsequent 2009 attacks from the August and September issues of the *Latin American Andean Group Report* and death-toll figures for 2003–2008 from the U.S. Department of State annual reports on human rights in Peru, available at www.state.gov.

62. Grupo de Opinión Pública, Barómetro Estudio 451 (4–5 April 2009), item 24.

63. McClintock and Vallas, *The United States and Peru*, 131–161.

64. "Fact Sheet on Stolen Asset Recovery," at http://go.worldbank.org/8VPOP4KJIO.

65. "El Caso Fujimori y la Opinión Pública," Instituto de Opinión Pública, Universidad Católica del Perú (April 2009): 2–5.

66. "Faltó la carne," *Caretas* 1716 (April 11, 2002): 30–31.

67. Webb and Fernández Baca, *Perú en Números 2008*, 599 and "La pobreza hizo click," *Caretas* 2079 (May 21, 2009): 34–36. The methodology for poverty calculation changed in 2001 and accordingly figures for the 2000s are not comparable with those for the 1980s or 1990s. For criticisms of these figures, see Richard Webb, "Quizás, Quizás, Quizás," *El Comercio* (June 2, 2008): editorial page.

68. The World Bank, *World Development Indicators 2008* (Washington, DC: The World Bank, 2008), 118–119, and the World Bank, *World Development Indicators 2009* (Washington, DC: The World Bank, 2009), 84–86.

69. The World Bank, *World Development Indicators 2008*, 68–69 and the World Bank, *World Development Indicators 2009*, 72–73.

70. www.latinobarometer.org, 2007 survey, from a presentation by Nora Lustig at George Washington University, March 2008.

71. www.latinobarometer.org, 2008 survey, from a presentation by Nora Lustig at George Washington University, March 2008.

72. Webb and Fernández Baca, *Perú en Números 2008*, 599.

73. Ibid., 345, and "Drama de Hierro," *Caretas* 1812 (February 25, 2004): 23.

74. "Commission to probe Amazon violence," *Latin American Andean Group Report* 9, no. 9 (September 2009): 11.

75. Webb and Fernández Baca, *Perú en Números 2008*, 677.

76. Ibid., 676.

77. Ibid., 691.

78. http://qesdb.cdie.org/lac/index.html, "USAID: Assistance Statistics for Latin America and the Caribbean," accessed January 5, 2009.

79. Instituto de Opinión Pública of the Universidad Católica del Perú, "Estado de la Opinión Pública" (November 2008): 6.

80. Ibid., 10–12.

81. Universidad de Lima Barómetro, October 2008, item 40.

82. The sub-title of the article "El año que el mundo hizo 'crack'" in one prestigious Peruvian newspaper was "La Crisis Financiera Originada en Estados Unidos Puso Al Mundo en Vilo." See *Peru 21* (January 3, 2009): 8l.

83. *Caretas* 2055 (November 27, 2008): 10–12; *Caretas* 2059 (December 23, 2008): 50–70.

84. Brian Scheid, "Bush Unlikely to Announce Full Implementation of U.S.-Peru FTA," *Inside Trade* (November 21, 2008): 3.

85. Ibid., 7.

86. Instituto de Opinión Pública of the Universidad Católica del Perú, 16.

87. Ibid., 9.

88. Base de Datos Turisticos at http://www.observatoroioturisticodelperu.com/mapas/usatrhrp.pdf, accessed May 22, 2009, and Webb and Fernández Baca, *Perú en Números 2008*, 1069.

89. "Los 4 fantásticos," *El Comercio* (January 4, 2009): A24.

90. Gustavo Gorriti, "Memo Para Corresponsales," *Caretas* 2054 (November 19, 2008): 37.

11 Relations between the United States and Venezuela, 2001–2009

A Bridge in Need of Repairs

Carlos A. Romero and Javier Corrales

In the 2000s, relations between the United States (US) and Venezuela became the most contentious of all bilateral relations in the region. President Hugo Chávez has earned the reputation as the head of state in the region that most virulently criticizes the U.S. government and its economic system. Chávez's animosity, evident in speeches and some policies, seems hard to stop. In September 2008 animosity reached new heights when Chávez, in a speech full of expletives, declared the U.S. ambassador in Caracas, Patrick Duddy, *persona non grata*. Even before president-elect Barack Obama took office in January 2009, Chávez was already accusing him of having the same "negative" attitudes as George W. Bush.

To understand the conflict between both nations, two questions need be addressed. First: What generates this level of conflict? This question takes us in the direction of analyzing the origins—ideological, political and structural—of conflict.

The second question goes in the opposite direction: Why have not the relations collapsed entirely? The U.S.-Venezuelan discord is mostly political and so far it has not spilled over into economics and trade. The United States remains Venezuela's main trade partner, and Venezuela complies with its foreign debt payments and sells oil uninterruptedly to the United States.

In this chapter we seek to analyze these contradictory directions in U.S.–Venezuelan relations. We begin with a descriptive account of the increasing number of disagreements between both countries, at the bilateral, regional and global levels. We show how this discord sometimes conforms and sometimes does not fit well with the concept of "soft balancing" used by some international relations scholars to describe conflict among certain states. We then focus on economic factors. Specifically we show that economic interdependence in some ways fuels this discord (contradicting what liberal theories of international relations would predict) and in other ways serves as a restraining force (in accordance with the expectations of liberal theories). We then assess the strengths and weaknesses of the different hypotheses offered by governments and analysts alike to explain the rise in tensions. We conclude with a discussion of possible scenarios in the post-Bush era.

Soft Balancing and Political Conflict between the United States and Venezuela

The Concept of "Soft Balancing"

"Do you really want to be my friend?" could have been the answer of President George W. Bush to the Venezuelan head of state, Hugo Chávez, when he informally asked the U.S. president during the 2001 Third Summit of the Americas whether he "wanted to be his friend."[1] Differences between the two governments had already surfaced.[2] But the relation began to deteriorate quickly after September 11, 2001.[3] Chávez was one of the few world leaders to forcefully criticize the U.S. invasion of Afghanistan. He refused U.S. assistance during a national emergency brought on by flooding. By 2004, Chávez was directly accusing the United States of supporting the April 2002 coup attempt, instigating the 2002–2003 oil workers' strike, of being behind several attempts to murder him, and generally of causing most of the domestic political unrest.

One way to conceptualize Chávez's political animosity toward the United States is to invoke the concept of "soft balancing."[4] Soft balancing refers to a country's efforts—short of military actions—to frustrate and undermine the foreign policy objectives of other more powerful nations.[5] This theoretical concept differs from more traditional forms of "power balance" in that the challenging nation seeks not to destroy the hegemonic country but to hinder its actions—*by increasing its costs.*[6]

There is some debate among scholars over factors that give rise to soft-balancing,[7] but there is little debate over the fact that Venezuela under the Chávez government is showing signs of soft-balancing in its relations with the United States.[8] These signs include: Avoiding systematic cooperation (i.e. not collaborating with efforts against drug trafficking), building alliances with nations that have exhibited strong anti-American foreign policies (i.e. Iran, Cuba, Belarus, Syria, Russia), creating obstacles to consensus building in international fora (e.g. the anti-U.S. "parallel summit" during the Third Summit of the Americas in Mar de Plata, Argentina, 2005), counter-offers in regional integration matters such as the Alternativa Bolivariana para las Américas (ALBA), created in 2004, and creating diplomatic "snags and ploys" (i.e. the joint military initiatives with Cuba and Russia in late 2008).

Nevertheless, as we show below, the concept of soft balancing only provides a *partial* explanation for Venezuela's behavior. In some areas, Venezuela's foreign policy towards the United States is too soft to be considered "balancing"—it is based more on talk than concrete actions. As indicated by Maihold, there is an enormous contrast between the "great pronouncements" and Chávez's modest concrete actions.[9] In other areas, Chávez's foreign policy has become too "hard" to count as "soft"-balancing. This is evident with respect to arms purchases, his lax attitude towards drug trafficking, and alleged secret ties with nuclear or terrorism-sponsoring states and movements. Furthermore, soft balancing is not always at the center of Chavez's foreign policy. He often resorts to alternative foreign policy objectives.

War of Words

Most of the confrontation between the United States and Venezuela is all words. Rhetorically, since the early 2000s Chávez has unearthed the old idea that developing nations need to fight off the empire and defend their sovereignty.[10] Chávez accuses the United States—the empire—of complete meddling in domestic affairs. Chávez also issues personal insults to U.S. presidents and high-ranking officials. Chávez stresses the need for a multipolar world, free of U.S. arrogance, and criticizes U.S.-based or U.S.-supported organizations that are dedicated to promoting democracy. He also criticizes local civil organizations that have ties across the hemisphere, while simultaneously supporting anti-U.S. social movements all across Latin America.

One of the most notorious episodes of verbal recrimination took place on September 20, 2006. Referring to Bush during a speech to the United Nations, Chávez expressed: "The devil was here yesterday. You can still smell the sulfur."[11] Although some countries applauded Chávez's words, the majority was appalled. This speech was so excessive that it might have cost Venezuela's chances to obtain the necessary number of votes to occupy a temporary seat in the Security Council, an objective that Chávez was keen on.[12]

Washington in turn accuses Caracas of cracking down on the Venezuelan opposition, undermining democracy and human rights in the country, and fostering a non-cooperative spirit—or refraining from cooperating—on vital hemispheric security issues, such as drug interdiction and counterterrorism.[13]

On several occasions, the Bush administration called for renewed dialogue. One such occasion occurred shortly after Chavez's electoral victory in December 2006. The then U.S. ambassador to Venezuela, William Brownfield, aptly described the status quo: "We have differences . . . serious, deep and ample differences in areas such as socialism, capitalism, free trade, hemispheric relations, relations with countries the likes of Iran and North Korea, and it is possible that such differences will not disappear tomorrow or the day after that." At the same time, ". . . we also share a second area where we have traditionally collaborated in matters such as the struggle against illicit drugs, energy, terrorism, trade affairs, etc."[14]

Brownfield became known for trying to institute a policy of dodging verbal accusations. He managed to earn the support of the State Department, and eventually the White House, on behalf of this approach. But ultimately, this policy had limited success. At times, Chávez showed moderation, saying for instance: "We are ready for dialogue . . ."[15] But by mid 2007, such moderation was increasingly rare. In Chávez's own words: "An understanding is not possible between our revolution and the Venezuelan oligarchy or with the government of the United States. Can we coexist? Yes! But will we ever embrace each other? . . . No, no, no. That is impossible."[16]

On March 2007, the United States appointed a new ambassador to Venezuela, Patrick Duddy, who attempted to sustain Brownfield's policy of dodging verbal accusations.[17] Yet again, Chávez did not show restraint. He continued to claim that the United States intended to include Venezuela in its list of terrorist-sponsoring nations. A State Department spokesperson, Adam Ereli, indicated that his office had "no intentions whatsoever" of taking such actions.[18] Chávez replied by indicating ". . . if the United States wants to end relations, it's up to them. I have no problem in shutting down the [oil] refineries. Then we'll see how they deal with high oil prices. We don't want to go there; we just want to be left alone. Let imperialism face the truth, Venezuela will not become a colony of the United States."[19]

Although it is true that during the second Bush administration the war of words became a bit more asymmetrical, with verbal attacks from Miraflores Palace becoming increasingly strident while verbal attacks from the White House became less frequent, other agencies of the U.S. government occasionally join this war of words. The U.S. Defense Department Southern Command, for instance, drafted a report which indicated: "Although the Southern Command is still in search of working opportunities with the Venezuelan Army, our efforts have been hindered by the Venezuelan authorities."[20] On January 2, 2006, the Venezuelan government informed the Bush administration that a navy officer assigned to the U.S. Embassy in Caracas, John Correa, had been declared *persona non grata* owing to alleged espionage.[21] Less than 23 hours later, the U.S. government declared Venezuelan Embassy diplomat in Washington, Jenny Figueredo, *persona non grata*. Sean McCormack, State Department spokesperson indicated on February 3, 2006: "We don't like this game of 'give and take' with the Venezuelan government, but they started this and the United States chose to respond."[22]

The State Department has also joined in. Its 2007 annual report on Human Rights in Latin America points out that the Venezuelan government "harasses the opposition and non-governmental organizations, and undermines judicial independence."[23] On April 6, 2007, the State Department indicated that "Venezuela and Cuba remain isolated from democratic norms in the hemisphere."[24] The department accused Venezuela of being one of the countries that least fought human trafficking and added that the country was "a source, a place of transit and destination of women and children for the purpose of sexual exploitation and forced labor."[25]

Nevertheless, the fact that the White House in general became, in the last years of the Bush administration, less willing to engage in a war of words, indicates that Chávez's incendiary rhetoric has lost its capacity to provoke high-level government officials in the United States. That is to say, the war of words is a means of exercising soft power that over time became too "soft." It seems to have decreasing impact on the United States, and may have even proven at times to be counterproductive, as Chávez's UN defeat in 2006 suggests.

Military Sanctions and Military Impulses

The one area where the United States has exercised some form of punitive policy is the military realm. The United States managed to persuade Israel to suspend maintenance services for Venezuela's F-16 aircrafts, Spain to stop supplying U.S. technology to C-295 aircrafts offered to Venezuela, and Brazil's Embraer to stop selling Super-Tucan airplanes to the Chávez's government.[26] On May 15, 2006, the State Department announced a ban on arms sales and military equipment to

Venezuela.[27] In September 2008, the State Department sanctioned sales from the Venezuelan Military Industry, CAVIM,[28] that could be used to help Syria, Iran, or North Korea to develop weapons of mass destruction or cruise or ballistic missile systems. As a consequence, CAVIM was banned from having commercial ties with any U.S. agency, participating in any assistance programs, and purchasing weapons or ammunition of any kind. All arms sales contracts were immediately canceled.

These military sanctions have provided the Venezuelan government enough reasons to seek alternative military suppliers, on the reasonable claim that it needs to reduce dependency on the United States for weapons modernization. However, Venezuela's effort to move away from U.S. military purchases predated these bans. It actually began as early as 1999 when Chávez decided to expel the U.S. Military Mission in Caracas and cancel all professional and educational cooperation programs, including outstanding military procurement. The Venezuelan Government also withdrew the Venezuelan Army from joint hemispheric and bilateral military exercises with the United States. Thus, the U.S. bans on arms sales do not really explain the start of Venezuela's military "divorce" from the United States.

Neither does it account for the extraordinary sums that Venezuela has allocated for weapon procurement in the last years of the Bush administration. In 2006 the country launched a process of modernization of its armed forces based on a six-year U.S.$30 billion investment. Plans called for purchasing and updating military equipment and technology, including supersonic aircrafts, 15 submarines, 138 ships, radars, and 600,000 GPS laser-led common and intelligent bombs. From 2005 to 2007, the Venezuelan government spent close to U.S.$4.4 billion in weapons imports,[29] which is an extraordinary amount (almost U.S.$220 per capita) in weapons alone.

Non-Cooperation with Narco-Traffic Interdiction

In some areas, Venezuela has taken steps that directly challenge some of the vital security interests of the United States. One such key step was the 2005 decision to expel the Drug Enforcement Administration (DEA). Less than two years after this expulsion, drug trafficking through Venezuelan territory multiplied by three, turning the country into the main cocaine transit "bridge" between South America and Europe (by way of Northern and Western Africa). Venezuela has become one of the countries in the region that does least against drug production and transport.

Venezuela denies the accusations that it is doing little to stop drug traffic. Yet, even Venezuelan official records indicate that cocaine eradication in the country dropped by 50 percent in the 2005–2008 period.[30]

Irrespective of the debate over figures and effort, the truth is that expelling the DEA alone had a disastrous impact in relations between the two nations, and has caused growing discomfort within the European Union as well.[31] For good or for evil, the battle against drugs is at the top of the U.S. national security agenda in the hemisphere. Once the DEA was ousted from Venezuela, the world of drugs in the Andean region gained in Venezuela a vast theatre of operations—free of U.S. vigilance. As drug trade increases (and oil revenues continue decline due to the slump in oil prices since 2008), Venezuela risks turning into a narco-state. This would represent a serious security challenge for the United States.

Maletagate and the Ambassadors' Farewell

Another event that indirectly strained relations between the two nations was "Maletagate" ("Suitcase-gate" in English, and known as "Valija-gate" in Argentina). This incident involved a suitcase containing U.S.$800,000 which was confiscated at the Aeroparque airport in Buenos Aires, Argentina, on August 4, 2007.[32] Venezuelan-American Guido Antonini Wilson took responsibility for the suitcase, but claimed to know nothing of its content. Antonini Wilson was traveling to Argentina in a corporate aircraft owned by Petróleos de Venezuela (PDVSA), Venezuela's state-owned oil company, leased to Energía Argentina Sociedad Anónima (ENARSA), the Argentine state-owned oil corporation. Several Venezuelan government officials and PDVSA executives were also on board.[33]

Following this airport incident, Antonini Wilson made contact with the U.S. Federal Bureau of Investigation (FBI), requesting protection. He repeated that the money was not his and that it was intended for the presidential campaign of Argentina's first lady, Cristina Fernández de Kirchner. On December 2007, the FBI announced the arrest of three Venezuelan citizens, charged on pressuring Antonini Wilson to accept that the bag belonged to him.

The case led to trial in Miami against the detainees. Two of them made a guilty plea, and a third pleaded innocence. One of the three, Franklin Durán, was found guilty and sentenced on March 2009 to four years in prison.[34]

The Maletagate incident is important because it suggests that an important component of Venezuela's foreign policy involves the illicit flows of monies from Venezuela into other countries for political purposes. This is becoming a matter of growing concern for the United States. The Treasury Department has already taken some punitive measures. On September 11, 2008, the department froze the assets in the U.S. pertaining to three Venezuelan government officers. The Treasury alleged that these individuals were assisting Colombian leftist irregulars, providing them with direct contacts with the Venezuelan government, facilitating a loan for 200,000 Euros to purchase guns, launder drug money, and obtain false documentation to travel across the Colombian border.[35]

Immediately after the "Suitcase-gate" episode, tensions between Venezuela and the United States escalated. Chávez declared U.S. ambassador Patrick Duddy *persona non grata*, giving him 72 hours to leave the country, and recalling Venezuela's ambassador, Bernardo Alvarez. Chávez did not exactly connect the Treasury with his decision to expel Duddy, but the public justifications he offered for the expulsion were not terribly compelling. The Venezuelan government justified the expulsion, first, by accusing the United States of participating in the alleged coup of 2002 and being behind assassination attempts against the Venezuelan president. Chávez never presented any evidence.[36] Second, the government also claimed to be acting in solidarity with Bolivia's president Evo Morales and his decision to expel the U.S. ambassador in Bolivia. It's hard to dismiss the idea that a possible trigger was the

Treasury's action. The United States retaliated by declaring the already-departed Venezuelan ambassador, Bernardo Álvarez *persona non grata.*

Expelling or recalling ambassadors is evidence of both the seriousness as well as the inane nature of the matter. On the one hand, it is not a common practice for Latin American presidents to expel U.S. ambassadors, and vice versa. To our knowledge, the last time a U.S. ambassador to the region was declared *persona non grata* was in 1973 (Vincent de Roulet in Jamaica).[37] On the other, expelling the ambassadors hardly affected trade relations between the two nations. There seems to be a pattern. Each nation grows increasingly frustrated with the other, and yet retaliatory measures don't amount to much.

Soft Balancing at the Regional Level

Chávez has attempted to convert the region into an arena for his soft-balancing policy. To compete against the United States for influence in the region, Chávez has developed an alternative to U.S. "soft power." Soft power refers to the values or goals that a country tries to promote abroad that might have intrinsic appeal among other nations. In the case of the United States, core elements of its soft power include the respect for democracy, the rule of law, human rights, and political minorities at home, and for some, the value of entrepreneurship. In order to compete against these liberal values professed by the United States, Chávez has developed what one of us has denominated as "social-power" diplomacy: the value of investing in social develop-ment programs and empowering new political groups above other goals. In promot-ing this social-power diplomacy, Chávez pays little attention to the actual results of the social programs he helps finance (i.e., he hardly worries about the cost-benefit ratio of his investments). He also shows no regard for preserving the system of checks and balances that limit the power for presidents, if such presidents have popular sup-port. And he privileges public sector without much regard for public transparency.[38]

Promoting social power—which entails both intangible (a strong dose of anti-imperialistic ideology) and tangible assets (plenty of economic subsidies)—has allowed Chávez to promote a model of governance that is different from the liberal values that the United States promotes, especially those agencies concerned with fostering development and democracy, all of which place a high value on govern-ment accountability. Call it "participatory democracy" (the preferred term during the early years of the Chávez administration) or "XXI Century Socialism" (the pre-ferred term today), the defense of unrestrained statism, not seen in Latin America since the early 1980s, is a hallmark of "chavismo."[39]

Spreading this model of governance in the region—through supra-national institutions, state-to-state relations, and support for leftist opposition forces—has had mixed results. On the one hand, it has allowed Chávez to create allies, or at least, tacit agreements with other governments not to criticize each other. This agree-ment includes even many non-radical governments. On the one hand, social-power diplomacy has failed to unite the region against the United States, and in some cases, has actually made political forces in the region turn highly critical of Venezuela, and in some cases, electorally victorious.

Supra-National Efforts: The OAS and Free Trade Agreement
of the Americas (FTAA)

Chávez has tried to use the OAS as an arena for his soft-balancing policy and especially social-power diplomacy. He has opposed most positions supported by the
United States and other nations regarding the organization's role as a guarantor of
democracy and human rights in Latin America and the Caribbean, including active
participation in electoral observation missions and support for non-governmental
organizations involved in electoral oversight.

Chávez has also attempted to block regional integration through the U.S-sup-
ported promotion of regional free trade. He calls instead for integration based on
state property (agreements among state-owned enterprises) rather than with private direct investment. This statism is a key element of ALBA.[40]

Since 2003 Venezuela has received enough oil revenues to develop an energy and
financial assistance program worldwide, especially for Latin America and the
Caribbean. Chávez disburses this aid through bilateral and multilateral schemes
such as Petroamérica, PetroCaribe and the San José Energy Agreement.
Venezuela's economic contributions to these programs are estimated to have
amounted to U.S.$40.3 billion, including a poverty fund for America, long-term
financing under privileged conditions of Venezuelan oil supply to more than fourteen countries in the region, infrastructure investments, purchase of other governments' debt papers; subsidized or free heating oil for low-income communities in
the United States through the Venezuelan state-owned CITGO, in collaboration
with U.S. municipal governments or non-governmental organizations.

State-to-State and State-to-Society Relations:
Ties with Other Left-wing Governments

At the start of the twenty-first century, Latin American politics experienced what
came to be known as the leftward shift, with the election of candidates and movements that campaigned on the left of the political spectrum. It soon became clear
that at least two "Lefts" emerged.[41] A Left that was more willing to negotiate with
Washington and undertake social change through democratic parameters while
preserving market forces, and a radical Left committed to statism and anti-party
politics, distrustful of checks and balances that may constrain the executive branch,
and repeating anti-American and anti-market slogans.[42]

Hugo Chávez's foreign policy objective towards the radical Left has been to
become its undisputed leader, and towards the moderate Left, to make it less critical of Chávez and less moderate, at least in its relations with the United States. In
order to achieve these goals, Chávez has resorted to two tools: (1) provision of subsidized "goods" (economic assistance, loans and subsidized oil) without many economic conditionalities, and (2) threatening the moderate Left with governance
problems by appearing capable of either stirring trouble or tempering domestic
tensions across each country's more radical factions.

The strategy's main achievements have been twofold. First, Latin America's radical Left—in power or in the opposition—certainly considers Hugo Chávez a

prominent leader, at least in economic terms. Second, many of these leftist presidents owe their electoral victories in part to technical and financial assistance from Venezuela: Evo Morales in Bolivia, Rafael Correa in Ecuador, Daniel Ortega in Nicaragua, Fernando Lugo in Paraguay, and Mauricio Funes in El Salvador. Néstor and Cristina Kirchner in Argentina and José Manuel Zelaya in Honduras may not owe their elections to Chávez's help, but once in office, they received substantial help. With Zelaya, Venezuela became the predominant external source of financing in Honduras.

The closest ties seem to be reserved for Bolivia. President Chávez provided financial, technical, and political advice (including personnel) to Evo Morales's campaign, and direct advice and financing during Morales's drive to change the Constitution (2006–2008). Chávez offered to create a bi-national company, PetroAndina, dedicated to oil development, to collaborate with the Argentinean-Bolivian project to build a liquid gas plant, to create the Organización de Países Productores y Exportadores de Gas del Sur, Opegasur (Organization of Gas producing and Exporting Countries of the South),[43] and to finance an unknown portion of the Bolivian state fiscal expenditure.

Ecuador has also benefited from Venezuela's assistance, although the relationship does not seem to be as close as Bolivia's. President Rafael Correa has indicated on several occasions that he accepts Chávez's "ideological package" and apparently also received counseling during the country's constitutional reform (2007–2008). Venezuela sponsored Ecuador's 2007 reentry into the Organization of Petroleum Exporting Countries, after a fifteen-year absence. Ecuador is now a member of ALBA and OPEC. Although Correa occasionally claims not to be aligned to Caracas, their foreign policies are similar, especially with respects to OPEC (supporting supply restrictions). The closest that Chávez has acted on behalf of Ecuador was shortly after the March 2008 conflict with Colombia, which prompted Venezuela to call for military mobilization against Colombia in solidarity with Ecuador; but less than a week later, Chávez retracted and lessened his support for Correa in his quarrel with Colombia.

Like Morales and Correa, Nicaragua's President Daniel Ortega owes his 2006 electoral victory to Chávez's support. But unlike Morales and Correa, he came to power with minority support: 38 percent. Ortega therefore has not been able to accumulate as much power as these other leaders, even though he has generated similar levels of polarization.

Despite these victories for Chávez, his policy of promoting the Left in the region has had major failures as well. Caracas has failed to convince the nonradical Left to align behind Venezuela, embrace its policy of soft balancing the United States, sever ties with the DEA, or turn its back on U.S. trade in general. A clear example of this failure was the vote for the two non-permanent seats in the United Nations Security Council in 2006. Venezuela lobbied hard for a seat, competing heavily against Guatemala, which had U.S. support. Neither country obtained a majority of votes and in the end, Panama won as a form of compromise.[44] One could even argue that Chávez has actually made some members of the moderate Left turn friendlier toward the United States: Luiz Inácio "Lula" da Silva in Brazil, Tabaré Vásquez in

Uruguay, Alan García in Perú are all closer to the United States than they were during their presidential campaigns, and Chile has maintained the same closeness to Washington since the beginning of 1990s. In many countries, Chávez has become a very unpopular figure, as unpopular as George Bush, according to some polls.[45] Chávez is more of a polarizing than a uniting figure across the Latin American electorate, with some of the deepest divisions within the Left itself, especially in Argentina, Peru, Colombia, and Mexico.

Furthermore, Chávez's foreign policy toward leftist governments in the region is not without competition. At the end of the Bush administration, Venezuela started facing a sort of soft-balancing response from Washington and Brasilia. One of the most remarkable changes in U.S.–Latin America relations, which began under Bush's and Lula's second terms, was a dramatic rapprochement between Washington and Brasília. In the United States, this rapprochement counts on the full support of the White House, Congress, the press, and many sectors of U.S. society, left and right. Although not openly expressed, analysts acknowledge that Brazil and Venezuela are clearly competing to establish their influence in the region,[46] and it is clear that the United States has placed its bets on Brazil, and that Brazil enjoys far more prestige in the region than Venezuela.

Another way in which the United States has tried to soft-balance Venezuela is by offering free trade agreements bilaterally. After failing to obtain hemispheric-wide free trade agreements, Bush switched toward a policy of bilateral trade negotiations with any takers. Many countries in the region have welcomed these negotiations, frustrating Chávez's desire to have an alternative trade association free of U.S. influence.[47]

Alliance with Cuba

Hugo Chávez's warm welcome in Havana on December 1994 and his electoral victory in 1998 marked the beginning of a new chapter in Venezuela–Cuba relations. This new chapter has had two parts, thus far. The first from 1999 to 2004 focused mostly on bilateral issues. Since 2004, the relationship has acquired a closer and more multilateral dimension.[48]

During a first stage, Venezuela committed to helping Cuba soften the impact of the U.S. trade embargo and the harsh economic conditions brought about by the collapse of trade with the USSR. Venezuela also committed to helping Cuba lessen its dependence on private foreign investment. These commitments became formal with the October 2000 Comprehensive Cooperation Agreement, calling for more trade, including "selling" 57,000 barrels of Venezuelan oil in Cuba at the subsidized price of U.S.$27 a barrel, with Venezuela paying for transportation and insurance costs. In exchange, Cuba began exporting to Venezuela initially 13,000 Cuban workers mainly from the health sector (physicians, nurses, and paramedics), and sports and education professionals.[49] The number of military personnel and intelligence exported is unknown, although certainly a much smaller yet much more influential group than the crew of social workers.

The second stage began with the launch of ALBA, initially signed only by Venezuela and Cuba in 2004 but since then signed by Bolivia and Nicaragua in

2006, Dominica and Honduras in 2008, and St. Vincent and the Grenadines in 2009. ALBA veered the relation with Cuba towards a regional strategy.[50]

Even in this new stage of greater multilateralism, both nations continued on their path toward deeper bilateral relations. In 2005, for instance, Venezuela increased its daily oil shipments to 95,000 barrels per day, which represent 54 percent of the total 175,000 barrels per day consumed by the island (Cuba produces some 80,000 barrels per day). Cuba is a member of PetroCaribe, a Venezuelan oil cooperation mechanism for the Caribbean created in 2005, and receives by this means an additional sum of 41,000 barrels.[51]

Overall, trade of goods and services between Venezuela and Cuba increased from U.S.$388 million in 1998 to U.S.$10.9 billion in 2008. Between 2007 and 2009 alone, trade almost doubled, from U.S.$2.6 billion to U.S.$5.3 billion. It has been estimated that some 39,000 Cuban "personnel" were in Venezuela in 2007, 31,000 of them in the health sector, which represents 75 percent of all of Cuba's international health staff.[52]

The relationship with Cuba has a military component as well. As soon as Chávez declared the United States the top enemy in Venezuela's war scenarios, the Venezuelan armed forces adopted a military doctrine to counter a potential attack from the United States commonly known as the asymmetrical war doctrine. Accordingly, Venezuelan armed forces receive technical and ideological training to fight a war and to inflict losses on a decidedly more powerful adversary. This war scenario includes the possibility of fighting the United States over Cuba. There is also a joint Cuban-Venezuelan proposal to create a defense block different from the Inter-American Treaty of Reciprocal Assistance, with the participation of Cuba but not the United States, and to provide strategic assistance to friendly governments and revolutionary movements in the region. Venezuela has also adopted a Cuban inspired military iconography (e.g., the new motto of the Bolivarian National Armed Force is: "Country, socialism or death").

However, it remains unclear whether, in the event of a Cuba–United States military confrontation, Venezuela would provide military support for Cuba, allow Cuba to use Venezuelan military facilities, or provide any type of advice.[53]

Ever since Raúl Castro succeeded Fidel Castro as president of Cuba, there is talk that relations with Venezuela have soured a bit. In September 2008, Raúl Castro seemed to have taken a stand toward the Bolivian situation that differed from that of Venezuela, making no reference to the deteriorating relations between Venezuela and the United States while still asking the U.S. government to allow for a six-month period for the purchase of U.S. goods by a credit line.[54] However, both countries deny that there are any rifts. The Cuban president officially visited Venezuela on December 13–15, 2008, his first visit abroad as president.[55]

There are good reasons to expect the Cuban-Venezuelan alliance to remain strong as long as Chávez and the Castros rule. To understand the strength of this alliance, it helps to think of a double analogy. For Cuba, Venezuela has become the "new Soviet Union," a provider of significant economic subsidies in exchange for no conditionalities on how the Castros run the island, For Venezuela, Cuba has become in turn a sort of issuer of a certificate of good "radical" conduct and an exporter of technical personnel. Thus, each country supplies the other with a set of assets that are inexpensive for the sending party but highly valuable for the receiving party.[56] This suggests that the relationship is stronger than any differences of personality between Chávez and Raúl Castro.

Soft Balancing Outside the Region: Iran, China and Russia

In his extra-hemispheric relations, and especially with authoritarian regimes, Chávez seeks to achieve (1) soft balancing of the United States, but also these other goals: (2) maximizing weapons acquisition; (3) finding trading partners who do business mostly through state-owned enterprises rather than private investors; and (4) cooperating with nations whose governments are not subject to democratic accountability.

These four objectives explain relations with Iran, and to some extent, Russia and China. Because Iran is an avowed adversary of the United States, links with this nation contribute to Venezuela's goals of soft balancing the United States. Links with Iran also provide arms and ammunition, and this has alarmed the United States, which fears that Iran may help Venezuela develop nuclear capabilities without international verification, or vice versa. Although nuclear arms cooperation between Caracas and Teheran has not been confirmed, it cannot be ruled out either.[57] Venezuela supported Iran's dispute with the United Nations regarding Iran's nuclear program and was the only nation to twice oppose the resolutions adopted by the International Agency of Atomic Energy sanctioning Iran in September 2005 and February 2006.

Iran also serves as a trading partner that does business through mostly state-owned enterprises. Trade between the two nations climbed from U.S.$1.1 million in 2004 to U.S.$50.7 million in 2006. In 2006 trade peaked at U.S.$37.4 million in Iranian exports to Venezuela and U.S.$13.3 million imports from Venezuela, a highly favorable trade balance for Iran. In April 2008, both nations signed 192 cooperation agreements in areas such as transportation, agriculture, auto manufacturing, health, and construction.[58] Iran's state-owned Petropars began surveys of oil reserves in the Orinoco Belt's Block 7. Both nations founded the joint venture Venezirian Oil Company and the Venezuela-Iran Petrochemical Company.[59] A joint Iran-Venezuelan company is producing tractors.

Relations with China comply with objectives 3 and 4, less so with objectives 1 and 2. Venezuela sees China through two levels: as an important trade partner, and as a potential "revolutionary" partner in international politics. However, China has been reluctant to join Venezuela's efforts to balance the United States or to supply Venezuela with significant arms. Venezuela has acquired fighting equipment and technology from China (24 K-8 airplanes and ten radars JYL1). China has increased oil imports from Venezuela (approximately 150,000 bpd). However, China is still a long way from buying the 1.5 bpd that the United States imports from Venezuela. China has also refused to join any form of strategic-military alliance, and has never really embraced Venezuela's "ideological package."[60]

Relations with Russia fulfill all four objectives, but the focus is on arms acquisition, and, increasingly on soft balancing.[61] Since 2005, Venezuela has signed more than twelve escalated arms purchase agreements worth over U.S.$4.4 billion with cash payment from Venezuela and a U.S.$2.2 billion credit line from Russia.[62] In 2007, Venezuela became the third world's largest buyer of Russian arms, after China and India. In arms imports per capita, Venezuela is by far Russia's best customer: in 2007, Venezuela spent $33 per person on Russian weapons; China U.S.$0.96 and India U.S.$0.79. In 2008, Venezuela was the eighth largest arms importer in the world (up from the 39th spot in 1999).[63]

Venezuela surprised many in late 2008 with the announcement of joint Russian-Venezuelan tactical communication maneuvers and navy exercises, the so-called Joint Venus Operation of November 29 to December 2, 2008. On September 10, 2008, the Russian government announced that the two Tu-160 strategic Russian bombers would fly the Caribbean air space for a few days, departing from a Venezuelan military base. During Russian president Dmitri Medvedev's visit to Caracas on November 26–27, 2008 to inspect joint military maneuvers and sign bilateral agreements, no reference was made whatsoever to possible military alliance.[64] However, there was talk of nuclear cooperation. Russia proposed to construct atomic power reactors in Venezuela. Atomstroyexport, the same company that constructed the Bushehr plant in Iran, confirmed its participation in negotiations for an agreement of nuclear cooperation with Venezuela. During Medvedev's visit to Caracas, an agreement was signed establishing "cooperation in the matter of controlled thermonuclear fusion, nuclear power plant security and development, construction of the experimental reactors and nuclear power plants." One of the elements briefed in the agreement is development of uranium.[65] In late 2009, Chávez announced his intention to acquire short-range missiles from Russia, capable of hitting Colombia and the islands of Aruba and Curaçao, where the United States operates surveillance flights.

So far, this military rapprochement with Russia has not set off too many alarms in the United States. The then U.S. Secretary of State, Condoleezza Rice, expressed that the alleged Russian advance in the region was "anachronistic."[66] Nevertheless, Russian-Venezuelan links are profoundly political, not just commercial/military. Unlike China, Russia has embraced Venezuela's open desire to build a multi-polar world and even end the so-called "dictatorship of the dollar." Consequently, we can expect greater cooperation. Venezuela supported Russia during the conflict with Georgia in 2008.[67] By September of 2009, Chávez visited Russia for the eighth time. This last time, Venezuela agreed to create a joint bank with Russia, and became one of the only three countries in the world (after Russia and Nicaragua) to recognize Abkhasia and South Ossetia, separatist republics of Georgia.

Economy and Trade as both a Driver and a Break on Soft Balancing

Economics is both the main driving force and the main restraining force on Venezuela's soft-balancing policy. The nation has benefited from two advantageous international developments: (1) the highest oil export revenue income in its history, close to U.S.$700 billion in a ten-year period, which is a staggering sum for a country of 26 million inhabitants, amounting to U.S.$27.000 per inhabitant, and

(2) the certainty that the United States will not declare an economic embargo on Venezuela.[68]

Venezuela oscillates between being the fourth and the fifth largest supplier of oil and oil derivatives to the United States (see Table 11.1) In 2008, Venezuela exported a total of U.S.$51.4 billion to the United States, or 55 percent of its total world exports (see Tables 11.2 and 11.3). The United States also supplied the bulk of

Table 11.1 U.S. Oil Imports by Country of Origin, 2008 (millions of barrels per day)

Canada	1.9
Saudi Arabia	1.5
México	1.2
Venezuela	1.0
Others (Nigeria, United Arab Emirates, United Kingdom, etc.)	4.2

Table 11.2 Venezuelan Exports by Destination (millions U.S.$)

Years	World	United States	European Union	Latin America	Andean Zone	Others
1998	17,564	9,181	1,926	N/A	1,953	4,504
1999	20,915	11,334	838	N/A	1,406	N/A
2000	34,038	18,650	2,350	4,506	3,902	N/A
2001	25,722	12,802	2,963	5,501	1,479	3,405
2002	20,515	10,853	3,076	N/A	2,191	2,915
2003	22,475	9,175	2,560	3,809	1,410	4,720
2004	36,630	11,655	4,580	6,053	2,333	11,699
2005	55,487	33,978	3,360	N/A	2,255	N/A
2006	65,210	37,133	6,000	N/A	2,535	N/A
2007	70,838	39,896	2,517	N/A	N/A	N/A
2008	93,500	51,423	N/A	N/A	N/A	N/A

Sources: MIC, BCV, Venezuelan Government.

Table 11.3 Venezuelan Exports by Destination (percentage of total)

Years	World	United States	European Union	Latin America	Andean Zone	Others
1998	100	49.2	10.9	N/A	11.1	28.8
1999	100	54.1	4.0	N/A	N/A	42.1
2000	100	55.3	6.7	22.6	9.5	N/A
2001	100	49.7	11.5	21.3	N/A	13.2
2002	100	52.9	14.9	N/A	10.67	14.2
2003	100	40.50	8.9	12.4	6.2	21.0
2004	100	45.20	10.1	16.8	6.3	21.8
2005	100	61.33	6.1	N/A	4.1	N/A
2006	100	56.95	9.2	N/A	3.9	N/A
2007	100	55.38	6.2	N/A	N/A	N/A
2008	100	55.22	N/A	N/A	N/A	N/A

Sources: MIC, BCV, Venezuelan Government.

Table 11.4 Venezuelan Imports by Place of Origin (millions in U.S.$)

Years	World	United States	European Union	Latin America	Andean Zone	Others
1998	14,816	6,545	2,661	2,320	1,094	2,196
1999	11,751	5,353	1,736	2120	1,082	1,460
2000	16,073	5,550	1,573	2,079	1,561	2,709
2001	18,534	5,976	2,803	3,015	2,123	3,210
2002	20,800	6,007	2,511	3,824	1,478	4,115
2003	22,584	6,840	2,412	3,505	1,001	4,806
2004	24,014	7,905	3,595	4,980	2,133	5,401
2005	23,955	6,879	2,813	8,700	3,115	2,448
2006	32,226	9,325	3,500	8,640	3,225	7,536
2007	52,987	10,199	2,561	22,678	2,957	14,592
2008	45,100	9,611	3,200	13,900	6,403	11,986
2009	31,664	8,552	2,800	8,756	4,990	6,556

Sources: MIC, BCV, Venezuelan Government.

Table 11.5 Venezuelan Imports by Place of Origin (percentage of total)

Years	World	United States	European Union	Latin America	Andean Zone	Others
1998	100	44.2	17.9	15.6	7.3	14.8
1999	100	45.6	14.7	N/A	8.1	31.1
2000	100	35.7	14.9	19.8	9.7	25.1
2001	100	32.5	15.0	16.2	11.4	17.3
2002	100	30.1	10.8	18.3	7.1	20.8
2003	100	32.8	9.50	19.3	4.4	31.4
2004	100	33.4	10.5	20.7	8.8	29.1
2005	100	25.5	11.7	36.7	11.2	14.9
2006	100	19.2	10.8	26.7	12.3	31.1
2007	100	19.2	2.9	42.8	5.6	29.4
2008	100	21.3	7.1	30.8	14.2	26.6
2009	100	27.0	8.9	27.6	15.7	20.8

Sources: MIC, BCV, Venezuelan Government.

Venezuela's imports of goods and services: 12.6 billion, or 28 percent of Venezuela's world imports (see Tables 11.4 and 11.5).

Venezuela's oil production is decreasing considerably, and exports to the United States have fallen in volume (they increased in dollar values, at least until mid 2008, because of increases in the price of oil, see Table 11.6). However, export revenues from other countries have dropped more than export revenues from the United States.[69] Consequently the Chávez administration is today more dependent on the United States for its exports than at the start of his administration (see Table 11.3). Venezuela's oil exports to the United States in 2008, the year that this oil price boom ended, still represented a 22 percent increase from 2007.[70] Furthermore, Venezuela does not have any major export other than oil and oil-derived products (see Table 11.7), which creates a double dependence: on one market (the United States) and one commodity (oil).

This dependence on the United States market serves both as driver and restraint on Venezuela's soft-balancing policy. The U.S. market remains guaranteed, which

Table 11.6 Price of Venezuelan Oil per Barrel in U.S.$ (annual average)

Years	U.S.$ price per barrel
1998	10.80
1999	16.00
2000	26.14
2001	20.21
2002	21.95
2003	25.62
2004	31.13
2005	45.39
2006	56.45
2007	65.74
2008	86.81
2009*	52.91

* Up to August 2009.

Sources: PDVSA. Venezuelan Goverment. El Universal: http://www.eluniversal.com/2009/10/09/en_eco_art_venezuelan-oil-baske_09A2873331.shtml.

Table 11.7 Venezuelan Exports to the United States by Type of Product, 2008

Product	Millions U.S.$
Oil	40,457.0
Oil Products	3,674.0
Fuel Oil	912.1
Bauxite and Aluminum	554.3
Organic Chemical Products	315.6
Iron and Steel Products	572.0
Car Spare Parts	32.6
Carbon and Carbon Products	181.0
Liquid and Natural Gas	3,636.0
Others	1,890.0
Total	51,423.0

Note: Oil, Oil products and Fuel Oil represents 88 percent of the total.

Source: FTD Webmaster, Foreign Trade Division, U.S. Census Bureau, Washington, US

provides the cash that finances Chávez's international deals, but it also means that Chávez has nowhere else to go to place its oil exports. There simply is no other oil market that is as large, as geographically close, and as equipped to refine Venezuelan oil. China could be the only possible replacement, but it is located at a substantially greater distance (considerably increasing transportation costs), does not have the oil tankers necessary to make trans-oceanic oil shipments affordable, nor does it have the necessary refineries to process Venezuela's special type of heavy crude.

The two areas in international economics where Chávez has met his diversification objectives are foreign investments and imports. Under Chávez, U.S. investments in Venezuela declined from 87 percent of total gross capital income in 1998 to 55 percent by 2007 within the decreasing tendency observed in recent years.

Imports from the United States declined from 45.6 percent of total imports in 1999 to 28.1 percent in 2008 (see Table 11.5) However, it is noticeable that some U.S.$150 billion in Venezuelan private hands are placed in bank deposits, financial products, and other financial instruments in different U.S. financial institutions or under U.S. registry.[71]

High oil prices between 2003 and 2008 enhanced the Venezuelan state's bargaining leverage vis-à-vis private energy multinationals as well. The state was able to impose business-unfriendly conditions on private energy companies (higher taxes and royalties, more discretionary terms, forced conversion of contracts into joint-ventures). However, the fact that U.S. oil companies remained and continued to invest in the country (see Table 11.8) despite these statist conditions is proof that the favorable oil prices granted the state the most bargaining leverage and still left room for private companies to make profits. To this day, U.S. oil companies are participating in joint ventures in exploration of oil and off-shore gas, in the Orinoco River Basin, Delta Platform, the Venezuelan Gulf and the Falcon state coast, by means of oil tankers for liquid natural gas (LNG) transportation; and, in the long term, through a gas pipeline through Colombia or an underground pipeline through the Caribbean and on to Florida, in conjunction with Trinidad and Tobago.

Venezuela's economic expansion cycle ended in mid 2008 with the drop in world oil prices and the global financial crisis starting in the fall of 2008 (see Table 11.9). This double shock (in price and demand) has somewhat impaired Venezuela's capacity to carry out soft balancing, and maybe even its approach to foreign private investors. By April 2009, the Venezuelan government was courting, for the first time since the early 2000s, private oil companies to invest in Venezuela, offering them the chance to own minority stakes in lucrative Orinoco River Basin oil projects.

Nevertheless, it is clear that Venezuela seeks two economic goals that are difficult to reconcile with each other: (1) increase capital and technology investments in the

Table 11.8 U.S. Investments in Venezuela

Years	U.S.$ millions
1998	622
1999	1,396
2000	3,798
2001	461
2002	150
2003	462
2004	−1,093
2005	2,073
2006	2,045
2007	1,229
2008	1,472

Source: Bureau of Economic Analysis, U.S. Department of Commerce: http://www,bea,gov/international/.

Table 11.9 Selected Macroeconomic Indicators for Venezuela and Latin America

	Venezuela: GDP Growth Rates	Venezuela: Annual Inflation Rate	Latin America: Annual Inflation Rate	Venezuela: Unemployment Rate	Latin America: Unemployment Rate	Venezuela: Exchange Rate (Official)	Venezuela: Exchange Rate (Parallel)
1999	-7.0%	20.2%	9.7%	15.4%	11.0%		
2000	3.8%	13.4%	9.0%	14.0%	10.4%		
2001	2.9%	12.3%	6.1%	13.4%	10.2%		
2002	-8.9%	31.2%	12.2%	15.8%	11.0%		
2003	-9.7%	27.1%	8.5%	18.0%	11.0%		
2004	17.9%	19.2%	7.4%	15.3%	10.3%	2.150Bs	
2005	10.3%	14.4%	6.1%	12.4%	9.1%	2.150Bs	
2006	10.3%	17.0%	5.0%	10.1%	8.6%	2.150Bs	2.500Bs
2007	8.5%	19.5%	6.1%	8.5%	8.0%	2.150Bs	6.100Bs
2008	6.2%	30.9%	9.30%	7.2%	NA	2.15BsF	5.10BsF
2009*	-1.20%	40.2%	6.00%	9.4%	NA	2.15BsF	5.91BsF

* Figures are provisional.

Source: Venezuela GDP, Inflation: Banco Central de Venezuela, http://www.bcv.org.ve/EnglishVersion/c2/index.asp?secc=statistinf. Latin America Inflation and Unemployment: ECLAC, http://www.eclac.org/cgi-bin/getProd.asp?xml=/de/agrupadores_xml/aes251.xml&xsl=/agrupadores_xml/agrupa_listado-i.xml&base=/tpl-i/top-bottom.xsl.

oil sector, which is something that can best by delivered by private energy companies, and (2) reduce dependence on private companies from democratic countries, since these are accountable to third parties (shareholders, governments, courts) which makes them unappealing to Chávez's anti-transparency administration. So far Chávez has privileged the latter objective. The sacrifice of capital and technology investments is one reason that Venezuela's oil sector is experiencing declining productivity and frequent industry-related accidents.

Hypothesis Revision

We can now return to our initial questions. What explains the rise in conflict in U.S.–Venezuela relations, and why haven't such conflicts culminated in a complete breakdown? In this section, we review four sets of answers.

The Aggressive Giant

The first hypothesis places most of the blame on the United States. The argument is that the lack of cooperation between the United States and Venezuela is the result of punitive policies applied by the United States against the Venezuelan government. The key idea behind this hypothesis is that the Venezuelan government would cooperate were it not for Washington's antagonistic attitude. The most relevant pieces of evidence in support of this hypothesis are the role played by the United States in the events leading to the 2002 coup,[72] the ongoing debate in the U.S. administration over Venezuela's alleged cooperation with terrorist organizations, the U.S. ban on arms sales to Venezuela, and sanctions against Venezuelan officials.

However, this hypothesis faces significant empirical difficulties. Venezuela's distancing from Washington began much earlier than the 2002 coup (Venezuela's refusal of U.S. assistance during the 1999 natural disaster in the state of Vargas and its severe criticism of the 2001 U.S. invasion of Afghanistan). Second, initially the Venezuelan government did not consider U.S. actions during the events that led to the 2002 coup to be all that relevant. Third, anti-Venezuelan rhetoric and policies by the United States have diminished since 2005 and, yet, the anti-American rhetoric and policies from Venezuela have increased since then. Fourth, the ban on arms sales to Venezuela may have driven the country to closer relations with Russia and maybe Iran, but it does not account for the expansion of Venezuela's arms spending.

The corollary to this hypothesis ("The United States is the aggressor") is that the United States sides with Chávez's domestic enemies (whom Chávez calls the "coup-plotting" opposition)[73] and regional rivals (Colombia), while harboring secret intentions, as Chávez claims, to invade the country or murder the president. Gregory Wilpert, for instance, analyzes this "side with the enemy" line by arguing that the National Endowment for Democracy (NED) has increased the amount of funds allocated to the opposition. According to Wilpert such aid climbed from U.S.$232,831 in 2000 to almost U.S.$10 million in 2003. Chávez accused the Venezuelan NGO "Súmate," which helped organize the recall referendum of 2004, of having received U.S.$53,000 from the NED and U.S.$84,840 from USAID.[74]

However, the aid provided by the United States to non-state actors seems puny in comparison to aid that other nations receive, and to the resources the Venezuelan government itself administers. It is estimated that, in 1973, the United States contributed U.S.$8 million in aid to opposition groups in the Chile of Salvador Allende,[75] which is equivalent to U.S.$36 million in 2006 dollars. This makes it hard to sustain the claim that aid to the Venezuelan opposition is significant.

Yet another corollary to the "US is the aggressor" thesis is based on the idea that Chávez is acting preemptively. The problem is that any argument based on preemption is hard to corroborate or disprove. It is based on information—real or imagined—that we have no access to. Nevertheless, the T-72 tanks that Venezuela is purchasing from Russia would be of no use against an alleged invasion from the United States, or for a campaign to invade Colombia given the topographical conditions of the country. In the end, one cannot rule out the possibility that all this talk of preemption is mere cover for a Chávez's own fabrication.

There Is no Aggressive Giant

If the conflict between the United States and Venezuela stems, at least, from Chávez's own fabrication, then the key question is: What does Chávez gain by provoking or sustaining this degree of confrontation? Two answers are possible. One is based on a thesis that is the exact opposite of the "the US is the aggressor" argument: Venezuela pursues soft balancing because it knows that U.S. retaliation—an economic embargo or even a military invasion—is unlikely.

This idea has theoretical and empirical support: The United States seems to be treating South America increasingly as a region of declining importance for national security. Commentators during the Bush years often talked about the administration's lack of attention to the region. The security threats posed by the Middle East and Asia overshadowed any problems from Latin America.

Nevertheless, it is easy to exaggerate the extent to which U.S. interest in the region is waning. No doubt, the region poses smaller threats in comparison to other world regions and fewer economic opportunities than Asia. This does not necessarily mean, however, that the United States has lost complete interest. Venezuela, for one, has incurred in domains that are vital to the United States: threat of oil embargos, alleged links to terrorists and nuclear regimes, inattention to drug trafficking, anti-Semitic actions, expropriation of private enterprises, and weapons acquisition, production and distribution. Historically, these types of actions would have drawn attention from high-ranking White House officials, Congress or both. Therefore, is it unclear whether U.S. policy of tolerance towards Venezuela is the result of the low salience of the issues at stake.

Generating Conflict for Different Political Reasons

A different explanation is based on an entirely different argument: the idea that conflict is instrumental to the party generating such conflict. This is based on the more traditional international relations theory that governments often pursue international conflict in order to neutralize and contain domestic unrest.[76]

The question then is: What domestic objectives does Chávez achieve, if any, by creating conflict with the United States? Two possible hypotheses may be explored. One is diversion: the state promotes external conflict in order to divert attention from domestic problems. The other is patriotism: The state pursues external conflict to encourage nationalism and win partisans at national and international levels.

The strongest evidence on behalf of this thesis is that conflict with the United States takes a turn for the worst precisely at a time when the Chávez administration is experiencing its worst political moment: the 2002–2004 period, characterized by massive rallies, the coup attempt, the oil workers' strike, and the fight for the recall referendum. During this period Chávez's disapproval rate exceeded his approval rates. In such a situation, it would not seem unreasonable to assume that Chávez discovered that resorting to conflict with the United States could help him overcome political weakness by gaining support from nationalists groups.

It is worth remembering that Hugo Chávez came to power with the idea of dividing Venezuela's democratic history into two periods, the so-called Fourth and Fifth Republics. He initiated a transforming process that displaced many of the traditional political actors and elevated the power of the president in a way that no other elected leader in Venezuela ever has. Likewise, Chávez abroad aspires to become a sort of *primus inter pares*, a political, economic and ideological leader among developing countries, not just Latin America.

However, this thesis does not account for the intensification of U.S.-Venezuelan conflict once political instability waned, from 2004 to 2008. Moreover, critical anti-American policies such as ending cooperation with the DEA, the United Nations speech, accusing the United States of murder attempts, and threatening the United States with an asymmetrical war have received little popular support, which makes it difficult to think that such stances have some electoral basis. His anti-American policies do earn him the support of radical groups—both at home and abroad—but it also earns him many detractors. It is a strategy that pleases radicals, but not a strategy that delivers majority support.

Structural Factors: The Impact of Economic Interdependence

Structural factors (not just political considerations) also influence U.S.–Venezuelan relations. First, Venezuela has practically no non-oil exports and, therefore, no alternative sources of hard currency income (see Table 11.7). Second, Venezuelan oil—which is heavy and has a high content of sulfur and other impurities—can only be processed in special oil refineries. Most of these refineries are in the United States. Thus, the Bolivarian Revolution has little choice but to continue to rely on the U.S. market.

The only other possible large-scale buyer is China. But China has alternative oil suppliers (in Central Asia and Africa), does not have any oil refineries to process the special type of Venezuelan heavy crude, and its shores are almost forty-four sailing days away from Venezuelan waters. For structural reasons alone, Chávez's threats of cutting off the oil supply to the United States are vacuous. Without U.S. oil trade, Chávez would have to sacrifice the Bolivarian Revolution.

On the other hand, structural dependence on the United States does help explain Venezuela's shift towards Iran, and to a certain point, towards Russia. With Iran, Venezuela seeks to balance Saudi Arabia and the United States In other words, Venezuela and Iran —both countries experiencing a fall in oil production—constitute a bloc within the Organization of Petroleum Exporting Countries (OPEC) that supports high oil prices through supply restrictions. Such a position goes, in effect, against Saudi Arabia and other OPEC members, not to mention the United States, which feels the goal should be to keep prices stable and affordable. As long as Venezuela is tied to oil sales to the United States, an anti-U.S. Venezuela will remain interested in high oil prices to extract as much revenue from the United States as possible. Likewise, economic factors explain Venezuela's veering closer to Russia. When OPEC reduces supply, Russia, a non-OPEC country, seizes the opportunity to increase its oil sales. One of Venezuela's objectives may be to favor Russia with arms purchases so that Russia would be more prone to cooperate with OPEC.

The First Six Months of the Obama Administration

The Barack Obama administration (2009–present) came to office promising a new era of "engagement," rather than "confrontation," with world nations in an effort to distance itself from what the world perceived as the more unilateral approaches taken by President George W. Bush. In Venezuela, this new commitment to engagement confronts a double problem.

First, the inherited policy from the last years of the Bush administration—avoiding direct confrontation with Chávez—is already pretty much in accordance with Obama's principle of avoiding unnecessary confrontation. In fact, the one major development in U.S.–Venezuela relations in the first six months of the Obama administration relations has been precisely the decision to retain the policy of dodging verbal attacks that former U.S. ambassador to Venezuela William Brownfield developed.

This continuity became patently clear during the April 2009 Fifth Summit of the Americas in Port of Spain. Chávez came prepared for a fight. He had spent the prior months issuing criticisms at Obama, even calling him an "ignoramus." He managed to get the ALBA presidents to state that they would not sign the Summit's final declaration, due to lack of unanimity on a number of topics. Yet Obama's conciliatory speech and clever avoidance of verbal attacks from Venezuela disarmed Chávez. Obama earned widespread praise from most presidents at the meeting.

As was the case under the latter part of the Bush era, this policy of deliberately avoiding engaging in "YOU did"/"no, YOU did" verbal exchanges with Venezuela does help to de-escalate rhetorical conflicts and isolate Chávez. But it also means that there is little room for change in U.S. policy toward Venezuela, since the inherited policy seems to be the preferred policy.

The second problem that the United States faces vis-à-vis Venezuela is that it is not clear that more "engagement" will work, especially since Venezuela either has no interest in a more engaged United States, or wants a type of engagement that the United States (or very few nations) would be willing to deliver.

For instance, in the first months of the Obama administration, there have been some signs of more engagement, or at least, closer alignment of U.S. policies with Venezuela's. The United States, for instance, went along with an OAS effort, led by Venezuela, to revoke the 1962 resolution suspending Cuba from the organization. And in handling the Honduras crisis since June 28, 2009, the United States has taken many steps that are directly in line with Venezuela's preferences: the United States condemned the coup, refused to recognize and imposed sanctions on the de facto government in Honduras; called for the restitution of deposed president and ALBA-enthusiast José Manuel Zelaya as a non-negotiable part of any solution to the crisis; and announced that it would not recognize presidential elections held by the de facto government. Sure enough, the positions United States and Venezuela held on Honduras were not identical. Perhaps the most important area of disagreement was their viewpoints on Zelaya's secret reentry into Honduras, with the United States calling it a mistake and Venezuela calling it a brilliant move. Nonetheless, there were far more points of commonality between the United States and Venezuela over the Honduras crisis than discrepancies.

And yet, the response from Caracas has not been that positive. To be sure, Chávez has moderated his words against Obama. At the September 2009 meeting of the UN, Chávez said "it doesn't smell of sulfur" anymore, "it smells of hope," in a clear attempt to highlight his contrasting response to the new U.S. administration. But in terms of policy, there has been very little change coming from Caracas, but rather an intensification of soft-balancing approaches. Since January 2009, for instance, Chávez has intensified his belligerence toward Colombia; has further increased spending on Russian military equipment by securing a U.S.$2.2 credit line to buy Russian weapons; recognized the independence of Russia's protégés, South Ossetia and Abkhasia from Georgia; congratulated Mahmoud Ahmadinejad on his electoral "victory," called Iran a "true strategic ally," and defended Iran's nuclear program, to the shock of many European nations. Domestically, Chávez's march toward concentrating more power continued, displacing elected opposition leaders, punishing dissenters, and silencing the non-aligned media.

Chávez essentially will tolerate no criticism. Thus, when Secretary of State Hillary Clinton warned Chávez in September that his weapons purchases could trigger an arms race, Chávez was quick to counterattack: "When efforts are made to improve relations with the government of the United States, the Secretary of State, Hillary Rodham Clinton, repeats the old practice of giving prescriptions and making judgments on Venezuelan democracy and the sovereign relations that our country has with other nations."[77] It seems that the only policy of engagement that Chávez will welcome from the United States would be a policy of political laissez-faire and total silence.

It is unlikely that the Obama administration will adopt a policy of strict political laissez-faire toward Venezuela. The security concerns are increasingly deeper, and the plight of the Venezuelan opposition increasingly dimmer, too much so for the United States to stay quiet. U.S. officials have already met with leaders of Venezuela's opposition; Hillary R. Clinton granted an interview to representatives of a television channel of Venezuelan opposition; the U.S. government signed an agreement of military cooperation with Colombia to continue using six Colombian military bases. Furthermore, as was the case under President Bush, agencies of the U,S. government will resume their criticisms of governance issues in Venezuela. For these agencies, issuing reports on the levels of cooperation from other governments is part of their routine standard operating procedures. In 2009 the U.S. Government Accountability Office, for instance, already complained about the lack of cooperation by Venezuela in the war against drugs. The U.S. press will also continue to report misconduct on the part of Venezuela, such as the revelation, already aired, that rocket launchers sent from Sweden to Venezuela mysteriously made it into the hands of the FARC.

Furthermore, Obama faces an opposition that is very different from the opposition that Bush faced: he has the conservatives on the other side of the aisle. For Bush, therefore, it was politically viable to maintain a policy of "dodging criticism" because he had the capacity to win the cooperation or tolerance of conservatives on this policy. It's unclear that Obama has that leeway among conservatives. Conservatives have already been quite unforgiving of Obama's relaxed policy toward Venezuela, even though this policy has not been that much different from Bush's policy toward the end of his second term.

Thus, even in the unlikely event that the White House takes a political laissez-faire approach toward Venezuela, it will still have a difficult time blocking other parts of the government, or American society, from offering critical judgments on Venezuela's conduct. This will trigger a predictable response: Chávez will use every one of those judgments to cry foul. Already the Venezuelan Ministry of Foreign Affairs officially responded that reports about ties to the FARC constitute "a political blackmail lacking scientific objectivity and methodological seriousness." In short, Chávez will continue to be able to find justification for his soft-balancing objectives, almost regardless of what the United States does, short of staying quiet.

Conclusion

We conclude with a discussion of three possible scenarios in U.S.–Venezuela relations in a post-Bush era: (1) reconstruction of relations; (2) increasing estrangement culminating in a definite rupture; and (3) more of the same: continued conflict without a major break. With regards to the first scenario, oil and—to a lesser extent— the low domestic popularity of Chávez's belligerence toward the United States constitute key factors pushing in this direction. Furthermore, as Chávez continues to suffer the ravages of rising crime rates stemming from drug trafficking, the regime may actually reconsider cooperation with the DEA.

With regards to the second scenario, there is no question that Chávez seems interested in provoking the United States for political gain. During the second Bush administration, United States responded by seeking to contain, ignore, or de-escalate tensions. If this policy of tension-containment is discontinued and the United States starts to take more retaliatory actions, it is easy to imagine Chávez responding in kind, leading to a deepening of conflict.

The third scenario—restrained conflict—depends on domestic politics. As long as Chávez perceives the domestic situation to be under control, he faces fewer incentives to generate greater conflict with the United States. As Venezuela's oil sector suffers the impact of declining production and world oil and gas demand, Venezuela may continue to realize that a stable trade relation with the United States is vital to its security.

Is it possible for the two governments to find a common ground? Is the Venezuelan government really up for normal relations or will it continue to use conflict for its own ends? Beyond any doubt, the current situation represents a comfortable balancing act for Chávez. Yet, equilibrium entails certain sacrifices. Perhaps the two most important sacrifices are the lack of investments in Venezuela's vital industry and climbing crime rates.

In general terms, the political bridge between Venezuela and the United States is in disrepair, but it has not entirely collapsed. A broken bridge is better than a collapsed bridge: repairs are often less expensive and easier to undertake than rebuilding an entirely new structure. The problem is that Chávez has few incentives to suddenly come out as a pro-U.S. world leader. He gains a lot by maintaining a certain degree of political conflict with the United States as long as economic relations remain intact.

Notes

1. Hugo Chávez Frías, "Programa Aló Presidente," November 3, 2001. www.embavenez-us.org/news.spanish/alopdte.
2. Janet Kelly and Carlos A. Romero, *The United States and Venezuela: Rethinking a Relationship* (New York: Routledge, 2002); Carlos A. Romero, *Jugando con el Globo* (Playing with the Globe) (Caracas: Ediciones B., 2006).
3. Janet Kelly and Carlos A. Romero, *The United States and Venezuela*; Jennifer McCoy, "Venezuela: Leading a New Trend in Latin America," *Revista. Harvard Review of Latin America* (Fall 2008): 52–56.
4. Javier Corrales, "Using Social Power to Balance Soft Power: Venezuela's Foreign Policy," *The Washington Quarterly* 32, no. 4 (October).
5. Robert A. Pape, "Soft Balancing against the United States," *International Security* 30, no. 1 (Summer 2005): 13; T.V. Paul, "Soft Balancing in the Age of U.S. Primacy," *International Security* 30, no. 1 (Summer 2005): 46–71; Andrew Hurrell, "Hegemony, Liberalism, and Global Order: What Space for Would-be Great Powers?" *International Affairs* 82, no. 1 (2006):1–19.
6. Stephen M. Walt, "Can the United States be Balanced? If So, How?," paper presented at the Annual meeting of the American Political Science Association. Chicago, Illinois (2004). Soft-balancing ought not be confused with "soft-power," the term coined by Joseph Nye to describe the magnetic power of a nation's values and agenda. See Joseph S. Nye, "Soft Power and American Foreign Policy," *Political Science Quarterly* 119, no. 2 (1994): 255–270.
7. Stephen G. Brooks and William C. Wohlforth, "Hard Times for Soft Balancing," *International Security* 30, 1 (2005):72–108; Stephen G. Brooks and William C. Wohlforth, "International Relations Theory and the Case against Unilateralism," *Perspectives on Politics* 3, no. 3 (2005): 509–524; Keir A. Lieber and Gerard Alexander, "Waiting for Balancing: Why the World Is Not Pushing Back," *International Security* 30, no. 1 (2005):109–139.

8. Mark Eric Williams, "International Relations Theory and Venezuela's Soft Balancing Foreign Policy," paper presented at the Meeting of the Latin American Studies Association, Montreal (2007); Mark Eric Williams, "The New Balancing Act: International Relations Theory and Venezuela's 'Soft Balancing' Foreign Policy," in *The Revolution in Venezuela*, ed. Jonathan Eastwood and Thomas Ponniah (Durham, NC: Duke University Press, forthcoming); Gregory Wilpert, *Changing Venezuela by Taking Power: The History and Policies of the Chavez Government* (New York and London: Verso, 2007).

9. Günther Maihold, "Foreign Policy as Provocation: Rhetoric and Reality in Venezuela's External Relations under Hugo Chávez," SWP Research Paper, Berlin, Germany, January 2009.

10. See the section on foreign policy in Hugo Chávez, Martha Harnecker and Chesa Boudin, *Understanding the Venezuelan Revolution: Hugo Chavez Talks to Marta Harnecker* (New York: Monthly Review Press, 2005).

11. Hugo Chávez, "Discurso ante la Asamblea Anual de las Naciones Unidas," *El Nacional*, 21–09–06:A/09.

12. Warren Hoge, "Venezuelan's Diatribe at U.N. May Have Backfired," *New York Times*, October 25, 2006.

13. Thomas Carothers, "The Backlash Against Democracy," *Foreign Affairs* 85, no. 2 (March/April 2006): 56–68; Moisés Naim, "La Internacionalización de Hugo Chávez, Epílogo," in *Venezuela y Estados Unidos. Coincidencias y Conflictos*, ed. Janet Kelly and Carlos A. Romero (Caracas: IESA-Libros del Nacional, Colección Minerva, 2005): 208.

14. William Brownfield, "Declaraciones," *El Universal*, 06–12–06: 1/4.

15. Hugo Chávez, "Declaraciones," in www.azcentral.com/lavoz/ 05.12.06.

16. Hugo Chávez, "Declaraciones," *El Universal*, 14–04–07:1/4.

17. *El Universal*, 02–03–07: 1/6.

18. Adam Ereli, "Declaraciones," *El Universal*, 31–01–06:1/8.

19. Hugo Chávez, "Discurso," *El Nacional*, 05–02–06: A/4.

20. General Bantz J. Craddock, *Informe al Comité de Servicios Armados del Senado de Estados Unidos* (Washington, DC: U.S. Congress, 2006).

21. República Bolivariana de Venezuela, Ministerio del Poder Popular para Relaciones Exteriores, "Comunicado," reprinted in *El Nacional*, 03–02–2006: A/2, A/10.

22. Sean McCormack, "Declaraciones," *The Daily Journal*, 04–02–06: 3.

23. *Reporte. Diario de la Economía*, 07–03–07: 22.

24. *El Universal*, 07–04–07: 4.

25. *El Universal*, 13–06–07: 1–4.

26. Ricardo Adrián Runza, "La construcción de una comunidad de Seguridad en América del Sur a la luz de la adquisición de armamento," Friedrich Ebert Stiftung, Program for Regional Security Cooperation, Policy Paper, July 20, 2008, www.seguridadregional-fes.org.

27. República Bolivariana de Venezuela, Ministerio del Poder Popular para Relaciones Exteriores, "Comunicado," 29–04–2008, www.mre.gov.ve.

28. Venezuelan Military Industries Public Corporation, CAVIM, by its Spanish acronym.

29. *El Universal*, June 2, 2008.

30. Reyes Theis, "Drug Smuggled Through Venezuela Increases," *El Universal*, February 24, 2009.

31. Michael Shifter, "Internal Dynamics of the Venezuelan Drug Problem," Washington, DC: Inter-American Dialogue (2007).

32. Hugo Alconada Mon, "Hallan culpable en Miami al acusado por el caso de la valija," *La Nación*. 04–11–08: 1, 6.

33. Ruth Berhrrenes, from Petróleos de Venezuela S.A. (PDVSA) in Uruguay, Nelly Cardozo, legal adviser of PDVSA, Wilfredo Ávila, protocol aide, Daniel Uzcategui Specht, a son of a vicepresident of PDVSA and María Isabel Specht, manager of Citgo Petroleum Corporation in Houston, Texas.

34. Hugo Alconada Mon,. "Hallan culpable . . ." (2008).
35. En www.eldia.es/2008012/venezuela/venezuela347; news.bbc.co.uk/hi/spanish/latin_ america/newsid.
36. Hugo Chávez, "Declaraciones," *Globovisión*, 11–09–2008, www.globovision.com/ - 48k.
37. In July 1988, the government of Nicaragua requested the departure of Ambassador Richard Huntington Melton, but they stopped short of declaring him persona non grata.
38. Javier Corrales, "Using Social Power . . ."; Schifter, Michael, "In Search of Hugo Chávez," *Foreign Affairs* 85, no. 3 (May/June 2006): 56.
39. See Javier Corrales and Richard Feinberg, "Regimes of Cooperation in the Western Hemisphere: Power, Interests and Intellectual Traditions," *International Studies Quarterly* 43 (March 1999): 1–36.
40. Alí Rodríguez Áraque, "Comunicación enviada por el Ministro de Relaciones Exteriores de Venezuela a la Presidenta y demás miembros de la Comisión de la Comunidad Andina de Naciones" (Caracas, Ministerio del Poder Popular para la Relaciones Exteriores de Venezuela, April 22, 2006), in www.mre.gov.ve.
41. Teodoro Petkoff, *Las dos izquierdas* (Caracas: Alfadil, 2005); Jorge Castañeda, "Latin American Left Turn," *Foreign Affairs* 85, no. 3 (May/June 2006): 28–43, at 40; Jorge Lanzaro, "La socialdemocracia criolla," *Nueva Sociedad* 217 (September–October 2008): 40–58; Jennifer Mc Coy, "Venezuela: Leading a New Trend in Latin America."
42. For an account on the origins of these governments, see Javier Corrales, "The Backlash Against Market Reforms, in *Constructing Democratic Governance in Latin America*, 3rd ed., ed. Jorge I. Domínguez and Michael Shifter (Baltimore: Johns Hopkins University Press, 2008).
43. Unofficial translation.
44. Carlos A. Romero, "Estados Unidos y Venezuela. De una relación especial a vecinos cautelosos," in *Venezuela. Del Pacto de Punto Fijo al Chavismo*, ed. Jennifer Mc Coy and David Myers (Caracas: Los Libros de El Nacional, Colección Fuera de Serie, 2007): 141–163.
45. Pew Global Attitudes Project, "Global Unease With Major World Powers; Rising Environmental Concern in 47-Nation Survey" (Washington, DC: Pew Research Center, 2007).
46. Sean Burges, "Building a global southern coalition: The competing approaches of Brazil's Lula and Venezuela's Chávez," *Third World Quarterly* 28, no. 7 (October 2007): 1343–1358.
47. Clare Ribando Seelke and Peter Meyer, "Brazil-U.S. Relations" (Washington, DC: Congressional Research Service Reports, RL33456, January 21, 2009).
48. Frédérique Langue, *Hugo Chávez et le Venezuela. Une Action Politique au Pays de Bolívar* (Paris: L'Harmattan, 2002).
49. Ministerio de Relaciones Exteriores de Cuba, "Relaciones Regionales, América Latina y el Caribe, Venezuela," www.cubaminrex.cu; Embajada de la República Bolivariana de Venezuela en Cuba, "Síntesis de las Relaciones de Cooperación entre Venezuela y Cuba," www.venezuelaencuba.co.cu/venezuelacuba/síntesis.htlm.
50. Alternativa Bolivariana para las Américas, ALBA, "Acuerdo entre el Presidente de la República Bolivariana de Venezuela y el Presidente del Consejo de Estado de Cuba, para la aplicación de la Alternativa Bolivariana para las Américas," December 14, 2004, www.cubaminrex.cu.
51. Agencia Rusa de Información (RIA NOVOSTI), "Presidentes Caribeños se reúnen en Cuba para profundizar integración energética," December 21, 2007, sp.rian.ru/analysis/20071221/93588754.html - 27k.
52. Embajada de la República Bolivariana de Venezuela en Cuba, "Síntesis de las relaciones de cooperación entre Venezuela y Cuba" (2008), www.venezuelaencuba.co.cu/venezuelacuba/síntesis.

53. Hugo Chávez, "Declaraciones del presidente Chávez sobre las Fuerzas Armadas del ALBA," January 27, 2008, www.esmas.com/noticierostelevisa/internacionales/698504.html; www.radiomundial.com.ve/yvke/noticia.
54. Raúl Castro Ruz, "Declaración del Presidente de los Consejos de Estado y de Ministros de la República de Cuba," September 13, 2008, www.granma.cu.
55. Aporrea, "Concluyó Raúl Castro visita oficial a Venezuela" (2008), www.aporrea.org/actualidad/n125584.
56. Javier Corrales, "Cuba's New Daddy," *Hemisphere* 17 (Fall 2006): 24–29.
57. Nima Ver Gerami and Sharon Squassoni, "Venezuela: A Nuclear Profile" (2008), http://www.carnegieendowment.org/publications/index.cfm?fa=view&id=22568.
58. Elodie Brun, "La place de l'Iran dans la politique étrangère du Venezuela," July 2008,http://www.wilsoncenter.org/index.cfm?topic_id=1425&fuseaction=topics.event_summary&event_id=454131.
59. http://comtrade.un.org/db/default.aspx (October 30, 2008); Elodie Brun, *Les relations entre l'Amérique du Sud et le Moyen-Orient. Un exemple de relance Sud-Sud* (Paris: L'Harmattan, 2008).
60. For more on relations with China, see Javier Corrales, "Why Venezuela is Trapped, for Now: Venezuela, China, Iran and Oil," In *China and Latin America*, ed. Alex Fernández and Barbara Hogenboom (under review).
61. Hugo Chávez, "Declaraciones," *Reporte. Diario de la Economía,* July 13, 2006.
62. Ian James, "Venezuela-Russia ties deepen despite US pressure," The Associated Press (2008), ap.google.com/article/ALeqM5j7DAfgieUqDDczqO; Ricardo Adrián Runza, "La construcción de una comunidad . . ."
63. Aaron Wodin-Schwartz, "Venezuela's Relations with Iran and Russia," Washington, DC: George Washington University, 2008, data from Stockholm International Peace Research Institute's Importer/Exporter TIV Tables. http://www.sipri.org.
64. "Medvédev y Chávez relanzan la cooperación bilateral," ("Medvédev and Chávez revamp bilateral cooperation"), *El País,* November 27, 2008: 6.
65. Michael Schwirtz, "Chávez Throws in his Lot with Russia" *The International Herald Tribune,* September 12, 2009: 3; Jaime López, "Rusia financia la compra de misiles en Venezuela," *El País,* September 15, 2009: 30; *Reporte. Diario de la Economía,* September 24, 2009: 20.
66. Condoleezza Rice, "U.S.-Russia Relations," address at the German Marshall Fund, Renaissance Mayflower Hotel, Washington, DC, September 18, 2008, www.state.gov/.
67. Hugo Chávez, "Declaraciones," *Reporte. Diario de la Economía,* July 13, 2006.
68. Carlos Mendoza Potellá, "Las tendencias actuales del mercado petrolero mundial y sus repercusiones para Venezuela," (Current trends of the world oil market and their repercussions in Venezuela), *Revista BCV* 22, no. 1 (January–June 2008): 105–136.
69. Ramón Espinasa, "The Performance of the Venezuelan Oil Sector 1997–2008: Official vs. International and Estimated Figures," Center for Hemispheric Policy, University of Miami, Task Force Policy Paper, March–May 2008.
70. Domingo Felipe Maza Zabala, "Dependencia de la Economía Venezolana de Estados Unidos," (Dependency of the Venezuelan economy on the United States), *Revista ZETA* 1680 (October 17, 2008): 21–23.
71. Ibid.
72. The idea of U.S. intervention in the coup is based on two arguments. First, that the United States knew, from 6 April, at least, of the coup and yet it did not warn the Venezuelan government (see http://www.democracynow.org/2004/11/29/cia_documents_show_bush_knew_of). Second, the White House issued an early statement that may be interpreted as supporting it. "Chávez supporters, on orders, fired on unarmed, peaceful demonstrators," White House press secretary Ari Fleischer said, referring to Thursday's violence that killed 12 people and wounded dozens more. "Venezuelan military and police refused to fire . . . and refused to support the government's role in human rights violations."

73. http://www.venezuelanalysis.com/news/560.
74. Gregory Wilpert, *Changing Venezuela by Taking Power*, pp. 169–174.
75. Lois Hecht Oppenheim, *Politics in Chile: Democracy, Authoritarianism, and the Search for Development* (Boulder, CO: Westview, 1993): 106.
76. Sarah McLaughlin Mitchell and Brandon C. Prins, "Rivalry and Diversionary Uses of Force," *Journal of Conflict Resolution* 48, no 6 (December 2004);Benjamin O. Fordham, "Strategic Conflict Avoidance and the Diversionary Use of Force," *The Journal of Politics* 67, no. 1 (February 2005); Gary Goertz and Paul F. Diehl, "Enduring Rivalries: Theoretical Constructs and Empirical Patterns," *International Studies Quarterly* 37, no. 2 (1993): 147–171; David Sobek, "Rally around the Podesta: Testing Diversionary Theory across Time," *Journal of Peace Research* 44, no.1 (2007): 29–47.
77. República Bolivariana de Venezuela, Ministerio del Poder Popular para Relaciones Exteriores, Communiqué, June 25, 2009, available at www.antv.gob.ve/m8/noticiam8.asp. See also Communiqué, July 8, 2009, available at www.mre.gob.ve.

Index